AMERICAN POLITICAL SCIENCE SERIES
LINDSAY ROGERS, *General Editor*

# MODERN POLITICS AND ADMINISTRATION

## A STUDY OF THE CREATIVE STATE

BY

### MARSHALL E. DIMOCK

ASSOCIATE PROFESSOR OF PUBLIC ADMINISTRATION
UNIVERSITY OF CHICAGO

☆
*AMERICAN
POLITICAL SCIENCE
SERIES*
☆

## AMERICAN BOOK COMPANY

NEW YORK  •  CHICAGO  •  CINCINNATI
BOSTON  •  ATLANTA  •  DALLAS  •  SAN FRANCISCO

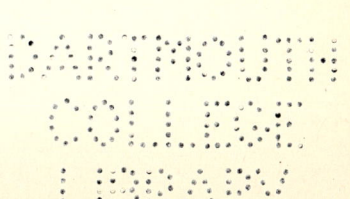

$2.70

COPYRIGHT, 1937, BY
AMERICAN BOOK COMPANY

*All Rights Reserved*

DIMOCK, MODERN POLITICS
W. P. 2.

320.15
D597m

OCT 16 1941
464505
John, Pol. Sci.

MADE IN U. S. A.

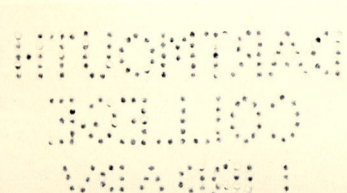

TO

C. A. DYKSTRA

*A pioneer in constructive government*

# PREFACE

☆ ☆ ☆

*"Governments have come to be engaged not merely in preventing wrong things from being done but in bringing it about that right things shall be done. A negative government requires only courage and consistency in its officials; but a positive government requires a constant supply of invention and suggestion."*
—GRAHAM WALLAS

THE EXTENSIONS of governmental responsibility which are taking place all about us represent in the eyes of many of our compatriots novel and untried experiments in state activity. Some of them are; but for the most part the positive functions of government, which are the subject of so much remark and of no little perturbation, are merely the logical extension of developments which have progressed continuously over a considerable period of time. It is not the functions which are new; it is the realization that our political theories have not followed the actual progress of political and social evolution. As Thurman Arnold has said, "Government itself has not been quite as stationary as thinking about government has been." What is needed, therefore, is a realistic analysis of the changes in our economic life and in society which have produced the modern state, with its positive responsibilities and its emphasis upon service.

The nature of the state has been changing rapidly since the beginning of the present century. Government, which was once thought of primarily as restraint or control, is now chiefly characterized by assistance and service. The principal relationships of government today are to economics and to administration. It is essential, therefore, that an interpretation of present-day government should emphasize public administration and political economy. Most of the treatises on state activity written in the United States have stressed politics, to the almost utter disregard of public administration, the services of modern government, and the central importance of political economy. In this book, I have tried to lay equal emphasis on both.

The treatment is functional and analytical. Government is considered a response to the immediate wants and persistent desires of individuals and groups. Institutional organization and procedures are examined from this point of view. An effort is made to combine the psychological, legal, and institutional approaches. Description is minimized, while an effort is made to use sufficient illustrative materials.

*Politics and Administration* is the title of one of Frank J. Goodnow's most influential books. He shows that government is divisible into two broad functions: the formulation of policy and its execution. The judiciary is an extraordinary arm of the administrative branch and also contributes to the evolution of public policy. Legislative, administrative, and judicial officers at one time take part in policy making, at another time in the execution of public programs. The division into politics and administration is in keeping with the functional treatment attempted here.

The traditional pattern for textbooks on American government deals with the federal government, then the states, and finally the local units. I have followed a different method in the present study. My principal concern is with problem and response, cause and effect, wants and satisfactions. I am not so much impressed with the question of which level of government exercises a certain power as with why the function is undertaken, how well it is performed, and whether improvement can be made.

Most of the important duties of government are shared by federal, state, and local subdivisions. Moreover, the legislative, administrative, and judicial processes are basically alike, irrespective of the level of government at which they are viewed. This is particularly true of federal and state governments. Obviously, then, we should seek the common factors, the intrinsic elements, the basic forces and explanations. This approach tends to prevent repetition, while any important differences between state and federal legislatures, for example, can readily be noted.

In this text, I have attempted to combine functional analysis and consideration of the most important questions of political theory and philosophy. The concluding chapter in Part I, as well as the last two chapters in Part II, is devoted entirely to theory, the questions under consideration being the ends of the state and the reconciliation of efficiency and popular control, and of liberty and equality. Throughout, an effort is made to raise philosophical issues which will provoke immediate discussion and additional study and reflection.

I began thinking about this book eight years ago while an instructor at the University of California (Los Angeles). There I was associated with C. A. Dykstra, who has since become City Manager of Cincinnati; at several points in my thinking, Mr. Dykstra's penetrating analyses have left an indelible mark. I wish also to acknowledge the helpfulness of another one-time colleague, Professor John M. Gaus, of the University of Wisconsin. The manuscript in whole or in part has been read by my colleagues, Charles E. Merriam, Louis Brownlow, T. V. Smith, and Lewis Meriam, to all of whom I owe a debt of gratitude. My own students, past and present, have been co-workers. To Dr. John H. Marion, one-time Fellow of the Social Science Research Council and now instructor in political science at Yale University, I am deeply indebted, because he helped to make available the material which was used in writing the treatise, and his co-ordinating activities and critical suggestions were beneficial at all times. Similar assistance was rendered by Dr. John McDiarmid, now instructor in government at Princeton University, and James L. McCamy, instructor in social science at Bennington College, Vermont. I acknowledge also the contributions of my present research assistants, Messrs. Howard K. Hyde, Robert W. Siebenschuh, and David B. Truman. Professor Lindsay Rogers, of Columbia University, has been both helpful and co-operative in his capacity as editor; I owe him a debt of gratitude. Without my wife's active co-operation and skillful planning, publication unquestionably would have been long delayed.

*Marshall E. Dimock*

Chicago, *January, 1937*

# CONTENTS

☆ ☆ ☆

## PART I—POLITICS

I. GOVERNMENT IN MODERN SOCIETY: 3
Social institutions—The institution of government—The theory of social lag—The *raison d'être* of government—Fundamental concepts: political science; political economy; the individual; group behavior; society; community; the state; government; politics; law; sovereignty; pluralism; pressure politics; representative government; democracy; the general will; public opinion; administration—The levels of government—Institution and dynamics—Some basic issues.

II. THE FUNCTIONS OF GOVERNMENT: 37
"Proper" functions—Recent views—"Public interest" as the test—Rival theories: the plutocratic position; aristocracy; the authoritarian state; liberalism; socialism; American social-democratic view—"The greatest good of the greatest number"—The appeal to history: American history—The dynamic theory—The theory of élites—The conspiracy theory—Contemporary power situations—Relieving tensions—A suggested classification—Distribution of powers among governments: federal functions; powers of the states; local services—Government as protector: police—The regulatory function—Government as assistance: education; health; housing; public welfare; assistance to business—The state as enterpriser—The door to service.

III. DEMOCRACY IN AN INDUSTRIALIZED COUNTRY: 69
Control and response—Difficulties and advantages of democracy—Varying interpretations—From agriculture to industry—Urbanism—Consequences of population congestion—Concentration in business—Wall Street—Relation between economic and political power—Results upon representative government—Can public control be expected to succeed?—Influence of technology—Control of public opinion—Obligations of a governing class—The middle class as the balance of power—"Practical socialists"—Remote control—Increased federal responsibility—Effect upon levels of government.

IV. PROBLEMS OF REPRESENTATIVE GOVERNMENT: 99
Possibilities of controlling the social environment—The electorate—Proposals to restrict the franchise—Non-voting—Increasing popular participation—Compulsory voting—Proportional representation—Political parties—Place of the party in the governmental process—Party membership—Economic interest and party affiliation—Handicaps of minority parties—Elements of party power—The machine—Pressure groups—Interest representation and political parties—Contributions of interest groups to the representative process—Interest representation and official independence.

V. THE LAWMAKING PROCESS: 131
Legislation and the representative process—Methods of apportioning representation—Equal representation in the Senate—City and country—Bicameralism—The American Senate—The functions of legislatures: internal organization; deliberation; enacting laws; criticism; selective process—Government by committees—Should legislative bodies be made smaller?—Greater specialization—The fact-finding process—Difficulties of improving efficiency—Methods of lobbies—Defense against pressure groups.

## CONTENTS

**VI. THE AMERICAN CONSTITUTIONAL SYSTEM:** 159
Types of constitutions—The American Constitution—Constitutional growth—Universality of basic charters—"A government of laws"—The American doctrine of judicial supremacy—Separation of powers—Responsible government—The city-manager plan—Difficult reforms—Irresponsible finance—Proposed constitutional reforms—Federalism—Problems of federalism—State versus Nation—Regionalism—Due process of law—The police power.

**VII. SOCIAL REFORM AND THE CONSTITUTION:** 187
Social legislation as an index—The judiciary as umpire—Periods of judicial review—The commerce power: uses of the commerce clause; navigable waters; anti-trust legislation; public control of business; the public-utility category—Entry into business—The interests of organized labor—Hour restriction and women workers—Taxation as a social instrument: "The power to destroy"; limitations on the taxing power—The "Gold Clause" case—Is reform necessary?—The amending process—Analysis of amendments—Expansion of federal power—Periodic constitutional conventions—Proposals to limit the Supreme Court—Legislative power of re-enactment.

**VIII. THE ENDS OF THE STATE:** 215
The nature of government—The importance of choosing objectives—Are ends real?—Traditional objectives—The contemporary objectives—The ultimate end—Society versus the individual—The significance of man—Elements of a reconstructed ideology.

## PART II—ADMINISTRATION

**IX. THE EXECUTION OF POLICY:** 229
The controlling influence of administration—Factors conditioning success—Administration as a concept—Relation of administration to the whole of government—Contribution to lawmaking—Administrators as policy makers—Administrative adjudication—Pros and cons of administrative justice—Administrative discretion—Legal remedies—Interest groups and administration—Public administration defined—Principles of large-scale organization—Organization principles—Rules for management—Central importance of organization—Four theories of organization—Modern theory—Administrative reorganization—Objectives—Causes of red tape.

**X. THE STRATEGY OF MANAGEMENT:** 257
Growing importance of administration—Reasons for neglect of management factors—Compromise versus principle—Inadequate organization arrangements—The dual executive—Consequences of inadequate attention to management—Adequate staff assistance a possible solution—Analogy to business corporations—Proposed department of general administration—A suggested plan—Qualifications of staff officials—"Top control"—Unity of management—Qualities of executive leadership: what the leader does—Spirited response—Relation of finance to top control: responsibility of the chief executive; two functions of financial management—The budgetary process: efficiency testing; public reporting—Public relations: objectives of public relations; the public and the executive.

**XI. MAN POWER:** 287
Human resources—Government as employer—Varieties of work—Administrative careers: improving career opportunities—Relation of political and administrative heads—Skills distinguished—An administrative corps—Objectives of the merit system—Parties and patronage—The neutrality of public servants—Taking stock of

civil service: adequacy of examinations; permanent tenure; inadequate use of probationary period; limitations on executives—Influence of employees' associations—Need for a complete program—Outstanding examples—Merits and demerits of classification—The problem of promotions—Theories of remuneration—Incentives—The future.

XII. ADMINISTRATIVE REGULATION: 315
Administration and the functions of government—Regulation versus public ownership—Implications of regulation for political theory—What public utilities are—Ambit of utility control—Extension of administrative regulation—A balance sheet—Economic results—The regulatory tribunal—Public control abroad—How expert are commissions?—Financial limitation—Limited jurisdiction—Summary of administrative deficiencies—The commissions and the courts—Holding companies—The rules of the game—Desiderata of public-service management—Future of regulation.

XIII. THE PROVISION OF ECONOMIC SERVICES: 341
Government as enterpriser—Causes of the change to public operation—Government holds the bag—Pioneering and risk bearing—Task of the political scientist—State enterprise abroad—Government participation in the United States—Size and administrative difficulties—Traditional shortcomings—Democratic control—Civil-service conditions—An excess of financial control—"Political" influences—Results of municipal trading—Objectives of businesslike management—The public corporation—Public-utility trust—Mixed undertakings—Relative advantages of the three types—General considerations—Decisive factors.

XIV. GOVERNMENT CONTROL OF THE ECONOMIC SYSTEM: 369
Recent economic theory—Shortcomings of *laissez faire*—Keynes's analysis—Planning in business—Gaps in planning—What is involved in planning?—Advantages that America possesses—Fashioning the instruments—Control without ownership—The self-government of industry—Government responsibility—Drawbacks of economic groups as governors—Organizing for planning—Providing the brains—Administrative reforms—National planning and international trade—The revival of political economy.

XV. THE EXPERT AND THE LAYMAN: 389
The reconciliation of efficiency and popular control—The indispensability of competence—Alternatives to effective popular rule—Problems to be solved—The machinery of popular control—Shortcomings of legislative procedure—Party responsibility and popular control—Legislative criticism, review, and confirmation—Judicial control—Citizen advisory committees—Directive boards—Necessity for long view—Inherent dangers of bureaucracy—Responsibility of the administrative corps—Democracy and a public-service philosophy—Popular participation—"Public persons"—Providing opportunities—Public values.

XVI. THE NEW INDIVIDUALISM: 409
Reconciliation of liberty and equality: liberty defined; equality defined; elements to be admixed—Regimentation—What is individualism?—Cultivating initiative—Inventive capacity—Freedom and inventiveness—The goal of community.

INDEX: 429

PART I ☆ POLITICS

CHAPTER I

☆ ☆ ☆

GOVERNMENT IN MODERN SOCIETY

*"The mould in which the modern state
was cast is broken or is breaking."*
—CHARLES E. MERRIAM

FEW OF THE BASIC social institutions rank with government in their importance to modern life. Government's significance relative to the institutions of the home, the church, and business has increased with great rapidity in the last few decades. A well-known sociologist has said that throughout most of modern history the home, the church, and the local community securely monopolized men's loyalties, but in fairly recent times the national state and organized business have moved to the center of the social stage, more or less dimming the importance of the others. Moreover, the relations between business and government have become so numerous and so close that it is hard to understand one without considering the other.

SOCIAL INSTITUTIONS

The rapidity with which government has forged to the forefront of men's considerations can be seen when it is recalled that the modern state goes back only about three hundred years. It is impossible to find an exact date of beginning, of course, but there is general agreement that the Treaties of Westphalia in 1648 saw the emergence of a system of sovereign states in the Western world. Not until the present century, however, did qualified persons begin to rank government and business as pre-eminent among the basic social institutions.

Is this just a passing phase? Will the powerful modern state shrink to its former proportions as other institutions and ways of life re-establish themselves? Will the artisan and the small merchant cause the huge corporate organizations to disintegrate? To pose these questions is to ask whether life in society may again become simple, rather than remain complex. Some people long for what they call a social organization of society rather than the present political system. One school of political philosophy believes that the state is merely a temporary expedient and that eventually it will be superseded. The syndicalists favor such a course of events. There are also suggestions of this in the writings of Karl Marx, and it was once thought that Soviet Russia would bring about the liquidation of the political state. Judging by trends in that country, however, nothing of the kind may be expected. The instrument of government is being found increasingly useful and indispensable. Soviet Russia has developed state socialism.

Instead of thinking wishfully about government, some students of social institutions attempt to base their analyses upon the cause-and-effect relationship. They project present social trends in an effort to predict what response will be required from institutions in the future. *Recent Social Trends,* a series of studies sponsored by former President Hoover, is a good example of this approach, and Charles E. Merriam and W. F. Ogburn, two of the contributors, have been prominent exponents of the method in their writings.

THE INSTITUTION OF GOVERNMENT

Government is largely a response to problems that society creates. It is probably still true that the institutions of family and business are more elemental, that is, closer to people, than is government. But when other institutions need help, when they are in disagreement, or citizens think that co-ordination and encouragement are necessary, the institution of government is called in. Government is an instrument. It co-ordinates. It can be thought of as being above other institutions, restraining, assisting, and performing some distinctive social functions of its own.

If a science of cause and effect could be worked out, it would be possible to tell what government should do and when the response should be made. But first of all we would have to have standards, yardsticks by which to measure what needed to be done. People might be hungry or sick, but unless the community, as well as the experts, knew that these conditions need not be and felt that something should be done about it, government or some other social institution would not be called upon. Moreover, there is frequently the issue as to which institution is the proper one to react to the need, or indeed whether the matter should not be left to the individual or to his family and relatives. Can valid criteria be established about these matters, or must they be settled experimentally and falteringly, depending upon the thoughts and feelings of the populace at any given time?

When the responsibilities and work of institutions are long-established and widely agreed upon, the relation between causation and response assumes more clear-cut lines. One can then say, "the city is failing to keep the streets clean," or, "the government should break up the powerful trusts." The social standard is what the law provides or what people have come to accept. Instead of saying that the government is doing too much, people frequently complain that it is not doing its duty. As a matter of fact, the investigations of social scientists, and especially those of Professor Ogburn, have led them to use the expression "social lag" as a description of government's habitual failure to keep abreast of what the social situation requires.

<small>THE THEORY OF SOCIAL LAG</small>

Between the time that the need arises and that when governmental response takes place, there is said to be almost always a time lapse. The stable is locked after the horse has been stolen from it. Energetic measures are taken to cope with depression only after the barometer hits bottom. Government attempts to organize industry, but cannot seem to reorganize its own administrative mechanism. Many instances will occur to anyone. But is this necessarily a reflection upon the institution of government? State action, as we have noted, is merely an instrument of the community. The reason government does not respond with scientific precision is not only because our yardsticks are inadequate, but because it takes the voters time to make up their minds. Deliberative bodies are not noted for their celerity. A democracy takes it for granted that reflection is a good thing. Moreover, the administrative services are not always as speedy as it seems they should be. But it must be recalled that they are expected to proceed according to law, that they are responsible, and that they must try to treat all parties equally. Under these circumstances it is difficult to act efficiently and with dispatch.

The theory of the social lag is a true and a useful one. The malco-ordination between institutions and the material conditions of life frequently makes the work of government much harder. You know the old statement, "an ounce of prevention. . . ." Abuses become fastened upon the body politic. Interests become vested. Dilatory litigation is resorted to. By the time the administrative machinery is organized, most of the damage may have been done. It is hoped that the reader will not get a false impression of government, one that is too pessimistic or cynical, at the very outset. Government does its work much better than most people usually give it credit for and the state is not always lagging behind the procession. Sometimes government is the pioneer, and often, particularly in recent years, it is the sponsor and creator.

If citizens understood the inherent nature of social lag, it might make them more vigilant of their interests as taxpayers and as beneficiaries of governmental services. They would give increased thought to the question of what government should do, and they would assist efforts to pass foresighted legislation. If government were viewed rationally, its program would be more consistently progressive and there would be fewer cases of injustice done to private interests that have become vested and to public interests that have been given insufficient attention. But here is another truth about statecraft: men should not be assumed to be predominately and consistently rational; yet, over long periods, they seem to come out with what appears to be the right result. If rationality were general, most of society's vexing problems would have been solved long ago. The calculating man, the voter or consumer with intelligent self-interest, is mostly a character in the learned treatises. All the more reason for attempting to add to the number of intelligent people! The difficulty of securing rational responses in a democracy is a problem with which we shall deal in a later chapter.

The necessity for government has varied as to both time and place, neither of which is independently determinative. The government of ancient Rome provided more and better services than are found in some modern countries. China in the twentieth century, as large as it is, places nowhere near the same reliance upon its political institutions as does little Norway or faraway Australia.

Historically, the principal characteristic of government has been supreme authority and its symbol, force. When in the settlement of individual disputes self-help no longer sufficed or was socially objectionable, the chieftain became enforcement agent and, later, referee and policeman. Early governmental activity immediately conjures up recollections of armies, taxes, and decree laws. It may be said that the primary function of government throughout recorded history has been to rule. This has carried with it the ancillary duties of preserving order, dispensing justice, defending the country, and sponsoring the country's trade and industry upon which the ruler's dominion and the people's welfare depended. At no period in history has government been merely a matter of force, of keeping the people subjugated, and of refereeing conflicts of interest. But the supreme authority of the state and the effective power of the government are as inherent in the political process today, and are every bit as necessary, as they ever were.

[margin: THE *RAISON D'ÊTRE* OF GOVERNMENT]

In the days of early Greece, Plato observed that "States originate because the individual is not self-sufficing but needs the help of many." Rendering assistance to groups and to individuals and supplying services to citizens have been functions of government from the earliest times. Recently these functions have become the dominant motifs. The police state has been superseded by the service state.

Government plays two primary roles in society: it rules the people and it serves the community. Although power, control, and coercion have been symbolic of the state's development—and although they are present and widely used today—the services of government have tended to increase so enormously in number and in importance that the control aspect of government appears less impressive in comparison.

The character of the state has changed very considerably in the last half century. Whereas during the nineteenth century it was considered mostly negative, today it has become also a positive, creative force in the life of the community. Irrespective of changes in party fortune, irrespective of the intrigues of groups and of individuals struggling for power and dominance, the primary services of government are so indispensable in this age of machinery and urbanism that the bulk of governmental work remains that of providing essential communal wants.

In its roles as ruler and servant, modern government performs four more or less distinct functions. These are protection, regulation, assistance, and direct service. Examples are police protection, public-utility regulation, provision of trade information, and water supply. We shall deal with the activities and responsibilities of government in the chapter immediately following, but a reference to the classification at this point serves to indicate how the ambit of state activity has expanded and, particularly, how the importance of service functions has increased, thereby changing the nature of the state itself.

Before we can deal understandingly with the nature of the state, the work of modern government, and the manifold problems of political science, we must define the fundamental concepts with which we shall be dealing. What is the state? Does it even exist? Should it be spelled with a capital "S" or a small one? Consideration of concepts and definitions not only will help our intellectual process but it will throw additional light on the importance of government in modern society.

FUNDAMENTAL CONCEPTS

Political science deals with the fulfillment of men's wants by means of public, i.e., political, instrumentalities. The maintenance of order, which is the principal manifestation of the control aspect of government, is a vital public necessity. Industry, commerce, the normal workaday processes of life, depend upon internal peace and the enforcement of the law. Hence, it is possible to combine the control and service aspects of government in one definition. Government is an instrument by means of which the people attempt to formulate and achieve common objectives and generally felt wants. In this process it is necessary that there should be citizens and officials, those who are governed and those who rule. Political science is therefore concerned with the art of ruling, with the

POLITICAL SCIENCE

techniques of control. Finally, the state has authority and power superior to that of any other institution. This is because the broadest or most common aims of the population can be achieved only by entrusting final power to some one agent. In order to preserve order and enforce the law, the government needs authority and power over any who might defy it.

Still another important aspect of government is the competition between the ins and the outs, between those who are ruling and those who would like to rule. Not until the last two hundred years or so has the struggle for succession by groups with conflicting programs been officially recognized and institutionalized. We now think of political parties, elections, and changes in government as being natural and necessary; but in the long record of known history this development is very recent. For that matter, there are several countries in the world today where opposition parties do not receive official recognition or legal sanction. This does not mean that opposition has not always, or nearly always, existed. It seems natural for men to disagree, if not about the objectives then about the means. It may be seen, therefore, that the struggle for position, the competition to gain control and to run the government, is a very important aspect of political science.

Another recognized fundamental of government is its method of working, its medium of formulating objectives and carrying them out. Government operates through law. In countries that have democratic rule, government is controlled by law; but law's age-old function is that of a medium. It is the connecting link between the will of the ruler and compliance by those who are meant to be controlled thereby.

Is it possible to construct a comprehensive definition of political science out of the basic characteristics and processes we have distinguished? Let us try. Political science is concerned with the state and its instrumentality, government, whose purpose is to fulfil the wants and expressed desires of the population within the bounds of legal authority; the state is assumed to have authority and power superior to that of any other association; there are those who hold political authority and those who are governed, those who have control of the government and those who seek its control; the medium by which the will of the government is given expression is called "law." This is a long definition, but it would be difficult to shorten it and still bring out all the important points.

If government is concerned with the fulfillment of fundamental wants, then how does it differ from political economy? The two subjects are difficult to distinguish. There are, however, logical bases of differentiation. Economics deals primarily with the market place, with the satisfaction of economic wants. It is concerned with the production and exchange of goods and services. Government, on the other hand, is interested in the totality of wants of all types, whether they be economic, social, or religious. Economics deals primarily with private economy, and government is concerned with public economy. The point at which the two meet is political economy, in the broadest and best sense of the term.

If the private-profit system in the liberal-democratic state produces disequilibriums and hardships that affect society and large groups of people adversely, the government is assumed to have a responsibility for setting things right. Moreover, governments now supply a growing number of services that were once private and that still are definitely "economic," i.e., they affect the price structure, profits, labor, competition, etc. In the liberal-capitalist state, in other words, the government assumes responsibility for direct economic services and for guiding, regulating, and rectifying some of the failures of private enterprise. So extensive has this responsibility become that the term "state intervention," once used extensively by economists and political theorists to describe opprobriously any interference of government that deigned to lay a hand on what was thought to be a self-regulating system, now sounds strange and out of place. There are no longer two systems, one private and the other public, existing side by side but independent of each other; they are now so intertwined and interdependent that one cannot be studied without considering the other.

POLITICAL ECONOMY

The common denominator in all institutional studies is the individual. Different groups owe loyalties to various institutions, but the individual is the individual. For his interest and support, all social groupings compete. For him, supposedly, all economic, social, and political services are made available.

But is the individual just an individual? Is he a unity? Is John Jones at one and the same time, citizen, owner, producer, consumer, church and club member? Or is he at one time a political man, at another time an economic man, and so on? This is not a side-trip into abnormal psychology. We are not interested just now in whether most people, or few people, deserve to be called "integrated personalities."

THE INDIVIDUAL

How shall we study government? Shall we assume that man can be segmented, divided, and that at one time, for purposes of study, he is a political man while at another he is an economic man? It is plain that practically, realistically speaking, we cannot do this. Men do not commonly dissociate their activities to any such extent. Moreover, it is usually hard to distinguish between one's economic and political interests. Quite properly, most people effect a unity of interests and psychological characteristics.

But why not create a hypothetical man, the imaginary political man? We could endow him with the characteristics of human nature that appear to be most pronounced and universal. Economics has hypothesized an "economic" man, one who is assumed to attempt to fulfill his wants with a minimum of sacrifice and a maximum of satisfaction. Why not say that the political man tries to do the same thing? Some political scientists believe that unless we take this step there cannot be a "science" of politics worthy of the name. Professor Catlin, the most outspoken champion of this approach, suggests that the cardinal truth about the human nature of the political man is his desire to control the wills of others and not be made to bend to others' wills.[1] This man has certain "persistent desires" that he hopes to satiate by means of controlling the machinery of government. Hence the political man attempts to win votes, just as the economic man tries to win

---

[1] G. E. G. Catlin, *The Science and Method of Politics* (New York, 1927), particularly Part II and Part III, and *A Study of the Principles of Politics* (New York, 1930), particularly chaps. I–III.

dollars. Politics, concludes Professor Catlin, is essentially a struggle for position, for power.[1]

This view of the process of government clearly emphasizes an aspect which is very important. In our definition of political science, we have already pointed out the important roles played by control and by the incessant struggle between the ins and the outs; but this is not the complete picture. If the concept of the political man is useful and desirable, a more complete analysis of political motivation and behavior needs to be given. Man also serves. What a libel on human nature it is to say that the basic fact about man's political activities is that he seeks position and power! It is to be doubted whether more than an infinitesimal proportion of the people of the country desire dominance and authority—at least for themselves as individuals. Their interests are close at home, simple, and largely concerned with animal comforts.

Men are altruistic as well as selfish. As groups, men do more outstandingly unselfish things than selfish ones; for instance, they die by millions for home and country. Men serve ideals, sometimes myths. They live by their emotions, their sympathies, their passions, more largely than by their calculating intelligence.

Government appeals to this side of man's nature. He is constantly encouraged by his fellows to do the "public-spirited" thing. The self must be sublimated for the common good. Thousands of men stand for office each year because they consider it their patriotic duty, rather than for anything they expect to get out of it themselves. Thousands more serve on school, park, recreation, and library boards with no thought other than a public service.

One difference between government and business is that the latter appeals primarily to the selfish streak in people and the former brings out the altruistic. This has become increasingly true since the functions of government have become so largely social-service ones. The governmental role is the father role, its assumption brings out in men some of the basic instincts and motives

[1] The most complete and penetrating analysis of this subject is found in Charles E. Merriam, *Political Power: Its Composition and Incidence* (New York, 1934).

found in parents. On the other hand, business is not ordinarily as selfish, as calculatingly so, as the writers on classical economics would make it appear. They have dignified selfishness by attempting to make it the self-sufficient explanation not only of why the economic mechanism runs, but of why it supposedly operates so well if left alone. Let it be hoped that political science will not make the same mistake.[1]

But supposing that we could assume self-aggrandizement to be the central, self-sufficient truth of political science, would we then know all the important things about political life? Obviously not. Individual psychology and social psychology have distinctive problems. Men behave differently in groups than they do singly. They are more easily moved by sentiment, passion, symbolism, myths, patriotic appeals. "Mass psychology" is no figment of the imagination. To understand individual psychology would undoubtedly help to solve the perplexing problems of political psychology. On the other hand, society is greater than the sum of its parts, i.e., the individuals who compose it. Institutions create customary responses, unthinking ways of acting, which sociologists call "mores." Institutions inculcate attitudes, ways of looking at things. Frequently they are emotionally colored, irrational, rather than logical and founded on fact. Overlook these considerations and political science cannot be fathomed; assume that self-interest is the self-sufficient truth of political behavior and the conclusions will be unrealistic. Political science should be satisfied with nothing less than an understanding of the real, the complete, man. This means that the predication of one motivation does not suffice; we must consider as many basic factors of individual and social psychology as are possible and applicable.

The bases of human personality are physical, geographical, economic, traditional, and psychological.[2] The individual's behavior and attitudes are determined by physical factors, such as biological heredity; geographical influences, such as climate and eco-

[1] My views on this subject are more fully explained in an article entitled "Scientific Method and the Future of Political Science" in *Essays in Political Science*, Part IV (Baltimore, 1937).
[2] The analysis that follows is taken from an unpublished address, by Peter H. Odegard, delivered at Colorado Springs, Colorado, in May, 1936.

nomic resources; economic forces, such as occupational status and security; traditional factors, usually referred to as the "social heritage"; and psychological forces, varyingly emphasized by such schools of psychology as the instinctivists, behaviorists, introspectionists, dynamists, gestaltists, and psychoanalysts.

Every person is born into a full-blown society which furnishes the customs, habits, traditions, and beliefs within which he grows and develops. Our social heritage—Protestant, frontier, equalitarian—naturally emphasizes individualism and democracy. The characteristic features of the American public mind,[1] as Professor Odegard has shown, can be understood only in the light of these controlling factors.

GROUP BEHAVIOR

There are various attempted explanations of the behavior of crowds and the influence of the social heritage upon social action. Three of the principal theories are those of unconscious imitation, consciousness of kind, and Freudianism. Walter Bagehot, Gustave Le Bon, Gabriel Tarde, and others have contended that crowd action is the result of unconscious imitation. Men and women follow the patterns established by dominant economic and social groups until a few bold individuals break through the "cake of custom" and create new molds. The gregarious instinct, or "consciousness of kind," is another explanation of group behavior, and has been emphasized by Wilfred Trotter, Franklin Giddings, and others. Man is so gregarious that he fears isolation, distrusts novelty, is almost wholly nonrational, and is intolerant of anyone whose conduct differs too markedly from that of the crowd. Everett Dean Martin, applying the Freudian theory, has concluded that crowds are devices through which individuals can satisfy their unconscious egoistic desires. Another writer, W. F. Vaughan, similarly emphasizes the relation of individual inferiority to social movements and points to the role of "compensatory drives" in social behavior.[2]

---

[1] *The American Public Mind* is the title of one of Professor Odegard's books.
[2] Cf. Floyd H. Allport, *Social Psychology* (New York, 1924); Gustave Le Bon, *The Crowd: A Study of the Popular Mind* (London, 1896); Everett D. Martin, *The Behavior of Crowds: A Psychological Study* (New York, 1920); and William McDougall, *The Group Mind* (New York, 1920).

Psychologists agree that human beings have fundamental hungers, variously denominated as instincts, unlearned responses, or prepotent drives. Among the "visceral hungers" are self-preservation, ambition, pride, love of family and freedom, patriotism, imitativeness, a desire to be a leader, and love of play. Some of these drives, such as the desire for security and the patriotic impulse, are more important in political behavior than are others. When social customs, institutions, or habits come into conflict with these fundamental psychological forces, when the individual feels a sense of frustration, the problem of social adjustment becomes acute.

Society encompasses all social institutions. (See Figure 1.) It helps one to understand political science and the political man when the concept of society and government's relation thereto are analyzed.

SOCIETY    Society consists of all the people and all the institutions and activities on a given portion of the earth's surface. When we speak of American society, we mean everything of human and social interest in the United States. The concept of society need not be territorially confined, but it is a convenience to do so. There is no reason, however, why the idea of world society should not be utilized and gain increasing currency. What would then be meant is all the peoples of the universe, with all their common patterns of institution and custom and all their diverse ones.

"Society" is not only a broader concept than "government," or even "state"; it is also more elemental. Students of sociology are concerned with the family, social customs, human nature in all its manifestations, normal and otherwise. Government, on the other hand, is more highly organized; it is built upon social foundations but represents a higher stage of social development. Sociology, for example, describes why and how men congregate gregariously, while political science tells us how their common affairs are administered. Historically speaking, the state appeared much later than the primitive, communal relationship with which the anthropologist and sociologist are largely concerned.

But sociology and political science have much in common. As in the case of its relationship to economics, political science finds it hard to draw a sharp line between its proper concerns and

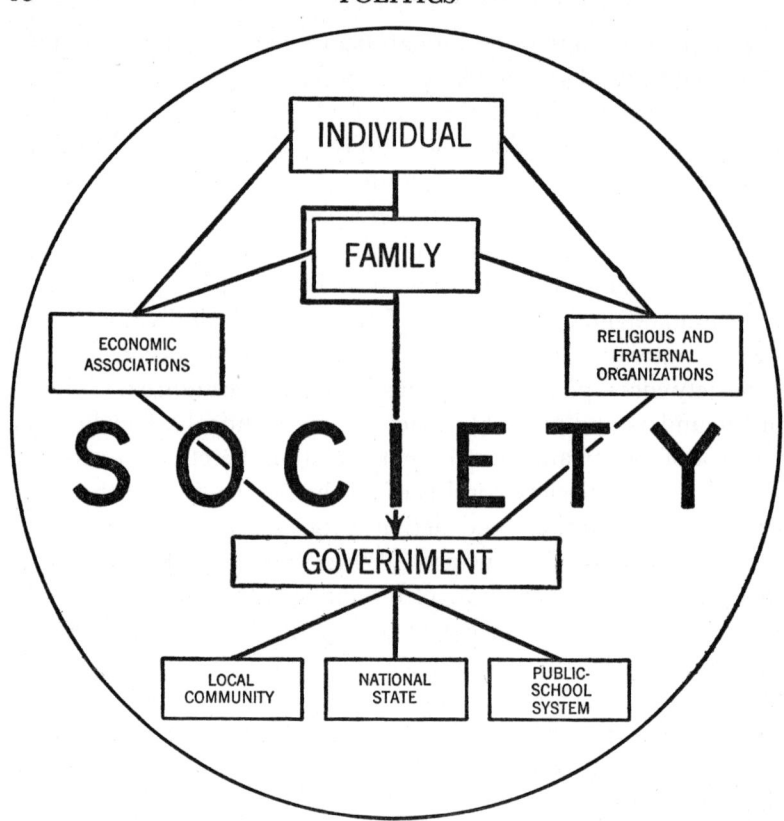

FIGURE 1.—INSTITUTIONAL ORGANIZATION OF SOCIETY

those of sociology. Anyone who has thought about the matter very much probably would not want to differentiate sharply in either case. A realistic political science will take adequate account of both social origins and economic desiderata. Unless the political scientist knows the basic facts about social patterns and community problems, he will be in the dark about how to deal with these matters. To a considerable extent, the task of the economist and sociologist is to indicate what is wrong with a particular social relation and what should be done about it; then the political scientist's responsibility is to recommend the method, the governmental remedy. This is merely a common-sense division of labor; but a basic knowledge of the other fields is necessary for effective work in any one. Sociology is not only a subject of study; it is an approach to other social studies, a method of attack. The sociological approach is a necessary one in political science because through it one attempts to get at the foundation matters upon which governmental procedures and techniques are properly constructed.

One significant concept that is shared jointly by both political science and sociology is that of "community."[1] Some suggestion of the general conception of that term is found in its application to local governments. The more generalized or ideal COMMUNITY definition is: a fairly large group of people living together under congenial conditions, these in turn being the result of common purposes and customs, making possible co-operative results and cultural conditions that are not dependent upon coercion. The power and control aspects of government are reduced to a minimum. Individuals are supposed to do the socially beneficial thing through natural impulse. Appropriate characterizations of community are "kindred spirits," "equal status," "mutuality of purpose," "freedom." The concept is not as Utopian or unrealizable as it sounds. Quite a few village and local governments and small national states have already approached such an ideal. Community should be the ultimate goal of the political state.

The state likewise is a conceptual creation, rather than something concrete that one can put one's hands on and watch operate in detail. It is no more imaginary, however, than society or community. It is probably even more necessary for THE STATE our thinking and understanding. The state has supreme authority over the population on a determinate portion of the earth's surface and operates through government to carry out the wishes and common aspirations of the community and those who govern for it. It will be observed that there is not a great deal of difference between this definition and what has been said about the component parts of political science.[2]

[1] The best book on this subject is one by Professor R. M. MacIver entitled, *Community* (London, 1917). See also his *Society* (New York, 1931).
[2] *Supra*, pp. 8–10.

The state is sovereign, legally supreme. Its jurisdiction extends to a definite territory and a definite part of the earth's population. The state finds concrete expression in its instrumentality, government. Finally, the state has duties, ends which organized society expects it to pursue. These ends differ; they are not always clearly formulated; they consist of the persistent desires, the common aspirations, the natural rights, the unwritten law. Like the state itself, the ends sought are hard to pin down, but there is no doubt about their powerful influence.

You may be thinking that in this discussion of society, community, and the state, we have dealt entirely with matters that are merely conceptual rather than with institutions that may be observed and analyzed objectively. The more skeptical may say that this is a flight into metaphysics. There is a good deal of justification for such an allegation, at least on first thought; but if we were to limit ourselves only to those matters that can be proved by actual observation, how circumscribed our study would become and how far from a complete understanding we should be! You may assert that there is no justification for continuing to use the concept of the state. Some political scientists have, directly or in effect, taken this view.[1] But does such a decision clarify one's thinking or, instead, limit one's comprehension?

Any idea or concept that is determinative of social behavior must be taken into account. Society, community, and state are terms that most people understand and that are employed in all parts of the world. Common usage and acceptance is, therefore, one reason for continuing to use the concept of the state. Then, too, the state serves a useful purpose. Government is merely an instrument and hence does not convey a complete understanding of all the basic elements that enter into the political compound. The most important of those that otherwise would be inadequately accounted for are the first and last terms in our definition, namely, supreme authority and ends or persistent desires. Sovereignty and ends are like law or religion—they cannot be fully proved by run-

---

[1] See, for example, G. E. G. Catlin, *A Preface to Action* (London, 1934); H. J. Laski, *Liberty in the Modern State* (London and New York, 1930) and *The State in Theory and Practice* (London and New York, 1935).

ning an adding machine or by looking at them through a microscope in the laboratory, but they are nevertheless real.

One potential danger in continued use of the concept of state is in idealizing it. A worshipful attitude may lead to a feeling of subservience and to uncritical adoration. Examples of this very thing exist today. Such extreme emotional demonstrations are not compatible with democracy and freedom. Just as eternal vigilance is the price of democracy, so a proper skepticism and independence form a desirable attitude toward the state. It is supreme, but even more importantly it is the common servant. Abject worship of the state can do great social harm, but an intelligent attitude to it may be the means of producing the ideal community.

Government consists of the fundamental framework of law, the organization and procedures by means of which effect is given to the desires of the citizenry and those who act as its agents. There is also a more generic sense in which the term GOVERNMENT "government" may be used. Thus, one may speak of the government of libraries, schools, fraternal organizations, or other associations. When so employed, it means the organization and administration of a common enterprise.[1] Our definition of political government is consistent with this generally accepted use; it is one example of the generic meaning, and by far the most commonly employed one.

There are two primary processes of government: the formulation of policy and program, and its execution. Government is politics and administration. As we shall soon see, however, there is far from being a sharp line dividing the two functions. One of our most important tasks will be that of showing how politics and administration are interrelated and interact. Law and policy run throughout the entire governmental framework.

Still another classification of governmental processes embraces legislation, administration, and adjudication—the tripartite division associated with the name of Montesquieu and found more prominently expressed in American governments than in those of any other country. This analysis is a necessary and valid one. It

[1]See, for example, a recent book by Carleton Bruns Joeckel entitled, *The Government of the American Public Library* (Chicago, 1935).

needs to be thoroughly understood and there is much to be said for it. For purposes of the present study, however, we prefer the dual division into politics and administration—an analysis which is widely accepted in Europe and one that has gained increasing favor among political scientists in this country. This approach first received prominent attention in the United States as the result of an influential book entitled *Politics and Administration*, written by Frank J. Goodnow, first president of the American Political Science Association. When the dual classification is used, the judiciary is shown to contribute to both the making of law and its enforcement. Emphasis is placed upon functions, and only secondarily is one concerned with whether the particular officer is associated with the legislative, executive, or judicial branch. The dual classification is accordingly in consonance with our attempted functional treatment of political science.

Government is not merely a matter of organization arrangements and customary techniques of realizing stated objects. It is equally a study of propulsions, problems, and goals. There is an unofficial government as well as a formal one.[1] Political parties, pressure groups, lobbies, voluntary associations, customs, these are only the more prominent of the forces which impinge upon the conventional framework and help it function or attempt to restrain it.

A study of government should therefore deal with all the agencies and influences which are contributory to framing policy or to seeing that it is carried out.[2] Nothing less can be called sociological or realistic.

There is still another sense in which the term "government" is sometimes used. That is to indicate the government of the day, the party in power. Hence, when a minister in the British Parliament states, "His Majesty's Government will give thoughtful con-

---

[1] There is coming to be quite an extensive literature of political science dealing with unofficial government. As readable examples, see Charles E. Merriam, *The Written Constitution and the Unwritten Attitude* (New York, 1931); William B. Munro, *The Invisible Government* (New York, 1928); and David Lawrence, *The Other Side of Government* (New York, 1929).
[2] On the administrative side, an excellent example of this treatment is found in E. Pendleton Herring's recent book, *Public Administration and the Public Interest* (New York, 1936).

sideration to the Honorable Member's point," he means—if he means it at all—that the responsible representatives of the majority party will take up the matter. This usage has become increasingly common in the United States. Still another variation may be noted. Increasing numbers of persons use the expression "the government" when they mean the federal government. It differentiates national government from state and local. This manifestation is clearly evidence of the generally recognized fact that the country has become "Washington conscious."

Three connotations of the word "politics" need to be examined. The first makes the term interchangeable with political science. The second is the historic meaning, namely, policy or statecraft.

POLITICS  The third connotation is the common American usage, a word used to describe one's efforts to get something through one's connections, by pulling the right strings, slyly. As thus employed, it is usually a word of abuse, an implied criticism.

As a description of the entire field of political activity, the term "political science" or "government" is to be preferred to the word "politics." There are more specialized or distinctive purposes which the symbol "politics" needs to serve.

Politics is more appropriately identified with the process of policy making. It deals with the agencies, the instrumentalities, and the results associated with the initial, i.e., policy-forming, stage of governmental activity. Politics is one-half of government. The other part is administration. We frankly admit that it is because this dual division is so meaningful and useful to us that we advocate a more specific, rather than the more general, use of the word. This may be done without interfering with accepted usage. No precise meaning of the word "politics" can be said to exist at present. The proposed application accords with the fundamental meaning which has been attached to it from early times and which is generally accepted in other countries today.

Little needs to be said about the corrupted meaning of the term "politics"—perhaps the less the better. What Americans have been taught to think and have been led to believe about the influences which control political life and the scheming methods which are used to get what selfish interest demands is a reflection of governmental mismanagement and low motives. It is anomalous that politics, which traditionally and correctly stands for the general interest, should come to suggest a special or unsocial interest. Like other perfectly good words in the American vocabulary, it needs to be made respectable for technical discussion; but we should not deceive ourselves about the length of time required for its eventual redemption.

"Law" has many meanings. It may convey the idea of justice or right. When used in connection with government, it suggests constitutions or basic rights. It may take the form of codes, as in countries where the civil law of Rome is found.

LAW    In common-law countries, lawyers customarily think of case law, of decisions which have grown from precedent to precedent. The largest body of law is that which the legislative bodies enact and put into our compiled and annual statute books. This body of law has a great deal of significance for the political scientist, because it represents the policies which the government has formulated and which the administration is expected to execute faithfully. Then there is what is known as "administrative law," dealing with the organization and functioning of the executive arm and the relation of government officials to citizens. The law of municipal corporations defines the fundamental powers and limitations of our local governments. Municipal councils pass ordinances, which are analogous to the statutory law of Congress and the state legislatures. This is all very confusing, not only to the preoccupied citizen but also to the employees of government who must execute the law and stay within its confines.

But law has still another connotation. It represents policy. The policy may be fundamental, relatively fixed, or temporary. In between there are various degrees of difference. The really important point is that law runs through all the framework and interstices of government. Government is policy, either in the making or in the execution. Law is a great unifying factor. It sets tasks. It imposes limits. Sometimes it seems to stand in the way of desirable activities or improvements. Law is, like government, an instrument. Men enact it to serve their welfare. When law fails to achieve the desired results, they expect to have a right to change it. Law is a servant, though sometimes it appears to be a relentless master. It is the nature of law to be conservative. All institutions have a naturally conservative influence; but none is more preservative of the past, perhaps, than the legal edifice.

Let us, then, take the sociological view of law. Law is policy. Law is a channel. It may be constitutional or statutory, codified or precedent, substantive or adjective—but the important thing is that it is the medium through which government works.

The early roots of political science were in law. Public law became political science and in European universities today the study of government is taught as a subdivision of law. The body of law is divided generally into private and public. Public law may be defined as the rules and principles that deal with the powers of government and the relationship between it and the citizens. Constitutional law is the principal subdivision of public law. From constitutional and administrative law, interest was gradually developed in political parties, actual administrative procedure, and all the newer emphases to which modern political science gives much of its time.

American political theory has been considerably influenced by the jurists. From them we derive the juristic theory of the state, with the concept of sovereignty occupying a central position therein. Of our contemporaries, W. W. Willoughby

SOVEREIGNTY is the most prominent exponent of this position.[1] The state is assumed to be a legal concept. The central truth about the state is that it is sovereign. Other fundamental concepts derive from this initial hypothesis.

Sovereignty is said to make the state illimitable. Citizens can hold the government responsible, it may be, but not the state. Its will is above that of everyone else. Each state is independent of every other state, because it is legally supreme. Even when a state has difficulty enforcing its will or is physically unable to do so, it is still sovereign. Sovereignty is inherent, ineradicable, illimitable, non-

[1] The best expression of his ideas is found in *The Fundamental Concepts of Public Law* (New York, 1924).

transferable. It is a legal concept, and hence the physical facts do not change it.

How much value is to be attached to this concept? What does it matter whether a state is assumed to be legally sovereign if the actual facts cannot be squared with the theory? Is it in the social interest to assume that the state has the mystical quality of illimitability? Even if one gives a negative answer to these questions, the concept of sovereignty is not necessarily cast aside.

Some political scientists have parted company with sovereignty.[1] They say the concept is untrue and that it expresses no idea which cannot be better conveyed by another word. Some suggested equivalents are supreme authority, immunity from liability, jurisdiction, and illimitability except when in conflict with international law.

Sovereignty is a fiction, but it seems to have some practical value. Sovereignty is a way of saying that the state is supreme within its borders. It has no power above it so long as it remains within its own jurisdiction. It cannot be sued unless it gives its consent. Some may think it is better to state these particular generalizations rather than to go on talking about sovereignty. This is clearly true if sovereignty is viewed as a mystical concept, almost incapable of definition or delimitation. If realistic connotations are attached to it, however, there would seem to be good reasons for retaining it as a useful and important term in political science.

The concept of sovereignty has lost influence as the ideas of the pluralists have gained increasing recognition. Pluralism points out that men have loyalties and strong attachments to associations other than the state and, hence, that authority is

PLURALISM simply a matter of degree. Political society is organized and ruled by a number of institutions, prominent among which are chambers of commerce, trade unions, and various agricultural and professional associations. It is an unreal myth to assume that men's chief attachment is to political

[1] See Harold J. Laski, for example, in *A Grammar of Politics* (London and New Haven, 1925) and *Liberty in the Modern State* (London and New York, 1930); but cf. his *The State in Theory and Practice* (London and New York, 1935).

government; their more immediate and natural loyalties are to those associations which assist them to make a livelihood. These organizations also bring cohesion and order into the social edifice. It is conceivable that one or another of them may rival the state for supremacy and even overshadow it. Pluralists, however, are prepared to accept the state as indispensable and to grant its superior authority. They simply protest against overemphasis, object to the concept of sovereignty, and insist that the plurality of social institutions which forms organized society should be given deserved recognition. There are many variations of this general position,[1] some going much further than others in their proposed curtailment of the state's influence.

This position is inclined to belittle the concept of citizenship; that is, the idea that men rise above their economic and personal interests and do many things for the common good and out of a sense of patriotic pride. It refuses to put citizenship on a pedestal, not because pluralism objects to public-spiritedness but because its proponents believe that human nature is not capable of such consistent behavior. Life is a matter of survival, of competition for the world's goods and gratifications. One's life revolves around oneself and one's immediate family. Hence the principal use man has for the state is that of assisting him to get out of life what he wants for himself.

Closely, almost inextricably, related to pluralism is the pressure-politics position, which has enjoyed increasing influence in recent years.[2] Government, like a clock, goes because of the motion which men give it. Government is a tool which PRESSURE POLITICS can be used to the advantage of any group powerful or influential enough to impress its demands upon the legislature and administration. Men vote their interests, represent these interests, exert powerful pressure through lobbies to force their desires to be transformed into law. Professor Herring feels that lobbies have assumed such a dominant place in our

[1] For a more complete analysis, see Francis W. Coker, *Recent Political Thought* (New York, 1934), pp. 497–517, 533–35; and W. Y. Elliott, *The Pragmatic Revolt in Politics* (New York, 1928).
[2] Cf. E. Pendleton Herring, *Group Representation Before Congress* (Baltimore, 1929); Harwood L. Childs, *Labor and Capital in National Politics* (Columbus, 1930); "Pressure Groups and Propaganda," *Annals*, V, 179 (May, 1935), edited by Harwood L. Childs.

representative system that he compares present conditions with the early guild system, in which man's life revolved around his vocation and representation was by estates.[1]

One of the central problems of political science is that of who shall control, in whose interest the government shall operate. There are many forms of government—monarchy, oligarchy, democracy, modern dictatorships, with variations in between; but in every case the central question is: Whose will shall be done, who is being represented and how well? In theory and outward form, the government may not be representative, but this fact does not keep citizens from thinking about their interests and well-being.

A system of representative government is one in which regular, legally established channels are provided through which the wishes of the citizenry can be registered at stated intervals. Representative government entails the privilege of voting, the holding of elections at frequent intervals, the choosing of legislators to represent those who elect them, and the assurance that those who are elected will be given the right to enact the will of the citizenry into law instead of being frustrated by a superior authority. Any definition of this form of government must of necessity be more or less arbitrary. Representation is a matter of degree and of outward form. There has always been disagreement about which form best represents the peoples' true interests. France's monarchists contend that a king is almost certain to be more far-seeing, wiser, and more honorable than the rabble who are foolishly given the right to vote. Fascist Italy contends that its system of representation, which centers all real power in the party, is best for the long-run interests of the people as a whole; but judged by our definition, Italy is not a representative government; her legislature is not independent and supreme—if she can be considered as having a legislature in any commonly accepted sense.

But representative government is not merely a matter of counting noses and of giving the legislature power to make laws. It needs to be viewed realistically, from the standpoint of actual results. When the majority expresses its mandate, is its will carried

[1] E. Pendleton Herring, *Group Representation Before Congress*, pp. 2–7.

out? Is the general interest furthered, or is it sidetracked for special interests? Decisions on these matters must, from the nature of the case, be more or less subjective and opinionated; but there seems to be no question about the importance of keeping such queries in mind.

There is a real difference between representative government and democracy, but in ordinary parlance most persons use the two terms interchangeably. Democracy is a system of government wherein policies are expressed and laws are enacted by direct action and participation of the citizens in common assembly. Representative government makes use of elected agents who enact the will of the body of voters into law. We shall deal with the difficulties of maintaining democratic government in a later chapter.[1] This will not represent the technical use of the term, but the conceptual use. Democracy is popular control, assurance that the majority's wishes will be carried out. In this general, or loose, use of the word, the distinguishing factor of law enactment by action of the citizen assembly is not present.

DEMOCRACY

One of the central problems underlying representative government is that of how large a segment of the total population is to control the government and how this collective will can best be ascertained. Popular control assumedly means public control. But what is the public? Does it exist, except as a fiction? What is public opinion? Is there a general will?

Rousseau contended that there is a general will which can be ascertained by getting the population to express its views on one side or the other of a question. The *volonté générale* consists, for all practical purposes, of what the majority decides to be the general will, and it is assumed by Rousseau that those who voted otherwise also agree with the general will; they would not oppose what was right and in their own interest; minority voters merely did not apprehend clearly. Is the general will the will of God? Is the majority always right?

THE
GENERAL
WILL

Political scientists have gone so far in their reaction against

---

[1] The concept and various meanings attached to democracy are more fully examined in chap. III, especially pp. 71–73.

Rousseau's analysis that there is a real danger of going farther than the facts warrant. Walter Lippmann has characterized the public as a "phantom."[1] It is contended, particularly among those who emphasize the pressure-group approach, that there is not a public but rather that there are "publics." There is no such thing as an opinion held by everyone but rather there are "opinions." Sometimes one wonders whether skepticism and assumed realism will be carried so far that man's ability to think will be denied. But on the whole, this skepticism is a good thing. It follows discoveries which psychology has made about how opinions are reached, how attitudes exert powerful influences on thought, and how action is controlled by propagandist tools.

The mere expression of a majority will may not be so important as the method by which the majority became a majority. The voters at an election may find that they were mistaken, either about the candidate, the important issue, or both. Many times in history the minority view has eventually proved right. Even the minority views of the highest court in the land sometimes become the majority opinions later.

If the public were assured of getting the facts and could protect itself against propaganda and misrepresentation, it would probably act wisely in most cases. The fact that it was swayed by emotion or sentiment would not necessarily mean that it would do the wrong thing. Man is largely, perhaps primarily, an emotional being. This part of his nature helps him to do the right thing as well as sometimes causing him to do the wrong thing. Sheer intelligence, divorced from emotion, is hard to imagine and probably would not be found satisfactory if it could be produced.

Because man is not pure intellect, and because he is so largely emotion, there is great danger in overemphasizing the concept of will in our thinking about the political man and the actions of government. The term "will" has differing connotations. It may suggest calculating intelligence, ambition; on the other hand, it is frequently asso-

PUBLIC
OPINION

[1] Walter Lippmann, *The Phantom Public* (New York, 1925); for limitations on public opinion and the influence of interested persons and groups, see also A. Lawrence Lowell, *Public Opinion and Popular Government* (New York, 1913) and *Public Opinion in War and Peace* (Cambridge, 1923).

ciated with stubbornness, determination. In the first case, a sense of direction is indicated, while in the latter instance, firmness or immovability is the thought. Suggesting spirit or temperament, the latter connotation is to be identified with man's emotional nature. Hence, in a realistic view of the term "will," one sees both calculation and feeling, a synthesis.

It is not too sanguine to expect that if voters are assured of reasonably accurate information they will usually reach the decision which proves to be best in the end. Moreover, particular results which prove to be wrong are usually rectified over a period of several years. The public is not as uncomprehending as some of our intellectuals seem to think. Such is our faith in democracy and the common man! It is not blind belief. What we say is much more likely to be true, of course, when educational opportunities are universally good and when sources of information are available which attempt to serve the interest of the general public.

Difficult it is to devise accurate methods of determining what public opinion is on a particular issue at any given time. What is the public? Every person, no matter what his age, condition, or intelligence quotient? Is it all voters, all registered voters, or all those who vote at a particular election? Yes, the difficulties are many; but the mere fact it is difficult to gauge or measure public opinion does not prove that it does not exist. The principal newspapers of a large city may be unanimously for the same candidate or the same issue, but there have been instances in which the grapevine method of enlightening others, combined with the common sense and the right instincts, has defeated the combined efforts of the press. Public opinion is elusive, but the evidence is not convincing that it is merely a phantom.

After the public has instructed its representatives and policies have been transformed into laws, there arises the problem of accomplishing the program, executing it. Every law that is passed creates a problem of administration. Machinery needs to be set up, unless that which exists can be used for the purpose. An organization must be perfected, employees provided to run it, and funds secured to carry on the work. A good deal of technical knowledge may be required. Popular compliance must be sought, co-operation invited. It is important to please the public, particularly the "public" that worked hardest to get the law enacted.

Public administration consists of the governmental organization, personnel, and procedures which are involved in giving effect to programs enacted by policy-making agencies. It is the state in action, government at work. The administrative services transpose plans into accomplishments.

ADMINISTRATION

They are the point at which the government most frequently comes into direct contact with the citizen. Administration exists to serve. It is established, regular, indispensable, practical. Administration is engineering applied to government.

Somewhere between politics and administration, there is an area in which they are meshed. They interact upon each other, forming a unity. Politics extends into administration, and administration reaches back into the realm of policy formulation. Both are equally concerned with control, with fulfilling wants, with obtaining compliance. Through both flows law. A government is likely to be no better than its administration. Men's fondest dreams may be enacted into law, but unless their execution is practicable, nothing but disappointment and disillusionment may come of the effort. The state cannot be expected to be creative unless it possesses a reliable administrative mechanism. If the mechanism is too bad, government may be hated and disregarded.

We speak of government as though it were a unity, and conceptually it is; but in actual practice there are many governments in a country, dozens of them. In the United States, it is estimated that there are as many as 175,000 separate governmental bodies. How to secure co-operation between them, prevent overlapping and conflict, accomplish all the things citizens expect of them, are some of the major problems of public administration.

The meshing of levels of government is especially difficult under federalism. Are the individual states sovereign or is the national government to be given ultimate authority? Jealousies and frictions are seemingly ineradicable. With changes in transportation, communication, and the size of business and banking units, adjustments appear necessary in the division of work and responsibility between levels

THE LEVELS OF GOVERNMENT

of government. It is desirable to keep government as close as possible to the people, but it is also necessary to provide governmental instruments which will secure effective public control and protection of the public interest.

In the American hierarchy of governmental levels, there are districts, townships, villages, incorporated municipalities, metropolitan governments, counties, states, and on top of them all the federal government. Even this enumeration does not include all the existing units. Of those mentioned, the major classification is into federal, state, and local.

One way of studying government is to analyze the federal government, then the states, and finally the local units. The traditional pattern for textbooks on American government follows this procedure. We shall follow a different method in the present study. Our principal concern is with problem and response, cause and effect, wants and satisfactions. Ours is a functional treatment. We are not so much impressed with the question of which level of government exercises a certain power as with why the function is undertaken, how well it is performed, and whether improvement can be made. The most important public functions are shared by two or more levels of government. The essentials of the legislative, the administrative, and the judicial processes are very much alike wherever found. This is particularly true of state and federal governments. If one knows the important things about either Congress or the state legislatures, differences in one or the other can easily be seen by superimposition. Unnecessary duplication is to be avoided. It is more important to examine the basic problems and the functional foundations than to catalogue and describe the minutiae of a complicated series of independent governments.

Government is a matter of both mechanics and behavior, institution and dynamics. From one point of view, it is a matter of social engineering. Such, for example, is the question of the

INSTITUTION AND DYNAMICS

proper relationship and co-ordination of the levels of government. Most of administration is a matter of engineering technique. The institutional emphasis upon government concerns itself with basic design, with construction, with smooth operation, with co-ordination, and with the fuel supply, which is law.

The motivation of men, group customs, collective behavior patterns, these are the concern of the sociologist and psychologist. From them, and from the historian, the political scientist learns how men have acted under comparable circumstances in the past. Statistics, too, is a very helpful tool in this connection. The combined emphasis helps the student of government to understand men's social desires, human nature, class competitions, the crowd mind, and how human beings are likely to act in certain political situations.

It is not suggested that there is a sharp difference between the institutional and dynamic approaches. The two need to be combined, so far as possible, in the education of the student and in research relating to government. Things which are not seen whole, from all essential points of view, often are not seen accurately and reliably. With the development and refinement of research in specialized fields, it is clear that students will need increasingly broad and well synthesized competences. The historical method tells the political scientist what society has done in the past, and from this, one gets some indication of what may happen under similar conditions in the future. Statistics gives us objectified knowledge of past social behavior, when counting or quantification is possible. Political economy indicates the policies which are best for society's material well-being. Sociology and anthropology give us insights into the past behavior of social and political groups and indicate the problems and probable limits of remedial action by government. Psychological method provides knowledge of why men act as they do and how institutional organization and technique need to be shaped if ample recognition is to be given to these behavior patterns. Law reveals to the political scientist the rules of organization and procedure and the principal policies which have been given official sanction. International relations shows us that the state is not necessarily the central fact in the institutional universe but that a larger society is taking form and that individual states have legal and practical obligations to that international community. Education provides knowledge of how intelligent citizens are to be produced in a democratic society and how civic education is to be supplied to adult voters.

It is obviously impossible for one person to know everything about all of these fields of study, but it is well to know what each has to contribute and to appreciate the desirability of as much co-operation and synthesis as possible. The basic factor is the existence of a social problem. In its solution, it may be that all the social sciences will need to make their distinctive contributions and that the ultimate formula will be a compound contributed co-operatively.

The attempted solution of society's problems gives rise to the most difficult theoretical problems of political science. How can public desires be fulfilled without doing injustice to individuals? Is every social gain necessarily a personal loss to someone? To what extent does an individual own social assets as well as purely private ones? Does the state interfere and destroy or are its actions usually constructive and just?

SOME BASIC ISSUES

Another difficult problem is that of the desirable balance between efficiency and a *laissez faire* policy. If government were consistently effective and efficient, would the results be better or worse? Is freedom jeopardized by extensive social controls, well administered? When the state commences to interfere, does the process continue automatically, irresistibly? Should one wish for inefficient government because then one's liberties are likely to be more secure? May not excessive sympathy toward state activity bring about a regime similar to that of Russia, Germany, or Italy? Obviously, a reconciliation is needed between efficiency and freedom. It will be well to keep these age-old but ever-pressing problems in mind as we proceed with our study.

### Selected Readings

Dewey, John: *The Public and Its Problems* (New York, 1927), chaps. I and II; a lucid and stimulating discussion of the philosophical concepts of state, government, law, and society.

Elliott, William Y.: *The Pragmatic Revolt in Politics* (New York, 1928), chaps. I–III, V, XII, XIII, and XVII; a consideration of the principal theories in revolt against political rationalism, with a discussion of Laski's ideas.

Finer, Herman: *The Theory and Practice of Modern Government* (rev. ed., New York, 1934), an encyclopedic comparative analysis and description of representative governments; read chaps. I and II dealing with relations between government and the state, with politics and economics.

Garner, James W.: *Political Science and Government* (New York, 1928), chaps. I, III, IV (pp. 46–69), VIII–XI, XIII, XIV; deals with definition of terms and discusses various concepts.

Laski, Harold J.: *A Grammar of Politics* (2d ed., New Haven, 1930), chaps. I, II, and VII; includes a stimulating consideration of some basic concepts, particularly of the state and of sovereignty.

———: *The State in Theory and Practice* (New York, 1935), presents Laski's later views in the field of political theory.

Leacock, Stephen: *Elements of Political Science* (rev. ed., Boston, 1921); chaps. I–IV, VII; written many years ago but is still interesting and suggestive; chaps. cited deal with the origin, theory, and form of the state and of sovereignty.

Lippmann, Walter: *A Preface to Politics* (New York, 1913); an excellent group of essays whose value lies in the author's ability to stimulate a critical attitude toward the governmental process.

McDougall, William: *The Group Mind* (2d ed., Cambridge, 1927); a treatise on the principles of group psychology as applied to the life of nations.

MacIver, R. M.: *Society: Its Structure and Changes* (New York, 1931), chaps. I, II, IV, and X; a sociological treatise including a discussion of the concepts of society, community, and the state.

Merriam, Charles E.: *A History of the Theory of Sovereignty Since Rousseau* (New York, 1910); not only traces 19th-cent. developments but sketches previous ideas in chap. I.

———: "Government and Society," chap. XXIX in *Recent Social Trends* (New York, 1933); an excellent brief discussion of the place of government in modern American society.

———: *New Aspects of Politics* (Chicago, 1925), especially chaps. I, III, and IV; an interesting study of the possible contributions of such sciences as statistics and psychology to a new method of politics.

———: *Political Power: Its Composition and Incidence* (New York, 1934); the outstanding analysis of politics as a struggle for power.

Watkins, F. M.: *The State as a Concept of Political Science* (New York, 1934); an able analysis of the concept of the state and its relation to the conquest of power as the basic problem of politics.

Willoughby, W. W.: "Political Pluralism," in *The Ethical Basis of Political Authority* (New York, 1930), chap. XXIII.

Willoughby, W. W.: *The Fundamental Concepts of Public Law* (New York, 1924), chaps. I–III, V, and VIII; an exposition of the older, juristic concept of the state, of sovereignty, and of the scope of political science.

Wilson, Francis G.: *The Elements of Modern Politics* (New York, 1936); a recent effort at a theoretical compilation and analysis; chaps. I and III–V deal with the theory and nature of the state, of sovereignty, and of politics.

*Encyclopedia of the Social Sciences* (New York, 1930–35); for a discussion of some of the points covered in this chapter and for further bibliographical suggestions, see articles under the following headings: "Administration, public"; "Community"; "Collective Behavior"; "Democracy"; "Economics"; "Lobby"; "Pluralism"; "Political Science"; "Politics"; "Public Opinion"; "Representation"; "Social Psychology"; "Society"; "Sovereignty"; "State."

## CHAPTER II

☆ ☆ ☆

## THE FUNCTIONS OF GOVERNMENT

*"The public, or at least a large portion of it, is ready for the extension of the functions of government in almost any direction where the general welfare may be advanced, regardless of whether individuals are benefited or not."*
—CHARLES E. MERRIAM

How WELL government performs its tasks and how much liberty is assured the individual depend in no small measure on the number and nature of the functions undertaken. This is almost axiomatic. Government is not a fixed process with an unalterable nature. Its successes and failures depend upon factors which are human and changing. What do citizens ask their governments to do? Is the activity a traditional one, and is legal compliance likely to be readily forthcoming, or will the function be resisted by a minority of considerable size and influence? One of Spinoza's shrewdest observations was to the effect that wise rulers take care not to promulgate too many laws involving difficulty of enforcement. Otherwise, he said, resentment against the ruler results and his authority and prestige suffer. Is this advice equally applicable to democracies, or is it, as some would doubtless say, the counsel of reaction?

The general question we want to consider is whether the scope of government is limited to certain "proper" activities, which, if not observed, will result in social maladjustment and loss and the impairment of governmental efficiency and prestige. The issue clearly cannot be dealt with adequately in a single chapter. For generations it has been a favorite theme of political philosophers. Disagreement engendered from the age-old argument, instead of diminishing, seems to be steadily increasing. This, however, may be too discouraging a view of the situation. Certainly men in most lands are ready to see government undertake a great deal more than in

"PROPER" FUNCTIONS

the past. Present disagreements are probably intensified because of the "crisis" conditions resulting from the most severe depression the world has ever seen, with the new and heavy burdens it has thrown upon government.

The most general contention is that government should be limited to "control," to the maintenance of the natural equilibriums of society, and that it should not attempt to provide direct services which bring it into competition with private enterprise. Government is the strategist and the referee. So long as it "sticks to its last," citizens will respect government and find its work efficient; but when the sovereign descends to the marketplace, becomes all things to all men, then government is bound to become unpopular. Thus proceeds the traditional analysis. Is it true that government should control but not attempt to assist? Is power the inherent characteristic of state activity, so much so that when government dons the cloak of service those who would otherwise be grateful subjects become disappointed recipients of improperly undertaken activities?

It is of the utmost importance to think as clearly as possible about the metes and bounds of governmental activity. If there are inherent functions, resulting from the nature of government and the requirements of social existence, we should know it. If we could tell what the responsibilities of government are going to be fifty, twenty-five, or even ten years from now, the task of the political scientist would be greatly assisted. The establishment of objectives and the analysis of future problems is basic to everything else. Even the manner in which government administers is determined in no small measure by the nature of the duty to be performed. But is there much that can be accomplished by thinking about this general question? Are the activities and limits of government the result of what men think or are they the product of uncompromising necessity? Do not men experience wants and seek satisfactions, a growing number of which can be served better, or perhaps solely, by social co-operation?

It cannot be said that there is any one set of assumptions regarding the appropriate and necessary functions of state activity which is held in the present-day United States. The political philosophy of President Roosevelt as expounded in his book, *Looking Forward*, runs counter to the presuppositions and tenets which political leaders had been enunciating for twelve years prior to the time he came into office. Their position had been more or less typical of the climate of opinion which had existed throughout a large part of American history.

RECENT VIEWS

The late President Coolidge expressed this fundamental position at frequent intervals during his presidency. The only legitimate functions of the state, he contended, are to protect its citizens from foes within and without and to act as an "umpire" in order to guide conflicts of interest.[1] If this theory of the proper functions and limits of state activity were accepted, then governmental action would be restricted to taxation, the maintenance of armed forces and police, and the passing of regulatory and restrictive laws calculated to preserve the balances and equilibriums which are assumed to exist in social systems.

The "umpire" state assumes no initiative itself, but is satisfied to exercise a restraining hand when classes and various interests threaten to disturb the peace and stability of the existing order. The "service" state, on the other hand, assumes that the purpose of government is to fulfill the wants of the community irrespective of what they may be. It is a planning, serving, creative force in human affairs. If it be pointed out that the actual activities of American governments already fit this latter description to a considerable extent, those who take a fundamentalist position with respect to the proper scope of governmental functions have a ready rejoinder. They assert that where government has exceeded its natural, inherent limits, private enterprise has suffered and objectionable social consequences have ensued.

To assume that the disagreement as to the proper functions of government can be resolved into the "police" and "service" emphases, admittedly oversimplifies the matter. Therefore, we must examine a wider range of political philosophies. Exhaustiveness cannot be claimed for the list of those with which we shall deal, but at least

"PUBLIC INTEREST" AS THE TEST

[1] Cf. Calvin Coolidge, "A Declaration for Economic Independence," *Nation's Business*, XVI (July, 1928), 19.

we can reasonably hope for a more complete insight into the principal views concerning the essential role of government.

Rival theories of the state have this much in common—all attempt to demonstrate that their respective programs will best redound to the public interest. Is it possible to attach reliable tests to the concept of public interest or must it remain a figure of speech, a word appeal which is utilized in rallying support to one's cause?[1] This is another of those questions requiring extensive discussion. We make no pretense of suggesting the answer in the following paragraphs. We shall be satisfied if the chief factors entering into competing philosophies can be made clear.

<small>RIVAL THEORIES</small>

In analyzing various views of the proper and most important functions of government, we shall only partially follow traditional classifications. Account needs to be taken of objectives and programs which, compared with the early classification into oligarchy, aristocracy, monarchy, and democracy, entail distinctive features. Permutations are sometimes better understood when new names are used in referring to them. In the United States, for example, what may be called the "plutocratic philosophy" has enjoyed great currency, particularly in the period of the last fifty years. This alone is reason enough for referring to it first. Then, too, an appropriate term needs to be coined for modern dictatorships; we shall use the word "authoritarian" to describe both the collectivist and the totalitarian programs. Differing views of the functions of government and of what constitutes the public interest are entertained by those whose philosophies may then be called plutocratic, aristocratic, authoritarian, liberal, socialist, and social-democratic.

That governmental policies which are designed to benefit a particular group, the owners and operators of business, will redound with most advantage to the whole country in the long run is the fundamental premise of what may be called the plutocratic position. Concrete illustrations of it are found in the principle enunciated by the United States Chamber of Commerce that "what is best for

<small>THE PLUTOCRATIC POSITION</small>

[1] See Herring, *Public Administration and the Public Interest, passim.*

business is best for the country" and, again, in the "sieve" theory of Andrew Mellon to the effect that if you enrich the captains of industry by means of low taxes and high tariffs, for example, their wealth will necessarily trickle down to all levels and individuals in society. By this method, it is argued, the country will be enabled to compete more successfully with foreign nations; there will be adequate provision of fresh capital for industry, making possible expansion and large-scale production; and the average man will be assured of constant work and increasing prosperity. In other words, the most important and necessary function of government, according to this view, is to strengthen the position of the owners and operators of the nation's business and render them special services.

Another position somewhat like the one just mentioned contends that a social class, the aristocratic group, should be nurtured. The most logical presentation of the theory in modern times is found in the writings of the French monarchists, ARISTOCRACY notably Charles Maurras and Léon Daudet. The general thesis is that permanence, progress, and value are assured in social affairs when an aristocracy is permitted and fostered. The justifiability of this policy is argued on social grounds. The aristocracy, it is said, enshrines honor, guarantees efficiency, is devoted to the public welfare, stimulates culture and aesthetic appreciation, and offers a worth-while example to which the humbly born may aspire. This aristocracy, it is usually said in these latter days, should be one of culture and public service rather than of blood and birthright; it should be, like the aristocracy of Great Britain, one which recruits the best talent of the middle class—the lawyer, the merchant, and, as Laski has phrased it, "the green-grocer."

A third view of the primary objective of the state, a social theory which has been struggling for supremacy particularly during the past ten years, is that the state should be used as the instrument THE of the political party whose members have ac- AUTHORITARIAN cepted a common social creed and program. Ref- STATE erence is made, of course, to the political systems of Soviet Russia, Fascist Italy, and Nazi Germany. One commonly accepted view in all these so-called dictatorship countries is that society will be benefited best and permanently only by the development of a party organization in which all the members have a common view of social and political objectives.[1] Their method of achieving orthodoxy is by means of confining the initial membership to persons who can be trusted and who believe in the tenets of the party. Those who are diametrically opposed to the program and who might conspire or have already conspired to overthrow it are rejected or liquidated. The third step, perhaps the most important of all, is the training of youth in the ideas and activities of the new regime. When these administrations are accused of using the state for the benefit of the few, that is, for only the official members of the party, the reply is that eventually the roster will be broadened by birth and education so that everyone is included. Only by beginning with an élite, by holding to a common philosophy and program, and by carrying out a doctrinaire educational curriculum, it is held, can the most widely cherished ends of the state be achieved and permanent progress be accomplished.

The liberal regards government as the adjuster of conflicts of interest and as the agency through which aid and assistance may be given to the less fortunate. When we refer to the liberal school of political thought, we have in mind the political ideas which have been the historical foundation stones of the Liberal party in Great Britain.[2] There is assumed to be a natural course of events in human affairs, a natural equilibrium which the state merely helps to maintain. According to the liberal view, the state should interfere with the individual as little as possible and should not render services which can be profitably undertaken by individuals. The state should be characterized by the disinterestedness and integrity which are expected of the judge. Its responsibility is to keep social affairs on an

LIBERALISM

---

[1] Perhaps it is unfair to refer to both communism and fascism in the same paragraph, for the control of the government and the ends sought are substantially different. Their authoritarian views of the role of government, however, are decidedly alike. At the same time, it should be recognized that communism may be considered under socialism.

[2] Cf. *Britain's Industrial Future*, which is the *Report of the Liberal Industrial Inquiry* (London, 1928); Ramsay Muir, *The Faith of a Liberal* (London, 1933).

even keel, but at the same time it must permit the motive power of social reform and the guidance of economic affairs to remain in the hands of individuals and interest groups.

Two distinct views of the primary purpose of the state are taken by the socialists. In the eyes of the guild socialist, the state is a rival whenever it attempts to go so far that it becomes the master of the trade unions, or *syndicats*. According to most guild socialists, the state has a necessary function in the transition period during which power becomes vested in the hands of the workers, but once the syndicalist organizations have established themselves in a position whereby they can govern through their economic organizations, the state as a controlling, dominating force will be expected to disappear.

SOCIALISM

State socialism, on the other hand, regards the government as the natural rallying point for social co-operation and as the instrument through which industrial progress and social values can be achieved. It assumes that an institutional medium is needed which is above any other economic or social group. State socialism is considered particularly necessary where there is a highly developed industrial system which requires integration and guidance and in which large urban communities find themselves completely dependent upon co-operative action which can best be supplied from municipal and other governmental channels. Hence, unlike the guild socialist, the proponent of state socialism not only believes that the state is the means whereby the ownership and control of the economic system can be acquired by the community but, indeed, regards the state as the indispensable, permanent, directive force in human affairs. Russian communism now takes substantially this position. The state owns, plans, and controls; individual industries carry out their appointed tasks. Little distinction is made between those engaged in work traditionally governmental and those employed in economic pursuits. Business and government have in this way been merged, but, contrary to some early expectations, the state has not been liquidated.

Another conception of what is meant by the public interest may be characterized as the traditional American view of democracy. It may also be called the social-democratic philosophy. The primary role of the state, according to an unbroken chain of American thought, is to guarantee equality of opportunity. The implications of this fundamental principle are many and far-reaching. The government is expected to destroy privilege and unfair advantage, to supply educational opportunities for all alike, and to take any action necessary to assure the individual every chance to capitalize upon whatever abilities and appreciation his birthright and industry have given him. This philosophy of government has been developed conspicuously by Jefferson, Wilson, and the two Roosevelts.

<small>AMERICAN SOCIAL-DEMOCRATIC VIEW</small>

It will be observed that what we have labeled the American concept of democracy views the state as a positive force. It goes somewhat further than the philosophical position of liberalism, but not so far as the economic position of the state socialist; however, it does recognize the indispensability and constructive nature of government. Particularly in the western states of the United States, the government is regarded as a community builder, a corporate instrument through which social assets, such as schools, playgrounds, libraries, and municipal utilities of various kinds, can be created and added to. There is a rather general appreciation of the facts that public improvements of this kind are a part of the permanent social capital of the community, and that through co-operative enterprise individual business will be improved and richer opportunities afforded for taxpayers and their children. Because of their confidence in municipal activities, Americans living in such western states as Wisconsin and North Dakota, for example, are sometimes called "socialistic."

Sometimes it is said that the public interest is to be found in "the greatest good of the greatest number"—a vague ideal, to be sure, and one which is not entirely clear until the problem of implementing it has been solved. The American view of democracy expresses this fundamental desire for the greatest good of the greatest number, but the fascists and communists insist that their philosophies and programs do, too. The matter becomes even further complicated

<small>"THE GREATEST GOOD OF THE GREATEST NUMBER"</small>

when we begin to examine precisely what is meant by "the greatest good." Are social values wholly matters of physical well-being and the equitable distribution of wealth, or do they also consist of people's individual liberties, freedom of choice, and right to do as they please? Are these psychological feelings and attitudes of men worth considering, or are they due to misunderstanding and unfounded fears? Is loss of liberty primarily attributable to cumulative extensions of governmental control or is the theory of "the social lag" an even more important explanation?

Those who maintain that the functions of government are inherently and precisely determined rely principally upon what history has to tell us about the evolution of states. The record is supposed to present convincing evidence for the view that the function of the state is domination and control. Have not various and sundry interests and élites, warriors, churchmen, business men, and socialists, captured the machinery of government at different periods in known history? The deduction is, therefore, that throughout the entire course of history there has been a central theme, the quest for power, and that the function of government has been that of control by the rulers over the ruled. Those who contend that the state should be merely umpire and protector also rely upon an appeal to history.

THE APPEAL TO HISTORY

There are two objections to this attempt at substantiation of a fundamental position by reference to historical data. The first is that the functions of government have never been so simple or restricted as the proponents of the control theory contend. The second objection is that, while history is able to tell us what has happened in the past, it is not a sure indicator of what may happen in the future. The latter point does not require a great deal of argument or explanation. Among historians themselves one finds, particularly in recent years, frank acknowledgment that history does not run in cycles and, hence, that future developments are not controlled by past events. It is obvious, for example, that the social and economic conditions which have determined what government needed to do—and was expected to do—during various periods in past centuries, have radically changed. It is also apparent that the urbanized, mechanized, corporate society which we find in the United States today differs so radically from the simple agricultural community of the revolutionary period that the resulting demands upon government are inevitably much different.

If, for purposes of argument, it be assumed that the long flow of history gives us an accurate indication of the functions and limits of government, and if it be assumed that what happened fifty, three hundred, or three thousand years ago is likely to be repeated under modern circumstances, it still can be pointed out that the role of the state has never been confined simply to that of control. Although history books used to deal almost exclusively with the battles and the political intrigues of ancient civilizations, sight should not be lost of the fact that early monarchs built public buildings and market places for the community, provided other essential services, promulgated extensive laws regulating trade, and supplied the rudimentary social services of early society. In the Greek city-state, one finds a great deal of evidence of a high form of civic pride and co-operation, of community programs and services—a social development which from the governmental standpoint clearly surpassed that of the medieval age in Europe. Jumping rapidly across the span of history, we may refer to the role of the state during the early stages of the modern period. All of us have heard of mercantilism and know that political economy was originally the fostering of trade and industry by political rulers. We are familiar with the guiding, directive hand of the state in the formation and activities of the East India Company and in the affairs of the American colonies. The state, prior to the time of Adam Smith, was not only a paternalistic, restrictive state but at certain periods it might even be called a positive state. The distinction between government and business was not clearly drawn; the economy was a national economy rather than merely one of the individual producer.

The variety of functions performed by government since the beginning of American history would appear to be so obvious that the limited interpretation we are examining would hardly seem

## THE FUNCTIONS OF GOVERNMENT 47

to require refutation. Government in the United States has never been merely a policeman, an umpire. The very groups which were principally responsible for the dissemination and acceptance of the "protection" view have, throughout the entire span of American history, been beneficiaries of government aid and assistance.

<small>AMERICAN HISTORY</small>

Modern historical treatises make it evident that the functions of the state were never merely those of protection and of control over competing groups. The emphasis upon the various functions of government has shifted during different periods of time. The number and the variety of governmental activities have grown—even in an individualist, *laissez faire* society. The power aspect of government has been less pronounced as the service functions of the state have increased. We have long since passed that stage of human development when it could be said with any substantial foundation in fact that "the prime function of the state was to protect property, maintain order, and defend the country" and that "the essence of the government was power." Service is the new emphasis in modern government. Speaking of this change, Charles A. Beard says:

> Today we have reached a point where the government is no longer defended on the ground of mere power. Justification has shifted to the basis of service. In truth in times of peace the acts of state are, in the main, acts of service, not of force. The civil servants of the United States Government outnumber the military servants more than two to one. New York City has about eighteen thousand policemen, but it has approximately one hundred ten thousand teachers, firemen, street cleaners, park employees, and other workers engaged in vital social services. Even policemen do more than maintain order.[1]

Unless one assumes a fundamentalism, an orthodoxy, which does not appear to be justified, the ascertainment of inherent functions of government once and for all seems impossible. This conclusion is in consonance with the basic theory that government exists for the purpose of fulfilling wants. Hence, when the conditions and the requirements of social life change, the number and variety of

<small>THE DYNAMIC THEORY</small>

---

[1] Beard, *American Government and Politics* (Macmillan, New York, 1931), p. 4.

governmental activities also are altered. It might be possible to find traces of determinate governmental functions running throughout the entire course of human history, but the differences in relative emphasis would be so great that such a discovery would be of little value. The growth of governmental functions depends upon the social and economic conditions which have developed in a given society and upon the demands of the population for activities of one kind or another. This might be called the "dynamic" theory, and it would seem to be realistic. On the basis of these conclusions, it is clear that any function of government is "proper" whenever there is a demand from the community for the government's assuming it, and whenever the responsibility is administered in an acceptable manner.

Political theory, on the other hand, continues to emphasize control and power as the central motifs of governmental functioning. Irrespective of what once may have been true, this now appears to be a mistaken emphasis, though it is an important one. We are counselling against overemphasis, not against proper consideration. As we have observed before, the power and service interpretations need to be juxtaposed, shown in their natural relationship and with due emphasis to each.

THE THEORY OF ÉLITES

In order to make our analysis of governmental functions as complete as possible, we need to give attention to the view which holds that government is almost entirely an instrument of domination. Government is said to be a struggle for position and advantage. It is the appropriation by élites of satisfactions which are secured by manipulating controls and symbols.[1] Élites are social and economic classes. They are large, well-defined interest groups. The ideology of those who take this position is similar to that of Karl Marx and other social theorists who have made the class struggle the foundation of their analyses. In the hypotheses of Professor Lasswell, however, it is not assumed that any par-

[1] This particular vocabulary is used primarily by Harold D. Lasswell. The reader is referred particularly to his *World Politics and Personal Insecurity* (New York, 1935) and *Psychopathology and Politics* (Chicago, 1930). G. E. G. Catlin employs substantially the same assumptions; see his books cited in the footnote on p. 11. Charles E. Merriam, *Political Power: Its Composition and Incidence* (New York, 1934), also deals with the dominance theory.

ticular élite is intrinsically superior to any other or that any one of them is predestined to remain in power. It is a matter of who gets what, when, and how. Whether the plutocrats or the proletarians are on top during a given period depends upon their success in manipulating the weapons of governmental control, particularly the symbols which shape public opinion. These, of course, are not the only implements of power seekers. They may use force, abnegation, ridicule, bribes, emotional appeals—any means that may be necessary to gain the prizes of the game at a given time and place.

The composition and confines of competing élites change from time to time. The middle class, for example, is found to be larger in some countries than in others and at one period than at another. Sub-classes are found within classes, causing friction and hampering the larger élites' struggle to gain control over the government. Political parties, as such, are not so important as the interests and classes which they represent and whose objectives they seek to achieve.

Government is an instrument by means of which élites seek to appropriate satisfactions. In order to do this, they must be able to control the government. Power techniques are employed to achieve this goal and are needed to keep the élite in control of the government. As one élite dies out and members of another group filter in, there is what is called a "circulation of the élites."

There is much of basic truth and importance in this general analysis. If one would hold governmental authority, one must learn how to secure it. If one would satisfy public opinion, one must learn how it reacts and why.

But there are some points of divergence between the élite theory of the function of government and the one we have been developing. Government rules and it also serves. Control over men's wills is only one aspect of government. The élite theory lays too much emphasis upon conscious design. It does not make allowance for those who are not seeking power. It fails to see that government has become largely a business enterprise, a matter of good administration.

The control and power aspects of government are less significant the nearer government is to the citizenry. Their importance graduates from the small local community, through the large city, the state, and the federal government. In other words, when applied to most governments, the élite theory does not have much pertinence. Hence, when it is made the central hypothesis in a political philosophy a distorted product results, because one element has been overemphasized.

Overemphasis on control and class lines brings one perilously close to what may be called the "conspiracy theory" of government. This term is not customarily employed in political science, but it best describes a position that needs to be identified. Franz Oppenheimer, who contended that the state is the instrument of economic domination and exploitation,[1] may be said to have been a proponent of the conspiracy theory. Anyone who assumes that social relations are governed almost solely by careful calculation and design, the laying of plans to gain advantage over others, may be said to subscribe to the conspiracy theory. It is a simple explanation of political behavior, and there is considerable substance in it; but there is great danger in trying to read too much into it. The élite theory faces the same hazard.

THE CONSPIRACY THEORY

The extent to which classes may be said to exist differs considerably as between countries and at various times in the same country. There is a general tendency for class lines to become more pronounced as a country gets older; however, the opposite tendency may be true. For example, class lines are not drawn so sharply in the Scandinavian countries today as they were fifty or a hundred years ago. Moreover, there is considerable reason for doubting whether class lines are ineradicable. Russian communism, by liquidation and education, expects to prove that they are not. But élites may survive even when there are no sharply differentiated classes. They are vocational or skill groups—farmers, laborers, executives, government employees. Men differ with respect to their abilities and talents; hence, even

---

[1] See Franz Oppenheimer, *The State* (New York, 1912), *passim*. Cf. his last chap. in which he points out that though the state in the past has been the instrument of economic domination, it need not remain so.

in a classless society, it is not unreasonable to expect that the skill group whose services were most prized might be accorded superior reward and social distinction, leading to differences between élites and possibly to jealousy.

But there is likely to be a good deal of fiction about the extent to which élites are differentiated and about their influence on governmental affairs. Does an élite exist unless it is fully self-conscious? To what extent do classes and groups calculatingly conspire to gain control of the government and use it for their own purposes? In British history, the "landed gentry" is commonly referred to as a group which for generations exerted powerful influence upon political policies. During all this time, did it act as a unit, think only of the interests of its own members? Such a suggestion is clearly foolish. One élite which is fairly well defined and which usually manifests considerable cohesiveness is the *rentier* group—those whose incomes are derived from investments. But the idea of large and small investors getting together for any length of time on a common political program has not proved itself in fact. In particular cases—for example, when public-utility profits are jeopardized by regulatory measures—they may rally their forces (a minority sufficiently interested and active to write its Senators), but this is about as far as the conspiracy theory holds. The proletariat—does it exist in the United States? As a fiction, yes; as an ill-defined force with greater potential power to influence government than has yet been exerted, the answer is clearly yes. But a united front, planning to grasp the reins of power, is hard to imagine today.

Men do not always vote their economic interests. Intelligent self-interest is not widely and consistently sought. If it were, the history of the world would have been considerably different. Economic determinism pushed too far becomes unreliable. The same thing is true of the élite theory and the conspiracy approach to government. The reason is the same in each case—people are not solely or even primarily guided by calculating intelligence. We are gregarious, easy-going, emotional creatures, living mostly for the moment, instead of planning how to rally together all those who have the same station in life.

52   POLITICS

In some instances, however, the conspiracy theory is no fiction. It may become stark reality, but these cases are the exception rather than the rule. Everywhere one finds a small minority of persons characterized by limitless energy, ambition, the desire to dominate. Some American business leaders have qualified for this classification. Some political leaders, past and present, also belong. Mussolini and Hitler are clearly appropriate examples. They began with a small following. The idea of seizing control of the government gradually germinated. Finally, they and their followers actually conspired, laid plans. In these cases the conspiracy theory is apparently confirmed.

<small>CONTEMPORARY POWER SITUATIONS</small>

But even here one should guard against oversimplification, should attempt to discover all of the important elements producing the result. It is difficult to make oneself do this. Usually we want to find *the* explanation, the one self-sufficient solution. It can be said, for example, that the political leaders of Nazi Germany[1] are psychopathic, almost madmen. Some persons contend in all seriousness that the German people are barbaric and blood-thirsty; but even if these contentions were true, they alone would constitute an unreliable analysis, because they need to be combined with other considerations. The personal and national pride of the German people has been deeply wounded. They sincerely believe that surrounding nations continually draw the ring of steel more tightly about the nation, threatening the people's security and national existence. The German people excel in science and industry, and hence they contend that it is their manifest destiny to penetrate foreign markets and share colonial possessions. When these and similar influences are calculated, the reason that the conspiracy theory worked out in Germany and that power and force are so much in evidence can be intelligently appreciated. Do not forget that with the adoption of the Weimar Constitution at the close of the World War political scientists highly praised the German fundamental law, particularly the bill of rights, which was the most comprehensive

---

[1] For a provocative treatise on Nazism, see Frederick L. Schuman, *The Nazi Dictatorship* (New York, 1935).

one to have been adopted in any country up to that time. This praise was merited. Glaring evidences of power and conspiracy may be but an incident in the life of a people!

Conspiracy and power may be expected to be in evidence when widespread dissatisfaction is present and when tensions exist which are almost at the breaking point. So long as contentment and normality exist, therefore, power situations and the conspiracies of élites may be expected to remain relatively insignificant. These observations point to an important truth: an indispensable function of government is that of correcting situations which cause dissatisfactions and dangerous tensions. This readjustment is part of the grand strategy of government. It can readily be seen, therefore, that government is not merely an engineer—it is a doctor. Part of the task of political scientists is to help diagnose social disturbances in order that government may seek to find a remedy which will restore normality and general contentment.

<small>RELIEVING TENSIONS</small>

A classification of governmental functions should be confined to a particular period of time. In recent years American governments have been performing at least four major functions. As we have previously suggested, government acts as protector, assistor, regulator, and as owner and operator. Having counseled against fundamentalism with reference to the scope and limitation of governmental activities, we must be careful to avoid an analogously rigid classification. Although the range of the classification we have indicated clearly includes a great variety of human enterprise, its potentiality for future expansion needs to be recognized. Moreover, it should be noted that in some cases the existing duties of government may be classified under two or more of the suggested functional headings. Health activities, which usually involve both protection and regulation, may be taken as a case in point. What government actually does can be discovered by analyzing the principal activities of the three levels of authority—federal, state, and local. Let us do this next.

<small>A SUGGESTED CLASSIFICATION</small>

Local governments are primarily concerned with the needs of the community which are nearest and most indispensable to the residents. The forty-eight states are, at least from the standpoints of theory and law, at the center of the system of governments. They create the municipalities and give them their authority; under the Constitution of the United States, they also retain any powers not specifically given to the federal government. The several states are primarily concerned with those matters which are of state-wide importance, such as the provision and maintenance of institutions for the poor, the insane, and the sick. The federal government is supreme in its own fields, that is, where the Constitution has given it express authority. It is primarily concerned with those matters which can be handled only on a national scale by a central agency. Among such functions are carrying mail, control over navigation and hydroelectric power on interstate streams, and provision of a common currency.

DISTRIBUTION OF POWERS AMONG GOVERNMENTS

But the division of authority is not so simple as the above analysis may seem to make it. There is intrastate commerce, as well as interstate commerce, and it is frequently very difficult to determine where one ends and the other begins. As a matter of fact, federalism creates a fiction. The assumption is that authority is parceled out among the several levels of government, primarily federal and state. But a functional analysis shows that the most important powers are usually shared by two, three, and sometimes four different hierarchies of government. In the United States at the present time, for example, federal, state, and local authorities all share jurisdiction over taxation, roads, police, schools, recreation, public works, public utilities, public welfare, and trade and commerce. Not many powers of importance are missing from this list.

Levels of government do not divide into watertight compartments; each is concerned with most of the important functions at its own level. This is not to say that, legally speaking, power is co-ordinate in all the cases we have mentioned. The term "co-ordinate power" has a technical meaning and has very limited applicability. What should be said is that federal, state, and local governments co-operate, their jurisdictions dovetail. In some cases, taxation for instance, their jurisdictions overlap and conflict. In a few cases responsibility is definitely monopolized, as exemplified by the federal government's complete authority over bankruptcy and the states' power over manufacturing.

But just at the moment we are more concerned with the scope and variety of functions than with the manner in which they are shared and divided. Let us look at the activities of the federal, state, and local governments to see how they are distributed according to our classification of governmental functions into protection, assistance, regulation, and direct service.

In the national government of the United States, no less than four departments—namely, Agriculture, Labor, Commerce, and Interior—exist for the purpose of rendering assistance to various interest groups and individuals. The Post Office renders a direct service in the form of carrying the mail. The War and Navy departments are the only ones whose historical role is primarily protective. The remaining departments—Treasury, State, and Justice—may be called "political" departments, inasmuch as they have to do primarily with the relational and housekeeping functions. If we should carry our analysis further and consider the functions of the independent establishments, we should find that of this group of fifty or so agencies, the great majority have as their purpose that of regulation, assistance, or direct service.

FEDERAL FUNCTIONS

The federal government is properly characterized as a great research and servicing agency. With the notable exception of the Post Office, federal agencies secure their results largely by indirect means. The departments in Washington, by means of their research and promotional activities, assist other governments. Research on crop pests, and federal aid for state highway construction are examples of these typical activities. Even the War Department's work is largely research, being preparation for possible contingencies. On the other hand, there are important control and regulatory agencies. These are usually found in the form of independent commissions, such as the Interstate Commerce Commission, the Federal Trade Commission, or the Securities and Exchange Commission.

"Although the variety of services now performed by the average state for its people is great," Bates and Field have observed in their *State Government*, "it is possible to group these activities into a few broad fields, each having somewhat distinct characteristics. . . . For convenience, the following classification is adopted: law enforcement, health, charities and correction, labor, education, business supervision, agriculture and conservation of natural resources. . . ."[1] The largest expenditures of state governments are for social purposes—education, health, and highways—through agencies which render assistance and service and which involve very little of the element of control. As a matter of fact, with the exception of law enforcement, which may be characterized generally as protection, and with the exception of business supervision, which involves regulation, all of the state functions enumerated by Bates and Field possess the social-service characteristic.

POWERS OF THE STATES

The activities of local governments, like those of the states, depend to some extent upon the size of the unit and the complexity of the social existence found therein. Generalization, however, is permissible. Lent D. Upson, in *The Growth of a City Government*, divides the duties of a municipality into the following nine groups: (1) general government; (2) protection to persons and property (including fire fighting, fire prevention, and safety engineering); (3) conservation of health; (4) sanitation and promotion of cleanliness; (5) highways; (6) charities, hospitals, and correction; (7) education; (8) recreation; and (9) public-service enterprises. The municipality, more than any other government, comes close to the citizen and meets his basic wants of daily life. The city is a corporation, analogous to business corporations.

LOCAL SERVICES

An inductive analysis of public functions reveals clearly that modern government is primarily a matter of providing assistance and fulfilling wants rather than one of power and control. The activities speak for themselves. Government is a public-service corporation, performing certain acts in a businesslike manner and charging for the services, usually in the form of taxes.

[1] (Harpers, New York, 1928), p. 303.

## THE FUNCTIONS OF GOVERNMENT

Protection is one of the most important functions of government and there are many ways in which citizens expect their governments to provide it. The prevention of tensions, which may cause loss of life or property, is one of these ways. Then there is the fear of attack from outside the borders; hence the principal expenditures of national governments are on preparations for war and on debts incurred in past struggles. The law breaker within the community is guarded against. Policemen cruise the streets in motor cars; prisons and courts are maintained for offenders. The fire department strives to keep fire loss at a minimum. Regulations are imposed upon building construction and maintenance in an effort to keep them safe, not only for occupants but for the public as a whole. The population is guarded against epidemics. Efforts are made in some instances to protect consumers against fraudulent advertising and unhealthful foods. Common carriers are forced to keep their equipment in a safe condition.

GOVERNMENT AS PROTECTOR

Government first got its reputation for paternalism by acting as policeman, judge, doctor, dietitian, and building inspector; moreover, this species of paternalism is usually applauded. It is only when profitable businesses are interfered with, as when pure food and drug acts are extended, that the cry "caveat emptor" goes up and "paternalism" takes on an unfavorable connotation.

When we think of protective activities, there usually comes to our minds the idea of physical force, compulsion, power. But the oldest, most traditional departments of government have been very much influenced by the general emphasis upon service. An excellent example of this is found in the modern municipal police department. Mr. Bruce Smith, America's outstanding authority on police administration, has pointed out that the role of police in modern society tends to become more difficult and more complex; that, whereas the early duty of the policeman was exclusively that of "thief taker," today he is characterized in American cities as "the vanishing patrolman." The reason that not more than one-fourth of the uniformed force is actually available for patrol

POLICE

duty and that only about one-twelfth of the total force is actually on patrol at any given time is that services rendered by police departments have expanded so greatly. "As an abstract proposition," says Smith, "the field of the police may be viewed as embracing all, or nearly all, of the administrative powers of government."

Among the special activities which are common to police forces in the United States are: regulating traffic; licensing; running public ambulances; registering voters; taking the police census; ice-breaking on navigable waterways; furnishing temporary lodging for the homeless, emergency relief for the destitute, free employment agencies, and neighborhood entertainments; operating dog pounds; examining persons for social diseases; and supervising paroled convicts. All these fourteen functions, with the exception of the last-mentioned, may be said to possess social-service characteristics, rather than the traditional one of protective power.

The regulatory power of government resembles the protective function. It is a manifestation of authority. It involves the display of power, either actual or threatened. Consider, for example, the regulation of business affected with a public interest—a subject that will be discussed in Chapter XII. It is designed to provide protection to the users, security holders, competitors, and employees. Regulation is frequently necessary as a control over monopoly power, which, if unrestrained, would almost surely be abused; however, monopoly conditions are not always present. Regulation may be used to protect health, safeguard morals, establish trade practices, prevent dishonest dealings, improve labor conditions, destroy undesirable businesses, and control the country's credit. The enumeration is incomplete. Regulation is inextricably related to the police power, which is the reserved authority of governments to adopt measures designed to safeguard and promote public interests in health, safety, morals, and general well-being. Regulation is closely associated with law. It is control. It bears the stamp of sovereign authority.

THE REGULATORY FUNCTION

But, as we have said, a sharp line cannot be drawn between

the control and the service aspects. Government as umpire not only coerces and referees but in many situations it thereby renders service. The regulated enterprise frequently enjoys the patronage and favor of government. For example, extremely valuable privileges are granted to the owners of public utilities, among them being the charter, the certificate of convenience and necessity, the power of eminent domain, and the prohibition of competition.

One of the principal corollaries of the general proposition that most things are private and that only exceptional matters are public is that government should lend its assistance and create satisfactory conditions in order that industry and private initiative generally will be more successful and profitable. According to the *laissez faire* position, public authority is supposed to assist, but it is not actually to provide the service itself. It is merely the administrative agent, while the prime mover is the economic system of private industry. The provision of various and sundry forms of assistance to the general citizen body and particularly to industry, trade, agriculture, and the professions has been one of the primary functions of government in the past and constitutes one large field of activity today. Nearly everyone cheerfully agrees that it is a "proper" function.

GOVERNMENT AS ASSISTANCE

When the government acts as the assistor of private enterprise, it does so in order that others may be better able to supply the necessary end products, in order that, as individuals and groups, they may be better able to perform their functions in society. When public authority furnishes the tools, it may be said to perform the function of assistance; when, however, it supplies fundamental wants directly, as in the case of water, light, and transportation, it becomes the proprietor of a public business.

It will not be necessary for us to enumerate all the forms of assistance which government renders to the general public. By way of illustration, however, we may profitably consider four concrete examples: education, public health, housing, and public welfare.

First should come public education—a universal service rendered by government in the interest of enriching individual life, developing good citizenship, and promoting the national welfare.

EDUCATION

From the time that the state first began to challenge the position of the church in community life, the slow but steady development of public education has accompanied the progress of Western civilization. In the United States, the nineteenth century witnessed the early struggles for free state schools, and subsequent advances have been so far-reaching that today, as I. L. Kandel has stated, public education "consists of schools and institutions as varied as the needs of the individuals that make up a state: Pre-school and child care institutions; primary and secondary schools; special schools for physical and mental defectives; part-time and full-time vocational schools at different levels corresponding to the great variety of occupations; colleges and universities; professional schools; institutions for the preparation of teachers; adult schools and courses as diversified as are human interests."[1] In addition to formal instruction, other services which contribute to the effectiveness of the educative process, such as food, medical treatment, library and museum facilities, and recreational opportunities, are included in the democratic concept of public education.

Public-health work, like education, is now a firmly established responsibility of government. Few people realize that fifty years ago it was in its infancy. Municipal and county health departments have rapidly expanded both numerically and geographically, and the funds expended by these agencies in curative, preventive, and educative health work are steadily increasing. State health departments aid and guide the local units, and attack specific problems of a serious nature. Typical state health departments include divisions dealing with communicable diseases, food and drugs (including milk production), sanitary engineering (concerning water-supply and sewage problems), tuberculosis, venereal disease, maternity and child hygiene, public-health nursing, laboratories, vital statistics, and sometimes mental hygiene and industrial

HEALTH

[1] *Encyclopedia of the Social Sciences* (Macmillan, New York, 1931), V, 418.

hygiene.[1] In the federal field, the United States Public Health Service performs a significant service in attacking interstate health problems, in assisting the state units, in conducting valuable research, and in disseminating health information.

No longer is "public health" a simple problem of treating disease and preventing the spread of epidemic germs. Today the program is a positive one, far transcending the work of the various health agencies proper, and embracing not only curative and preventive activities but in addition a multiplicity of functions looking toward better living conditions, proper infant care, wholesome recreational facilities, and the wide dissemination of health education of every type. The results of this service are to be found in the increased security, longevity, and happiness of our citizens. The way is open for even greater strides in the future.

The housing problem affords another example of government's efforts to provide conditions conducive to health, work, and enjoyment. While for many years the construction, sale or rental, and ownership of homes was considered exclusively a HOUSING private, and almost personal, concern, citizens today are growing more and more conscious that slum conditions, squalid and unhealthy tenements, and overcrowded shacks present a problem directly affecting the general welfare. In a concerted and public attack upon these evils, the United States has lagged far behind most European countries, but there is now almost unanimous agreement in this country that the responsibility for leadership in the housing campaign must fall upon the government.

Differences of opinion still exist as to the method by which desired ends should be reached—whether through government construction and operation, through encouragement and subsidies to nonprofit or limited dividend private corporations, or through guarantee of favorable credit terms to private enterprise. Activities of the war-time Housing Corporation and the contemporary Emergency Housing Corporation illustrate the first method; New York State housing laws, the second; and the insurance functions of the Federal Housing Administration, the third. Increased

[1] C. E. A. Winslow, "Public Health," *Encyclopedia of the Social Sciences*, XII, 656.

governmental action along these or other lines is a clear indication of present tendencies and widespread opinion.

Whatever form they take, the activities of government in eliminating slums and fostering salutary housing conditions represent a positive service in the public interest, and lead us farther and farther away from the narrow concept of the "police" state.

In public welfare we find another striking example of the transference of a function from private to public responsibility. Recent developments in this field have been summed up as follows: ". . . the laying off of employees by private business and industry has resulted in placing a heavy burden on government. Providing food and clothing for needy unemployed prior to the depression was largely the concern of community chest agencies. In recent years, cities and counties have established public welfare departments and practically all relief work is supported by public funds. In 1929, public expenditures for family relief represented 60 per cent of the total; in 1930, 71 per cent; and in 1934, 95 per cent of all expenditures for unemployment family relief came from public funds."[1] During this period, the growth in federal responsibility for public-welfare work was even more rapid, and billions of dollars were spent in a relatively short time in an effort to maintain the bare necessities of life for millions of Americans.

<small>PUBLIC WELFARE</small>

Assistance is the most important and the most rapidly growing of the state's functions. From an early time, government has supplied poor relief and charity, but today almost every individual and every group is either directly or indirectly a beneficiary of government aid. In the United States at the present time we find that banks, insurance companies, industrial corporations, and local governments are financially assisted by the Reconstruction Finance Corporation; the American merchant marine is subsidized by huge grants of public revenues; farmers receive crop and property loans in addition to a variety of educational services rendered by

<small>ASSISTANCE TO BUSINESS</small>

[1] William Anderson, *The Organization and Functions of Municipal Government* (mimeo., Chicago, 1935), p. 183. This is one of the courses of study of the Institute for Training in Municipal Administration conducted by the International City Managers' Association.

the Department of Agriculture; workmen are the beneficiaries of industrial accident insurance and, in some cases, old-age and unemployment insurance. The unemployed and improvident are succored by the Works Progress Administration and the social-service administrations of local governments. In other words, from the top to the bottom of the social structure, public authority renders direct aid to individuals and groups. Business itself, the principal proponent of the view that governmental functions should be confined to protection, has been the direct recipient of a large number of government boons and services; one needs simply to mention the work of the Bureau of Standards, the Patent Office, the Bureau of Foreign and Domestic Commerce, and the various subsidies and loans which individual enterprises have received from the beginning of American history.

Contrary to the representations which are usually made by chambers of commerce and various other conservative groups, the expansion of governmental activities has rarely been the result of pressure from within the city hall, but rather a response to the demands of individuals and groups of citizens, chief among which has generally been the organized business association.

So successful have organized business groups been in securing various and sundry forms of assistance from government that one of their foremost champions, Samuel O. Dunn, editor of the *Railway Age*, has stated that "practically every increase in taxes and in government interference with business is due more to our business men than to our politicians." This situation has been very well summarized by Professor Anderson: "From Hamilton's day to the present, in this matter of governmental functions, our principal leaders have been consistently inconsistent. While holding to the theory of individualism, Hamilton advocated (and achieved) a protective tariff, the creation of a national bank, and the assumption of state debts. The government was plunged into business. Holding firm to the doctrine of a strict construction of national powers, Jefferson yet could not resist the annexation of Louisiana with its consequent great and unavoidable expansion of governmental activities."[1]

[1] William Anderson, *op. cit.*, p. 185.

The state acts also as owner and operator; the role of planner, builder, developer of the economic life of the country, is another and by no means entirely new public function. The state as entrepreneur is not a development of recent years. Political economy, as we have observed, was originally the economy of princes. In our analysis we shall give a good deal of attention to these economic functions—regulation, planning and co-ordination, problems of ownership and administration. Any attempt at this point to enumerate or to discuss these problems would be wholly inadequate. It may simply be observed that in the building, planning, enterprising field of conduct, the state is most clearly seen as a positive, constructive force in human affairs.

THE STATE AS ENTERPRISER

No period in human history fails to reveal the encouraging hand of the government in promoting economic interests. In this connection it is important to note that a large part of the pioneering work which has been done in commerce and in trade is attributable to governmental experimentation, subsidy, and risk taking. The concept of the creative state—the constructing, initiating, guiding state—is not a new one. Governments have historically led the way and paved the road. Until recent times the state has done more paving than pathfinding. That is to say, the government has been used by powerful financial and business groups, usually large corporations. In their pamphlet entitled *Less Government or More*, Louis Brownlow and Charles Ascher give the following instances as exemplifying the pioneering work of government:

> Note, too, the way in which private enterprise asks the government to pioneer, to spend public monies in building up a service to the point at which profitable operation becomes possible . . . then clamors for less government in business. It is sometimes hard to remember that our basic railroads were made possible only by huge grants of public lands, supplemented by grants of local credit which eventually caused a crisis in public finance. Today, the federal government spends nearly ten millions a year in maintaining frequent airway beacons and emergency landing fields every thirty miles from New York to San Francisco, and more millions in air mail contracts that are frankly subsidies to struggling commercial air lines. It is a safe prophecy that within a few years

huge air transportation companies will decry governmental regulation, which, they will say, is stifling private enterprise.[1]

How private are some private enterprises!

Eloquent evidence of the effectiveness of group-interest demands upon the expansion of governmental activities is to be found in the departmental organization of any government, particularly the federal government of the United States. The Department of Agriculture was established at the insistence of the agrarian population. The establishment of the Department of Commerce was the result of the business community's insistence upon similar consideration and special attention by the government. Later the Department of Labor was set up as an independent department because labor argued successfully that its interests should be of at least as much concern to the state as those of business men and farmers. A more complete analysis of federal organization and, just as significantly, a consideration of reasons why reorganization has not taken place, reveal that the expansion of governmental services and the organization of administrative units occur primarily in response to the effective demands of organized pressure groups.

The functions of government are whatever the citizens and their interest groups succeed in getting public authority to undertake. The "proper" activities are apparently limited only by the desires of the people and the ability of government to fulfill them more adequately than can individuals or other groups. This fundamental is clearly expressed by Professor William Anderson, who, with particular reference to the activities of cities, says:

THE DOOR TO SERVICE

> No door to service is closed so tight that it cannot be reopened. There is no complete and final list of what cities should do, nor a separate list graven in brass of functions which they should not perform under any circumstances. Whoever renders a service, whether private individual, private corporation, or the government itself, should be on trial at all times. If a better agency can be found to perform the service, the people served have a right to employ that agency, whether it means taking a function from the government or putting another upon its shoulders. When a public function demonstrably fails to be of any substantial

[1] (American Library Association, Chicago, 1933), p. 7.

public good, it should be dropped forthwith. When the weight of the evidence shows that the public can do better for itself what others are doing poorly for it, the city, county, or state authorities should not be held back by ancient prejudices from undertaking the service.[1]

But does not government perform some functions better than others, and cannot those which are most successfully administered be said to constitute the "proper" activities? This question is very difficult to answer to everyone's satisfaction. Those considering the same evidence probably would not come out with the same answer. What we do hope to do, however, is throw light on this question at various points throughout the book.

### SELECTED READINGS

Anderson, William: *American City Government* (New York, 1925); chap. XVI; an illuminating discussion of the widespread functions of the modern municipality.

Beard, Charles A.: *American Government and Politics* (7th ed., New York, 1935); chaps. I and XXIX; entire book emphasizes the modern "service" state, the chaps. cited being particularly devoted to it.

Coker, Francis W.: "American Traditions Concerning Property and Liberty," *American Political Science Review*, XXX, No. 1 (February, 1936), 1-23.

Coolidge, Calvin: *Foundations of the Republic* (New York, 1926), chaps. XIII and XXIX; sets forth the idea of the "umpire" government.

Croly, H.: *Progressive Democracy* (New York, 1914); an early and convincing plea for the positive theory of government.

Douglas, Paul H.: "Proletarian Political Theory," in *Political Theories: Recent Times*, Charles E. Merriam and Harry E. Barnes, editors (New York, 1924), chap. VI.

Finer, Herman: "State Activity Before Adam Smith," *Public Administration*, X, No. 2 (April, 1932), 157-78.

———: *The Theory and Practice of Modern Government* (New York, 1934), chaps. III and IV; presents views of state activity based on the historical and on the analytical approach.

Garner, James W.: *Political Science and Government* (New York, 1928), chap. XVII; presents a discussion of the theories of the functions of government, particularly the *laissez-faire* policy and socialism.

Haider, Carmen: "The Italian Corporate State," *Political Science Quarterly*, XLVI, No. 2 (June, 1931), 228-47.

———: "The Meaning and Significance of Fascism," *Political Science Quarterly*, XLVIII, No. 4 (December, 1933), 556-64.

---

[1] William Anderson, *The Organization and Functions of Municipal Government*, pp. 190-1.

Huxley, Thomas H.: "Administrative Nihilism," in *Critiques and Addresses* (London, 1890), pp. 2–32; an old but stimulating discussion of the arguments for the "police" state, organismic theories, and the propriety of publicly supported schools in England.

Lasswell, Harold D.: *Politics: Who Gets What, When, How* (New York, 1936); a good exposition of the élite theory by one of its principal students.

Leacock, Stephen: *Elements of Political Science* (Boston, 1921), Part III; contains an interesting discussion of individualism, socialism, and the province of government in the modern state.

Mellon, Andrew W.: *Taxation: The People's Business* (New York, 1924), chaps. I, III, V, VII; an excellent example of the plutocratic position.

Mill, John Stuart: *On Liberty* (first published, 1859); effectively distinguishes between interference which restrains the individual and that which is designed to help him.

Ortega y Gasset, José: *The Revolt of the Masses* (trans. from the Spanish, London, 1932); a modern exposition of the aristocratic theory.

Roosevelt, Theodore: *The New Nationalism* (New York, 1910); an inspiring plea for an extension of governmental functions.

Schuman, Frederick L.: "The Political Theory of German Fascism," *American Political Science Review*, XXVIII, No. 2 (April, 1934), 210–32.

Smith, Adam: *Wealth of Nations* (first published, 1776); the classic argument for the *laissez-faire* state.

Smith, Thomas V.: *The Promise of American Politics* (Chicago, 1936), chaps. I, III, IV, and VI; while the chaps. cited here deal with individualism, fascism, communism, and Americanism, perusal of entire book will be time well spent.

Tugwell, R. G.: "Design for Government," *Political Science Quarterly*, XLVIII, No. 3 (September, 1933), 321–32.

Willoughby, W W.: *The Ethical Basis of Political Authority* (New York, 1930); chaps. IV, VIII, and XVI include a discussion of the functions of government as seen by socialists, communists, and fascists, as well as the author's own opinions of the legitimate sphere of state activity.

Wilson, Francis G.: *The Elements of Modern Politics* (New York, 1936), chaps. XXI, XXIII–XXVI; discusses various theories of governmental functions, including the authoritarian state.

Wilson, Woodrow: *The State* (Boston, 1896), chaps. XV and XVI; presents an interesting and balanced discussion of the functions of government.

Wooddy, Carroll H.: "The Growth of Governmental Functions," chap. XXV in *Recent Social Trends* (New York, 1933); an illuminating account of the recent changes in governmental functions in the United States.

## CHAPTER III

☆ ☆ ☆

## DEMOCRACY IN AN INDUSTRIALIZED COUNTRY

*"Popular government cannot continue if faith is lost. All such qualities depend in some large degree upon economic and social security."*
—C. A. DYKSTRA

CONTROL
AND
RESPONSE

THE LOCUS of effective control determines in no small measure whether the functions of government are to be limited and static or numerous and responsive. Statecraft is properly defined as the response of government to social need; but it should be obvious that whether the response takes place at all, and whether it is delayed or prompt, involves the willingness of those in authority to put the governmental machinery into motion. When social problems are numerous and popular control is extensive, public responsibilities are almost sure to be many. When a selfish minority is steering the ship of state, concessions to the popular will usually have to be fought for, and official activity is characterized by control and power. A responsive, popular government can afford to minimize the display of power. It begets compliance by co-operation and appreciation rather than by fear and deference.

Minorities are not always selfish, and majorities do not invariably act wisely. Those who rule in monarchies, in oligarchies, and even in dictatorships may be sufficiently shrewd and public-spirited to give the people the most important things they demand, to prevent dangerous tensions, and to take special pains to ingratiate themselves with the populace. Minority government has certain theoretical advantages over popular government. It is likely to realize the necessity of recruiting intelligence; it can act with greater dispatch; there are usually fewer divided counsels and hence more positive measures may result; and governance is characterized, as a rule, by efficiency and honesty. Popular government, on the other hand, sometimes produces the opposite results; it encourages debate and deliberation, consults minorities, changes leadership frequently, starts many programs that are never completed, and tends to rely upon the average man.

Government in which control is widespread among the citizenry is the most difficult to make work successfully. Democratic methods of governance develop slowly, because they depend upon more widespread popular understanding, general intelligence, traditions, and other basic factors which are not easily produced. For the short run, or when crisis conditions prevail, popular control is definitely not the best choice. But as a goal, democracy must clearly be rated first. It gives the greatest assurance that over a period of time the wishes of the community will be transposed into action. It keeps officialdom responsive to changing needs and desires. It is the only sure way of building social solidarity and tolerance, because it starts from the bottom. Finally, democracy encourages individual self-respect and adult responsibility by giving every voting citizen an effective part in operating the popular processes. It treats people as adults rather than as children. Democracy emphasizes the worth of individual personality, the highest compliment that can be paid any form of government. With so much disillusionment abroad in the world today, it is well to reflect on the imperishable values of popular government.

[margin note: DIFFICULTIES AND ADVANTAGES OF DEMOCRACY]

The problem of self-government is that of superimposing upon the foundation of democratic responsiveness and respect for the individual the advantages which are associated with less democratic but more efficient systems. This is difficult, but not impossible. It takes time, and sometimes it seems as though pressing social conditions will not permit democratic peoples the uninterrupted period in which to perfect their institutions, social education, and basic traditions of co-operation, tolerance, and progressivism. But intelligent leadership can be produced under democratic conditions, if the citizenry can only be educated to avail itself of that leadership. Minority-controlled governments have no monopoly on efficiency and honesty, although the problem of combining these characteristics with popular rule is immensely more difficult. Greater alacrity and more positive accomplishments than are common at present are possible under popular governments, but sight should not be lost of the fact that they will always be relatively less because of public lethargy, the principle of democratic responsibility, and the desirability of combining expertness and citizen participation. If a democratically inclined people gives sufficient thought to ultimate objectives and the inherent difficulties of reaching them, the task is a possible one, despite countercurrents of great force which are surging in other parts of the world.

There are a number of essential requirements and conditions of democracy. Some of these are general educational opportunities; traditions of co-operation, tolerance, and community pride; an impulse of social equality; opportunities for citizens to inform themselves reliably on public issues; honest elections; and a sufficient amount of leadership coming from all ranks of the population.

Within the last generation, the meaning and implications of the term "democracy" have become increasingly vague and varied. The widespread discussion during the World War about making the world safe for democracy has been interpreted by some as war-time propaganda and hysteria; by others as a deep-rooted, universal aspiration. Since the War our political thinking as to a precise definition and a workable program seems no nearer general agreement. Democracy is still a mendicant with a multiplicity of connotations. To some—Mussolini, for instance—this lack of definiteness is proof that political democracy is a snare and a delusion, "a bastard mistress."

<small>VARYING INTERPRETATIONS</small>

Democracy is frequently referred to as a social attitude, meeting one's fellows on an equal footing. This is not the political connotation of the term but is basic to it. In its general use, democracy implies a common willingness to approximate social equality. A halo is thrown around the "democratic way of life." Looking at the matter negatively, one may say that social snobbery and class exclusiveness will limit, if not make impossible, political democracy. The feeling of equality and fraternity is therefore the well-spring of the institutional expression of democracy. The United States, with its tradition of the "melting pot," fares far better in this respect than countries in which social distinctions are strongly established.

Democracy and tolerance are invariably found together. Peter Odegard has said: "Democratic government involves essentially a broadening of the basis of consent and may be said to rest upon the twin rights of association and advocacy. It is based upon a recognition of the diversity of interest which at any given time may be found within the community, and the right of these diverse interests to representation. The day of direct government by a small clique was done when the framework of an agrarian feudal society was shattered by the steam engine, the factory system, and the modern city." Reactionaries and extreme radicals view with undisguised contempt the babel of voices which is a logical incident of democracy.

The term is sometimes used to denote the method whereby the will of the people may be ascertained and put into effect. Democracy is expected to satisfy the needs and desires of the entire citizenry, to achieve the ends of the state. As Abraham Lincoln said, the government should be *for* the people. It should be controlled by, and be run in the interest of, the many rather than the few.

Before the World War, most of the emphasis was upon the external form and procedures. The framework of representative government was studied assiduously. Democracy meant an elected chief executive, bicameralism, and universal suffrage. This view was conventional rather than critical; it went not to the substance and the results but merely to the machinery. From the extension of the franchise alone, wondrous things were expected.

At least one desirable result of the intellectual ferment which has resulted since the War has been the emphasis upon underlying forces and ultimate ends. Framework means less; more attention is attached to general education and traditions. Voting is still considered an indispensable requirement, but a more realistic view is taken of the importance of the mere act of marking a ballot. The semblance of voting is retained in Fascist Italy; in isolated instances voting is sometimes as much a pretense in countries which have adhered more closely to democratic moorings.

Since the War the emphasis has been largely on social democracy. It is contended that political democracy cannot exist where there is not industrial democracy.[1] If great differences of economic position exist, political forms will be helpless to prevent loss of equality and freedom. The two go hand in hand. A consideration of one necessarily leads to an examination of the other. Economic control is political power.

Other interpretations of democracy might be mentioned, but the ones we have emphasized have a direct bearing upon the particular problem we are examining, namely, democracy in an industrialized country. We have pointed out that the older view of democracy was concerned too largely with the form and mechanics of government. The importance of these public processes should not be minimized today, and there is no inclination to do so. What has been said is that the modern approach to democracy goes under and beyond the mere framework of representative government to the dynamics, the economic implications, and the ends which society attempts to achieve.

It is difficult to realize the ideals of democracy, or even to hold the ground that has been gained, in a country which has become highly industrialized. Political democracy needs to be looked at from the sociological point of view. The basic factors to be considered are the concentration of economic power, and the change from an agricultural, individualistic society to an urbanized, collectivist one.[2]

FROM AGRICULTURE TO INDUSTRY

When society is simple, governmental requirements are simple; when society becomes complex, the responsibilities of government grow accordingly. Men living in an agricultural society tend to remain self-sufficient as far as the fulfillment of their wants is concerned. They may produce most of their own food, make a

---

[1] See, for example, Norman Thomas, *America's Way Out* (New York, 1931), chap. entitled, "What Is the Matter with Democracy?"
[2] These questions have been admirably considered in Charles A. and Mary Beard's *Rise of American Civilization*, 2 vols. (New York, 1927), and Lewis Mumford's *Technics and Civilization* (New York, 1934).

large part of their own clothing, and provide their own entertainment. Co-operative effort is usually called forth in the provision of education, in the building and maintenance of roads, and in the performance of rudimentary governmental functions—but in the main, rural dwellers can rely upon their own efforts rather than upon an outside agency, whether that agency be government or business. In the matter of regulation, too, the demands upon government are usually negligible. So long as farmers are owners rather than tenants, there is no particular disposition to call upon the government as a means of leveling down differences in wealth or income.

The less industrialized a country and the more self-sufficient its citizens, the less indispensable the government and the fewer its functions are likely to be. This does not mean that farming communities are necessarily conservative and individualistic in a political sense; the radical movements in our own western states and the examples of Australia and western Canada are instances of the demand for social co-operation which will instantly come to mind. With the industrialization of farming and the growth of co-operative marketing in agriculture, the reliance of the rural population upon the government has grown very rapidly in the United States. As might be expected, the farmer's dependence has increased with the substitution of machine for manual labor, with the growth in the number of tenant farmers, with the habit of purchasing clothing, groceries, and even fresh vegetables instead of producing them on the farm, and with the development of co-operative finance and marketing as the means of combating the city bankers, brokers, and distributors.

Hence, it is not entirely accurate to state that agricultural communities are self-sufficient and independent of government for the protection of their well-being. Nor is it true that an agricultural country will necessarily be a democratic one, socially, economically, or politically. Lord Bryce did not say that an agricultural economy necessarily produces democracy; but in *Modern Democracies* he did observe that the achievement of real democracy is much more likely in a country of farmers than in an industrialized, urbanized commonwealth.

## DEMOCRACY IN AN INDUSTRIALIZED COUNTRY

The industrialization of a country has the result of bringing the population to the cities, where urban dwellers are dependent upon outside agencies for the fulfillment of almost all their wants. Nearly two-thirds of the citizens of the United States now live in municipalities rather than on farms or in unincorporated rural places. The city dweller, unlike his country cousin, has no choice in the matter of fulfilling the everyday necessities of life. He becomes a cog in a highly complex and synchronized machine; he becomes completely dependent upon the services of others in order that he may take advantage of community living.

URBANISM

The urbanite counts upon the milkman to have his cream on the doorstep at the same time every morning; he relies upon the city water department for an adequate and pure supply of drinking water; he purchases his food from the nearby grocery store whose stock on hand would run short in a few days if anything should block the highly organized and sensitive wheels of distribution; his schooling, library requirements, and outdoor recreation are made available, for the most part, by public provision. For his knowledge of affairs in the outside world, he must depend upon newspaper press services, the radio broadcasts, and the motion pictures, trying as best he can to sift the propaganda from the truth and discounting what he reads or hears in the light of his knowledge of the agencies' bias; for the protection of his person, his belongings, and his economic position in society, he must pin his faith upon the effectiveness and statesmanship of government. Anomalously, the city dweller finds himself a very small part in a very large mechanism, becoming almost completely dependent in order that he may enjoy the larger opportunities afforded by organization, co-operation, and culture.

Man's reliance upon the state is in direct ratio to the complexity of society and the congestion of population. How few city dwellers are aware of this fact! It is to be doubted whether the mad bustle of our business centers induces clear thinking and an appreciation of what constitutes the individual's real interest. How can democracy succeed when citizens become as mechanized and as specialized as the machines which they operate during their day's work?

During the decade of the twenties, the central cities of metropolitan areas, as a whole, grew only about half as fast as the rest of the areas. Urban dwellers are constantly pushing out farther into the suburbs and neighborhood shopping centers are growing up. Industries are beginning to move from the more populous areas to sparsely settled or even rural ones. There they find lower taxes and a supply of rural workers who will accept lower wages than city dwellers. The work, moreover, can be carried on under more healthful and congenial conditions. The decentralization of industry has been one of the policies of the Roosevelt administration. It finds concrete expression primarily in the Tennessee Valley Authority and the Rural Resettlement Administration. The underlying idea of the program is to produce a "balanced economy," consisting of small industries and processing concerns in the center of farming areas. These populations will then be able to work part of the time in industry and another part in the soil. They can work under city conditions during the day and enjoy the outdoors during off-hours. This is an admirable ideal, which the government does well to sponsor. In many ways, too, it is to the financial advantage of the owners of industries.

Can decentralization of industry be carried so far that huge metropolitan centers of a million, or seven million, will shrink substantially in size, reversing the trend that has accompanied America's change from a predominantly agricultural country to a highly industrialized one in an astonishingly short period of time? In 1800 the percentage of the population of the United States living in places of 8,000 inhabitants or more was only 4.0; in 1850, 12.7; and in 1880, it was still only 22.7. By 1900, however, the proportion had risen to 32.9 per cent, and in 1930 it was 49.1 per cent of the total population.

Some of the very largest cities may lose population, or their rate of growth may be retarded, but the cities as a whole will probably continue to attract newcomers from rural areas. Men are gregarious. Modern invention gives urban life attractions which are universally appealing. The financial opportunities for young people of promise are incomparably better in large cities. Farming has become mechanized, with the result that more work can be done with far less human effort. It is the suburbs that will probably continue to grow at the fastest rate. Electrical power, free from dirt or odor, can be used to turn the wheels of suburban industries. "Garden cities," of which there are already several, here and abroad, will be the result. The government of metropolitan areas has already become one of the most important and difficult fields of political science.[1]

Governmental problems would naturally be much simpler if municipalities were automatically limited to a certain size. This, of course, is only theoretically possible. The optimum size of a city is a debatable question. Some would say fifty thousand, while others could make out a good case for an urban center ten times that large. At the latter figure, the largest cities would be about the size of Cincinnati or Buffalo. How much better that would be!

CONSEQUENCES OF POPULATION CONGESTION

Extremely large metropolises make men impersonal in their dealings. The individual feels swallowed up in the mass of milling men and the hubbub of ceaseless activity and noise. He meets so many people; he knows none very well. Moreover, when man loses close contact with nature he loses some of his natural qualities. He is more artificial, sophisticated, calloused. The basis on which he makes decisions is changed. In the city the personal factor is minimized. The person becomes part of a system. It is larger than he is and demands his compliance. Then, city people begin to talk about "the thing to do," "the rule of the game," "everybody else does it." Group customs and standards hold sway; individuality is submerged. It is entirely different with the farmer who knows everybody in his valley; when life is simple and human acquaintances are few, action is controlled primarily by personal considerations—regard for the man you know.

These considerations have an important bearing upon government. Democracy depends upon individual choice and discernment. It is individualistic rather than mass acting. It expects the individual to learn, weigh, and criticize. These things are hard

[1] Cf. Merriam, Parratt, and Lepawsky, *The Government of the Metropolitan Region of Chicago* (Chicago, 1933); also Paul Studenski, *The Government of Metropolitan Areas in the United States* (New York, 1930).

to do when one is caught up in mass activities, and when fashions and views are more or less stereotyped. Even our best-educated and well-to-do city dwellers rarely know how to vote intelligently, especially on candidates. How can they be expected to, when there is little possibility of knowing the candidate and when one's own business customarily takes all of one's time? The setting is ideal for the political machine. It does not prey upon ignorance alone. It can count also upon general bewilderment and anemic individual interest and responsibility. The person feels so helpless! Many succumb to cynicism and defeat; others vote automatically, as the ward boss or the favorite newspaper suggests. Citizenship becomes an irksome duty rather than an opportunity for self-expression. Several years ago Frederic L. Howe wrote a book entitled, *The City, the Hope of Democracy*. There is a question as to whether or not his optimism was justified.

The congestion of population has largely followed the industrialization of the country and the concentration of economic power. The central factor in business life is now the large-scale corporation. It has changed the character of private property and of social relations generally.

CONCENTRATION IN BUSINESS

The business corporation, like large cities, is artificial. Business has become depersonalized. When business life was less highly developed, the man who began an industry also owned it and managed its affairs. Now, in an increasing number of business enterprises, ownership and operation are in entirely different hands. Corporations have thousands of stockholders. The American Telephone and Telegraph Company, for example, is owned by about two-thirds of a million persons. Our economic life is now dominated by the "semi-public" corporation, or one in which a large measure of separation of ownership and control has taken place through the multiplication of owners.

Developments in government and business run almost parallel. Formerly close to the people, they are becoming farther and farther removed. Both tend to grow in size, to work through larger units of organization. Democratic control continues to wane. The largest business corporations now have "management control"; the paid managers actually run the corporation's affairs because the stockholders are so numerous and any one individual holds such a small proportion of the total ownership that voting control loses its effectiveness.

An understanding of the modern business corporation and the resulting developments in economic power is essential to a comprehension of the difficulties of democratic control on the political level. Berle and Means point out that "at least 78 per cent and probably a larger proportion of American business wealth is corporate wealth. Since the largest 200 non-banking corporations controlled approximately 49 per cent of all corporate wealth, the rough calculation would indicate that they controlled 38 per cent or more of all business wealth."[1] The concentration of control has advanced with great rapidity. In 1909 the assets of the 200 then largest non-banking corporations amounted to only 26.0 billion dollars; by 1919 they had reached 43.7 billions, an increase of 68 per cent in ten years; and in the next decade they increased to 81.1 billions, an increase of 85 per cent. In 1929 there were 300,000 non-financial corporations in the country; 200 of these, or less than seven-hundredths of 1 per cent, controlled nearly half the corporate wealth.[2] "This dissolution of the atom of property destroys the very foundation on which the economic order of the past three centuries has rested. . . . In creating these new relationships, the quasi-public corporation may fairly be said to work a revolution. It has destroyed the unity that we commonly call property—has divided ownership into nominal ownership and the power formerly joined to it. . . . On the basis of its development in the past we may look forward to a time when practically all economic activity will be carried on under the corporate form."[3] Challenging words, these, almost staggering in their social and political implications!

Many important questions immediately cry out for answers. The first is whether democracy can flourish except when individual ownership and its accompanying independence are the general characteristics of the economic order. Conversely, it may be asked

---

[1] Adolf A. Berle and Gardiner C. Means, *The Modern Corporation and Private Property* (Macmillan, New York, 1932), p. 31. It is strongly recommended that the reader who has not done so acquaint himself with this illuminating book.
[2] *Ibid.*, pp. 32, 33.     [3] *Ibid.*, pp. 6, 8, 17.

whether concentration in business does not inevitably result in narrower control of government. If, as appears to be largely the case already, the industrial system becomes almost entirely corporate, will not this fundamental change be reflected in the operation and control of government?

In election years there is a good deal of talk about the power of Wall Street. Many times the picture is overdrawn. All the big business men do not get together and lay plans to control Congress and the state legislatures. Business is too much divided. It is the nature of the competitive system for every enterprise to attempt to get the upper hand over rivals. Hence, a combined assault upon the stronghold of government is rarely in the nature of the case. Business executives are too absorbed in the pressure of running their own businesses to have much time for conspiracy. Moreover, Wall Street executives are not greatly different from other people. One of their number has said, with much truth, that "they are a pretty simple-minded lot." Picturing them as octopuses or supermen is fantasy.

*WALL STREET*

Yet when it is averred that the "real rulers" of America are the three or four hundred men who manage the largest businesses and wield concentrated power through holding companies and interlocking boards of directors, there is just enough truth in the assertion to make one give it respectful consideration.

Ownership and political power interact. The individual who controls the economic destinies of banks and businesses is often more powerful because of the special favors and immunities which he can obtain from government than because of his wealth as represented in investment securities. If he can obtain a liberal charter of incorporation, special tariff favors, lax enforcement of the "blue-sky" or public-utility laws, and tax exemptions, or if he can defeat the enactment of regulatory measures which would limit vested interests or monopoly privileges, the political power thus represented may be the principal factor producing financial success.

It has become increasingly clear in recent years that the well-being of all economic interests, large and small, depends upon the policies of government. This is particularly true of big business. Banking laws, the rediscount rate, tariffs, anti-trust laws, monetary policy, public works, governmental indebtedness, regulatory and restrictive laws, all count more heavily with banking, manufacturing, and public-utility enterprises than with small businesses. Public policy is the determining factor between prosperity and failure in the case of a growing number of large-scale enterprises. Hence it is entirely natural that their owners and managers should take a growing interest in government and attempt to increase their influence over its decisions.

The representative system of government is dominated by the party system, and the major political parties are dependent upon campaign funds which are principally subscribed by those who relation between economic and political power are best able to contribute—the business and financial leaders of the country.[1] Candidates who willingly or unwillingly accept these sources of financial support must expect to comply with the wishes of those by whom they are elected or else face the prospect of political oblivion. Under such circumstances, the fulfillment of the ends of the state becomes a slow and discouraging process. When one considers the vast sums that have been available for campaign purposes, it is surprising and reassuring that the United States has not had more "bought" governmental officials than it has had. Professor Munro is responsible for the statement that "the money power in politics" rules government and that when it "loses out" it soon re-establishes itself.[2] If this is true, then the concept of the general will is seen to be illusory.

The average business leader does not draw a sharp line between business and government—except when he considers his interests adversely affected. Otherwise, everything is business with him; and electing candidates who will be manageable, spending large sums to defeat legislation, and influencing officials who are responsible for the enforcement of regulatory laws are all part of the process of making profits for the company; if government gets in the way or can be used, the business man shapes his course of

---

[1] James K. Pollock, *Party Campaign Funds* (New York and London, 1926).
[2] William Bennett Munro, *The Invisible Government* (New York, 1928), chap. entitled, "The Money Power in Politics."

action accordingly. In many specific cases, such as a united effort by insurance companies to defeat a proposed piece of legislation, the conspiracy theory is much more plausible. At various times there has been a general campaign by official business to restrict the functions of government, particularly when they impinge upon the established interests of business men. One prominent aspect of this campaign is to discourage the public's putting too much confidence in government and to convince citizens that public agencies are not capable of performing their functions efficiently. A former president of the United States Chamber of Commerce once wrote: "The best public servant is the worst one. . . . A thoroughly first-rate man in public service is corrosive. He eats holes in our liberties."[1]

Another difficulty impeding the achievement of a democracy in a highly industrialized country is the stealthy and sometimes insidious influence of lobbies. Those maintained by business are the best financed and among the most effective.[2] When large corporations stand to gain millions of dollars, a few thousands contributed to lobbyists are considered an exceptionally good investment. When, as the Federal Trade Commission investigation of recent years shows, public utility interests go so far as to sponsor or to fight candidates, and attempt to control educational institutions and the press, popular control is in great danger.[3] The economic pressure group is an undemocratic influence because it ties the hands of representatives whose natural inclination might be to support the larger public or the larger interest; it encourages the use of government for narrow and selfish purposes; it strengthens the invisible government and hence prevents the correction of inadequacies in the official government; it acts secretly and

RESULTS UPON REPRESENTATIVE GOVERNMENT

[1] See my article "Do Business Men Want Good Government?" *National Municipal Review*, XX (January, 1931), 31–7.
[2] Cf. E. Pendleton Herring, *Group Representation Before Congress* (Baltimore, 1929), especially chaps. v, vi, and xiv; and Harwood L. Childs, *Labor and Capital in National Politics* (Columbus, 1930).
[3] See Federal Trade Commission, *Utility Corporations*, No. 71A (Washington, 1934); Report on "Efforts by Associations and Agencies of Electric and Gas Utilities to Influence Public Opinion." For interpretation of F. T. C. findings, consult Jack Levin, *Power Ethics* (New York, 1931); Ernest Gruening, *The Public Pays* (New York, 1931); Mosher and others, *Electrical Utilities* (New York, 1929), chap. v.

connivingly, lessening governmental responsibility and the opportunity for knowledge and criticism; finally, it opens the door to corruption and anti-popular control over the instrumentalities and purposes of government. But is not the lobby a natural accompaniment of private ownership and an essential phase of free government?

A country does not deliberately choose industrialism, nation-wide trusts, and concentration of financial power; they just naturally grow up. Business complexity is the result of many factors, including improved transportation, mechanical invention, division of labor, growth of investable wealth, and the rapid exploitation of national resources. Government seems powerless to prevent further concentration. The first anti-trust law was passed in 1890, and another with sharper teeth was enacted in 1914. Some proposed consolidations have been forbidden, but over the wide front business corporations have continued to expand rapidly. The most recent stage in the development is "banker control." Salaried managers run a manufacturing business or public utility and the profits are turned over to the banker owners. This form of control is found particularly in the transportation and electrical utility industries.[1] The trend to banker control has been accompanied by the widespread use of the holding company device. Companies are pyramided, with the result that a relatively small amount of capital can control operating enterprises representing vast totals. The holding company is thus able to "skim the profits." Ultimate control is far removed and it is sometimes hard to put one's finger on the actual apex of the pyramid. Under these circumstances, the government finds it difficult to prosecute unlawful combinations, regulate profits, and fix responsibility for efforts to evade the law or influence legislation.

CAN PUBLIC CONTROL BE EXPECTED TO SUCCEED?

If these business developments are natural, if they seem to inhere in economic development, why not let them alone? Perhaps it is a mistake for government to interfere. It may be there is a point

[1] The technique has been extended also into other fields. The Du Ponts, for example, are bankers in their relationship to General Motors and use banker methods in the management of the rest of their enterprises. See "Du Pont II: A Management and Its Philosophy," *Fortune*, X (December, 1934), 86 ff.

beyond which concentration would naturally come to a stop and the opposite tendency would set in. If monopolies were left alone, say others, the people would become dissatisfied and would call upon the government to take them over and operate them. Socialism would be the result.

But government also has "natural" functions. One of these is protection. People become fearful of power, whether it be economic or political. They ask government to check the tendency toward monopoly and to regulate essential businesses. They call upon public authority to prevent monarchy and dictatorship in business because they suspect that if they do not, popular government will be threatened. But the plutocracy becomes increasingly strong, while the threat to democratic institutions grows. This is the dilemma of democracy. Is the solution a benevolent business aristocracy? Can popular control be safeguarded despite trends in the economic order?

Industry is built upon invention and technological improvements as well as upon capital investment. These in turn create many of government's most difficult problems. Physical discovery outstripping social invention is the principal cause of "the social lag."[1] The telegraph, telephone, and radio have brought New York and Los Angeles within split seconds of each other. Airplane travel has reduced three thousand miles to a day's trip; but the fundamental laws and processes of government have not been correspondingly improved. Modernization is difficult in the political realm. Industry, with power which constantly grows because of inventions and improvements, is presumably regulated and controlled by government, which finds it difficult to progress. Must we, then, conclude that physical invention and technology are foes of democratic control? Not at all. It is clear, however, that governmental improvement needs to take place at somewhere near the same rate as physical discovery or public authority cannot be relied upon as an effective instrument for preserving popular government.

INFLUENCE OF TECHNOLOGY

[1] See the excellent article by Professor W. F. Ogburn entitled "Technology and Governmental Change," *Journal of Business of the University of Chicago*, IX (January, 1936), 1–13; also his chap. on "Influence of Invention and Discovery" in *Recent Social Trends* (New York, 1933).

Technology intensifies the competition for control of the instruments of public opinion. The discovery of the radio is the best illustration of this point. Broadcasting is now the most effective medium in political campaigns and has a great deal of influence on all public questions. Radio helps determine people's attitudes toward government and business. Those who have access to what goes over the air therefore wield an enormous power. Popular decisions, intelligently arrived at, now depend in no small measure upon the manner in which broadcasting is controlled and administered.

American broadcasting differs fundamentally from that in most other countries. Our system is private, competitive, and supported by advertisers. Most other countries have created a government monopoly and the programs are financed by taxes on listening sets. There are over six hundred broadcasting stations and seventeen million receiving sets in the United States. What part does radio play in molding political opinion, and how much influence do advertisers have on the character of what goes over the air?

It is often said, "Whoever controls the press, controls public opinion." It has become increasingly clear that the primary purpose of the modern newspaper is to make money for its owners. Financial solvency depends upon the sale of advertising, which occupies the bulk of newspaper space. Publishing daily journals, like other businesses, has felt the influence of economic concentration. Although total circulation has increased, the number of newspapers has declined. In 1917, there were 2,514 daily papers; in 1931, there were approximately 2,000. Chain newspaper development is the order of the day. According to *Editor and Publisher Year Book* for 1935, 341 newspapers were controlled by 63 chains. This number, it will be observed, is approximately one-sixth of the total number. The Scripps-Howard chain with 25 papers in 25 cities and the Hearst group with 22 dailies in 18 cities are the largest two. In 1931, the aggregate circulation of the Hearst press was about four million a day, or 10 per cent of the total newspaper circulation of the country. In 1933, of 1,305 cities with a population under 100,000, only 163 had two or three dailies published by independent companies; in 1,142 of these cities, or 87 per cent of the total, one paper or one company had a monopoly. Two news-gathering syndicates, Associated and United, each supplied news to some 1,250 papers.

In a democracy, widespread knowledge is the fulcrum on which the power of government should rest. Affording educational opportunities to the individual is the initial consideration, of course. In the United States this is done quite satisfactorily; but, in addition to that, the citizen must be provided with reliable and constant information on public affairs. Live issues will be brought to him principally through the newspapers, the motion pictures, and the radio. When the press is dependent upon advertisers, when the motion-picture industry is largely owned and controlled by investment bankers, and when radio broadcasting is supported by selling time to large business concerns and many of the newscasters themselves are hired by advertisers, most of what the citizen reads and hears may be expected to be tinctured with the outlook and interest of the leaders of industry and finance.[1] The extent to which editorial opinions have been injected into the news columns in recent years makes some American newspapers openly biased. They have an axe to grind. Radio broadcasts are sometimes subject to the same criticism.

<small>CONTROL OF PUBLIC OPINION</small>

In a highly industrialized country, the means of supplying information concerning public affairs and of controlling citizens' attitudes toward controversial issues tends to be dominated by the nation's business leaders. The power thus made available to shape public opinion and to limit the effectiveness and functions of the state is another of the obstacles in the road of popular rule. Its significance is hard to overestimate.

In short, the industrialization of a country tends to concentrate political power in the hands of the few rather than to increase the base of those who are politically effective; it creates a governing industrial system which challenges the authority of the political state and even at times tends to overshadow it; the state is used frequently for the advantage of economic groups; and, through the control of, or influence over, instruments of information and

[1] See S. McKee Rosen, *Political Process* (New York, 1935), chap. entitled "The Press."

propaganda, popular attitudes and views are fashioned in the interest of the business community. The net result is that there sets in a countercurrent to what we have called "the surge of democracy."

The inhibiting effect of a business man's civilization upon democratic government may be just as real but it is not so obvious nor so likely to cause strategical mistakes when those who control the nation's economic life have developed a governing class skilled in the art of government. As a matter of fact, in a country wherein the democratic surge is pronounced and in which industrial concentration is also highly developed, it is doubtful whether the existing system of industrial and governmental control can continue unless among the nation's business leaders a strong corporate sense is developed and a governmental career is made the highest ambition of the sons of "ruling" families. Effective government, resting upon compromise and social service, is the indispensable requirement of those who would retain a high degree of industrialization under private ownership and control.

<small>OBLIGATIONS OF A GOVERNING CLASS</small>

It is sometimes asked whether there is more democracy in the United States than in Great Britain. The answer clearly is that there is more of the surge and the actuality of social equality in the United States than in Great Britain, but that those who control the latter nation's economy are more adroit in the technique of political rule. In the long run, we should prefer the former to the latter, but at this particular point we are being quite Machiavellian.

Those who have governed Great Britain for generations, as Laski has pointed out, constitute a corporate-conscious aristocracy founded upon the landholding class and later strengthened by, and controlled primarily in the interest of, the business and financial community. The art of political rule, of compromise while retaining the prizes of conservatism, of giving the larger public enough to keep it fairly well satisfied while holding on to the control and profits of industry, has reached a higher point of perfection in Great Britain than in any other Western country. The economic interest group which has governed Great Britain has made political democracy as satisfactory as possible in order to sidetrack the issues of social and economic democracy.

It is a mistaken and unfair view to assume that the cultivation of political democracy by the nation's economic leaders has been wholly a deep-dyed conspiracy aimed at popular quiescence relative to social and economic matters. The rational character of the matter, however, should not be underestimated. Britain's leaders early learned to think in terms of the nation's economy. If Great Britain's government were not in wise hands, the nation's foreign trade and investments could not be expected to flourish; if the country's affairs were not properly managed, the trade and investments of the owners of industry could not be expected to be secure. Thereupon it became recognized that government is of more importance than business, because the latter is so completely dependent upon the former. Naturally enough, the most promising sons of British ruling families went either into politics or into governmental administration; but this was not all.

Britain's governing class developed a philosophy of public service, the credo of which goes somewhat as follows: Service to the state is the most desirable vocation in life; in all that concerns the state, public officials must be scrupulously honest and as effective as possible; the essence of government is compromise, the ability to maintain stability and equilibrium in society; and finally, the country and its rulers are secure only insofar as government is popular and effective.

The conservatives of the United States have not been so understanding or so far-seeing. They have shown very little appreciation of the fact that economic power means governmental responsibility or that service for the state is the highest career, and they have belittled government and made it appear as inefficient as possible. In so doing they have clearly not known on which side their bread was buttered.

The basic weakness of the philosophy of self-interest is that it is almost inevitably short-sighted. Unfortunately there is much evidence to support this observation in the United States. Britain's rulers have been somewhat more astute. The explanation of the difference is to be found largely in the British governing class's comprehension that privilege entails social obligation. The British aristocrat has a feeling of paternalism for his constituents. If they insistently demand free-school education, unemployment insurance, or the municipalization of local utilities, the conservative leaders usually come around to the popular point of view. Compromise, particularly if it can be accompanied by a counterbalancing gain in another direction, is the stuff out of which successful political domination is molded. The British conservatives have almost invariably obtained their *quid pro quo*. The nationalization of electricity, the unification of London transport, and other utility services were fought for by the Labor party, for example, but the conservatives put through these measures and took care to see that a large number of gilt-edged securities were made available for the investing public, the bulwark of conservatism. Machiavelli would say that the greatest victory is the one that benefits the governed while further strengthening the position of the governor!

Industrialization causes class differentiations to be more pronounced. Differences in economic and social status tend to be intensified. Laborers organize to offset the power of employers and to seek a larger share of the national income. This results in increased emphasis upon the power aspect of government and less likelihood of democracy based upon equality and co-operation; but such consequences are seemingly inherent in the system. The class struggle does not automatically become more aggravated; but if deep divergences are to be prevented, popular control must retain its vitality, and government must be intelligent and positive.

A democracy should be classless. Even in countries where class lines are not sharply drawn, however, as in the United States, the wage-earning and salaried group, with its moderate savings, is commonly referred to as the middle class. Some writers on social problems have stated that the size of the middle class is the index of democracy.[1]

THE MIDDLE CLASS AS THE BALANCE OF POWER

[1] The best analysis of the importance of the middle class is to be found in the writings of Professor Arthur N. Holcombe. See his book, *The New Party Politics* (New York, 1933), especially chaps. IV and V; and "Foreword" in his *Government in a Planned Democracy* (New York, 1935). Read also the interesting book by Lewis Corey entitled, *The Crisis of the Middle Class* (New York, 1935).

In the political equation, as historical instances abundantly illustrate, the middle class occupies a strategic position. Generally, the middle class has acted as a balance between the radicalism of the right and the radicalism of the left. At times it has suffered at the hands of the rich, and at other times its status has been lowered by an uprising of the proletariat. When a strong middle class begins to be submerged, a violent social adjustment is likely. The most recent example of the social importance of the middle class is Nazi Germany, where, according to reliable interpreters of the German scene, the usually stolid middle class espoused National Socialism when it found its economic status being lowered to that of the proletariat.

Not only is the middle class the balance of power (as in postwar Germany) and at times the most numerous group in the country (as in the United States) but, within the realm of political ideology, its influence is of unequalled importance. As middle-class America thinks, so goes the country! The same observation may be made of the British electorate or of the electorates in some other countries.

It has been frequently remarked that the middle class is a conservative force in government. This generalization is usually supported by the observation that the person who owns ten shares of stock is frequently more fundamentalist and reactionary with regard to state activity than is the financier who owns ten thousand shares. The bourgeoisie is sometimes said to be merely the duped prop of the exploiter.

One can probably think of concrete instances in which each of these allegations has been confirmed. There is, however, another side of the picture. The middle classes of the several countries are not exactly alike. The middle class in the United States is more distinctive than any other; it has more spirit; it fights more fiercely for equality; it is not so stolid; it is idealistic and reformist. Middle-class America is the tradition and spirit of America. Its beliefs and thinking are frequently uncritical, but its instincts and emotions tend toward fairness and equality.

The most representative expression of American middle-class views and political behavior is found among the rank and file of small business men. Being typically American, these men state as their credo that governmental functions should be narrowly circumscribed; but in practice they extend the field of state activity whenever it appears to be for the community's interest. According to Samuel O. Dunn, one of the most outspoken champions of official business, the rank and file of America's business men are "practical socialists." Mr. Dunn is right. "Practically every increase in taxes and in government interference with business," he has pointed out, "is due more to our business men than to our politicians. . . . Our danger is not from the theoretical socialist, but from the practical socialist. . . . A practical socialist is a man who will favor almost any form of governmental action, however socialistic, which he believes will benefit him." Local business men are responsible for larger and better city halls, social services, and local utilities. As Mr. Dunn reminds us, "the woods are full of practical socialists."[1]

"PRACTICAL SOCIALISTS"

Despite the costly and continuous campaign that has been carried on in the United States, aimed at the prevention of public interference with business and the acceptance of the belief that government is by nature inefficient, the average American still acts in a rational and practical manner when traditional American equality is threatened or when the community can be benefited by co-operative undertakings. Americans do not follow all the false leads that seem to attract them, and in the long run they usually come out on the right side of public issues.

We may agree with Mr. Dunn that "nobody wants any of his own territory taken in" by an extension of public economic services. By making use of government, however, the small business man has helped his own venture. This observation applies particularly to the states which were involved in the western movement. Until the time came that satisfactory streets, law and order, a supply of water, adequate public buildings, and other community services were available, the town could not be expected to attract settlers, with the resulting improvement of business. Private undertakings were dependent upon, and directly

[1] *Nation's Business*, Nov., 1928, pp. 17–18.

aided by, community improvements. Conservative Los Angeles has long operated the largest municipally owned electricity undertaking in the country, because an adequate supply of water and cheap power were imperative to the community and to individual business men. This is the realistic and progressive tradition of a large part of the United States.

The individual fortitude of the pioneer and the business prowess of the Hills, the Goulds, and the Astors have been emphasized to such an extent that we fail to recognize the degree to which community co-operation and governmental assistance were involved in the building of America. Particularly during the period of business expansion that set in following the Civil War, government was the instrument which made business possible, which protected the business man after he had become established, and which permitted him to expand his business as the community became a more attractive place in which to live. During this period of three generations, the United States, particularly western America, has learned a great deal about the advantages of community co-operation. Americans became "practical socialists" without even being conscious of it.

Nation-wide trusts began to take form about 1880, and the process of concentration set in. Then the small business men turned to the government as their protector; the functions and agencies of government were multiplied; regulation became the most emphasized duty of the state. The surge of democracy and the passion for equality were asserting themselves. The Sherman Anti-Trust and the Interstate Commerce Commission acts were passed. The increase in governmental expenditures which took place during the next generation was largely attributable to the efforts of small business men, farmers, and laborers to protect their interests through the agency of government.

Despite such efforts and notwithstanding the regulatory laws and the enforcement agencies which have been brought into operation, the concentration of industry and finance has continued to gain momentum. One need simply read Harry Laidler's *Concentration in American Industry* to learn the extent to which small proprietors have been eliminated and the nation's economic life pyramided. Reliance upon the state has grown accordingly.

What will the future bring? The American tradition of equality has retained much of its vitality; the western expansion taught the people the benefits of community co-operation; the growth of big business has made the middle class increasingly reliant upon governmental protection; public control of businesses which are essential and inclined to be monopolistic is in line with American traditions and in the interest of middle-class business men.

The growth of big business has the effect of removing government farther from the people and of making the national government more important. This is due to one of the axioms we have mentioned; namely, "When society is simple, governmental requirements are simple; when society becomes complex, the responsibilities of government grow accordingly." Big business results in big government, if there is to be a degree of popular control over the economic order. There cannot be said to be complete coincidence and synchronization, however. We have already referred to the theory of the social lag. In addition, the federal government is prohibited from free expansion because of constitutional limitations. Yet it is true that concentration in business has meant the increase in federal authority and relatively less power close to home.

REMOTE CONTROL

The farther government is removed in terms of distance, the more difficult it becomes to control. Things close at hand are much more likely to be democratically handled. Only within the compass of a small area is direct participation possible. When electoral areas become large and business is transacted far away, the citizens usually know little about the candidates or what they do after being elected. Democracy exalts the individual and the small jurisdiction.

But when industry and finance become national there is only one satisfactory method of attempting to regulate and control—to use the government which covers the same area. The principal extensions of governmental power in the last fifty years have occurred in the federal realm. This is because business became national during the period following the 1880's. Let us mention some of the govern-

INCREASED FEDERAL RESPONSIBILITY

mental responses to social and economic situations which citizens decided needed the restraining or encouraging hand of federal authority. First, there were many railway subsidies and regulatory acts. A single standard of currency was established. National jurisdiction was extended further into banking and bankruptcy. Laws were passed prohibiting and regulating articles sent in national commerce. Certain laborers engaged in interstate commerce were given protective legislation. Efforts were made, as has been said, to prevent unlawful monopolies. Grain elevators, stockyards, and many other enterprises associated with the national flow of trade were made subject to governmental regulation. Water-power sites were made a matter of national concern. Telephones, telegraphs, and radio were brought under public control. Banking and the sale of securities were added to the list of federally regulated enterprises. Pure-food-and-drug legislation was enacted. Labor's rights to organize and bargain collectively were recognized. Businesses, large and small, entered into code agreements. Certainly the growth of federal power is clearly indicated by these illustrations.[1]

Measures enacted between 1880 and the present helped to protect the people's economic and social interests. There was no choice about what to do. Industry, transportation, and finance became nation-wide; some of the practices of big business were objectionable; and economic power instilled fear in the people. The problem-response relationship could then be seen at work. People may have regretted the concentration of power in Washington, but it was both natural and necessary.

It is no more likely that this development will be reversed than that business will again become small and local. As a matter of fact, further accretions of authority may almost surely be expected. The federal government has become banker not only to other governments but also to corporations and individuals. An extension of this activity, in the form of either regulation or direct management, seems quite possible. Constitutional amendment may be necessary; but as business goes so government may be expected to go, or at least attempt to go.

[1] See Carroll H. Wooddy, *Growth of the Federal Government* (New York, 1934).

The growth of federal authority, following industrialization, has changed the relative importance and interrelationships of the levels of government. The several states have waned in their
EFFECT UPON LEVELS OF GOVERNMENT
relative influence and rate of growth. Counties have been "going down hill," too, except in a few isolated areas. The principal relationship is now between the municipality and the federal government.[1] Local services and relief duties have expanded. All federal functions have grown: assistance (primarily relief), regulation, protection, and ownership and operation. During the depression, when emergency conditions existed and time was precious, federal agencies made it a common practice to deal directly with municipalities instead of clearing through state channels. This is probably a practice that will continue and be further extended.

Government is growing at its two extremes—at the local level and on the national plane. Rapid industrialization has a great deal to do with the explanation in both cases; it brought people to cities, and it created problems of national regulation. If economic trends continue, therefore, we may expect to see municipal and federal governments increasing in relative importance to state and county units.

We began this chapter by pointing out that democracy is very difficult to achieve even under the most favorable circumstances. It takes time for traditions to develop, for general enlightenment to be attained, and for habits of active citizen participation to grow. When, therefore, the difficulties of achieving democracy are made enormously more difficult by developments in business growth, patriots may well become increasingly concerned about the prospects of popular control and the realization of the dream of community.

Industrialization concentrates economic power and increases the likelihood that it will be transformed into political affluence. Industry helps to produce huge urban agglomerations. Both industry and urbanism are characterized by individual dependence; the submerging of personal responsibility; the delegation of power; a feeling of impotence; acceptance of crowd attitudes,

[1] Cf. Paul V. Betters, *Recent Federal-City Relations* (Washington, 1936).

styles, and beliefs; narrow control over the instruments of information; the increasing importance of interest representation; development of class lines; less direct participation; and the growth of government farther away from the people.

Let us not minimize the difficulties of preserving popular control and of achieving a true democracy in our modern complex society. But, in spite of the handicaps, it is possible to make better use of the instruments and opportunities available.

SELECTED READINGS

Barker, Ernest: "The Social Background of Recent Political Changes," *Sociological Review*, XXVIII, No. 2 (April, 1936), 117–32.

Beard, Charles A., and William: *The American Leviathan* (New York, 1930), chaps. I, IV, and XII–XX; a study of effects of machine age on the federal government; chaps. cited deal with the increased responsibilities resulting therefrom.

Beard, Charles A., and Mary R.: *The Rise of American Civilization*, Vol. II (New York, 1927); chaps. XX–XXV, XXVII, XXIX, and XXX deal with the great industrial expansion in the United States after the Civil War and its effects on democratic government.

Berle, Adolf A., Jr., and Means, Gardiner C.: *The Modern Corporation and Private Property* (New York, 1932), Books I and IV; the best study of the development and consequences of concentrated economic power in the United States.

Boas, George: "Technic of Mob Rule," *Harper's*, CLXX (May, 1935), 755–61.

Chase, Stuart: *Men and Machines* (New York, 1929); presents a good introduction to the social problem of modern technics.

Childs, Harwood L.: "Rule by Public Opinion: Fourth Stage," *Atlantic*, CLVII, No. 12 (June, 1936), 755–64.

Dewey, John: *The Public and Its Problems* (New York, 1927), chaps. III–VI; discusses some of the problems before modern democracy, based on Dewey's view of the need for participation and communication.

Dykstra, C. A.: "The Challenge of Urbanism," *Public Management*, XVI, No. 11 (November, 1934), 333–39.

Filene, Edward A.: *Successful Living In This Machine Age* (New York, 1931), chaps. I, V, XXII, XXIII; the philosophy of a successful business man who has the intelligence and courage to face the implications of modern society.

Frankfurter, Felix: *The Public and Its Government* (New Haven, 1930), chaps. I and III; a stimulating discussion of government's place in modern society.

Herring, E. Pendleton: "A Prescription for Modern Democracy," *Annals*, CLXXX (July, 1935), 138-48.
Holcombe, Arthur N: *Government in a Planned Democracy* (New York, 1935); a discussion of the importance of planning and administration in a democracy which aims at a balance among the conflicting forces of modern society.
———: *The New Party Politics* (New York, 1933), chaps. I, IV, and V; presents the thesis that as class politics tends to supplant sectional politics in America, stability and justice will best be furthered by middle-class politics.
Laski, Harold J.: "The Élite in a Democratic Society," *Harper's*, CLXVII (September, 1933), 456-64.
Lasswell, Harold D.: "The Moral Vocation of the Middle Income Skill Group," *International Journal of Ethics*, XLV, No. 2 (January, 1935), 127-37.
Lippmann, Walter: *The Phantom Public* (New York, 1925), *passim;* an interesting but somewhat pessimistic view of public opinion.
Morris, Charles W.: *Pragmatism and the Crisis of Democracy*, University of Chicago Public Policy Pamphlet No. 12 (Chicago, 1934).
Myers, William S.: "The Meaning of Democracy," *Annals*, CLXIX (September, 1933), 153-58.
National Resources Board: *A Report on National Planning and Public Works* (Washington, U. S. Government Printing Office, 1934), pp. 1-88, *passim;* effectively illustrates the increasing responsibilities of the federal government.
Odegard, Peter: *The American Public Mind* (New York, 1930), chaps. I, II, V-VII, and IX; a remarkably objective discussion of the merits and deficiencies of control by public opinion in America.
Odum, Howard W.: "Orderly Transitional Democracy," *Annals*, CLXXX (July, 1935), 31-9.
Ogburn, William F.: "The Influence of Invention and Discovery," *Recent Social Trends* (New York, 1933), chap. III.
Russell, Bertrand: *Freedom versus Organization, 1814-1914* (New York, 1934), Part III; an analysis of the lag between industrial technique and social invention; part cited discusses democracy and the concentration of wealth in America.
Shepard, Walter J.: "Democracy in Transition," *American Political Science Review*, XXIX, No. 1 (February, 1935), 1-20.
Smith, Thomas V.: *The Democratic Way of Life* (Chicago, 1926); a beautiful and effective statement of the ethics of democracy as a means to an end in our modern society.
Wallas, Graham: *The Great Society* (New York, 1914); a plea for understanding modern society and its large problems, by a pioneer in the field of social psychology.

CHAPTER IV

☆ ☆ ☆

## PROBLEMS OF REPRESENTATIVE GOVERNMENT

*"Those who concentrate on the defects of democracy are blind to what history discloses of the weaknesses of alternative forms of government."*
—FELIX FRANKFURTER

AMERICA IS STILL YOUNG. Compared to the ontogeny of the individual, she is about nineteen years of age.[1] Just before reaching maturity, America grew very rapidly—almost too fast, perhaps. At the age of sixteen agricultural simplicity still dominated her countenance; at nineteen the United States is the world's leading industrial nation.

The problems of adjustment which come with maturity are somewhat difficult for a country, as well as for human beings. Adult responsibilities come suddenly. Parents (or nature) no longer provide, and one needs to take stock of resources and prospects. It seems as though there would never be a chance to play again. One begins to wonder whether one has the ability and the preparation to make a success in life.

For this period of trial and doubt, America was well prepared. Her population came from pioneer stock, from people who were not only unafraid to venture into the unknown but were, in POSSIBILITIES OF CONTROLLING THE SOCIAL ENVIRONMENT fact, thrilled by it. The early settlers were a red-blooded and self-confident race. They left settled communities to find opportunity, freedom, and greater equality.

Moreover, a virile democratic spirit is the American heritage. The pioneer vitality is by no means dissipated. There is reason for believing that the democratic spirit still has considerable vitality, even though it does not manifest itself as patently or as frequently as in days past.

[1] Analogies to biological life are usually misleading. But what a temptation! André Siegfried has written a book entitled *America Comes of Age* (New York, 1927), said by some to be the best treatise on American democracy since De Tocqueville.

Fundamental changes in the life of the country have not yet had time to react fully upon the spirit of the people and the operation of their political institutions. We are now in the testing period, in which social and political direction is likely to be determined for a considerable period. It will probably be fifty years yet before the technological and corporate developments of the last fifty years are fully registered on our social institutions. During that time, Americans will reveal whether the democratic tradition and equalitarian spirit are strong enough to enable them to make effective use of the country's governmental machinery in resisting undemocratic influences. If this attempt is to be successful, there must be far more understanding of governmental problems and much wider use of popular processes than there has ever been before. Government will need to be made a more effective instrument. The shortcomings of representative government in the United States will require immediate and remedial action.[1]

Basic factors, such as industrial and urban concentration, have enormous determinative potentialities. Trends which are already manifest have a tendency to gain momentum unless something interferes. But immediate causes and social trends cannot be relied upon exclusively in making social analyses. There are other factors—traditions, the spirit of a people, and human intelligence. Man is distinctive because of his outstanding ability to contrive, to shape his destiny. He bends nature to his ends, changes the course of events which seem almost predestined. If trends are carefully analyzed and intelligence is applied to directing society toward objectives which are more desirable, the concept of community may still be attained. If man's social contriving can be made as successful as his physical discovery, this will be a highly satisfactory world.

A democracy should broaden the base of those who are politically effective. This objective, except in very small communities, must be sought through representation instead of by direct participation in lawmaking. The system is one of agency, of giving an elected representative a proxy to act in one's stead; but the analogy

---

[1] The last chapter in *Recent Social Trends* (New York, 1933), presents this challenge in a very gripping manner.

is not entirely accurate. In representative government the measures to be considered are more numerous than in a business enterprise and hence the discretion of the person elected must be relied upon to a much greater extent than is that of the agent.

We have been taking it for granted that popular control should be as wide as possible and that free universal suffrage is unquestionably desirable. Perhaps this assumes too much. Occasionally an intelligent person in the United States openly questions whether the privilege of voting should be as widespread as it is and feels pretty certain that it should be restricted to "responsible" people. It was not so long ago that property qualifications were demanded of voters, and even now these limitations still exist in some states for persons voting on municipal bond issues. For general elections, such qualifications were found in the early history of the United States and are required in some countries today. A generation ago, half the population, the feminine half, did not possess the privilege of voting. Instead of assuming that voting is a right, something that every adult should share, perhaps we should say that universal suffrage is still on trial.

THE ELECTORATE

Only responsible persons should be allowed to vote. But what is the meaning of "responsible?" There are several meanings. Age is one. The assumption is that when men and women reach the age of twenty-one, they have attained adulthood and hence should be able to assume the responsibility of voting as well as other privileges of maturity. Occasionally it is contended that this age is too low. Another assertion is that only citizens are responsible. Aliens who have not had enough interest or loyalty to take out citizenship papers should not be allowed to vote in any election. Similarly, it is argued that residence requirements are too liberal in most electoral jurisdictions. Instead of demanding a fixed residence for a few weeks or months, before permitting adult occupants to vote, the requirement should be universally extended to a year or more. Underlying assumptions are that newcomers should have sufficient time to make up their minds about candidates and issues and that temporary residents cannot be expected to take a responsible attitude.

Most proposals for limiting the franchise are usually made in private conversations. Rarely do any of them break into the printed page. People are jealous of the right to vote, even when they rarely exercise it. The re-establishment of property qualifications is the suggestion which is advanced most cautiously; but it is sometimes heard, particularly since the crash of 1929 which made millions propertyless and dependent upon relief. The argument is simple. If a person does not have property of his own, he will recklessly vote for new taxes, realizing that those who do possess will have to bear the burden.

PROPOSALS TO RESTRICT THE FRANCHISE

Other suggestions for restricting the number of those permitted to vote are less well defined and infrequently heard. Only persons whose mental age is above a certain point should be allowed to exercise the most important privilege of citizenship. This statement has been made more frequently since the World War conscription, which through tests made at that time, revealed to Americans the appalling percentage of low mentality and of those who were illiterate. If a man cannot even read and inform himself, it is argued, how dangerous it is to allow him to share responsibility for the country's policies.

If voters do not use their right to vote, they should be divested of the privilege. This contention, too, is heard rarely; but the reasoning underlying it is very interesting and makes the proposal worth our attention. If the franchise were limited, it would be prized. This psychological observation about human nature has a great deal of truth in it. It is difficult to bring out the vote merely by appealing to people's pride and patriotic duty, but when the fear response is struck, when the loss of the franchise would affect adversely the individual's interests and social standing, then the privilege of voting becomes something to fight for. This being the case, it is probably a great pity that proposals to restrict the franchise are not brought out into the open more frequently than they are.

The use of the franchise has admittedly been disappointing.[1] A turnout of about 50 per cent is the usual showing in American

[1] See Charles E. Merriam and Harold F. Gosnell, *Non-Voting* (Chicago, 1924).

elections. It takes a hot campaign or very colorful candidates to secure 70 per cent or 80 per cent participation. The United States compares unfavorably with other countries in this matter.[1]

NON-VOTING
A number of smaller countries, such as Denmark, Holland, and Australia, fairly consistently bring out 90 per cent or more of the registered voters, while England and France probably average 20 per cent to 30 per cent higher than the United States. This is surprising, when one considers that we literally fought for popular government, and that the democratic spirit is still strong; but countervailing influences also have had their effect. Government has not been taken so seriously in the United States as it has been in the countries mentioned. Perhaps, until recently, it did not need to be. While the westward movement was being completed, Americans were intent upon "empire building" and getting rich; voters were like carefree youths. Why bother to vote when everything else is getting "bigger and better" and when government does not cut a particularly important figure? Now that the picture has changed, the use of the franchise may increase. There is some evidence of this already.

Participation in elections by those who are entitled to vote is patently essential to democratic control. Voters and voting need to be made more intelligent. There is almost universal agreement on these points, but there are wide differences of opinion about the best methods of securing the desired results. Those who would limit the number who may exercise the franchise in order to make voters more responsible and the privilege of casting a ballot more highly prized, take what seems to be a short-sighted and reactionary view. The more constructive procedure is to organize popular interest, improve the honesty of elections, and further educate the citizen to his responsibilities and real interests as a member of society.

Even though a large percentage of the registered voters is not sufficiently informed and the average intelligence quotient is discouragingly low, it is better that the right to vote should be general than that a substantial minority should be disenfranchised.

[1] Harold F. Gosnell has written a book entitled, *Why Europe Votes* (Chicago, 1930).

Humanity in the main knows what is to its general interest and, as we have stated previously, the public will eventually express itself correctly, though frequently only after a period of trial and error. To move falteringly is better than to segregate a minority which will chafe because of its disbarment. Class strife and social revolution are invited by disenfranchisement. The least that can be said for universal suffrage is that it is a safety valve.

Constructive methods have been invented for getting out the vote and for enabling those who have only a patriotic, rather than a selfish, interest to cast their ballots intelligently. Considerable progress has been made along these lines since the war, giving cause for new hope. Neighborhood voters' leagues, women's organizations, business men's service clubs, nonpartisan informational publications, educational broadcasts, free speakers' bureaus, and the governmental news circulated to members of chambers of commerce and trade unions are some of the more prominent methods of informing the citizenry.[1] In the last decade, the work of the League of Women Voters, alone, has done more to increase knowledge and to formulate constructive programs than any two similar agencies in the ten-year period prior to its establishment. Women's clubs and professional women's associations also have been energetic. The emancipated suffragists bid fair to wield the larger share of political power and to do for government what the male member of the family has not been able to do in more than 150 years of American history—make it a consistently reliable tool of the popular will.

INCREASING POPULAR PARTICIPATION

This view of citizen education and participation may be too sanguine. The principal advances have benefited middle-class voters, the professional and business people, and the skilled workers. The informational media available to unskilled workers and farmers have not shown corresponding improvement—and this group, of course, needs it most and casts a large proportion of the total vote. The rural population, however, is rapidly developing reliable channels of knowledge and effective methods of group activity. Agricultural organizations, journals, and radio stations

---

[1] This question is admirably considered in a book by Charles E. Merriam entitled, *The Making of Citizens* (Chicago, 1931).

all serve the farmer's interests. The county agent is a powerful educational medium and spearhead of activity. The greatest neglect, therefore, is among the masses in the large cities. The foreign-speaking populations and the subsistence-level groups are the inert, helpless portions of the citizenry. Here we find ready ground for bossism and political machines.

The participation of almost the entire number of registered voters would be obtained if compulsory voting laws were enacted. When a man must give an acceptable excuse for not casting his ballot or pay a fine, the percentage of stay-at-homers becomes very small. It is rarely more than 10 per cent and usually less than 5 per cent. Moreover, there is now ample precedent for compulsory voting in the laws of other countries. The system has worked with remarkable success in Belgium and Australia, two of the countries we mentioned as leaders in well-nigh universal election response.

COMPULSORY VOTING

Government has as much right to insist upon voting as it has to require the payment of taxes and the conscription of eligibles in time of war. Democracy is at stake. Representative government is built upon the assumption that everyone entitled to participation will take advantage of citizenship's greatest privilege. But would Americans look at it in this way? They hate compulsion and penalties. Neither taxes nor conscription is exactly popular, and the analogy is easily noted. The existence of obligatory voting in Germany and in Italy will not help its popularity here.

But is 100 per cent voting an important democratic ideal, after all? People will vote when they feel that it is in their interest to do so. They are much more likely to cast a ballot when they feel sure that everything is "on the level" and that a vote one way or another makes some difference. Moreover, it is possible to overemphasize the mere fact that a certain percentage of people do or do not vote. The extent to which citizens go to the polls is not an infallible measure of democratic results. The way in which a majority became a majority is more important than the mere fact that it exists. What made people vote and what kept them from doing so are basic considerations. In other words, non-voting is a symptom; it points to something basically wrong or to the fact that people do not consider the stakes important. Voting is a good thing in itself, but no one, after the experience of the Western world, should think for a moment that it is a panacea.

One deterrent is the bewildering number of issues and choices among candidates that the voter is expected to act upon. An honest, conscientious man hates to stamp a ballot blindly. He would rather not vote at all. Many people who go to the polls vote "no" on a large percentage of issues because that is the easiest way of disposing of a question they know nothing about. The way issues are worded usually does not relieve the voters' general bewilderment. Hence the movement for short-ballot reform is decidedly in the right direction. The reasoning is that the voter should not be expected to do so much, but in what he is called upon to decide there should be a greater understanding. The short ballot includes only the candidates for the most important offices and the propositions which are of basic importance. It results in popular decision on fundamental matters and the delegation of greater discretionary powers to those in office. Short-ballot reform is usually a condition precedent to administrative reorganization, especially in state governments, which are among the chief violators of the principle of integrated control.

Popular dissatisfaction also results from too few alternatives, as well as from the necessity of making too numerous choices. There are usually several sides to every question. Election laws usually permit of but two choices, "yes" or "no." In the case of candidates, the decision is "for" or "against." Narrowing the range of choice is one reason why some people vote negatively; they are against something or somebody. Liberals, particularly, are dissatisfied with election laws, because they see many shades of opinion, rather than just plain black and white.

PROPORTIONAL REPRESENTATION

Proportional representation permits a wider range of choice in the selection of elected officials, for minorities are given that percentage of the total number of places to which their voting strength entitles them. If they have a real following, they are sure of winning at least one seat in the legislature. The chances of self-expression and interest representation are therefore greatly increased. Issues are more likely to be sharply drawn, or at least more points of view on the same issue can be reflected. These being some of the substantial merits of proportional representation, it is surprising that American governments have not adopted it in a larger number of instances. The actual number of cases is very small, and confined to municipalities. In Cleveland and Cincinnati, it accompanied the council-manager form of government; Cleveland later rejected both, but Cincinnati has retained them. In municipal government, proportional representation is a definite aid in shifting attention to issues and reform and in withdrawing attention from national party politics. This is decidedly to the good.

Proportional representation also has drawbacks. It is a complicated electoral system, and the results of an election are not immediately determined. People usually do not become enthusiastic over a thing they do not understand very well; but this criticism is not nearly so important as another one: the system increases the number of parties or factions, and hence it becomes more difficult to get a workable majority with a commonly agreed-upon program. The net result is that responsibility is therefore lessened. The choice is the same as in the case of multiple parties versus the two-party system: which is more important, more complete representation of political viewpoints or the greater responsibility and longevity of a steam-roller majority? These considerations bulk large in state and national affairs, but they lose much of their force in municipal governments. Balancing advantages against disadvantages, then, there is much to be said for wider acceptance of proportional representation in local governments. It is an aid to democracy.

Where democracy exists, there parties are found. Political parties are devices for doing indirectly in democratic nations what is done directly in dictatorships. They control the approaches to public power and provide instrumentalities by means of which organized interests are able to carry out their programs. They serve to mobilize individuals and to determine what persons shall wield public authority.

POLITICAL PARTIES

The founding fathers were on the whole hostile toward party

government. George Washington, it will be remembered, warned his countrymen against the dangers of factions. "Among the numerous advantages promised by a well-constructed system," said James Madison, "none deserves to be more developed than its tendency to break and control the violence of faction. . . . Complaints are everywhere heard . . . that our governments are too unstable, that the public good is disregarded in the conflicts of rival parties, and that measures are too often decided . . . by the superior force of an interested and overbearing majority."

The framers of the Constitution of the United States hoped to provide effective checks upon party government in the separation of powers, checks and balances, federalism, express limitations, the amending process, and the methods of electing the President and Senate. "It is this lack of power to shape the entire policy of the government," J. Allen Smith has pointed out, "which more than anything else has given form and character to the party system of the United States." Only against this background of early hostility to parties and the constitutional provisions resulting therefrom can the political history of the United States be adequately understood.

The political party is one of the principal instruments of representation.[1] Standing for certain principles and objectives, its banner is a symbol around which men of like views can rally for the purpose of effectuating a program. It not only attempts to carry out a common policy but it has its own ideas about the best means by which this will be possible. At its best, the political party formulates basic principles to which it adheres with consistency, applying them to new problems which arise in the course of social change. This, however, is a more or less idealized view of partisan programs, because a high degree of consistency is found only over a relatively brief period. In the history of the United States, both major parties have shifted their positions on most major issues rather considerably—in some cases diametrically. The same observation may be made of conservatives and liberals in Great

PLACE OF THE PARTY IN THE GOVERNMENTAL PROCESS

[1] Cf. Edward Logan (editor), *The American Political Scene* (New York, 1936); Charles E. Merriam and Harold F. Gosnell, *The American Party System* (New York, 1929); and E. M. Sait, *American Parties and Elections* (New York, 1927).

Britain or Canada. Consistency in group action is more of an ideal than an actuality.

Party politics combines certain emotional and irrational factors with ones which are highly practical and reasonable. The political party, although it has grown up without constitutional provision and although it may be said to have forced its own recognition, is one of the three or four most important parts of the representative process. Others are voting, legislation, and pressure politics. The political party is the connecting link between the franchise and policy making. It is more than this. Parties promise to carry out programs, thereby introducing one of the most important elements of responsible government into the constitutional system. Elected individuals make promises, too, but only group action, such as the party can provide, gives adequate assurance that the program will be put into effect. The party is a continuing agency. If it succeeds, it will live much longer than any individual; hence, it needs to be careful of its reputation. When it makes promises, the voters expect that efforts will be made to carry out the stated program. Otherwise, the party is subject to the voters' resentment and possible repudiation in the next election.

Politics is a spasmodic interest of most people. Economic and social groups function as part of the party organization only at election time. Each of the major parties includes farmers, workers, owners, Protestants, Catholics, and Jews. Most voters, whether in a union, trade association, church, or fraternal organization, are too busy, ignorant, indifferent, or lazy to maintain an active and continuous interest in the affairs of the political association. Consequently, the actual work and decisions devolve upon a small minority. Theodore Roosevelt once remarked that the boss in politics is like the boss in any other enterprise—his function is to get things done. To the party faithful, the head man is the "leader," while to their enemies he is the "boss." In a very real sense, public officials who owe their election to the party leader are his creatures. He makes them and breaks them. Obedience is usually the price of political success. Only the strongest can go their own way. "I have always believed," said Tom Platt, "that a political organization should be as well disciplined as the army and the navy. An officer of either who proves unfaithful is sure of punishment. The traitor is rarely treated with mercy. . . . In choosing my lieutenants and candidates I invariably insist upon the qualification that the man must know enough to stand when hitched."

The party is the connecting link between policy formation and its execution. It proposes, and the voters elect, the chief executive. He is then party chief, recommender of legislation carrying out the party promises, and head of the administrative establishment.

Three very practical and important functions of the political party within the framework of the governmental system have been differentiated. It proposes a program; it enacts all or parts of the platform; and its responsible leader administers the policies which have been given the force of law. Under the American system of government, however, the legislature may be controlled by one political party and the executive branch by another. When such an impasse occurs, party responsibility is naturally confined to the first two steps. In actual result, however, real responsibility goes up into thin air. Each branch points an accusing finger at the other.

The least that may be said is that party government introduces a measure of responsibility into American governments which would not be found there otherwise. Checks and balances, not co-operation and smooth performance, are characteristic of our political institutions. How fortunate it is, then, that parties supply direction, co-ordination, and motive power.

It would be a great exaggeration, however, to suggest that the party keeps all its promises, or even most of them. Platforms are not solely an expression of what adherents stand for and what they propose to do. They are the means of capturing votes. They are meant to be appealing to as many interests and to as many shades of opinion as possible. The main idea is to have the ticket win or to be returned to power. Winning votes fills the same place in the success and survival of a party as winning business does in that of a commercial house. Hence, there is always the danger of emphasizing too strongly the theoretical contributions of political parties. They provide essential processes, but they also play a game. Not a game in the juvenile sense (although at times the resemblance is striking), but a game of competition and victory. The stakes are sometimes high, and the methods used in winning them are subject only to the rules proverbially linked with love and war; however, the sporting side of political parties can be overemphasized. Government is serious business. Socialists, particularly, protest vigorously when politics is laughingly referred to as a game. It is too important for that. If the essential process of government is belittled, its use as the medium of economic reform becomes exceedingly difficult. Ridicule is the surest method of destruction.

A major premise in the ideology of party politics is that all men are born, or soon become, either conservatives, liberals, or radicals. In this idea, as in the concept of party consistency, there is a measure of truth. Men are likely to cast their lots with the associations with which their parents and acquaintances are identified. Thus, if one's father is a Republican or a Democrat, one is likely to enroll under the same banner. This is particularly true in areas where one party is overwhelmingly dominant, as in the "solid" South or in the Green Mountain area. In these one-party regions, social pressure almost forces adherence to the group symbol. Nonconformists are considered dangerous or socially unacceptable.

PARTY MEMBERSHIP

In other sections, where party ranks are more nearly equal, there is considerable shifting back and forth. Massachusetts, once a solid Republican stronghold, has swung over to the Democratic column in recent years. This shift, however, may be explained in large part by the changing character of the population—the growth of textile towns and the influx of immigrants whose interests and sympathies differ from those of the early British settlers. Other states have passed through the same metamorphosis, or are in the process of doing so.[1]

Even within the same family, disagreements on party affiliation seem to be increasing in number. Husband and wife cancel each other's votes, father and son cast ballots for different candidates. In other words, it cannot be said that the circumstances of birth

[1] These shifts are analyzed in *The American Political Scene*, pp. 22 ff.

settle the matter of party affiliation once and for all. The increasing volatility of the electorate is the most significant feature of modern parties. In most people's acquaintance, there are individuals who have changed loyalties two or more times; but permanent shifts are relatively few. Party connection tends to a fixed loyalty, analogous to that to family or church. It feeds on the same psychological food. Party affiliation is usually a social and sentimental matter rather than a critically intelligent one.

Party strength depends in large measure upon symbols and myths. These factors are particularly important in maintaining constant allegiance over a lifetime. They can be counted upon to win elections save when opposition issues or candidates are so appealing that they overcome men's traditional and emotional reactions.[1] Leaders of renown become party symbols.[2] Thomas Jefferson, Abraham Lincoln, Theodore Roosevelt, and Woodrow Wilson are probably appealed to most frequently. Personality is one of the most potent of all the symbols; it can be idealized, and the individual can imagine himself filling the place of his hero. Symbols such as the donkey and the elephant, on the other hand, merely amuse. They have the same appeal as the three monkeys.

The term "symbol" is used in a variety of ways, often with a resulting clarification of our thinking about political processes. There are symbols of *identification*. Thus, we speak of the East, the West, the North, and the South—geographic loyalties. We may also identify economic and religious groupings, such as farmers, business men, Christians, and Mohammedans. Then there are symbols of *demand*, examples of which are "production for use," "a living wage," and an "American standard of living." Furthermore, political parties rely heavily upon symbols of *expectation*, upon slogans, such as "the new freedom," "a new deal," and "freedom for individual initiative."[3]

Myths also are part of the equipment of the political party. When one group or another is in power, it claims to engender

---

[1] Cf. Frank R. Kent, *The Great Game of Politics* (New York, 1923).
[2] See a little book by Charles E. Merriam entitled, *Four American Party Leaders* (New York, 1926).
[3] See Peter Odegard, *The American Public Mind* (New York, 1930), especially chaps. V–VII.

spontaneous stability or to achieve by divine inspiration the deepest aspirations of humanity. It keeps us out of war, or it keeps the dinner pail full. All such thoughts are so pleasing that most people would chide themselves for dispelling the illusion. Moreover, they appeal to the individual's ego. "I am filling the dinner pail by voting the right way," many individuals would probably be saying, if one could only delve into the obscure recesses of their minds.

There is far more rationality in the institutional function performed by the political party than in the behavior of those who make up its membership. Not only are individuals dominated by tradition, symbols, and myths, but most of them fail to give primary consideration to their economic interest in aligning themselves with party organizations. There are, of course, interests other than economic, but material well-being is supposedly the realm in which man acts with the greatest amount of intelligent self-interest. This supposition, however, is enormously overweighted in economics. Evidence of it is seen in the surprisingly low correlation between individual economic interest and party affiliation. Conservatives win political victories not by their own numbers but by the staunch support of small shopkeepers and laborers. In England, for example, a strong foreign policy makes a far greater appeal than the socialists' plan of economic reform. True, the conservatives have leadership, money, organization, and greater unity in their ranks than is usually found among liberals and radicals. These factors help to explain the wide support which the wealthiest group in the country receives. Then, too, as we have already remarked, the Tories of Great Britain have learned that it is wise to make liberal reforms when the popular desire therefor becomes sufficiently strong.

ECONOMIC INTEREST AND PARTY AFFILIATION

In the United States, economic interest and class consciousness have played less part in drawing the lines of party support than in any other great nation. There are several possible explanations of this. The country is relatively young. Sharp class lines have not had time to form. The middle class has been large and well satisfied. Labor has been relatively better off than in other countries; its organization has been weak and there has not been much pressure to establish a party of its own. Third parties have sprung up in various parts of the West but have never lasted very long. The last statement needs to be qualified, however, if it be assumed (as seems warrantable) that there has been a continuous existence of the progressive forces from the Roosevelt campaign in 1912 to the present organization led by the La Follettes of Wisconsin. The Socialist party also has had a continuous existence for many years, even though it has always polled a tiny percentage of the votes in a national election.

During times of business depression and rapid social change, much more conscious attention is likely to be given to economic and class considerations. In such periods, the idea of self-interest operates to a greater extent than it does at other times, and there is likely to be less traditional voting. Men register their discontents. If depressed economic conditions were to continue for a considerable period of time, as they have in some countries since the World War, then fundamental changes in party strength might take place. England, France, and Germany, for example, have had socialist prime ministers in the post-war period. In this country, there seems to be more likelihood of a labor party in the near future than there ever has been before, for there is more talk about it and more pressure in that direction from within the unions themselves.

Our analysis must not be interpreted as suggesting that there is no connection between economic interest and party choice, or that class differentiation may not be the ruling consideration. Since 1917, these two factors have been the dominant ones in Soviet Russia. Labor has been in control through most of Australian history. Agricultural aristocracies have been known to monopolize political power in some of the Balkan countries. Spain had her populist uprising, as well as her "popular front" government; Mexico's affairs are still run by a farmer-labor alliance.

The real point is that economic interest plays nowhere near the determining role that one might be led to expect. We are not interested at the moment in the desirability or undesirability of such social behavior. In understanding politics, it is important to know that men are largely controlled by symbols, myths, and the skillful techniques of arousing party loyalty and emotional exultation which professional leaders manipulate. Most of us are victims of emotional exploitation through propaganda and very few develop even partial immunity. We are born vulnerable.

Would life be happier and social conditions be better if men were actually controlled by intelligent self-interest? Class lines would be more consciously drawn, and the number of parties could be expected to increase. In this imaginary situation, oratory would fall on cold reason, and symbolic and mythical idols would shrink to their reasonable stature. The hypothetical economic man would come to life. Economic determinism would take on real substance. What would the final result be? Would classes eventually disappear, along with political parties? But there is no point in further indulging our fancy. The point is that a wider application of intelligence is undoubtedly desirable; but as in everything else, the golden mean is a balance of the factors entering into the situation. If human personalities were better integrated, political behavior would produce more satisfactory social results.

One of the principal reasons for the failure of minority parties to grow more rapidly is that individuals are fearful of "wasting a vote," when they know there is no chance of winning. As a result, there

HANDICAPS OF MINORITY PARTIES

are "vested interests" in politics just as there are in the economic realm. It is difficult to get a large number of people to adhere to principle, irrespective of the prospects of immediate success. Expediency is a controlling factor in political behavior. How frequently one hears it said, "I should like to vote for party C, but if I do not support B, then A will win."

This explanation seems nearer the truth than the contention that two parties, and two only, are of the nature of representative government; yet there are strong arguments for having only two major parties. A responsible majority is needed, and a strong minority also is highly desirable. One group should be in power trying to carry through its program, and the other should be in opposition, criticizing the majority and advancing alternative proposals. If the government of the day is a coalition of blocs, division in the ranks may occur before much of anything is accomplished. If there is not a strong minority, criticism may not be effective and justifiable doubt may be entertained about turning to the opposition for responsible leadership.

But when, as sometimes happens, the two major parties become so much alike that there is little to choose between them, a realignment within the dominant parties or real opportunity for rapid growth by a third party would seem to be indicated. Yet the history of the United States, as well as situations in other countries, show that this does not take place—or if it does, the shift proceeds with surprising slowness.[1] Why is the longevity of the major political parties so great?[2] Why do not new constellations emerge and individual planets grow dim?

"The most striking characteristic of the two great parties in American politics," said Arthur Holcombe in 1936, "is their longevity. The Democrats have now been operating under their present name and with a continuous organization for more than a century; the Republicans, for more than eighty years. The present is the twenty-first consecutive campaign which the presidential candidates of the major parties have waged against each other. The issues which originally divided Republicans from Democrats have long ceased to hold the attention of the voters. Even the campaign orators now show little interest in them; but the parties continue on their way."[3]

A party which has "arrived" can count on fixed loyalties, traditional responses. Its symbols and myths have been stamped on the public consciousness; but these are not the only reasons that established parties remain on top and smaller ones find it difficult to climb. It is said, "whosoever hath, to him shall be given." Money is a very important factor. It buys time on the radio, space in the press, oratorial eloquence, and even votes. Some of

[1] Frederick E. Haynes, *Third Party Movements since the Civil War* (Iowa City, Iowa, 1916).
[2] Cf. William Starr Myers, *The Republican Party* (New York and London, 1928); and Frank R. Kent, *The Democratic Party* (New York and London, 1928).
[3] Arthur Holcombe, "Present-day Characteristics of American Political Parties," in *The American Political Scene*, Edward B. Logan, ed. (Harpers, New York, 1936), p. 1.

the largest business and financial concerns make it a policy to contribute substantially to both the major parties, because then they cannot lose. They can ask favors and immunities from the winner. This is one reason—an important reason—that differences tend to disappear between dominant political groups.

Complete organization is the bulwark of party strength.[1] A well-organized municipal machine resembles the hierarchy of the army or the church. Within the precincts are the local workers, while above them are ward leaders, county and assembly district chairmen, culminating in the state and national committees. There are wheels within wheels, machines within machines. Party leaders advance from a lower to a higher plane in the hierarchy. Precinct leadership, in large cities at least, is usually the reward of faithful labor in getting party adherents to the polls, organizing meetings, running errands, and being generally useful to the ward, county, or state chiefs.

Election laws favor the older parties. They draft these laws and hence it is natural that obstacles should be put in the way of upstarts. It requires much money and time to build up an organization covering the entire country. A hierarchy of control from neighborhood clubs, through municipal, county, and state units, to the national committee must be put in smooth working order. This calls for the peculiar skills of party organizers and manipulators, and in this work, as in other professions, experience counts for a great deal. Such leadership can be paid for by the major parties, whereas the minority groups are handicapped in purchasing this particular skill.

Success not only brings financial contributions but it also assures the opportunity of putting loyal party workers in strategic positions. This is one form of reward—a very important one,

ELEMENTS OF PARTY POWER

although it would be a mistake to assume that patronage is the only stake that makes men work hard for the political party. This is true, however, of the skeleton organization of the major parties. The party could not well dispense with the services of its key workers, and

[1] Cf. Edward Logan, "Party Organization in the United States," in *The American Political Scene*, chap. II.

the reward of appointment to a governmental position is considered a small price to pay. Among the parties that have never tasted power, however, no such inducement can be held out. The interest and unselfish devotion of active workers must be relied upon almost exclusively. Moreover, patronage results in "planting" people who can be relied upon to attempt to influence their friends at election time. Hence, the party in power is assured of a certain number of "safe" votes—sometimes a very large number —in advance of the test of strength.

Small parties also have difficulty in producing candidates and executives whose ability will win the confidence of the voting public. This is particularly true of the parties of the left, whose leaders usually do not have the social and educational advantages enjoyed by those who lead the older parties. The British Labor party has experienced this difficulty, and Laski and others have made quite a point of it. British labor is particularly deficient in lawyers who understand constitutional law. In order to operate a governmental system, one must know its rules. When a party can recruit into its inner circle men of letters—writers, speakers, lawyers—and leaders of proved executive capacity, its chances of rising to the top are greatly enhanced.

Two additional obstacles stand in the way of successful bids for power by third parties and minority groups generally. One of these has been discussed: those who control the leading parties have access to the principal instruments of information, such as the press, motion pictures, and radio. The use of soap boxes and leaflets is a slow road to success; but other channels of persuasion and propaganda are expensive and hence can be used only to a limited extent. A second difficulty is that breaks in the ranks are found more frequently among minorities than in the major parties. This is more often true on the political left than on the right. A united front is difficult to achieve and even harder to maintain. Parties that rally around myths and symbols are much more cohesive than those that emphasize intellectual analysis. Liberals particularly, because they try to be intelligent and honest, are usually overwhelmed because of their divisiveness. On the other hand, a major party may be a hodgepodge of disagreeing economic, sectional, and social interests and yet keep the party machinery intact. They know that division means defeat. Success is too sweet to be lost simply for a fight over abstract principle.

The inability of liberals and radicals to agree is one factor that encourages attempts to seize control of the government by force. Knowing that the advantages enjoyed by dominant parties are so great, and having learned from bitter experience the seeming impossibility of getting a solid front on the left, radicals conclude that revolution is the only path open to them. As is well known, however, this is only one of the factors entering into the revolutionary analysis.

From one point of view, the machines that have grown up in some large American cities represent minority activities.[1] They are protective. The Tammany Wigwam has long taken bewildered "foreigners" under its roof and given them assistance in many forms. Party organizations in Chicago and Philadelphia also carry on charitable activities; they "look out for their own." The neighborhood social club is about the only place people in congested areas can go to have a good time without its costing them money. When a good party follower falls into the toils of the law, the offense can often be "fixed." Moreover, city bosses make good use of the appeal to class and social differences. "Vote for the man of the people or you will be ruled by the rich."

THE MACHINE

These same leaders sometimes turn around and make shady deals with the very interests and individuals they tell their followers to fear. This is the aspect of bossism that "nice" people hear most about. Contract-letting Tammany administrations and traction franchises between Insull and Thompson are familiar instances of machine mismanagement. The highest and the lowest (on the social ladder) have been known to make "deals." There is general denouncement of such sharp dealing, and well there may be; but, before placing all the blame on

---

[1] M. R. Werner, *Tammany Hall* (New York, 1928); also Harold F. Gosnell, *Boss Platt and His New York Machine* (Chicago, 1924); John G. Salter, *Boss Rule: Portraits in City Politics* (New York, 1935); Charles E. Merriam, *Chicago: A More Intimate View of Urban Politics* (New York, 1929).

individuals, the social situations lying back of such shameful "sellouts" need to be fully understood.

"Cheap labor" was brought to American shores to fell forests, work mines, tend blast furnaces. The larger part of this immigration wave naturally settled in the large cities. There America has duplicated the squalid conditions found in the worst slums of Europe. Not understanding the new language and customs, newcomers were easy prey for exploiters. National groups were naturally drawn more closely together. Unity in race, religion, and politics became more pronounced. The political machine has given such stranded minorities protection and philanthropy. In return, no questions are asked about the ethics and practices of the recognized leaders. When attaching blame for what happens, however, we should realize that every American shares the responsibility for bringing these peoples here, despite the fact that it lowered labor standards and the prospect of democratic successes.

Men of lowly birth have been catapulted into positions of financial power. Not being used to so much affluence, they sometimes become drunk with success and make mistakes. They make deals with political bosses. The truth eventually comes to light. But men born into "the four hundred" also connive. No class has a monopoly on high character or on low ethical standards. Those who are not used to power, however, are more likely to err and to be found out.

Machine politics is discouraging to those who live in large cities. The situation seems to perpetuate itself. When one sees garbage dumped in alleys, streets that are never swept, traffic laws that are never enforced—and sees these and many other evidences of low morale day in and day out—one's senses become dulled. If a person is born into such a situation, he is not likely to feel a strong desire for anything better—he has no basis of comparison, knows nothing better. Sometimes, one wonders if the essential spark which distinguishes man from animal does not die out among such surroundings.

But neither the present nor the future is absolutely dark. New generations replace the old; wider educational opportunities are afforded; and both racial and national exclusiveness begin to break down. The government builds playgrounds, libraries, museums, vocational schools. American customs are adopted, while older social traditions are weakened. If the economic side of the picture could only be improved, the life of the urban masses might be brought up to the early American standard in the next fifty or one hundred years. Is the original vitality sufficient to carry through? Can the people use their governments on a wide enough front and with sufficient effectiveness to transform slums into habitations fit for human beings?

Several factors are at work lessening the influence of the major political parties. Continued unemployment strengthens radical movements. Eastern conservatives and Western progressives find it difficult to pull together. The socially conservative "solid" South and the sidewalks of New York form a queer pattern. Sectionalism is a disrupting force in both of the principal parties. Some political scientists and journalists are saying that we must surely have a new alignment into conservatives and liberals. This has been prophesied before, and as desirable as such a realignment would be from the standpoint of responsible government and realistic representation, it cannot be expected with anything like certainty. It should not be forgotten that American parties are holding companies for sectional blocs, and that the presidential system discourages third-party movements.

Group representation, acting through the lobby, has tended to lessen the relative importance of party government. Like the party, it has grown up outside the official constitutional framework, but has jockeyed itself into a position of central importance.[1] Professor Herring hardly exaggerates when he calls it part of the "official" government. Some go so far as to call it "the third house" of the legislature.

PRESSURE GROUPS

It is important to differentiate group representation and lobbying. The former is more comprehensive, including all efforts by

[1] S. McKee Rosen has written an excellent little book entitled, *Political Process* (New York, 1935). See particularly chaps. v–vii, inclusive, dealing with business, labor, and farmer pressure groups. The reader is referred also to Peter Odegard, *Pressure Politics* (New York, 1928).

organized interests to influence governmental policy. Persuasion may merely take the form of one person's talking to another. The lobby, on the other hand, is a special form of pressure upon governmental bodies. It is the agency of the organized interest through which contact is made with the official representatives of the citizens. Usually, the person directing the lobbying is located in the capital city; however, not all organized interests which attempt to influence legislation maintain lobbies.

Group representation takes place whenever an organized interest of any kind wants something from the government or wishes to prevent action which is thought to be hurtful. Every conceivable group finds itself in this situation at one time or another. Most interests are constantly concerned with what is going on at city halls, county courthouses, state capitols, or Washington. It is estimated that the average number of lobbies in Washington alone is well over five hundred. Interest representation is as comprehensive as social groupings, and would necessarily include industry, trade, finance, labor, farming, professions, clubs, churches, philanthropies, patriotic organizations, and peace societies.[1]

It is only when an organized group appoints someone to get in touch with governmental officials, usually at the capitol, that lobbying may be said to occur. There are two principal steps in pressure politics: solid support must be organized back home, and the results of this organized opinion then need to be registered on the public officials. The lobbyist directs both, but his distinctive function is that of contact man and pressure applier. Some lobbies are permanent and some transient; some rent office space and others do not. The more important and permanent ones are listed in the telephone directory.

Interest representation has a decided advantage over the political party when the latter stands for nothing in particular. The pressure group has a definite interest, knows what it wants and what should be resisted. This is one important reason for the increased importance of group representation, as compared with the representative function of the political party.

[1] See the classification of interest groups in E. Pendleton Herring, *Group Representation Before Congress* (Baltimore, 1929).

Political parties make promises to most interest groups, but many of their pledges are never carried out. Many of those that are fulfilled are largely the result of pressure applied during legislative sessions by the lobbyists of the interests concerned. This is an important reason for the growing influence of pressure politics. The lobby applies "heat" where it will be most effective and at times when matters of interest to it are up for consideration.

Another reason for its increasing power is that the American electoral system invites pressure politics. Representation is by area, the accepted idea being that the elected person represents the interests of that particular piece of the earth's surface. County, state, and federal elections all are based upon this plan. Moreover, another feature of the American electoral system is that a person making his abode within the area to be represented is the only one who can stand for the office. A person from outside is not eligible. This differs from the system usually found in other leading countries, whereby a candidate may live in one electoral district and run for legislative office in another.

Areal representation means that legislators are not identified primarily as party men or as able individuals. They symbolize a state, a county, a city; where they come from is more important than what they are or what they can do. This system results in neglect of party consistency, insufficient emphasis on recruiting the country's best ability, and failure to make political life a career. One of the principal observations made by foreign observers is that our governmental leaders are here today, gone tomorrow. In other leading countries politics is the honorable career of a lifetime. If a good man loses in one constituency, he is entered by his party in the race for another seat. This promotes regularity and national interest and helps men to rise above local and selfish interests. Unless America can overcome provincialism and logrolling, and can develop career opportunities and the larger interest, there is reason for great concern about the future of our representative process.

What the political party should stand for is a compromise between different sections and their corresponding interests. The pressure group is more specific. It represents textiles, steel, coal, cotton, corn, or oranges. There is no need to compromise. It invites logrolling. Interest A promises its support to legislation desired by B, if the latter, in turn, will get behind a measure wanted by A. These agreements are reflected on the floors of legislatures. The legislator is virtually helpless. If most of the voters in a congressman's district are citrus growers, for example, he must spend most of his time working for legislation favored by the organized interest; otherwise he stands no chance of re-election.

<small>INTEREST REPRESENTATION AND POLITICAL PARTIES</small>

Interest representation is invited also because American legislatures are not particularly effective in safeguarding themselves from the constant thrusts of lobbyists. Here, again, the governmental process provides the principal part of the explanation. In the United States, we do not have "responsible" government. We do not draw a line between "government" bills and "private" bills. We do not have a change of ministry when the legislature fails to support the program of the cabinet. Individual legislators may sponsor as many bills as they please, whether or not such bills be in accord with the general program of the party in power. Logrolling by individual members is largely prevented under a system of responsible government. Appropriations cannot be raised or lowered without the consent of the cabinet. One very important implication of responsibility is that group or private interests must be subservient to and consistent with the general program. Party then means something; it can be held responsible for sins of commission as well as for faults of omission.

Individual legislators receive specific demands from lobbyists and general advice from party leaders. Our system results in the legislator's not being effectively bound by the party, and at the same time being left wide open to the dictates of the pressure group. Under these circumstances, it becomes difficult to realize important goals of good government, namely, national interest, general welfare, sound finance, and real responsibility.

Although pressure politics makes responsible leadership difficult, it makes distinct contributions to more effective representation. Lobbyists are the eyes and ears of the country's major interests; they are charged with the responsibility of learning when legislation of concern to the group membership is about to be fostered. Word is then sent back home. Greater opportunity for discussion is provided than would result merely from press or radio accounts. The larger lobbies publish periodic leaflets giving a résumé of bills which are of special importance. Citizen interest and participation are thereby increased.

<small>CONTRIBUTIONS OF INTEREST GROUPS TO THE REPRESENTATIVE PROCESS</small>

The group's watchdog exhorts his constituents to write to their legislator, expressing their views on the pending measure and reminding him of their particular interest. Baskets of telegrams frequently await the lawmaker when he goes to his office in the morning. Sometimes, they ask him to champion the bill and almost as frequently they beseech him to fight the legislation to the last ditch. In many cases, the wording of telegrams is identical; it has been sent out to the member of the association by the legislative agent; but even such a stereotyped method as this carries much weight with the elected official who is making up his mind.

Lobbies sometimes contribute to the improvement of governmental procedures. Most of them are interested in economy; therefore, when a reform in organization or method would help to save taxpayers' money, the interest group may press for the needed change. The United States Chamber of Commerce, for example, has been instrumental in furthering several such bills; among them, the Budget and Accounting Act of 1921.[1] The total amount of such activity, however, is relatively small. Governmental economy is usually the concern of taxpayers' associations and privately financed bureaus of governmental research. The interest groups are too completely immersed in their own day-to-day affairs to give much thought to such general and complex matters as institutional organization and procedure. Moreover, they fear that, if existing agencies are brought under the spotlight, some unit of government rendering special services to the group may be limited as a consequence of the economy drive. Every bureau has its own clientele!

[1] Cf. E. Pendleton Herring, *op. cit.*, pp. 93-4.

The increasing power of pressure groups makes even more important the basic queries which have always accompanied a discussion of representative government. How can elected officials be guaranteed sufficient independence to act in behalf of the general welfare and yet be the channel for registering the will of those who constitute the community's dominant interests? The most important decisions in government are between the group and the national interests, the welfare of society and the well-being of the individual. Group representation tends to make the official the rubber stamp of the particular interest or interests which help him secure election and which instruct him after entering into the duties of office. It would be untrue to suggest that any such situation exists generally today, but trends in that direction are observable.[1]

Perhaps it is a mistake to assume that representative government should be more than the tool of interest groups. Government is merely a matter of who gets what, when, and how. The concept of general welfare may be just a nice-sounding phrase. Officials are foolish to risk their political futures simply because they have a childish idea about being able to do something for the community as a whole. Why should an elected representative have independence, so-called? The idea of agency, which is tied up in the term representation, precludes independence. The judgment of the individual lawmaker should not be substituted for that of the interest he serves.

*INTEREST REPRESENTATION AND OFFICIAL INDEPENDENCE*

If this idea fastens itself on the system, democracy can never be achieved. The general welfare cannot be defined to everyone's satisfaction, but it is necessary that elected representatives should strive to conceptualize and concretize it as well as possible. It may be merely a fiction to assume that it is government's responsibility to put public interest above that of any special interest;

---

[1] In 1924 William Allen White referred to the pressure groups as "a vast, uncontrolled, but tremendously powerful, invisible government—the government of the minorities.... The Congress of the United States and the legislatures of all the states are used as Olympic bowls for these great contests between the powers of invisible government. And the legally constituted members of governments are kicked around, tramped upon and sometimes thrown carelessly into the discard by the great unlegal forces that stage the combat." From his book, *Politics: The Citizen's Business* (New York, 1924).

but fiction or not, such a concept is widely held and clearly necessary. It underlies all thought on self-government. To retreat from it invites tyranny and strife.

The public interest is both fixed and changing. It has been defined in certain fields of social interest. For example, minimum standards are widely accepted in matters of health, safety, and education. Individual interests which conflict with these social interests must either conform or step aside. But public interest will never be completely defined, and it is best that it should not be. Society changes and government needs to respond. The adjustment involves changing ideas of general welfare. In the agricultural era, it was in the public interest for government to keep its hands off housing. Now that slums are prevalent, government will shirk a plain duty unless remedial action is taken.

Someone has defined the task of the public official as that of keeping just ahead of the average. He who is too much in advance of public opinion will bump his head and experience disillusionment. He who lags behind encourages stagnation. He who is just ahead of what the public is ready to adopt helps to lead and has the privilege of engaging in construction activities. This is not meant to minimize the necessity and desirability of a due share of reformers and martyrs, men who are far ahead of the procession.

Unless government can attract men of principle and independence, the state will be denounced as a tool of the exploiter, as it already is by many. If government is to be respected and men remain free, the people's representatives must be given encouragement to place the general good above the group interest. To do this involves more than the continued breeding of a strain in which social sympathy and incorruptible principle are prominent characteristics; it involves also the correction of obvious weaknesses in our machinery of representative government. The best man available should be permitted to run for legislature, no matter where he resides, and party government needs to be made responsible. The "unofficial government" should be brought out into the open. Let no one be deceived about the difficulties involved in achieving any one of these objectives.

SELECTED READINGS

Beard, Charles A.: *American Government and Politics* (7th ed., New York, 1935); chaps. IV and XXIV deal with the national and local party machines.

Brooks, Robert C.: *Political Parties and Electoral Problems* (3d ed., New York, 1933); discusses the history and operation of the American party system, including such problems as the short ballot, proportional representation, and patronage.

Childs, Harwood L.: *Labor and Capital in National Politics* (Columbus, Ohio, 1930); an exhaustive study of the techniques of labor and business pressure groups.

——— (ed.): "Pressure Groups and Propaganda," *Annals*, CLXXIX (May, 1935).

Douglas, Paul H.: *The Coming of a New Party* (New York, 1932); an interesting, somewhat optimistic, prediction of a new party alignment, including some of the difficulties involved.

Finer, Herman: *The Theory and Practice of Modern Government* (New York, 1934), Part III; an enlightening discussion of the problems and practices of the parties and the representative system.

Garner, James W.: *Political Science and Government* (New York, 1928); chap. XIX deals with the significance of the electoral function.

Gosnell, Harold F.: "The Political Party versus the Political Machine," *Annals*, CLXIX (September, 1933), 21–8.

———: *Why Europe Votes* (Chicago, 1930); a study of the European voting characteristics, including a discussion of compulsory voting in Belgium and Switzerland.

Gruening, Ernest H.: *The Public Pays* (New York, 1931); an interpretation of the Federal Trade Commission investigations into the pressure and propaganda activities of the power companies.

Harris, Joseph P.: "The Practical Workings of Proportional Representation in the United States and Canada," *National Municipal Review*, XIX, No. 5 (May, 1930), 337–83; presupposes a knowledge of how the Hare system works.

Haynes, Fred E.: *Third Party Movements Since the Civil War* (Iowa City, Iowa, 1916); the most authoritative study, although somewhat outdated.

Herring, E. Pendleton: *Group Representation Before Congress* (Baltimore, 1929); the best and most complete study of the activities of pressure groups in the national capitol.

Hoag, C. G., and Hallett, G. H., Jr.: *Proportional Representation* (New York, 1926), chaps. I–VIII; a complete discussion of the various forms of representation, favoring the single transferable vote.

Logan, Edward B. (ed.): *The American Political Scene* (New York, 1936);

a concise, up-to-date analysis of present conditions in American politics, by six able students of various phases of the field, such as parties, campaigns, and pressure groups.

Merriam, Charles E., and Gosnell, Harold F.: *The American Party System* (New York, 1929); chaps. I, II, VI, VIII, and XIV–XVI deal with the composition and place of the party and with the tendencies toward a reconstitution; an outstanding book.

———: *Non-Voting: Causes and Methods of Control* (Chicago, 1924); an interesting study based on an elaborate interviewing technique.

Mill, John Stuart: *Considerations on Representative Government* (1861), a classic and in many ways the most brilliant discussion of the subject in the English language.

Munro, William B.: "The Boss in Politics—Asset or Liability?" *Annals*, CLXIX (September, 1933), 12–20.

Odegard, Peter H.: *Pressure Politics: the Story of the Anti-Saloon League* (New York, 1928); a case study of the most effective pressure group of our time.

Peel, R. V.: "The Political Machine of New York City," *American Political Science Review*, XXVII, No. 4 (August, 1933), 611–18.

Siegfried, André: *America Comes of Age* (New York, 1927), chaps. XVIII–XXII; an excellent view of the American scene by a distinguished French student; chapters cited deal with the party system.

Wallas, Graham: *Human Nature in Politics* (3d ed., New York, 1921); the significance of this book is its plea for a conscious and systematic effort of thought in social matters.

Wilson, Francis G.: *The Elements of Modern Politics* (New York, 1936); chaps. XII, XIII, XIV, and XVIII deal with the principles and problems of the party, representation, and citizenship.

CHAPTER V

☆ ☆ ☆

## THE LAWMAKING PROCESS

*"How to reconcile speed of action with reflection and individual rights is perhaps the major problem of government which has not yet been solved."*
—CHARLES A. BEARD

GOVERNMENT has a dual relationship to law—it makes it and then enforces it. In the formation of policy, which is the primary stage, many forces and instruments play their part. (See Figure 2.)

LEGISLATION AND THE REPRESENTATIVE PROCESS — Citizens express their desires and provide for the fulfillment of some of their wants when they go to the polls and exercise the privilege of voting. Political parties help to transmit the mandate of the voter and assume responsibility for directing the lawmaking and executive processes through which the citizen will is given effect. Pressure groups supplement the representative capacity of parties and also make a direct impact upon all the official governmental agencies.

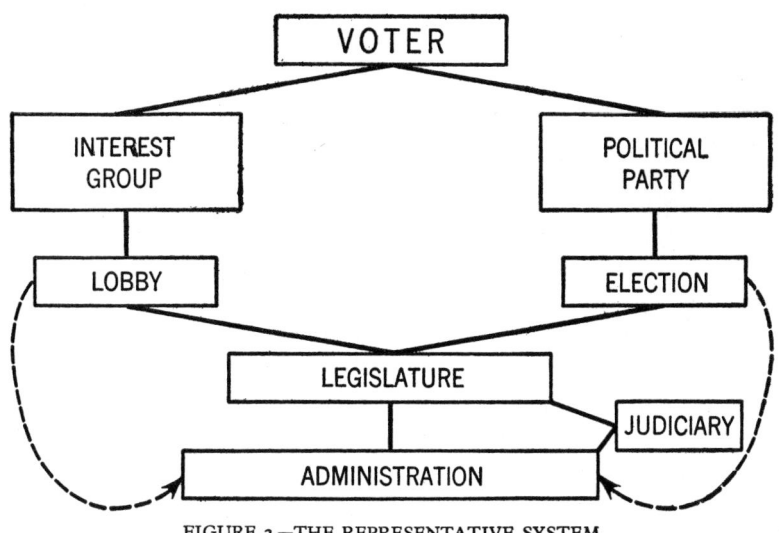

FIGURE 2.—THE REPRESENTATIVE SYSTEM

The legislature is the center of the representative process. It is there that pressures converge, that public policy is officialized, that the authority of law is stamped upon those measures which have been successfully fostered. The legislative stage lies between social pressures and administrative execution.

In a democratic government, the legislature is the dominant department. This is true both analytically and historically. By the nature of the case, it must be supreme; because, in the making of policy, the sovereign will is expressed. Either the citizens in body assembled or the elected representatives convened in the legislature must determine what government is to do, how its activities are to be financed, and to whom is to be entrusted the responsibility of accomplishing the agreed-upon objects. If either of the other departments, the executive or the judicial, were to assume the supreme command, popular government would cease to exist.

In the development of democratic institutions, legislative supremacy has always marked the victory in the people's struggle for self-government. Monarchy may be "limited," but unless the king is actually subject to the legislative will, democracy in the realistic sense of the term could not be said to exist. British constitutional history bears out this point. Not until Parliament had complete authority to control expenditures, pass any laws it pleased, choose the efficient executive, and legislate regarding royal succession and emoluments did representative government reach fruition.

Having profited from this lesson in political science, the American settlers took care to curtail the powers and possible ambitions of their chief executives; but the founding fathers did not expressly recognize legislative supremacy. Congress has never had as complete power as Parliament; however, care was taken to assure legislative control over the purse-strings and authority to impeach the President should he attempt to seize power. The fundamental question of departmental supremacy was left purposely undefined. In preference, all three departments were assumed to be equal, each one independent within the boundaries established by the Constitution. To guard against the supremacy of any one, numerous checks and balances were written into the fundamental law. Since the legislature was not expressly granted supremacy, does it follow that complete self-government has not yet been attained in the United States? The stock answer is, of course, that the Constitution is supreme.

What has been said about the necessity of legislative hegemony, if popular rule is to be a reality, is fairly obvious; but it is well to remind ourselves about the central importance of legislation. Democratic assemblies are unpopular even in our own country. Some of the country's leading newspapers apparently believe they are registering popular sentiment when they express thankfulness at the adjournment of the legislature. Congressmen are the butt of many a joke. Much of the ridicule is well deserved, but behind it all there is a more serious side. If legislatures fail, self-government will disappear. If men who can command the respect of the people are not elected, it is a reflection upon the citizens who cast the ballots. Those who laugh, laugh also at themselves. Are public amusement and dismay the reactions to an inferior brand of lawmaker? Is not the general average of intelligence and ability among legislators higher than ever before? It may be, then, that legislative practice and institutional backwardness are principally to blame for the shortcomings of legislatures. Some part of the explanation may be found in the operation of the "social lag."

When democracy receives a setback and reaction prevails, it is usually difficult to determine what part of the explanation is to be found in human frailties and what portion is attributable to institutional deficiency. Italy and Germany, under their present dictatorships, may be taken as examples. In some ways, both countries were socially advanced, in both legislation and institutional method, in the period immediately following the World War. There seemed to be a fairly successful adjustment between social problems and governmental remedies. Today they both are regimented. Voting is a pretense. Legislatures have no power. What is the explanation? Fascists contend that those who formerly ran the country were frequently corrupt and pusillanimous. Nazis claim that the Social Democrats were merely spineless job holders. Naturally, they are prejudiced. What, then, is the real explanation? We must content ourselves with merely raising questions. Was leadership deficient? Were institutions inadequate? It is alleged that the legislators spent all their time talking and, as a consequence, nothing was ever accomplished. Or, as is sometimes claimed, are these peoples not ready for self-government, because, childishly, they worship the sabered man on horseback? Or was the collapse of democracy in Germany and Italy attributable to world-wide tensions and maladjustments which may in time cause breakdowns in other countries? These questions are pertinent. Every one of them has a possible bearing upon our own situation.

America has a host of legislative bodies—so many it is difficult to count them all or to keep track even of those which affect us. There are selectmen, councilmen, assemblymen, congressmen, not to mention county supervisors, school-board members, and those who serve on policy-forming boards which control some departmental activity. There are approximately 175,000 separate political jurisdictions in the United States.[1]

Representation in the principal legislative bodies—municipal, county, state, and federal—is a complex matter. On grounds of theory, it would seem that electoral districts should be divided in METHODS OF APPORTIONING REPRESENTATION such a way that they contain equal numbers of the population. In many cases they do. But other methods of dividing representation in legislative bodies are not so democratic. Four principal methods of distributing seats may be differentiated: each governing unit may get the same number of places, irrespective of population; districts roughly equal in population may be established; the number of seats apportioned may depend upon the proportion that the population of the electoral district bears to the total population and the number of seats to be divided; and competition may be area-wide, that is, representation at large.

Let us take up these systems in inverse order. The last mentioned method does away with the emphasis upon limited areal

[1]This statement is found in *Better Government Personnel* (New York, 1935), p. 87, published by the Commission of Inquiry on Public Service Personnel; for a detailed analysis, see the pamphlet by William Anderson, "The Units of Local Government in the United States" (Public Administration Service, Chicago, 1934).

representation. The only requirement is that the candidates live in the jurisdiction holding the election. The purpose in area-wide representation is to elect the best men irrespective of where they happen to reside in the district. Its use is confined to county and municipal governments, though it is not the only system in either of these units. It is usually found in undistricted election areas, such as small towns and villages. As large a city as Cincinnati, however, uses the area-wide basis. It is well adapted to county government because equal representation among townships would produce a board of supervisors (or county commissioners) of unwieldy size.

The proportionate basis is best illustrated in the distribution of seats in the House of Representatives. Of the 435 places, each state theoretically gets that number to which its proportion of the total population entitles it, with the constitutional provision that no state shall have less than one representative. This method is indicated when there is a fixed electoral area whose boundaries cannot be changed as changes in population occur.

The division of electoral districts so as to give each an equal number of representatives is the most common method. It is the technique used in a large number of municipalities. In Chicago, for example, ward lines are drawn corresponding to the number of seats in the council and with equal population in each electoral area. The charter usually provides for a redistricting at stated intervals thereafter. The state governments also divide their territories into election units for the purpose of selecting congressmen and members of the State legislature. Different areas exist for each. Reapportionment is usually supposed to take place after each decennial census, but the state government frequently shirks its duty—when it would be to the disadvantage of the party in power to carry through the redistricting.

The fourth method is that of granting equal representation to governing units, irrespective of population. The best illustration is the procedure of giving two seats in the Senate to each of the forty-eight states. This method, however, is not confined to the federal government. While theoretically population is the basis of distribution, state senates frequently give equal representation to each county, although representation is sometimes by senatorial districts or by towns. New York City accords each of its boroughs equal representation on the Board of Estimate and Apportionment, which is in some respects a second chamber of the council.

This system is a concession and reflects sovereign jealousy. Equal representation of unequal populations is a repudiation of democratic principle, but expediency is sometimes not too high a price to pay for results which otherwise would have been impossible. The original thirteen states were jealous of their independence and prerogatives and consented to federal union only on the condition that they should be equally represented in the Upper House. So important did they consider this matter that each state's having two Senators in Congress is presumably the only provision in the Constitution that cannot be changed by amendment.

EQUAL REPRESENTATION IN THE SENATE

The issue of equal representation is still the source of much latent discontent. Thirty-five states have come into the union since the Constitution was adopted. They are far from equal in size, population, wealth, interest, or influence. The smallest state does not have one-twentieth the population of Greater New York; yet the populous states have no more voice in the affairs of the nation's leading legislative body than those in which 50 to 90 per cent of the state area is in public lands owned by the federal government. In recent years, protests have been more frequent and outspoken. But what method could be substituted which has a reasonable chance of approval—even assuming that the constitutional prohibition is not absolute? Moreover, has not the the present system produced a more democratic spirit and more progressivism than could have been expected from the dominance by populous urban areas? To ask whether exception to the democratic principle is ever justifiable is like asking whether circumstances ever make it excusable to tell a lie.

Representation in the United States is unequal in other respects. Failure to give large cities the share of control in the state legislature to which they are entitled is probably the most glaring shortcoming. When legislatures were established, constitutions adopted, and election laws originally framed, the rural population in every state greatly outnumbered that of any city. As cities such as New York, Chicago, Philadelphia, and Detroit have grown, they have failed to get their corresponding share of representation in the state legislatures. Reapportionment has been almost consistently resisted by the rural majority in control of the Lower House; but even when partial victories have been won in the representative chamber, the door has been closed to complete adjustments. The Upper House was never meant to be representative of population; hence, the rural areas apparently will continue to dominate state senates no matter how much urban centers may grow.

The issue of farmer-controlled cities is somewhat similar to the one over equal representation in the Senate. The metropolis complains that it is not given enough home rule, that the legislature hems it in with too many restrictive provisions. Before it can put its own house in order, the city must be made independent and responsible. Urban dwellers resent being taxed for services and improvements which only rural people enjoy. On the other hand, rural representatives contend that state laws should be equally applicable; no exceptions should be made for cities. Urban populations live off the countryside and, hence, part of the unearned increment should be returned in the form of public improvements. Moreover, city dwellers frequently do not know what is in their own self-interest and hence the legislature should make no exemptions. This view obtains particularly when moral questions are involved. Which view is more defensible?

*CITY AND COUNTRY*

Equal representation and farmer-controlled legislatures both tend to hold us to the original American traditions. But do they encourage governments to adapt themselves to a system in which technology, industrialism, and urbanism are the principal characteristics? Do not city people deserve equal representation and local self-determination? As we stated in the preceding chapter, a fundamental issue in American life is whether people should be represented on an area-wide basis or whether political boundaries and dominant interests attached thereto should be the controlling influences.

Instead of reforming representation in state legislatures, other methods of setting the cities free may be found more fruitful. City-county consolidation helps to give the metropolitan center control over all essential interests. Philadelphia and San Francisco have been greatly benefited by this reform. Another proposal is that new states might be hewn out of the largest metropolitan areas.[1] Presumably this would apply only to New York and Chicago. There is much to be said in favor of such a proposal. After all, these cities are far larger in population than most existing states. The difficulties of making their powers coextensive with metropolitan problems by other methods are discouraging; but realization of such a goal seems to be in the realm of fancy. The Constitution provides that before a new state can be brought into existence, approval of the states out of which it is formed must be secured. And state legislatures are rurally controlled! How to represent city populations fairly, how to govern metropolitan areas, and how to bring about better understanding between city and countryside are among the most important problems of the future.

The legislature is a very interesting institution. It develops customs, traditions, and atmosphere. After the members are first elected, they find themselves freshmen on a strange campus. In their own electoral districts, they may have felt like big frogs in little puddles, but in Albany, Springfield, or Washington, the individual is lost in the shuffle. Particularly when he is new, the lawmaker is simply a man who has an office (if he is lucky) and who has his vote counted when the clerk calls the roll; but, as likely as not, the name of the political subdivision will be intonated, rather than the legislator's name. At first sight, the legislature appears to be a formal, utterly impersonal procedure. It seems to have a life of its own, which is not dependent upon the men who come and go. The trip-hammer staccato of the speaker, the rap of the presiding officer's gavel, and the rather musty, venerable atmosphere are characteristic of legislative assemblies everywhere. The members of the assembly are sent to represent

[1] This suggestion has been made, as one of several alternatives, in the metropolitan region studies conducted at the University of Chicago.

their present-day constituencies, but the institution itself belongs only to itself and to past generations.[1]

The difficulty one first experiences in understanding the legislature is increased because of the fact that it is usually in two parts. An assembly so divided is called "bicameral"—literally, "having two chambers." The upper and lower BICAMERALISM houses meet in separate places (although usually in the same building), are different in size, and are almost invariably jealous of each other. This is inevitable. In general, the smaller chamber has the feeling of greater exclusiveness and, in both theory and practice, is more conservative. The lower house, on the other hand, is conscious of being the more democratic and of having greater authority to initiate financial measures. He who controls the purse strings runs the government!

The indispensability of bicameralism was once considered virtually unquestionable. In English-speaking countries, particularly, it was assumed that two houses and representative government were one and the same thing. In early American history, even municipalities had two chambers of the council. How odd New York City's bicameralism seems today! In the field of municipal government, it has been discovered that a single council is far more sensible than two bodies. Nobody would think seriously of going back to the old system. This fact has made people wonder if we may not be under the same delusion about the desirability of bicameralism on other levels, particularly the state. Nebraska, the first state to cut loose and experiment, now has a single-chambered legislature; we shall soon be able to judge whether the results compare favorably with those obtained in municipalities.

The advantages claimed for bicameralism cannot lightly be brushed aside. A single assembly might act rashly, inadvisedly. Under the dual system, its hastiness and bad judgment can be checked by the other chamber. The Lower House is likely to be

[1] H. G. Wells has written a colorful and amusing description of Parliament's environment and procedure. It is more or less applicable to legislative assemblies the world over. See his book, *The Work, Wealth, and Happiness of Mankind*, II (New York, 1931), 622–37.

swept off its feet; the conservative Upper House is a moderating influence. In the former, bills are hastily considered and mistakes get by; but the second chamber can be counted on to catch most of them. Moreover, when an area is as vast and as important as in the United States, a second house should be retained for the purpose of giving an adequate voice to political subdivisions. The Lower House is a machine. Debate and deliberation are not its characteristics. Therefore, the Upper House is needed as a supplement, because debate is freer and detailed duties are fewer. The membership of the upper unit attracts men who are older and more experienced; hence, they are more responsible and the welfare of the country is safer in their hands.[1]

Bicameralism is based upon a historical situation which has no pertinence today. With the growth of the middle class in England, the townspeople and traders began meeting apart from the aristocracy and ecclesiastics, theretofore the only members of Parliament. The lower house, the Commons, eventually became the dominant one. In 1911, the powers of the House of Lords were greatly curtailed, and much serious consideration has been given to its complete abolition. All Englishmen are now politically equal; aristocrats have been divested of special privileges; the King's powers are nominal.

Bicameralism is a vestige of the undemocratic past; it throttles the popular will. Men in a single legislature can act just as responsibly as those in two houses. If democracy acts rashly, let its leaders learn sobriety by experience, not by handcuffing. Moreover, the idea that a popular assembly will run riot is merely a bogey built up by those who resist popular government for selfish reasons. A single chamber would be a financial saving. It is analogous to the short ballot in that it simplifies government and hence enables citizens to exercise more intelligent and effective control. Bicameralism is one of the too numerous checks and balances. Government in the twentieth century must seek effective action. Purposeful handicaps need to be removed. Is there not much to be said for unicameralism in most American states?

[1] Cf. H. B. Lees-Smith, *Second Chambers in Theory and Practice* (London, 1923).

## THE LAWMAKING PROCESS

**THE AMERICAN SENATE**

The United States Senate is the most distinctive and most successful upper chamber in the world.[1] It simply does not run true to form. Instead of being "an assembly of old men and elders," it is consistently younger (in ideas and actions) and more progressive than the House of Representatives. It stirs things up. In the last hundred years, it has taken over the investigatory function and made itself the censor of the executive department.[2] The Senate accounts for more than its share in the introduction of important legislation. It wields an important influence over foreign affairs, and may check the President on all his important appointments. Notwithstanding all this, the Senate has more freedom for deliberation, and more important things are said there, than in any other legislative chamber in the world—with the possible exception of the House of Commons.

To be sure, there is also much nonsense aired in the Senate. Particularly during "morning business," some Senator may be given "leave to print" a long harangue, for home consumption, which few in the Senate would condescend to hear. This is not the only time when much seemingly pointless talking takes place; but the balance of factors is heavily on the Senate's side. It performs such a useful function for American democracy that one is inclined to forget that the system on which its membership is based does violence to the theories of representation according to population or by economic interests.

The eminence of the Senate is explained in no small part by its traditions. It is not an exclusive social club, as it is sometimes described. It is a burly, virile institution. Speakers hit hard and do not pull their punches. There is neither fear of the "interests" nor undue deference to the President. Even the Supreme Court is sometimes taken off its pedestal and neatly dissected. The Senate combines the ruthlessness of the East, the hardiness of the North, the culture of the South, and the blunt sincerity of the West. The Senate is a galaxy of American sectionalism. It is the caustic, fearless critic of society and government.

[1] Lindsay Rogers has written a sparkling book entitled, *The American Senate* (New York, 1926).
[2] See my study, *Congressional Investigating Committees* (Baltimore, 1929).

The Senate comes close to doing what should be expected of a legislature. It puts its own house in order, discusses and deliberates, gives due attention to matters of high policy, criticizes those who deserve it (and some who do not), disciplines members of the official family, selects and elevates public men, passes laws, and votes appropriations. It is not the function of a legislature to administer—that responsibility needs to be delegated. Its responsibilities are to authorize action, after suitable consideration, and to criticize and control those agents to whom are entrusted the authority and power to carry out the program. Although we usually think of lawmaking when we think of legislatures, we should realize that the passing of new laws creating rights and duties on the part of the citizens is only one aspect—though obviously the important one—of the legislative process. The legislature is the hub of the governmental wheel: there pressures center; plans materialize; action is supervised.

THE FUNCTIONS OF LEGISLATURES

Before a legislature can make rules for others, it must establish rules for itself. One of the oldest and most important functions of lawmaking bodies is that of internal organization. So much depends upon rules and procedures.[1] Traditional processes tend to become so rigid that sometimes the legislator finds it more difficult to know how to carry through a measure than to determine the point of policy involved. That is why experience is so necessary to the effectiveness of legislators and why the old members have so much power. The fundamental principle of internal organization is that the legislature has inherent power to preserve itself and to prevent interferences with its lawmaking process, dignity, and independence. Back in 1821, Congress arrested a man and kept him incarcerated because he was in contempt of legislative independence. The Supreme Court ruled that power to protect the lawmaking process is an inherent prerogative of a legislative assembly.[2]

INTERNAL ORGANIZATION

[1] Cf. Robert Luce, *Congress* (Cambridge, 1926); Paul DeWitt Hasbrouck, *Party Government in the House of Representatives* (New York, 1927).
[2] This was the case of Anderson *vs.* Dunn, 6 Wheaton, 204 (U. S., 1821); it involved the offer of a bribe. For this and later cases, see my *Congressional Investigating Committees*, pp. 53 and 121-3.

Legislatures usually have the power to test the qualifications of those elected, decide contested elections, and keep out anyone who cannot satisfy the assembly with his credentials. They can discipline their own members, eject them, and even disbar them for cause, such as bribery. Likewise, visitors in legislative halls are subject to reprimand, ejectment, and even arrest. Organization for survival is the first law of legislative life.

The deliberative aspect of legislative procedure is the one which provokes the greatest amount of public criticism and disdain. Legislators talk to hear the reverberations of their own voices; they say foolish things. Why not act more and talk less? But if justice is done to the discussion stage, one of representative government's greatest needs is met. Debate brings out the weaknesses in proposals; it makes majority action responsible; it educates the citizens, for politics receives more space in newspapers than any other single subject.

Sometimes it is said that speechmaking in representative assemblies might better be discarded. Decisions are made in caucuses and committee rooms. Debates never change votes. Members talk to the folks back home instead of to their colleagues. These statements have merit.

DELIBERATION

The diagnosis is correct, but the prescription would be a mistake. The success of representative government depends upon keeping the citizens interested and informed. Public debates help. The fact that legislators speak for publication, for their constituencies, is all to the good. By this means, citizen influence may be registered on a pending measure. Memories of where men stood on important issues help citizens to support or oppose those who took sides in public debates.

What is urgently needed is more and better deliberation. Too many legislators never commit themselves publicly for fear that it may cost them support in some quarter. These men are untrue to representative government. Freedom and progress both depend in no small measure on honest differences of opinion courageously expressed.

A legislature needs to discipline itself in such a way as to have ample time for matters of high policy. It is easy to fritter away time on inconsequential details, and most legislative bodies do; then legislation of consequence is rushed through during the last days, or hours, of the session. In this respect, the United States Senate is no exception.

Passing new laws constitutes a small proportion of the output of legislatures. Most enactments modify existing statutes, relate to private matters, or apply to the organization and procedure of government. It is estimated that American legislative bodies turn out approximately 25,000 enactments each year. It is doubtful, however, whether a fifth of this number represent new policies and programs. On the other hand, the consideration of new matters obviously takes much time. Hence, in social importance and in time consumed, if not in numbers, the enactment of new policies is the outstanding concern of representative assemblies.

ENACTING LAWS

The policy body also plays the part of critic and censor. In some ways, this is its most important task. Criticism helps fulfill the educative function. It prods the administrative branch and holds it accountable. In both these ways legislative criticism is an aid in the preservation of liberties. The legislature cannot execute its own laws. It does not have the organization and the personnel; but it can observe how its agents perform their administrative tasks and reprimand them or amend the legislation if not satisfied. How to succeed in this, without hindering efficient administration, is one of the most difficult adjustments of democratic government.

CRITICISM

Still another function of legislatures may be called the selective one. Men are tested, and those who survive are sometimes elevated to positions of greater importance. Councilmen become assemblymen; and assemblymen, congressmen. Legislators who distinguish themselves have a chance of being chosen mayor, governor, or even President. This is what is meant by the selective function. It is of less importance in the United States than in countries where political careers and cabinet government are established features. When the cabinet is created out of the legislature, those who have won recognition as parliamentarians are elevated to executive positions

SELECTIVE PROCESS

in the cabinet. In another sense, legislatures test and select when they are called upon to give their approval to executive appointments. The Senate is especially influential in this respect. Joint responsibility for appointment helps to bridge the gap between the legislative and executive departments. The selective function is extremely important in this country, and needs to be made increasingly so.

Summarizing, we have distinguished five important functions of legislative assemblies. They organize, deliberate, legislate, criticize, and select.

The important procedures and decisions of representative bodies tend increasingly to take place where the public eye cannot see. This is not a sweeping accusation of connivance and conspiracy. Most of the legislature's work is transacted in committee sessions. Extensive hearings occur during this stage. Real deliberation takes place. Moreover, when a bill is reported out favorably by the appropriate committee, it is almost certain to be passed. When the third and final reading occurs in the chamber, the result of the forthcoming vote is commonly a foregone conclusion.

Woodrow Wilson characterized the American system as "government by committees,"[1] and their present number and importance substantiate his observation. In most other leading countries, however, legislative committees have virtually disappeared. Cabinet rule and committee rule do not mix, for the cabinet itself is a committee. If other committees could run counter to its wishes, conflict would occur; responsibility would be divided and tend to disappear. France has learned this lesson. On the other hand, committees are at the center of the English system of local government. They are numerous, active, powerful, and, on the whole, well liked. The difference is that the principle of responsibility does not apply to municipal governments in Great Britain.

GOVERNMENT BY COMMITTEES

American legislative procedure is complex and uncertain. Any member can introduce any number of bills on any subjects he

---

[1] See Woodrow Wilson, *Congressional Government* (Boston, 1885), an American classic that deserves thoughtful consideration by all.

wishes. They need not deal with questions of public importance. Importuning friends and persistent lobbyists account for a large number. This welter of proposals is distributed to the appropriate committees. If the bill is of sufficient importance, the committee will hold hearings at which interested parties are allowed to present evidence for and against. Most matters, however, are disposed of in executive session. Many bills never leave the committees. They are buried there, pigeonholed, and a resolution is required to call up a bill which a committee refuses to relinquish. The committee's stamp of approval, on the other hand, means a victory won. The committees thus have great power; they are little legislatures.

Individuals are powerful within legislative halls insofar as they come to occupy important committee assignments. The party in power naturally has a majority of its own members on every committee. Committee chairmanships are distributed primarily on the basis of seniority and the holder of one has far more influence than any other member. Chairmen of such Senate committees as those dealing with the judiciary, interstate commerce, and foreign relations rank close to the President of the United States in the amount of power and influence they wield.

Even in the House of Representatives—where party discipline is enforced, debate is limited, and steam-roller tactics are employed—power is widely distributed among those holding important committee posts. The Speaker and the floor leader exert considerable unifying influence, but the legislative process is basically segmented. However, party control over legislatures in all parts of the country has tended steadily to increase. Committees and individuals are given less leeway, and legislative calendars are adhered to more closely. Consideration of appropriations is centered in fewer committees. If responsible government is desired, however, the process will need to proceed much farther than it has.

How efficient should a legislature be before discipline interferes with ample deliberation? The answer depends in part upon the number of enactments which are considered desirable. There is also disagreement about how much is accomplished by debate.

The point that should not be overlooked, however, is that the people should know who sponsors bills, who furthers them in the legislature, and who accepts responsibility for passing them. Is it a party measure or a bill hammered through by a lobby? When committees are so numerous and power is so divided, even members of the legislature are sometimes in doubt about these matters. It is infinitely more difficult for public-spirited citizens to keep informed of what happens and why.

One possible method of increasing popular understanding and control would be to reduce the size of the legislative body. If such a move were to accompany a change to unicameralism, there would be assurance of greatly increased understanding. On the other hand, defenders of the *status quo* can point out that a smaller membership would inevitably mean each member's having to represent larger numbers of people and territorial areas. The individual and his neighborhood would not be likely to receive as much special consideration; but this argument, in turn, is offset by the increased ability of legislators and by the lowered cost of running the assembly which could be expected if the size of legislatures were to be reduced. The cost factor, however, is not an important one, because any decrease in numbers of salaries would probably be offset by much-needed increases in the emoluments of those under the new plan. Here, again, municipal experience is instructive. Where the city-manager plan has been introduced, small councils have been much more satisfactory than large ones. The former increase the likelihood of public understanding, add to the personal responsibility of councilmen, and diminish the likelihood of "back-stairs" control.

<small>SHOULD LEGISLATIVE BODIES BE MADE SMALLER?</small>

There is no doubt about the necessity of making legislative bodies more effective, but speed is not the highest consideration. It can be bought at too high a price. Steam-rollers flatten out deliberation and the expression of minority positions. One need, however, is greater responsibility, which was discussed in the preceding chapter; a second is greater specialization. The conservative nature of the legislature presents another type of problem. Organization, procedure, and rules change very slowly. In consequence, there is a strong resemblance between deliberative bodies of today and those of a hundred years ago. The improvement of the legislative process, like government generally, has not kept pace with developments in other fields.

The division of labor applies to governmental functioning, as well as to economic processes; but it has not been so clearly recognized nor so consistently followed. Government consists of processes which determine what the distinctive contribution of its component parts should be.

<small>GREATER SPECIALIZATION</small>

The legislature determines policy, the executive enforces it, and the judiciary settles controversies which arise in the administration of the law. Some of the latter's decisions also make policy. It is clear, then, that the legislature should concentrate upon policy, avoiding all unnecessary tasks which interfere with this basic consideration. This admonition does not mean that the legislature should be unmindful of how satisfactorily its laws are administered. The success or failure of existing laws determines very largely what needs to be done in the future.

The legislative process is a problem in administration.[1] The problem is that of adjusting the organization and procedure to the requirements of the job, but headway in this direction has been discouragingly slow. A valid generalization of political science is that a governmental body almost invariably leaves to the last the improvement of its own efficiency. Since everything on the calendar is rarely taken care of in sufficient time prior to adjournment, this means that the reforms on which the effectiveness of everything else depends go by the board.

Some improvements may be noted, but they are in the direction of delegated responsibility rather than toward greater specialization. Some legislatures now engage as regular employees of the assemblies draftsmen whose task it is to phrase bills skillfully. Usually there is only one such person. This move has saved the time of members, tended to standardize statutory phraseology, and to prevent lawsuits due to careless drafting. It is a service which should be made universal. Some technical improvements

---

[1] W. F. Willoughby shows it to be so in *Principles of Legislative Organization and Administration* (Washington, 1934).

THE LAWMAKING PROCESS 149

have also been experimented with in recent years. In at least one state legislature, an electrical device has been employed to register the votes. This device saves many hours of the assembly's time, and since oral roll calls are numerous and lengthy, any contrivance that can reduce routine procedures is greatly to be desired.

Some improvement has been made in the fact-finding procedure. It is clearly important that debates and laws should be based upon facts, but it is very difficult for legislators to assemble the facts quickly and reliably when so many technically involved questions are up for consideration.

THE FACT-FINDING PROCESS

Modern legislation deals with the most complex questions of science and society. Moreover, when social-control legislation is being considered, information is sometimes difficult to get because interests affected by the proposed legislation are averse to giving it out. One method of securing such data is by means of the investigating committee. This device is as common in state legislatures as it is in Congress, where over four hundred of these committees have been empowered by the two houses. The investigating committee has power to demand the production of pertinent records and the presence of necessary witnesses. Failure to comply means fine or imprisonment.

The original intention of regulatory commissions was that of assisting the legislatures in gathering facts about public businesses. In theory these bodies—now extremely numerous and important—are but appendages of the lawmaking assembly. Whether they actually operate in this fashion, we shall see in a later chapter. There is no doubt, however, that they have relieved the legislature of detailed responsibilities, that direct regulation by the legislature would be quite out of the question, and that the studies of *ad hoc* commissions have helped the lawmaking process.

The problem of gathering reliable information is far from a satisfactory solution. The legislative reference bureau, either publicly or privately maintained, is one source which could be used to better advantage. A publicly maintained library, such as the Library of Congress, can perform an analogous service. Trained researchers are placed on the library's staff and are available on short notice to look up questions of concern to legislators; but instruments in addition to these are clearly needed. The legislature should create fact-finding committees to study basic problems on which legislation is contemplated or to investigate the administration of laws causing dissatisfaction. Specialists in law, economics, engineering, and other professional fields should be attached to these commissions, and only a portion of the membership should be drawn from the legislative body itself. Greater objectivity would thereby be secured and at the same time some official representatives would be included who could present the findings and support them in the assembly. This is substantially what the Royal Commissions do in Great Britain. Analogous practices have been developing in American legislatures, but the practice should be perfected and universalized.

Fact-finding and deliberation are the core of the legislative process. If they are to be given increased emphasis, further delegation and specialization need to take place. Too much time is devoted to private bills, to matters which either affect only one person or deal with a property or money adjustment of some kind. Pension claims are an example. The time of the entire body should not be consumed on such matters. The creation of the Court of Claims, the Veterans' Administration, industrial accident commissions, and administrative agencies dealing with public lands, has relieved Congress and the state legislatures of some of the burden. Despite such delegations of responsibility, however, there is a serious question as to whether a separate procedure within the legislature is not necessary for bills of a private character. Special committees could handle matters of a nonpublic nature, reporting back to the entire legislature for confirmation of their findings and recommendations. The manner in which Parliament handles private bills[1] roughly approximates what seems to be advisable for relieving the legislative burden in this country. If all such matters, however, could be handled through administrative channels, and if the political party could assume real responsibility for dividing pending measures into "official" and "private-member" categories, giving the former

[1] The procedure is described in William Bennet Munro, *The Governments of Europe* (New York, 1931), pp. 188–92.

the right of way, the result would be preferable to a further extension of the committee system.

Legislatures need to divest themselves of responsibilities which are essentially administrative. Operation of the United States Printing Office, the Library of Congress, and the Smithsonian Institution are instances of administrative preoccupation on the federal level. The choosing of major generals, "Kentucky colonels," and names of battleships are matters which should never engage the time of an entire assembly.

Self-discipline is difficult for legislatures, especially if it means self-limitation. Institutional pride and jealousy must be reckoned with. With the increase of executive authority, the legislature has been increasingly suspicious of any proposal which would limit its responsibilities. Even when specialization would be clearly to the assembly's own interest, the actual carrying out of the reform is sometimes never accomplished. Institutions (political and nonpolitical) are, unfortunately, loath to relinquish any authority once gained; they seem, indeed, ever anxious to extend the scope of their governance.

DIFFICULTIES OF IMPROVING EFFICIENCY

The lobby tends to diminish the autonomy and independence of legislative bodies. It makes the members look outward. It divides loyalties, for the institutional claims of the legislature are less compelling. The lobby would use the lawmaking body as a servant. On the other hand, it is the nature of legislatures to feel sovereign and aloof.

Too much institutional independence would be a bad thing for democratic government; but it is even more important that a legislature should control rather than be controlled. In other words, if the power of lobbies becomes so great that citizens find it difficult to tell why decisions are made as they are, and if legislatures are virtually helpless against the assaults of browbeating lobbyists, then legislative independence is seriously threatened and people will soon lose confidence in their governmental system.

METHODS OF LOBBIES

Sometimes it is very difficult to safeguard the autonomy of the legislature and the independent judgment of its members. Most pressure politics is indirect and subtle; but some is direct and forceful. For example, in his study, *Pressure Politics*, Peter Odegard tells about the whip-snapping methods of the Anti-Saloon League. The situation he depicts is by no means unprecedented, either in Congress or in the legislatures of the several states. In recent years, several lobbies have received reputations for buttonholing tactics. Prominent among them are the farm groups and the veterans. Legislators are literally coerced; they are told that if they do not vote as directed, every effort will be made to defeat them at the polls. Very few men who hope to remain in politics can stand up under this kind of assault. They know that hard-working minorities elect candidates and defeat those whom they disfavor. The listless majority is pushed around by militants who know what they want.

Lobbying tends to become a polished art. Clubbing methods are not used so frequently as they once were, and stopping a legislator in the corridor or buttonholing him outside the door of his office is usually considered too obvious and crude. Yet, much of it still takes place. In some state legislatures, lobbyists are known even to show themselves on the floor of the chamber, where they "confer" with individual members. The timid, reticent man does not have what it takes to make a successful legislative agent.

Some methods are so old that they are traditional. Lobbyists' dinners are still in vogue, but their character has changed. Usually, the identity of the interest doing the entertaining is under cover; "one of the boys" gives the party; liquid refreshments are not so much in evidence; and, if "business" is mentioned, it is usually to make an appointment to discuss a "matter of mutual interest." Then, too, the giving of emoluments "in appreciation," and the outright acceptance of bribes are not so frequently brought to light, which probably means that there is less of this sort of sinister influence. In 1857, four members of the House of Representatives were summarily dismissed for having taken money in return for their votes. "Trying to bribe a professional politician," it has been said, "is the same as letting yourself in for blackmail. He can hold the deal over your head and keep gouging you as long as he is in office. The best policy is to watch your morals when you're dealing with politicians."

The lobbying of pressure groups is increasingly done through regular and open channels. Most of those who appear before public sessions of legislative committees represent some interest or other. They ask for time to present their viewpoint or evidence. When the spokesman is called, he states candidly that he is connected with a trade association, trade union, or other organized interest. Frequently, persons appearing before committees speak for several organizations which have interests in common. This is the most constructive aspect of interest representation, for it is entirely in the open. Moreover, legislatures receive enormous benefits from the testimony presented by interest-group spokesmen, because, as a rule, it is very well prepared. Information is looked up and bills are even drafted by these same spokesmen, sometimes on the interest's initiative and often at the invitation of the committee. The United States Chamber of Commerce is outstandingly successful in activities of this kind. Instead of sending its own employees, the Chamber secures some business man who then speaks for his industry and his area, as well as for the association itself.[1] Legislators usually dislike paid lobbyists, just as public-utility commissions look with disfavor upon highly paid attorneys. They particularly dislike former members of the legislature who turn lobbyist and attempt to capitalize upon friendships. The layman, therefore, scores heaviest. Use of his services by the United States Chamber of Commerce and other interests is evidence of the growing sophistication of pressure groups.

Lobbies resist as well as sponsor. When they are out to kill a bill, they move with deadly effectiveness. Their presence is harder to uncover than when they are pressing for action. Defense brings together a solid phalanx of interests which might otherwise be competing with one another. When weighed in the social balance, lobbies' resistances are frequently more important than their pressures.

[1] Its methods are described in Herring, *Group Representation Before Congress*, pp. 78–94; see also Harwood L. Childs, *Labor and Capital* (Columbus, Ohio, 1930), *passim.*

What can legislatures do to protect themselves and their individual members when the power of surrounding groups makes their position like that of an unarmed platoon surrounded by machine-gun nests? A walk of five minutes in any direction from a legislative building convinces one that lawmakers are completely hemmed in by pressure groups.[1] We have tried to make it clear in this chapter and the preceding one that group representation has its constructive side as well as its antisocial one. Only when pressures result in coercion, invisible influences, and the overwhelming of the legislator's independence and judgment can the lobby be said to constitute a threat to representative government. To attempt to legislate lobbies out of existence, however, would undoubtedly be more ineffectual than the restrictive legislation known as the Eighteenth Amendment. Registration holds possibilities and has been used in some cases already. The lobby is required to fill out a blank giving such information as what it is, where it is located, and who speaks for it. This step is clearly so desirable that it is surprising that every legislature has not passed a registration law. Lobby investigations have been rather frequent, and although Congress has made some sweeping ones,[2] it is doubtful whether these inquisitions have made lobbies reform appreciably. The facts, however, usually prove helpful to the legislature and the publicity sometimes makes the interest "let up" for the time being.

DEFENSE AGAINST PRESSURE GROUPS

Lobbies are kept under control much more satisfactorily in other leading countries, Great Britain and France, for example, than they are in the United States. What is the explanation? Does government have more immunity, derived from greater respect, in these countries? Are interest groups less well organized? Even if both these questions are answered in the affirmative, the most important explanation remains undisclosed. In these

[1] "Among only the more important national associations, it has been estimated that there are thirteen representing industry and commerce; ten, agriculture; eight, labor; nine, women; eight, "reform"; and eleven, defense and disarmament." S. McKee Rosen, *Political Process*, p. 26.
[2] In 1913, and again in 1929–30, Congress conducted extensive lobby investigations. Mr. Rosen makes several references to their findings and influence in *Political Process*, especially on pp. 23, 26, 42, 118, and 140.

representative systems, the cabinet introduces legislation, not the individual member. To attempt to influence the entire cabinet would be a task of some magnitude, even for the most influential person speaking for the most powerful interest. So England and France have group representation, but not high-powered pressure politics, such as we find in the United States. One of the surest ways of putting public interests above private interests is to make party government responsible. But one must not fail to emphasize the importance of traditions in these countries. Some things "just are not done."

Instead of attempting to put the pressure group in its place and hoping that legislatures can be made more highly principled and more public-spirited, some may ask, why not recognize the inevitability of group representation and the important role it plays by converting legislatures into bodies officially representative of interests? For the present bases of population and area, there would be substituted a system of organized interest representation. "The third house" would be made official. The present system would be either supplemented or superseded. Some of the germinal ideas of the Italian corporative state would be utilized.

As one of the world-wide currents of thought, this proposal needs to be taken seriously. Discontent with the shortcomings of representative processes makes people look for new methods. Moreover, group representation has grown rapidly in favor during the last ten years. An example of this enthusiasm for unofficial interest representation is found in a recent pronouncement of a United States Chamber of Commerce spokesman:

> There has developed a recognized third house: not the third house of fraud and bribery, but the third house that states its desires openly and frankly. This third house is composed of organizations such as the United States Chamber of Commerce, the National Education Association,—the labor groups, and the agricultural groups. These bodies openly and intelligently further the interests of those whom they represent.[1]

If pressure politics becomes more significant and controlling than

[1] This statement is quoted by Peter H. Odegard in the article entitled, "Majorities, Minorities, and Legislation," *Annals*, CLXIX (September, 1933), 32. This number devotes considerable attention to group representation and is well worth reading.

political parties and the formal framework of government, sooner or later there will probably be a movement for its official inclusion in the representative system.

A legislature representative of interests would be "realistic." It would be expressive of social interests which are closer to the individual than is government. Political science could then be truly defined as a study of the struggle for position and preferment. But before making this bow to "realism," the consequences of introducing the corporative principles into legislatures need to be weighed. The effort to make "public persons" out of individuals would be abandoned. The system would not encourage a broad view of public affairs and human welfare. Almost of necessity, it would seem to require some person or body, with power superior to the legislature, deciding what constitutes the national interest and steering the ship of state. In short, the ends of the state sought by democracy are hardly to be sought in a governmental system based upon interest representation.

Vigilance is not the only price of democracy. If fundamental principles of popular participation and control are to be preserved, the people and their agents must expect to improve the legislative process when theory and actual practice openly conflict. In theory, it is the people who are served; increasingly in practice, it is areas and interests. One need not assume that developments along these lines are inevitable and unalterable; but fundamental changes in our social and economic life, combined with widespread disparagement of popular assemblies, will inevitably change the character of our representative system unless remedial steps are taken. Three important factors stand out. The citizenry needs to be educated concerning what is at stake and what institutional improvements seem to be desirable. Secondly, party government and the legislative process need to be made more responsible. At the same time, increased attention must be given to training for political leadership. Men of principle and independence are not accidents. The home, the school, the total environment produce them. If more people realized that the enjoyment of everything in modern life—home, business, art, recreation—depends upon sound governmental policies

THE LAWMAKING PROCESS 157

honestly administered, more of them would have the courage and determination to go into politics. Theodore Roosevelt said that our most capable young men must be effeminate, or they would go into politics because it *does* have a reputation for being a dirty business. To clean it up and put it on the plane where it belongs is the biggest man-sized job in the country.

SELECTED READINGS

Beard, Charles A.: *American Government and Politics* (7th ed., New York, 1935), chaps, v, vi, and xxv; treats of the organization and operation of the state and national legislatures.

Chamberlain, Joseph P.: *Legislative Processes: National and State* (New York, 1936), chaps. i, iv–vi, viii–x, xii, and xiv; concentrates on the legislature's duty of making law; chapters cited deal with internal organization, procedure, developments of the fact-finding process, and the role of the party in legislation.

Dicey, Albert V.: *Law and Public Opinion in England* (2d ed., London, 1914); lectures 1–3 of this classic series deal with the relation between law and public opinion and the characteristics of that opinion in 19th-century England.

Dimock, Marshall E.: *Congressional Investigating Committees* (Baltimore, 1929), chaps. i, iv, and vii; these chapters deal with an exposition and criticism of the relation of investigations to the lawmaking process.

Finer, Herman: *The Theory and Practice of Modern Government* (New York, 1934), Part IV; discusses the problems of modern legislatures, including second chambers.

Garner, James W.: *Political Science and Government* (New York, 1928); chaps. xx and xxi are an analysis of the history, functioning, and problems of the legislative organ.

Gosnell, Harold F.: "British Royal Commissions of Inquiry," *Political Science Quarterly*, XLIX, No. 1 (March, 1934), 84–118.

Hasbrouck, Paul D.: *Party Government in the House of Representatives* (New York, 1927); a thorough study of such elements of party government as the caucus, the committee system, and the influence of the electorate.

Laski, Harold J.: *A Grammar of Politics* (2d ed., New Haven, 1930), pp. 80–88 and 311–40; these sections include a discussion of the consultative function of government and the place and organization of the legislature.

Lepawsky, Albert: *Home Rule for Metropolitan Chicago* (Chicago, 1935); chaps. i, ix, and x cover the problems of urban-rural relationships, especially reapportionment.

Logan, Edward B.: "Lobbying," *Annals*, CXLIV, supp. (July, 1929), 1–89.

Luce, Robert: *Legislative Assemblies* (Boston, 1924); concerned with the manners and make-up of national and state legislatures.

———: *Legislative Principles* (Boston, 1930); concentrates upon the history and theory of lawmaking by representative governments, with examples cited from his own experience.

———: *Legislative Procedure* (Boston, 1922); deals with parliamentary practices involved in passing statutes. This and the two Luce citations above are peculiarly valuable because of the author's long service as a legislator in Massachusetts and in the national capitol.

———: "Petty Business in Congress," *American Political Science Review*, XXVI, No. 5 (October, 1932), 815–27.

Marriott, Sir John A. R.: *Second Chambers* (New ed., Oxford, 1927); an inductive study of this controversial subject.

Norris, George W.: "The One-House Legislature," *Annals*, CLXXXI (September, 1935), 50–58.

Odegard, Peter H.: "Majorities, Minorities, and Legislation," *Annals*, CLXIX (September, 1933), 29–46.

Rogers, Lindsay: *The American Senate* (New York, 1926), especially chaps. I and III–VIII; these sections cover the various contributions of the Senate to the lawmaking process.

Rosenbaum, B. B.: "The Urban-Rural Conflict as Evidenced in the Reapportionment Situation," *Social Forces*, XII, No. 3 (March, 1934), 421–26.

Unsigned: "The United States Senate," *Fortune*, XI, No. 2 (February, 1935), 47 ff.

Walker, Harvey: *Law Making in the United States* (New York, 1934), chaps. VII–X and XI–XIV; these sections deal with the process from the formulation of public opinion through the procedure of legislative bodies.

Willoughby, W. F.: *Principles of Legislative Organization and Administration* (Washington, 1934), chaps. I, III–V, XII–XV, XVII–XXVIII, and XXXIII–XXXVI; this exhaustive study covers: legislative functions; relation of the legislature to electorate and administration; the structure, organization, and procedure of the legislature; party leadership; and fact-finding aids.

Wilson, Woodrow: *Constitutional Government in the United States* (New York, 1921); chaps. I, III–V, and VIII are particularly applicable to a consideration of the lawmaking process.

CHAPTER VI

☆ ☆ ☆

## THE AMERICAN CONSTITUTIONAL SYSTEM

*"Governments were in process of formation in the United States when eighteenth-century ideas of checking and dividing powers were uppermost in political thought."*
—CHARLES G. HAINES

THE POPULAR will must find expression through a framework, through an integrated series of processes. Of these, the legislative stage is only one. Thus far we have not attempted to analyze the entire superstructure; our approach has been inductive. We have asked ourselves, "What do citizens expect of government in twentieth-century America? How do they go about giving effect to these desires? How complete is the correlation between public need and governmental response?"

The framework of government is described as its constitution. More accurately, the constitution is a body of law, custom, and practice which sets forth the general organization and powers of government and defines its relation to the citizens. It can readily be seen, therefore, that a constitution is an accumulation. It may develop rigid tendencies, it may be flexible, or it may be something between these two. The British constitution is largely unwritten. It consists of some basic acts of Parliament, such as the Bill of Rights, the Act of Settlement, the Parliament Act of 1911, statutes on the suffrage, and judicial decisions. But these formal expressions of law are the smaller part of the entire constitution. The larger portion consists of the customs, the established practices, the limitations upon government, and the inherent rights of citizens which have been recognized for generations.

Lord Bryce classified all constitutions into those which are either rigid or flexible, written or unwritten. The Constitution of the United States, therefore, was considered rigid; and the unwritten British one, flexible; but this division is too simple. One American author has written a convincing book about the living

Constitution;[1] and another has shown that there is the written Constitution and the unwritten attitude.[2] However, Bryce, in *Modern Democracies*, does make it clear that a written constitution is not so likely to be changed and expanded when social needs suggest it as is one consisting of custom and general understanding.

TYPES OF CONSTITUTIONS

Most of us have belonged to a social group of some kind in which the question has come up of whether to draft a written constitution or to leave the fundamental rules and purposes in the realm of common agreement and understanding. In such cases, the written constitution is usually chosen if the society's rules are not clearly understood, or if there is a feeling that some members cannot be "put on their own." However, when all the members are used to working together and understand one another's purposes and points of view, they usually regard a written constitution as something of a nuisance. It cramps the freedom of the membership and seems to reflect upon their ability to work together.

These same factors have their bearing upon political constitutions. A written constitution externalizes and formalizes common agreements; one not completely written continues to emphasize custom, general understanding, and unwritten rights. The written constitution is not necessarily more protective. Fundamental rights are nowhere more secure than in Great Britain. Freedom of assembly, speech, and press are more jealously guarded and more completely exercised there than in any other major nation. Their existence is founded upon the people's sense of fair play. It is an attitude rather than a legal formulation; it is largely a reflection of the Britisher's love of sports. In the long run, the greatest assurances that citizen rights will be respected are to be found in binding traditions, in the feeling that social justice prevails, and in tolerance and fair play that have been put to the test. A written constitution has greater presumptive authority than an unwritten one; but constitutions, like treaties, have been treated as "scraps of paper." A constitution's protective

[1] Howard Lee McBain, *The Living Constitution* (New York, 1927).
[2] Charles E. Merriam, *The Written Constitution and the Unwritten Attitude* (New York, 1931).

power, however, depends upon whether it remains a satisfactory social instrument and whether it is buttressed by social solidarities.

The Constitution of the United States consists of three general types of provision. The first type includes the preamble, the Bill of Rights (first ten amendments), the Fourteenth and Fifteenth (Civil War) amendments, and the Nineteenth (Woman's Suffrage) Amendment, dealing with the purposes of government and the rights and privileges of the individual. Legally speaking, the first ten amendments are merely limitations upon the federal government, but their practical effect is to guarantee individual rights. The second body of subject matter, and by far the longest, deals with the framework of government and the distribution of power. It is with this part of the Constitution that we shall be primarily concerned in the present chapter. The third type of provision consists of temporary or transitional arrangements and can be forgotten as quickly as it is mentioned. Illustrative is the statement about the importation of slaves, which since the date mentioned, 1808, has had no further importance. Hence, it may be said that the federal Constitution consists of a small number of temporary provisions and two sets of permanent stipulations—one relating to individual rights and the other to governmental framework and powers. All of the so-called "permanent" provisions, however, can be changed by constitutional amendment, with the exception of the one mentioned in the preceding chapter, namely, equal representation by states in the United States Senate.

*THE AMERICAN CONSTITUTION*

To some people, a written constitution suggests the idea of something finished. It symbolizes the truth revealed at a given time and place and remaining all-sufficient for an indefinite period thereafter. The kind of functional analysis we have suggested shows that constitutions are highly practical matters, as well as charters of human liberty. There is a good deal to be said for the contention that the Bill of Rights and the preamble set forth ideas of inalienable rights which we inherited from our forbears and which we mean to preserve in the future. The rules for organizing government and regulating its procedure, however, would seem to fall

*CONSTITUTIONAL GROWTH*

into a somewhat different category. They are merely matters of mechanics. These provisions express the knowledge of the time concerning the manner in which the instrument of government is best operated.

Government is a response to social needs which change with invention and human contrivance. On the other hand, if a constitution were to set forth provisions for a government with an organization and powers which were meant to be unchanging, it can clearly be seen that this view and our analysis would be contradictory. A constitution, like the whole of government, is a social instrument. Moreover, it is to be expected that the development of knowledge about government, like that in any other field, continues to be added to gradually. Plato and Aristotle did not know all about government any more than Copernicus fully understood astronomy. It is to be expected that better constitutions can be drafted as knowledge about statecraft increases. It is important to reiterate, therefore, that although human rights (as set forth in constitutional provisions) may be fixed and inalienable, the same presumption does not apply to the mere machinery of government and the tasks which it may be expected to undertake. To say that everything of importance was known about government in 1787 is like contending that nothing has been learned about transportation since the day of the horse and buggy.

But, as Professor McBain has pointed out, ours is a "living constitution," even though all people may not agree that bodily growth has occurred fast enough. It has been added to by amendment, supplemented by extra-legal agencies such as political parties, changed by customary methods of institutional procedure, expanded when popular desire therefor became great enough, and altered in the process of judicial construction. All three departments of government—legislative, administrative, and judicial—must construe the constitutional provisions in the course of their work. This process has gone on for 150 years, during which time a remarkable amount of adaptation to changing conditions has been found possible. In this process, not the least part of the change due to construction has been by "judicial legislation." The application of old rules to new cases gradually changes the law. This process is most pronounced in the field of constitutional law, where rules are not so complete and where dynamic social forces impinge most sharply. Judges engage in policy formation as well as in its enforcement.

The important question is not whether constitutions change, but whether their degree of flexibility is such that government's powers and methods are adequate when new needs arise. Few people, indeed, would deny that some change does occur or dispute the fact that constitutional adaptation is necessary. The real question is one of degree. For this reason it is important to take the sociological approach to political science. A study of causes and needs will indicate the extent to which institutional response is effective. The functional approach puts all government's instrumentalities, including constitutions, on trial.

A consideration of the sheer number of constitutions in the United States tends to confirm one's belief in the functional approach. Professor W. W. Willoughby, in his book entitled, *The American Constitutional System*, devotes much space to a consideration of federalism, the relation between national and state authority. Constitutions form a *system* of government. The federal Constitution is "the law of the land." The state constitution is the highest law within its own jurisdiction. The municipal charter is the fundamental law for the city. All of them together, and no one separately, give us the rules for organizing government, the division of jurisdiction among the various levels, and the relations between public authority and the citizen. We hear so much about the federal Constitution that we are inclined to overlook the fact that a similar basic instrument is found in each of the states. The distinction between "fundamental" law and "statutory" enactment, or constitutional and legislative law, is found everywhere in American governments. The federal Constitution merely serves the largest area and is "supreme" whenever state or local laws conflict with provisions in the federal charter.

UNIVERSALITY OF BASIC CHARTERS

The city charter is indeed the basic law of the municipality, but there is one important difference between it and state and federal constitutions. The latter are drawn up and ratified by a constitutional convention consisting of delegates selected for the purpose by the citizens. The municipal charter, on the other hand, is framed and ratified by the state legislature. In legal theory, the municipality is merely a corporation, a creature of the sovereign state. In practice, however, increasing numbers of cities are getting "home-rule" charters, which increase their discretionary powers and free them from some of the state controls.

Every American school child has heard the famous comparison between "a government of laws and a government of men." Many are the conclusions that are derived therefrom. The usual moral is that only the separation-of-powers system assures a government controlled by law. But the concept in the large is so important and has had such a profound influence upon people's attitudes and thinking that we need to examine it first.

"A GOVERNMENT OF LAWS"

Does government make law or is law above government? We know that constitutional conventions, such as that of 1787, frame constitutions; that legislatures pass statutes telling citizens what to do and what not to do, on pain of falling into the toils of the law; and that judges declare the law. They are all agents of government. The natural law theory, which can be traced back into Graeco-Roman times, is the concept that there is a higher law, a sense of reasonableness and justice, existing independent of institutions and of ordinary man-made law. Hence, law is superior to government and controls it. Professor Charles G. Haines has shown the influence that natural-law theory has on American constitutional law.[1] There can be no doubt that this mystical concept deeply affects the ideology of people generally.

Nowhere in their thinking are men likely to be so uncritical as where law is concerned. Law is law. It stands for justice and right. To ask how law became law or what influenced those who administered it in a particular case is considered rank disrespect. No other realm of government enjoys such deference, and it is not a healthful thing for legal institutions themselves.

[1] Cf. Charles G. Haines, *The Revival of Natural Law Concepts in American Constitutional Law* (Cambridge, Mass., 1930).

Human beings, of course, make law, administer it, and are affected by it. What may reasonably be meant by the phrase, "a government of laws," is that the persons who execute the law should themselves be controlled thereby and, hence, not act arbitrarily. Government operating through fixed and widely understood rules; and administrators who will not discriminate between individuals—these phrases also express possible connotations, and very desirable ones.

When amenability of government to its own rules and equal treatment of all persons are the implications of the famous phrase a "government of laws and not of men," it is synonymous with "the rule of law" in Great Britain. This unwritten constitutional principle, as A. V. Dicey has said, means that all persons, official as well as lay, are subject to the same law administered in the same courts, without fear or favor. Happily, this principle is followed also in the United States.

What is usually meant by "a government of laws" is that the constitution should be supreme. Officers of the government, rather than acting without authority or in an arbitrary fashion, should follow the rules. Ready agreement is found on this requirement of constitutional government; but we need to push the analysis even further. Constitutions are not self-executing or self-interpreting. Irrespective of whether or not there may be a transcendental law, substantive law requires instrumentation. This means that ultimately some person or agency must be supreme.

Government controls. When citizens disagree and interfere with the work and peace of society, public authority steps in and adjusts the controversy. Likewise, the departments of government sometimes disagree as to the interpretation of the Constitution. Some one of them, therefore, must have the power to decide. In Great Britain, Parliament is the agency which decides; the legislature is supreme. In the United States the highest court of each governmental jurisdiction decides; the judiciary is supreme.[1] The Constitution is what those who interpret it say it is.

[1] Charles G. Haines has written a great book entitled, *The American Doctrine of Judicial Supremacy* (rev. ed., Berkley, 1932).

All three departments of government interpret the Constitution. When two of them disagree, or when a citizen challenges an act of any one of them, the question of constitutionality may be raised. In common-law theory, a person brings a case or controversy to the appropriate court. If, in the course of the court's examination, it finds that the law is not authorized by the Constitution or that it conflicts with a provision of the fundamental law, said law ceases to have effect. In constitutional practice, cases are frequently brought to the Supreme Court with the very definite purpose of testing the constitutionality of an act, and when one is declared unconstitutional it immediately becomes null and void.

The power of the courts to declare legislative acts unconstitutional is the outstanding feature of the American governmental system. It is obvious that any power to pass finally upon what government is permitted to do is of the greatest importance. The highest court has "the last guess" as to whether an act is in conformity with constitutional provisions. If the tribunal rules that it is not, the Constitution must be amended before the same law can be re-enacted and given legal effect. There are several aspects of American government that have attracted attention abroad, among them the separation of powers, presidential government, the influence of the Senate, and the city-manager form of government. But in its internal importance and in the amount of attention that has been given to it by publicists in foreign countries, the judicial review of legislation stands foremost. Yet, with the exception of some of the South American countries, other nations do not seem inclined to emulate our example.[1]

THE AMERICAN DOCTRINE OF JUDICIAL SUPREMACY

Higher courts invariably have the power to review the acts of lower courts. The right of judicial tribunals to take jurisdiction over cases and controversies involving administrative action was established in common-law courts prior to the adoption of the American Constitution. But judicial review of legislative acts is typically American and still fairly new. In 1803, the Supreme Court of the United States enunciated the doctrine in the opinion rendered by Chief Justice Marshall, in the case of *Marbury* vs.

[1] Cf. Charles G. Haines, *The American Doctrine of Judicial Supremacy*, chap. 1.

*Madison.*¹ Professor Haines has pointed out that there were preceding cases in which state courts had reviewed the acts of state legislatures. It seems clear, however, that the court in this case went out of its way to establish the right of the Supreme Court to review acts of Congress.² Be that as it may, *Marbury* vs. *Madison* established the doctrine. Then it was laid aside until after the Civil War. Since that time, and particularly in recent years, judicial review has been of the utmost social and governmental importance. About seventy congressional acts and more than three hundred state acts have been declared unconstitutional by the Supreme Court. To this number must be added a large number of state and congressional statutes ruled out by the lower federal courts and the highest courts of the several states.

The real significance of judicial review is not in the number of legislative statutes invalidated. More important is the fact that governmental action declared null and void in one jurisdiction will probably meet the same fate everywhere else. Decisions of the federal Supreme Court are binding in all the states. Most of the cases involving a declaration of unconstitutionality by the United States Supreme Court have dealt with social legislation enacted by the states. Thus, judicial review discourages social legislation. Adverse decisions relative to one subject may, by analogy, control what may be done in another field. Reversals upset governmental administration and hurt the morale of those responsible for attempting solutions of social problems. Months after laws are enacted they may be declared null and void. Moreover, there are coming to be "no man's lands" wherein neither the federal government nor the states are allowed to act. Legislation attempting to control the minimum level of wages may be taken as a case in point.³ But, if the courts did not check the legislatures, would not constitutions be changed?

For how long a period may a constitution be assumed to serve a people without being reconsidered in the light of changed

[1] *1. Cranch* 137 (1803); Cf. Robert E. Cushman, *Leading Constitutional Decisions* (New York, 1929), p. 155; the best treatise on constitutional law is that by W. W. Willoughby, *The Constitutional Law of the United States*, 3 vols. (New York, 1929).
[2] Cf. Andrew C. McLaughlin, *A Constitutional History of the United States* (New York, 1935), and Charles G. Haines, *The American Doctrine of Judicial Supremacy*, pp. 193–203.
[3] Cf. *Morehead* vs. *Tipaldo*, 298 U. S. (1936) 56 Supreme Court 918.

conditions? Even though Thomas Jefferson probably did not foresee the rapid technological changes which were to occur in the United States, the Sage of Monticello was of the opinion that a constitutional convention should be called about every twenty years; but Jefferson's advice has apparently never been taken seriously. A federal constitutional convention has not convened since the original one in 1787.[1] Conventions in the states have been few and far between. Jefferson was considered a radical in his times and apparently is still so considered in some respects today.[2]

In a system which assumes that a written constitution is supreme, the separation-of-powers doctrine takes on a significance not found in countries where legislative finality is definitely established. In constitutional theory, all three departments in the United States are equal and independent. Each operates in its own bailiwick. The Constitution coalesces their work. Montesquieu, whose writings influenced the American fathers to implant this principle at the center of the system, thought he saw this practice at work in British government. We now realize, however, that Montesquieu's analysis of the essentials of English government was incorrect.

SEPARATION OF POWERS

The separation-of-powers principle is a cornerstone in representative governments elsewhere, but with important differences in emphasis and qualification. In France, home of Montesquieu, for example, the emphasis is upon division of labor and specialization of function. The separation of powers in this sense is a principle of the British constitutional system; but outside the United States, the separation of powers is qualified by the important principles of legislative supremacy, the necessity of close co-operation between the legislative and executive departments, the centering of initiative in the cabinet, and undivided responsibility for the program and actions of the government of the day.

[1] Concerning the personnel and purposes of the Philadelphia Convention, see Charles A. Beard, *An Economic Interpretation of the Constitution of the United States* (rev. ed., New York, 1929); Andrew C. McLaughlin in *Constitutional History of the United States* takes issue with Beard's view.
[2] Cf. William S. Carpenter, *The Development of American Political Thought* (Princeton, 1930), chap. IV.

Realistically analyzed, the American system is not separated in practice as much as it is in theory. Every department exercises powers and procedures which, judged by their nature, adhere to the other two departments. Congress, for example, has the essentially judicial powers of impeachment, of testing membership qualifications, and of investigation. In its internal organization and procedure, and also in its sharing responsibility for appointments, responsibility of an administrative nature is constitutionally provided or necessarily implied. The executive shares in the legislative process when he recommends legislation, promulgates ordinances having legal force, and exercises the power of veto. Administrative agencies perform numerous acts having judicial characteristics, such as holding hearings at which rights are adjusted and penalties are imposed. The courts administer property, manage the judicial system, and shape public policy. Historically, the judiciary derives from administration and became separate only when specialization of function and personnel became necessary.[1]

The chief objective of the separation of powers is to prevent the concentration of too much power in the hands of any one person or agency. This is clearly a necessary safeguard to democracy, but there are other goals of representative government which should simultaneously be sought. The best division of labor is one of them. In this respect, American governments have achieved substantial success. Still a third desideratum is the assured co-operation between the legislative and executive branches in order that programs authorized by the voters may be effectively carried through. In this respect the American system is not so reliable as the cabinet system. In the fourth place, the political party holding power and the executive representing it need to be made responsible for both what they do and what they fail to accomplish. In this test, too, the American machinery of government falls short of a desirable standard.

RESPONSIBLE GOVERNMENT

Woodrow Wilson did not hesitate to recommend the adoption

---

[1] The practical exceptions to the separation-of-powers theory are excellently analyzed by W. W. Willoughby in *The Constitutional Law of the United States*, III, 1616–35.

of cabinet responsibility in the United States,[1] and it is safe to say that most American political scientists have been convinced of the desirability of the responsibility principle. In recent years, however, there has been less open advocacy of a definite change in this direction. Americans are no longer inclined to be receptive to principles which are transplanted from abroad. We hold that our institutional procedures are superior. Moreover, self-confidence and pride, unless carried so far that they become blind complacency, are admirable characteristics. But what are the prospects of an increasing measure of responsibility without a complete shift to cabinet government? Attempt at reform within an established system is usually surer of results than advocacy of a complete change. This seems to be the present temper of political scientists.

Executive participation in the lawmaking process has increased. Strikingly illustrative of greater initiative is the appearance of President Roosevelt in Congress to confer on the "state of the Union." Moreover, recent presidents have made extensive use of "the White House spokesman" as a means of influencing public opinion and securing compliance from Congress.[2] The White House breakfast, at which key congressmen are told what the Chief Executive desires, is an established institution. Corresponding developments are observable in many American states. The names of Al Smith, Gifford Pinchot, Harry Byrd, the late Floyd Olson, Paul McNutt, and Philip LaFollette clearly suggest that "strong" governors are on the increase. Legislatures are not allowed to go their own sweet ways. Cities, too, evidence the same tendency, although perhaps not so extensively. New York's Mayor La Guardia and Milwaukee's Mayor Hoan are two of the "strong" type.

The city-manager plan of municipal government represents a movement away from the separation of the legislative and executive departments. It is more analogous to responsible government as found in other countries. A city council is elected and it in turn chooses the manager. He is appointed for an indefinite

[1] Cf. Woodrow Wilson, *Congressional Government*.
[2] See the last chapter in Lindsay Rogers, *The American Senate* (New York, 1926).

term, and is removable at any time. In other words, his period of office, like that of ministers in countries having the cabinet form of government, depends upon his ability to retain the confidence of the legislative body. Unlike this system, however, the manager is not chosen from the council. In cabinet government, the executive is created out of the legislative body; in city-manager government, the appointee may be secured from some other city. The idea is to get the best available man for the manager's post. Then, after appointment, the manager is given complete freedom to operate the purely executive end of the city government.

*THE CITY-MANAGER PLAN*

The city manager hires and fires, submits a budget to the council, executes contracts, has complete control over all administrative departments and officers. He meets with the council members, and, because of his knowledge of and familiarity with it, is relied upon heavily by the council when it comes to the policy-making stage. Although the manager must be careful not to be "political," he nevertheless exerts a great deal of influence upon the city's plans and programs. Like the cabinet system, the manager plan usually includes a dual executive, an elected mayor with nominal powers who presides over the council and takes care of the ceremonial functions, and the appointed manager who does the real work. Although this system came into existence only a generation or so ago, it now numbers about 450 cities on its roster and has become international in its scope.[1]

Administrative reorganizations in over a third of the states have tended to increase the amount of actual governmental responsibility. The powers of the governor have been strengthened.[2] Some now have cabinets which are actually subject to their control, as in the federal government. Moreover, the executive budget centers in the governor the responsibility for recommending a legislative program.

There are additional improvements and reforms which would

[1] Cf. William Anderson, *American City Government* (New York, 1925), chap. XIII; Clarence E. Ridley and Orin F. Nolting, *The City Manager Profession* (Chicago, 1934); and Leonard D. White, *The City Manager* (Chicago, 1927).
[2] See the essay by George W. Spicer entitled, "From Political Chief to Administrative Chief," in *The Law and Practice of Governmental Administration* (Baltimore, 1935), Haines and Dimock, editors.

increase the amount of co-operation and responsibility and still not change the separation between the legislative and executive departments. As the result of experience, executive budgets may come to be treated with greater respect by legislative bodies. For years there has been a suggestion that members of the President's cabinet be given *ex officio* seats in Congress, where they would be available to answer questions and to make statements. This could be done without giving them a vote or allowing them to enter into debates. This single device, if widely adopted, could do much to secure better understanding and closer co-operation.

There are some problems of "unresponsible" government which are seemingly insoluble, short of a change in fundamental constitutional theory. There is no protection against electing a legislative majority of one party and a chief executive of another. New York, Empire State of the Union, has done so several times. The situation in the federal government is even worse. A President may come into office with a safe majority in Congress, as Wilson did, and at the biennial election see that majority in the House turned into a minority. One House may be controlled by the executive's party and the other one by the opposition forces. The system does not make sense. Nowhere outside of government would anyone think of trying to run human affairs in such an odd fashion.

DIFFICULT REFORMS

A second seemingly ineradicable difficulty is that of securing responsible leadership in legislative assemblies. As pointed out in the preceding chapter, the party steers, but cannot completely control what takes place. Anyone can introduce any kind of bill. Committees dominate the chamber. Members sometimes filibuster against their own party. Caucus decisions frequently do not bind all members to a united program. The legislator is made an easy prey of the lobbyist.

The third problem is a result of the uncontrolled legislative process. In the United States we have irresponsible spending. This may sound more like a party campaign cry than the sober statement of a political scientist; but it is true. A cabinet government is responsible for the total amount spent. In England especially, the executive budget cannot be altered during the legislative stage without the permission of the cabinet; otherwise the Government will fall and the people will be called upon to decide. In American legislatures, the budget can be increased whenever enough votes can be mustered. We have an official appropriation bill, followed by several emergency appropriation bills. There are "ordinary" budgets and "emergency" budgets. In all this process, each lobby is hard at work, trading support on a proposed expenditure sponsored by another for votes on one it desires. "Logrolling" is the term. States compete, municipalities vie with each other. "If you vote for our harbor bill, we will vote for your river-deepening program," legislators say, following the procedure commonly called the "pork barrel."

IRRESPONSIBLE FINANCE

Each interest tries to get as much as it can for itself. The total amount to be spent is the result of all such pressures which become effective. When the two-billion-dollar veterans' bonus was being considered, President Roosevelt said the measure would jeopardize the nation's credit and that he was against it; but it was passed over his veto. In a responsible government, such a proposal either would have been voted down or the government of the day would have decided to "go to the people."

Professor Corwin has pointed out the enormous possibilities contained in the federal spending power.[1] The federal government is limited, but the power to appropriate money for "the general welfare," as well as for other more express purposes, is not limited. It is quite possible that in order to make use of the money when it is available, the federal government will have to turn it over to the states, the municipalities, proprietary corporations, or some other agency which does have the requisite power to engage in the activity. In the meantime, federal expenditures and the national indebtedness continue to mount. The same thing can happen in the governments of the states.

Irresponsible finance, more than any other factor, is likely to gain support for responsible government. Under it, the executive and legislative branches working together would make every interest prove its case and reach a decision on the basis of what

[1] E. S. Corwin, *The Twilight of the Supreme Court* (New Haven, 1934), chap. IV.

seems relatively more important and what seems totally possible.

Cabinet government assures responsible finance. It protects members of the legislature from the onslaughts of pressure groups; it forces parties to stand on principle rather than to retreat into expediency; and it guarantees co-operation between the legislative and executive branches. This cannot help but happen, for the cabinet is created out of the legislature. Can these results be achieved by reforms within the system of divided powers?

An additional factor to be reckoned with is the growing jealousy between the legislative and executive departments. Lawmaking bodies have delegated or surrendered some of their prerogatives, while the executive has been gaining authority and prestige. There is a general feeling in legislative halls that this process has gone far enough, and in a sense the attitude is justified. We have already tried to make it clear that the legislature is the center of government and that free government depends upon its continued health and effectiveness. At the same time, there are sound reasons for increasing executive power and responsibility. If effective co-operation between the two branches can be secured, both legislative control and executive power should be equally possible. If the two branches fight one another, either legislation or administration is bound to suffer; and when either is adversely affected the whole government gets out of gear. What are we going to do about it?

Professor W. Y. Elliott has proposed certain remedies, which, although they require action by a constitutional convention, he considers quite within the realm of possibility. Realizing that

PROPOSED CONSTITUTIONAL REFORMS

"any realistic approach to constitutional reform must begin with our spending mechanism," he suggests that the President be given the legal right to veto any separate items in any bill carrying an appropriation, and that no bill should be allowed to have a "rider" attached to it that has no connection with the title or the aims of the bill.[1] The President could then "represent the national will as against group and sectional raids on the Treasury."

[1] William Y. Elliott, *The Need for Constitutional Reform* (McGraw-Hill, New York, 1935), pp. 31, 32.

Other proposals would be more far-reaching in their institutional ramifications. Professor Elliott proposes that the President should have the right to force the House of Representatives to stand one general election during its term of office, while the terms of Congressmen would be increased from two to four years. Dissolution would "help party discipline, but it would not render Congress slavish." The Senate would be limited in two important respects: it could delay the passage of money bills for only a month, but in no case beyond the end of the session; and its power over bills appropriating money or raising money would be taken away.[1] The Senate, he says, "is the entrenched stronghold of lobbying pressure groups, the most unrepresentative body, from the point of view of population, in the world today."

Perhaps some such compromise between the *status quo* and a complete cabinet system is the best way out of our difficulties. The cabinet system, however, has its faults. In war-time or in national emergencies, the cabinet is found to be too large. The presidential system, on the other hand, is readily turned into a highly concentrated and efficient machine. Then, too, when cabinets fall, both government and business are upset. This need not happen frequently, of course, and in England it does not. In France, there are frequent changes of cabinet, but they are not so upsetting as might be expected. Most of the ministers remain in the new cabinet, while the permanent civil service carries on the government. The most important change is that of the person holding the premiership. There need be no general election oftener than every four years in France or every five years in England.

Moreover, the cabinet system provides for a dual executive, one nominal or ceremonial and the other actual or efficient. Great Britain has King and Prime Minister; France, President and Premier. Our American President, on the other hand, is almost killed by the rigors of his position. Too much is expected of him; he must be party head, legislative leader, administrative chief, ceremonial figure. Perhaps the United States should have both a president and a prime minister.

[1] *Ibid.*, pp. 32, 33.

Revealing his awareness of cabinet government's greatest fault, Professor Elliott has summarized the arguments in favor of his own proposals:

> This is not so hair-trigger a system as the parliamentary system. It leaves room for adjustment between the executive and the legislature along the lines of presidential leadership and compromise. But it does give our President, as a national leader, a power that would make our party system far more responsible, for with it he could resist pressure-group legislation successfully. A Congress that overrode him would have to face what amounted to a national referendum on his policy.[1]

Clearly these are the objectives that should be sought, irrespective of how much we may differ about the best means!

Another fundamental constitutional principle comes from historical origins and from geographical peculiarities, as well as from legal provision. Federalism has been a problem since the earliest days of the Republic; and, so far as anyone can foresee, it will continue to be so for an indefinite future. The enormous size of the country seemingly makes numerous political subdivisions necessary. Diversity of interests leads to sectional rivalries and jealousies. When it is considered that the Pacific coast states are three thousand miles from the national capitol, and that desert, rivers, and mountain peaks intervene, it is surprising that national unity has developed to the extent that it has.

FEDERALISM

A federal system invariably leads to difficult problems of governmental co-operation and national solidarity. Canada has experienced more controversies over the relative authority of the provincial versus the national government than over any other public question.[2] Under the Republic, Germany's efforts at social control were bound up with the rival claims of the *Länder* versus the *Reich*.[3] Most of Australian political history has been concerned with the struggle between the states and the federal

---

[1] *Ibid*, p. 33. Other proposals for constitutional reform are summarized on pp. 30–32.
[2] Cf. W. P. M. Kennedy, *The Constitution of Canada* (London, 1922); chap. xxiv; also, Edward Porritt, *The Evolution of the Dominion of Canada* (New York, 1918), chap. ix; and Robert M. Dawson, ed., *Constitutional Issues in Canada, 1900–1931* (London, 1933), chap. ix.
[3] Frederick F. Blachly and Miriam E. Oatman, *The Government and Administration of Germany* (Baltimore, 1928), chap. ii.

government, particularly over labor regulation.¹ Similarly, Switzerland, Mexico, South Africa, and New Zealand have been perplexed by the difficulty of reconciling two parallel systems of government.

A federalism is a political system in which the total governmental authority is divided between a central government and provincial entities, both of which have independent and autonomous jurisdiction within their spheres. A unitary government, on the other hand, monopolizes all authority, merely creating districts or administrative units for the sake of convenience. France and Italy are examples of governments which center all authority in their national capitals. The unitary government simplifies the problems of hierarchy and authority, but it leads to centralization and lessened local responsibility.² Federalism, on the other hand, has been found to produce duplication, increased expense, and areas of conflict and ineffectuality.

A federal union is responsible for other constitutional and administrative results. Agreement upon the division of authority between the states and the central government encourages reliance upon explicit constitutional provisions. The written charter, in turn, throws upon the federal judiciary the responsibility of upholding federal authority when the states attempt to invade its sphere and of preventing the national government, in turn, from bursting its bounds. In short, federalism is a contributing factor to judicial supremacy.

Federalism is one of the most difficult of dilemmas. The preservation of the states is argued on grounds of local participation in government, the essence of political democracy. People form attachments to the state symbol. Rare is the man who is not proud of the state of his birth or present residence. In theory, at least, governments close to the people are more easily controlled by the citizenry. National

PROBLEMS OF FEDERALISM

---

[1] W. P. Reeves, *State Experiments in Australia and New Zealand*, 2 vols. (London, 1902); also A. P. Conoway, *The Failure of Federalism in Australia* (London, 1930); and K. O. Warner, *An Introduction to Some Problems of Australian Federalism* (Seattle, 1933).
[2] See Edward M. Sait, *Government and Politics of France* (New York, 1926), chap. VIII; and Robert K. Gooch, *Regionalism in France* (New York, 1931); on centralization in Italy, see H. W. Schneider and S. B. Clough, *Making Fascists* (Chicago, 1929), pp. 24–7.

centralization, on the other hand, removes processes and controls to a distant point, increasing the dangers of unresponsiveness and abuse of power. The larger the institution, the greater the potentialities of domination and tyranny.

But national centralization is not always a matter of design; sometimes it is determined by the natural course of events. When the problems with which government is expected to deal become as large as the country, it is obvious that only a national government can hope to cope with them successfully. As we have stated, this is the explanation of centralizing trends in the United States. Moreover, a large institution, if ably administered, is more efficient and economical than a large number of smaller, unrelated ones. This is particularly true as the positive functions of government increase. Planning, for example, inherently involves central research and thinking. When a pattern becomes too complex, it cannot be fitted together properly. Moreover, it is very costly to maintain 175,000 separate governmental units in the United States. Duplication, ineffectuality, and expensiveness are an unpopular trilogy.

"There is no relief in sight for taxpayers under any deal, old or new," states Elliott, "unless, by a constitutional revolt like that of 1787, they call constitutional conventions over the heads of the vested interests of politicians and spoilsmen, rationalize the machinery of government, and reorganize the men who run the machine. . . . The only way to stay the march of bureaucracy is to cut out useless duplications. . . . " But he is not so hopeful about the prospects. "The vested interests of office holders are the most unassailable of all vested interests."[1] Professor Elliott's position is sound. But what form should governmental simplification take? Should it be confined to local units, or should the reform extend higher up?

The federal Constitution gives the central government express powers, and all others belong to the states or to the people. This is stated explicitly in the Tenth Amendment. Congress's powers are enumerated in the third article. Are these express provisions comprehensive enough to take in all the responsibilities which

[1] W. Y. Elliott, *The Need for Constitutional Reform*, pp. 30 and 31.

the federal government now exercises, is in the process of absorbing, or should assume? Let there be no mistaking the amount of honest and vigorous disagreement the attempted answer to this question immediately calls forth; however, an enumeration may be suggested, simply for purposes of comparison: The national interest is now dominant in the fields of transportation, communications, electrical power, banking, business trusts, insurance, labor, social security, housing, national resources, and planning.[1] How many of these are found in article three? Many implied and derived powers have been given judicial approval;[2] but how much further can the Constitution be stretched without amending those provisions which divide governmental powers between the nation and the several states?

STATE VS. NATION

Socially, economically, and geographically considered, the several states are no longer at the center of the governmental firmament. The municipality and the federal government more nearly qualify. The state's strength is in the position guaranteed it by the federal Constitution. Few administrative or problem areas, however, coincide with state boundaries.[3] Most of them are found to be local, regional, or national. Geography is not a respecter of political boundaries. The dust problem extends across parts of several states; watershed-improvement schemes necessarily involve whole drainage areas; the cotton belt blankets the south; steel and automobiles are produced where iron, coal, and cheap transportation find a meeting point. In other words, governmental problems are largely regional.

Regional commonwealths, midway between the local units and the federal jurisdiction, would make a logical and efficient governmental pattern in the United States.[4] They would more nearly

[1] See the suggestions by Charles A. Beard, *The Open Door at Home* (New York, 1934), especially the last chapter; also Stuart Chase, *Government in Business* (New York, 1935), chap. VII.
[2] Read John Marshall's exposition of the doctrine of implied powers in the case of *McCulloch vs. Maryland*, 4 Wheaton 316 (1819).
[3] This appears plainly in a study entitled, *Regional Factors in National Planning and Development* (Government Printing Office, Washington, D. C., 1935).
[4] Possible regional boundaries are mentioned in the publication referred to above; see especially chap. xv. Six regions are suggested and defended by Howard W. Odum in his fascinating book, *Southern Regions* (Chapel Hill, N. C., 1936), chap. III.

correspond with the governmental problems induced by technology, improvements in transportation and communication, and the necessity of taking steps to conserve our national resources. Regional governments would be a substitute for increased centralization in Washington. They would make it possible to simplify and rationalize the areas of local government; moreover, they already have reality. Regional consciousness and pride are found in every section of the country. New England, the South, the Middle West, the Mountain Empire, the Northwest, and the Pacific coast are well-recognized regions. Prominent visitors on leaving the United States frequently remark that in reality we are several units rather than one. Regional vitality, moreover, has increased very decidedly in recent years and has the prospect of gaining additional force. The administrative convenience of regionalization is reflected in the existence of 106 cases of regional organization in the federal departments and independent establishments.[1]

REGIONALISM

One of the principal reforms advocated by Professor Elliott is the establishment of regional groups of states, which groups would be given representation as such in the national legislature.[2] Regional government is by no means a new idea among political scientists. William Bennett Munro pointed out its desirability ten years ago.[3] Frederick Jackson Turner, the great historian of the westward movement, first laid great stress upon it. Geographers and sociologists have long been aware of its advantages. Here, again, the advantages of a constitutional change seem apparent, but what of the prospects of any considerable reform?

Attachment to established political subdivisions is a strong tie. Loyalty to the name of a state is in the same category as that to home and church. Moreover, our constitutional system is built upon the central idea of states. The members of Congress are drawn from them. The electors who choose the President speak in the name of the several states. It seems quite unlikely that regional governments will be realized unless the popular demand

[1] Cf. James W. Fesler, "Federal Administrative Regions," *American Political Science Review*, XXX, No. 2 (April, 1936), pp. 257–68.
[2] W. Y. Elliott, *The Need for Constitutional Reform*, pp. 191 ff.
[3] William B. Munro, *The Invisible Government* (New York, 1928), chap. vi.

becomes exceedingly strong and necessary changes are authorized by means of a constitutional convention.

The very size of the United States makes government complex, limits democratic control, and, therefore, increases what must be expected of the citizen. Differences in racial origin, language, and customs, added to the enormity of the territory and its geographic diversity, make the development of a national culture extraordinarily difficult. Even though our regional patterns become increasingly distinctive, which seems likely, the sense of national unity and interest must not be allowed to suffer in consequence. Federalism requires mixed loyalties, a sort of cosmopolitanism.

Our federal judiciary has been a great unifying force. Unlike other English-speaking countries, the United States from the beginning has had courts of the national government in all parts of the country. During the first seventy-five years of American constitutional history, this was a fact of considerable importance. Most states wanted to pay no more attention to the federal government than they had to. The district court of the United States, presided over by a judge selected from the locality, stood as a symbol of national unity and federal authority. If there had been only a Supreme Court in Washington, and no inferior federal courts supporting it, the history of the United States might have been much different. We would then have had to rely upon state courts for cases involving national law, as is done in Canada and other federalisms in the British Empire.[1] The federal courts, moreover, have helped to make possible the expansion of federal, legislative, and judicial powers. This they have done by means of the doctrine of implied powers, the principle of the superiority of national law over that of a state in case of conflict,[2] and extensions of expansive concepts, such as due process of law.

The due-process provisions are the most important ones in the federal Constitution. They have made the judiciary a policy-making agency of enormous influence. They have made judicial supremacy the most important constitutional principle. They

[1] Felix Frankfurter and James M. Landis, *The Business of the Supreme Court* (New York, 1928), chap. 1.
[2] For example, see the leading cases of *Fletcher* vs. *Peck*, 6 Cranch 87 (1810), and *Houston, East and West Texas Ry. Co.* vs. *U. S.*, 234 U. S. 342 (1914).

have radically changed the Constitution of 1789. These statements may sound sweeping, but they are nevertheless true.

The two clauses, found in the Fifth and Fourteenth Amendments, are worded as restrictions. The first is binding upon the federal government, and while the other applies to the states, the wording is almost identical in each case. No person shall be "deprived of life, liberty, or property, without due process of law." The due-process clause became of first-rate importance, however, only after the adoption of the Fourteenth Amendment in 1868.

DUE PROCESS OF LAW

Due process of law is derived from the *lex terrae* of Magna Carta and "the rule of law" which has developed in Great Britain as a result. Until the adoption of the Fourteenth Amendment, due process of law, like the rule of law, was a restriction primarily upon the judiciary and secondarily upon administrative officials. Due process had no applicability to legislative enactments and has none in Great Britain today. When applied to courts and administrators, it seeks to guarantee such things as impartiality, notice of the proceeding, opportunity to be heard, and freedom from duress. As the phrase itself suggests, due process originally had to do with procedure. It was not concerned with substance. Judicial and administrative officials were required to observe certain rules of fairness or a higher court would intervene.

After the due-process clause had been written into the Fourteenth Amendment, a new application was found for the power. The clauses were applied to legislative acts, both state and federal. Due process has made the judiciary what it is today. The due-process and "equal protection of laws" provisions, both in the Fourteenth Amendment, give rise to most of the important decisions handed down by the Supreme Court. Today the highest court's leading cases deal with economic and social questions, as a direct consequence of the importance which has been given these two provisions, neither of which was in the original Constitution.

The Thirteenth, Fourteenth, and Fifteenth are the so-called Civil War Amendments. They were adopted in order to safeguard the "life, liberty and property" of the recently emancipated slaves and in order to give them the privileges of citizenship, but they have rarely been used for this purpose. Instead, a fiction of law has entered in to help give the clauses their present importance. The business corporation is a legal person, and the courts have decided that when legislation deprived any (legal) person of life, liberty, or property, due process gave them the right to review said law, and, if found "deprivatory," to declare it null and void. After the Civil War, the case of *Marbury* vs. *Madison* took on real importance. Judicial review, considered a dead issue, except for the Dred Scott Decision of 1857, suddenly came to life just at the time social legislation was beginning to increase with rapidity. Railways were being pushed through to the West; nation-wide businesses soon followed. These developments led to regulatory laws affecting railways, stockyards, grain elevators, and other undertakings "affected with a public interest." In their path emerged the due-process clause of the Fourteenth Amendment.

Then the process of judicial construction set in. Due process of law cannot be defined. It must be understood by reading thousands of cases, the largest percentage of which are decided in district and circuit courts. Due process of law, like equity, is capable of infinite expansion. It is more flexible than equity, because, in equity proceedings, the plaintiff must be able to show that there is no other remedy. Due process is comparable to such words as "reasonable," "just," and "proper." It means what the judges say it means. The word "life" has come to include the use of one's limbs and all the faculties. "Liberty" means not only freedom from restraint but freedom to do such positive things as to make contracts with employees. "Property" includes not only real estate and tangibles but the use of them, which of course includes interest and profit. If a business "person" can prove to the court that, as a result of a legislative or other act, his freedom of contract or his profits are being interfered with, the due-process doctrine begins to operate. As in any other field, precedents are gradually built up; but the varieties of social legislation are so numerous, modern life is so complex, and judicial discretion is so broad, that one scarcely knows what act will be challenged under the due-process provision or what the result will be.

Judicial review of legislation concerns what may be thought of as a competition between due process of law and the equal-protection clause, on the one hand, and such important powers as those dealing with commerce and taxation on the other. The judges must decide whether a piece of social legislation withstands the due-process test. The courts are called upon to deal with political theory's oldest and most difficult problem, public right versus private right. This issue is drawn in the conflict between the police power and the due-process provision. As we have explained previously, the police power is the reserved authority of the several states to pass laws protecting the safety, health, and morals of the population. Like due process of law, it is undefined and expansive. It is government's right to do anything that society's interest seems to require. Due process of law also protects a society. It upholds processes and liberties which make society's interests secure; but it does this by protecting the individual. Often it is his property or his vested economic interests which are involved. This is how the clash between public right, represented by the police power, and individual right, expressed in due process of law, comes to occupy the center of the judicial arena.

THE POLICE POWER

Does the state have the right to regulate the weight of loaves of bread, the manufacture of ice, the preservation of fish life, the sale of theater tickets, the earnings of street-railway systems? In some cases, yes, and in others, no. Where it does have the right, due process sets limits beyond which governmental control is not permitted to go; for example, limiting the return on the stock of the Baltimore Street Railways to 6.26 per cent is "confiscatory," and the percentage was accordingly raised by a Supreme Court decision to 7.44.[1]

The American judiciary has the final word as to whether government's attempted solutions of social problems conform to constitutional limitations and the courts' construction of due process of law. For this reason, the judicial department necessarily participates in the policy-making process. It has the power of life or death over the legislature's most progressive measures. The

[1] *United Rys. and Electric Co. of Baltimore* vs. *West*, 280 U. S. 234 (1929).

American constitutional system is a "government of laws" in which judicial supremacy has become the outstanding principle.

#### SELECTED READINGS

Arneson, Ben A.: *Elements of Constitutional Law* (New York, 1928), *passim;* a readable discussion of the elementary principles of constitutional law in America.

Arnold, T. W.: "Apologia for Jurisprudence," 44 *Yale Law Journal,* 729 (March, 1935).

Black, Forrest R.: "Constitutions and Democracy," *Annals,* CLXIX (September, 1933), 1-11.

Corwin, E. S.: "The 'Higher Law' Background of American Constitutional Law," 42 *Harvard Law Review,* 149 ff. and 365 ff. (December, 1928).

Cushman, Robert E.: "Constitutional Law in 1934-35," *American Political Science Review,* XXX, No. 1 (February, 1936), pp. 51-89; author presents an article on this subject each year in this journal.

Elliott, William Y.: *The Need for Constitutional Reform* (New York, 1935), chaps. I-X; covers implications of recent developments, problems of industrial control, and those of judicial supremacy; these sections will be found very stimulating.

Graves, W. Brooke: "The Future of the American States," *American Political Science Review,* XXX, No. 1 (February, 1936) 24-50.

Haines, Charles G.: *The American Doctrine of Judicial Supremacy* (2d ed., Berkeley, California, 1932); covers background and development of judicial review in the United States, including proposals to remedy its defects.

———: *The Revival of Natural Law Concepts* (Cambridge, Massachusetts, 1930), chaps. III-VIII and XII; these sections, though no more valuable than the rest of the study, are concerned with the effect of natural-law concepts on the theory and practice of American public law.

Holmes, Oliver Wendell: *The Dissenting Opinions of Mr. Justice Holmes* (New York, 1929), especially chap. III; this section deals with the issue of federal encroachment upon the states.

———: *Representative Opinions of Mr. Justice Holmes* (New York, 1931); chaps. II and VII deal with federalism and the regulation of public utilities.

Llewellyn, K. N.: "The Constitution as an Institution," 14 *Oregon Law Review,* 108 (December, 1934).

McBain, Howard L.: *The Living Constitution* (New York, 1927), chaps. I, II, and IV-VII; the sections cited from this valuable little book are concerned with the nature of constitutions, "government of laws," problems of the federal and presidential systems, and judicial control.

McCorkle, Stuart A.: "Our New Line of Federalism," *South West Social Science Quarterly*, XVI, No. 2 (September, 1935), 53–60.

McIlwain, Charles H.: "Government by Law," *Foreign Affairs*, XIV, No. 1 (January, 1936), 185–98.

McLaughlin, Andrew C.: *A Constitutional History of the United States* (New York, 1935); chaps. xiv, xv, xxiii, xxx, and xlix–li are concerned with the constitutional convention, the influence of Chief Justice Marshall, and the problems following the adoption of the Fourteenth Amendment.

Merriam, Charles E.: *The Written Constitution and the Unwritten Attitude* (New York, 1931); chaps. i and ii discuss a dynamic theory of the constitution and the new regionalism.

National Resources Committee: *Regional Factors in National Planning and Development* (U. S. Government Printing Office, Washington, D. C., 1935), especially Parts I and II, which state the ramifications of the problem of regionalism.

Odum, Howard W.: *Southern Regions of the United States* (Chapel Hill, North Carolina, 1936); chap. iii of this significant study discusses a new type of regional analysis used by the author.

Powell, Thomas R.: "Common Sense and the Constitution," *Current History*, XLIII, No. 5 (February, 1936), 484–89.

Spicer, George W.: "From Political Chief to Administrative Chief," *Essays on the Law and Practice of Governmental Administration*, edited by Charles G. Haines and Marshall E. Dimock (Baltimore, 1935); deals with the changed status of the governors of the several states.

Unsigned: "The Honorable Supreme Court," *Fortune*, XIII, No. 5 (May, 1936), 79 ff.

CHAPTER VII

☆ ☆ ☆

## SOCIAL REFORM AND THE CONSTITUTION

> "*The first requirement of the Constitution of a progressive society is that it keep pace with that society.*"
> —E. S. CORWIN

IN A MATURE COUNTRY, the extent of social legislation is an indicator of the people's democratic virility. When, in the development of social and economic institutions, need, injustice, or lack of opportunity appear, voters turn to government's ameliorating and protective powers for remedial legislation. The states exercise their police power. The federal government, chiefly through the commerce and taxation provisions, enacts laws which have the same effect as those enacted under the police power. Counties and municipalities pass zoning laws, provide for family welfare, make playgrounds and hospitals available. The list of what governments do to protect society's health, safety, morals, property interests, and aesthetic values is constantly growing. This is seemingly inevitable, because industrialization and urbanism multiply social needs.

<small>SOCIAL LEGISLATION AS AN INDEX</small>

Social legislation is not merely protective; it also creates higher standards of individual well-being and adds to the number of public assets. This is a very important side of the picture and one that is frequently overlooked. Social legislation usually suggests actual need and suffering. On the other hand, it is frequently progressive rather than merely of an emergency nature. Hence, there may be a national standard of education: all children under sixteen years of age must attend schools; all teachers must have the required credentials; and the federal government will step in and assist if localities fall below the established minimum.

Progressive standards apply to other fields, such as health, sanitation, fire protection, housing, and road building. Social legislation also adds to the number of public buildings, instructional agencies, recreation centers, and public services which are equally available to the entire public. The desirability of living in a particular community depends in large part upon the number and excellence of the parks, schools, libraries, museums, playgrounds, art galleries, swimming pools, and other amenities which are so essential to modern life. When used by large numbers of people, they can be provided and maintained at a lower average cost to the individual. The more such services a community provides and pays for, the greater the social assets of its citizens, for a person's total wealth consists of what he has accumulated, plus the *pro rata* portion of community property which is equally available for his enjoyment.

Social legislation sometimes represents a concession on the part of the dominant group exercising the greatest influence over the government. Legislation has to be fought for, in some cases, every inch of the way. Laws restricting the number of hours of work, or prohibitions against employing women or minors, usually meet with such resistance. Moreover, social legislation, like lawmaking generally, requires a sponsoring group. Enactments seeking to preserve nature's beauty spots require the united efforts of Isaak Walton Leagues and every other organization interested in getting the most enjoyment from the out-of-doors. The reason for resistance is that someone is affected adversely, or thinks he is, by every piece of social legislation. For example, one of the natural preserves just mentioned might very well have been the Cumberland Falls in Kentucky, where the Insull interests wanted to locate a hydroelectric generating plant, but after a bitter fight, the spot was finally set aside in perpetuity as a state park.

Social legislation differs from other enactments in that it evokes more of an instinctive, widespread public response than do other questions submitted to voters. Frequently it affects one's children, concern for whose well-being is a fundamental instinct. Public welfare legislation takes care of the needy and weak, appealing again to inherent familial and sympathetic responses; moreover, patriotic pride and altruism are both involved.

These matters are of great importance to political theory. Social legislation represents the people's efforts to achieve the goal of community. It is a democratic impulse. The readiness with which such legislation is secured is a good indicator of popular control over the instrumentalities of government. The widespread existence of social legislation makes one realize that self-interest and domination are by no means the only important aspects of government. There are interests which are broader and less well defined, but which, nevertheless, possess great vitality.

During the 150 years of its history, the Supreme Court of the United States has changed from a common-law court, trying cases which were of individual concern, to a truly constitutional court, deciding the country's most important social and economic issues.[1] It began in a basement; it now occupies a marble palace. Throughout most of its history, the court has been greatly overworked. The docket was never cleared at the end of the term. In recent years, however, Congress has taken steps to limit the amount of business going to the supreme tribunal, and some classes of cases coming under the court's original jurisdiction are now dealt with in lower federal courts. But the most important reform is that appeals can no longer be taken as a matter of right; they will be accepted only at the discretion of the justices after it has been made clear that a constitutional issue is involved. Speaking in the lawyer's terms, the writ of error is no longer used in state cases; appeals may be taken only by use of a writ of certiorari. This means that justices of the Supreme Court refuse to hear cases coming from lower federal courts or the highest tribunals of the states unless the controversy relates to a constitutional provision. The most important decisions, as we have said, usually turn on the due process of law clauses.

THE JUDICIARY AS UMPIRE

Between 1789 and 1803, the Supreme Court decided several important cases, but in no one of them was there a suggestion of judicial review of legislation. Then came *Marbury* vs. *Madison*, regarding which, it may be recalled, President Jefferson said, "The Federalists have retreated to the judiciary." Later, when tension over the slavery issue was at white heat, the court handed

[1] For its institutional development, see Frankfurter and Landis, *The Business of the Supreme Court.*

down the Dred Scott decision,[1] invalidating the Missouri Compromise. It had been hoped that this law would avert the threatened rift between the North and the South. In this instance, an anti-Federalist, Chief Justice Taney, handed down the decision. After the adoption of the Civil War amendments, as we have explained, judicial review took on new significance. It was directed at state legislation in particular; however, not all the decisions, by any means, restricted the state police power or the authority of Congress.

The importance of judicial review of legislation, as it developed in the period following the Civil War, lay in the court's assuming review power over all legislation, both state and federal. Thereafter, it was not only interpreter of the Constitution, but umpire of social reform. Whether a majority of the justices were conservatives or liberals, former corporation attorneys, or lawyers from rural communities became questions which people quite naturally looked into. The farmers feared the railways and the trusts, and business was desirous of maintaining or extending its scope of control and influence.

There has been a constant stream of judicial review of legislation since the Civil War. Unlike the earlier period, there have been no long breaks, but there have been terms when the court has been particularly active. Around 1890, several important cases were decided. In the decade before the World War, some of the most momentous decisions were handed down; immediately after that war there was a wave of review. Following this, constitutional lawyers and publicists began to wonder if judicial review was on the way out. There were few cases of invalidated social legislation. Justices were described as "docile" and the Supreme Court was thought to be going into its "twilight," but the prediction was premature. The court took on new force and importance after the advent of the "New Deal." In rapid succession, and with greater frequency than ever before in its history, the highest tribunal rendered null and void several of the principal measures which the administration had enacted to combat the depression. What will the future bring?

PERIODS OF JUDICIAL REVIEW

[1] 19 Howard 393 (1857); see McLaughlin, *A Constitutional History of the United States*, pp. 552-64.

The "commerce" power has become the most important one belonging to the federal government. This is entirely natural because the country's future is wrapped up in the relation between government and business. The working out of the relationship between social need and governmental response is strikingly illustrated in the history of the commerce power. For almost a hundred years after the Constitution was put into effect, the federal government made no positive use of its authority to regulate foreign and interstate commerce. Very few cases involving this power were decided by the courts. In *Gibbons* vs. *Ogden*,[1] John Marshall upheld federal authority over interstate navigation, when a monopoly granted by New York would have infringed upon that authority. But for the most part, cases such as *Cooley* vs. *Port Wardens*[2] sustained the right of the states to regulate commerce indirectly by means of their police power, so long as Congress did not choose to pass legislation covering the matter.

THE COMMERCE POWER

The passage of the Interstate Commerce Commission Act in 1887 marked the beginning of the present importance of the commerce power. Since that time, the courts have been called upon to define the line between state (intrastate) and federal (interstate) jurisdictions. This question remains one of the most important issues for future determination. The Shreveport Case[3] and the Minnesota Rate Cases[4] sustained the federal government's power as supreme when state laws caused discriminations which adversely affect interstate commerce. In actual effect, they extended national authority, and railway transportation is now almost entirely a federal concern. But in the first child-labor[5] and N.R.A. cases,[6] the decisions were adverse to federal power. In both cases, it was held that the national government was trying to control the manufacturing or production stage, whereas this control is reserved to the states. Interstate commerce begins only when a commodity is actually moving in traffic between states. Congress cannot reach back into the particular state and attempt to control the labor conditions and

[1] 9 Wheaton 1 (1824).      [2] 12 Howard 299 (1851).
[3] 234 U. S. 342 (1914).      [4] 230 U. S. 352 (1913).
[5] *Hammer* vs. *Dagenhart*, 247 U. S. 251 (1918).
[6] *Schechter Poultry Corp.* vs. *U. S.*, 295 U. S. 495 (1935).

processes which are involved in producing goods which are destined for shipment outside the state.

But are not these the very aspects of social reform which are most important? If state laws do not impose equal requirements upon industry, the efforts at control usually break down. Two manufacturers in different states, one of whom employs only adult labor and the other of whom employs minors, will soon find a disparity in their labor costs. Can public control of business practices or the rationalization of industry be expected to succeed unless business is considered a continuous process from production to consumption? To what extent are industrial conditions different now, compared to what they were when authority over commerce was parceled out between state and nation? The attempted extension of federal authority over industry will probably be the most important issue of the next generation. It is desirable, therefore, that independent analyses be made of the basic questions we have raised.[1]

As technological developments and improvements in transportation have occurred, the federal power over interstate commerce has received broader application. Not only are railways, motor trucks, and waterways subject to federal jurisdiction but so, too, are radio, interstate telegraphs, telephones, pipe lines, and the transmission of electrical energy.[2] Surely these matters are of great importance and cover a wide field. Is it not reasonable to expect the federal government to prove that its jurisdiction over transportation and electrical utilities can be effectively discharged before extending its power into the field of manufacture? But can "social security" be realized without coping with national problems of production, distribution, real wages, and social insurance through the only agency that is comprehensive enough, namely, the federal government?[3]

USES OF THE COMMERCE CLAUSE

---

[1] An excellent point of departure is the article by Thomas Reed Powell entitled, "The Scope of the Commerce Power," in the book edited by Haines and Dimock, entitled, *The Law and Practice of Governmental Administration*, pp. 197–226.
[2] There is a good brief analysis of the scope and limits of the federal commerce power in Benjamin A. Arneson, *Elements of Constitutional Law* (New York, 1928), chap. VI.
[3] This question is the main one considered in W. Y. Elliott's treatise, *The Need for Constitutional Reform*.

The federal authority over interstate commerce has been used for purposes closely resembling those served by the state police power. Laws of Congress have sometimes had the effect of prohibitions. Under the commerce power, the interstate transportation of liquor, lotteries, impure foods, and white slaves has been made illegal, and all the laws have been upheld by the Supreme Court of the United States. The Constitution has been stretched for the benefit of the community as well as for individuals resisting governmental interference.

From the commerce power is derived the "navigation" power. The federal government has jurisdiction over all "navigable" streams within the United States. This jurisdiction has been the means of greatly expanding federal power and authority. It makes possible the licensing and regulation of hydroelectric projects. The power over navigation was used in upholding the constitutionality of the Tennessee Valley Authority.[1] Upon it is placed the chief reliance at the present time for regional planning schemes. From the navigation power, federal jurisdiction over soil erosion and afforestation on watersheds has been further inferred. Unified control of soil, water, and power makes effective conservation of natural resources possible. Largely by the invention of legal fictions, the Constitution has been expanded to meet new needs.

NAVIGABLE WATERS

The commerce power has provided also the legal peg on which to hang legislation attempting to prevent business combinations in restraint of trade. The Sherman Anti-Trust Law was passed in 1890, followed by the Clayton Act and the Federal Trade Commission Act in 1914.[2] These legislative enactments represented the efforts of the community to keep business small, economic life competitive, and social life simple. Legally, they were justified as measures of preventing "restraints" upon commerce which the Constitution gave

ANTI-TRUST LEGISLATION

[1] 297 U. S. 288 (1936); also cf. the case of *Arizona* vs. *California*, 283 U. S. 423 (1931), upholding the Boulder Dam agreements.
[2] Cf. Milton Handler, *The Federal Anti-Trust Laws* (Chicago, 1932); Dexter Keezer and Stacy May, *The Public Control of Business* (New York, 1930); chaps. i–iv; J. M. Clark, *Social Control of Business* (Chicago, 1926); Myron W. Watkins, *Industrial Combinations and Public Policy* (Boston and New York, 1927); N. B. Gaskill, *The Regulation of Competition* (New York, 1936); and T. C. Blaisdell, *The Federal Trade Commission* (New York, 1932).

Congress power to regulate. Government's effort to stay economic forces, however, has been largely unavailing. The law states that *all* combinations in restraint of trade are illegal. Severe penalties, including dissolution of the combination and the assessment of triple damages, were provided. But what constitutes the offense mentioned in the Act was not defined. The lawmakers apparently assumed that restraint and conspiracy had been adequately defined in common-law decisions. For the first twenty years, the Sherman Act was applied by the courts rather literally and effectively. The high level was reached in 1911, when the Supreme Court ordered the dissolution of both the Standard Oil Trust and the American Tobacco Company combine. But in the Standard Oil case, the court introduced "the rule of reason."[1] Not all combinations are unreasonable and unlawful, argued the tribunal, but only those which by their practices and intentions produce results which are uneconomic. Henceforth, of course, illegality has depended upon the majority's opinion of what is unreasonable.

Three years after the Standard Oil decision, the Clayton Act was passed, supposedly strengthening the trust-breaking program, and the Federal Trade Commission Act created a commission by that name which was given the duties of preventing unfair methods of competition and serving as the administrative enforcement agency. Nevertheless, nothing seemed to retard the steady growth of nation-wide businesses. Then, in 1920, the original intentions of the legislation were practically nullified by the decision in the steel case.[2] The Supreme Court ruled that size is not a reliable test of the existence of unlawful restraint; for, as a matter of fact, consolidation may actually result in greater efficiency. Before there can be an unlawful restraint, there must be illegal acts. It needs to be shown, for example, that higher prices have resulted, that competition is actually (not merely potentially) lessened, and that the actions of the company are "unfair." Since this historic decision, the emphasis has been almost entirely upon acts of unfair competition, with size and potential danger left out of the picture.

[1] *Standard Oil Company* vs. *U. S.*, 221 U. S. 1 (1911).
[2] *U. S.* vs. *U. S. Steel Corporation*, 251 U. S. 417 (1920).

SOCIAL REFORM AND THE CONSTITUTION 195

The social objectives of the anti-trust laws have not been achieved. From that standpoint, they are "dead." The holding company device, banker control, and the services of trade associations all add to the concentration of control and the tendency to produce areas of inflexible prices. These new developments in the business world are not even touched by the anti-trust laws. If a trade association executive goes around quietly instructing all members to fix identical prices, competition is almost as effectively removed as though all units of the business were absorbed by the same corporation. The law as interpreted does not reach such practices. It would be almost impossible to enforce if it did.

Political demand for strong anti-trust laws remains constant. "Independents" on many fronts are on the retreat. They cry for the government's help to stop the concentration movement. Will it be given? Could it succeed? The answers to these questions will leave a deep mark on representative government in the United States.

Federal regulation of public utilities is based almost entirely upon the commerce power. State and federal control over public businesses frequently comes into conflict with the due-process clauses, and the results of judicial review are probably more widely criticized in this field than in any other. One reason for this is the failure of legislative bodies to define with sufficient clarity the rules of valuation and rate making which the regulatory bodies shall follow. This puts the responsibility up to the courts. Their efforts to define "the law of the land" for public utilities have been stumbling and inconsistent. The so-called "rule of valuation" laid down in *Smyth* vs. *Ames*,[1] for example, was no rule at all. It was merely an enumeration of a number of elements that, in the court's opinion, should be considered in arriving at a valuation figure. Hence, at various times courts have seemed to favor one or another of the three principal methods of valuation, namely, historical cost, prudent investment, or reproduction cost. The Interstate Commerce Commission had been making railway valuations for twenty-five years and then had all its work swept aside by a

PUBLIC CONTROL OF BUSINESS

[1] 169 U. S. 466 (1898).

single decision.[1] Rate disputes have been allowed to drag on for ten years and more.[2]

Public utilities are expected to earn "a fair return on a fair value," but the word "fair" is as vague as the word "reasonable." If either the valuation or the rate base fixed by the regulatory body is too low, in the utility's opinion, an appeal can be taken to the courts. They then decide whether the company's property is being taken without due process of law.

The courts are expected to decide some of the most technical questions of engineering and finance. For example, they may be called upon to determine whether the capital structure has been "watered." Is the depreciation reserve too high or too low? Under existing conditions in the investment business, what rate of return should gilt-edged utility stocks bear? If the courts make a mistake on the valuation or the rate of return, it frequently means a difference of millions of dollars in the pockets of either the users or the investors.[3]

In theory, the legislatures entrust regulatory powers to administrative tribunals, which supposedly have conclusive authority on questions of fact. But due process allows no immunity from review, from trial *de novo*. Administrative finality is on the decline. The judges substitute their own ideas of fairness for those of commissioners who are presumably "expert."[4] Public-utility regulation, as we shall see in a subsequent chapter, has produced results which leave much to be desired.

The vagueness and unpredictability of judicial construction of due process of law have severely handicapped the regulation of enterprises affected with a public interest. Due process also beclouds the question of how far governments may extend public control over businesses of considerable social importance. Clearly,

---

[1] *St. Louis & O'Fallon Ry. Co.* vs. *U. S.*, 279 U. S. 461 (1929).
[2] This was true in the New York Telephone case. See Felix Frankfurter, *The Public and Its Government* (New Haven and Oxford, 1930), pp. 94–108; the decision in *Lindheimer* vs. *Illinois Bell Tel. Co.*, 292 U. S. 151 (1934), is also illustrative.
[3] The financial results in the famous case of *Ohio Water Co.* vs. *Ben Avon Borough*, 253 U. S. 287 (1919), may be taken as an example. See John Dickinson, *Administrative Justice and the Supremacy of Law* (Cambridge, 1927), pp. 195–202.
[4] In addition to the Ben Avon and O'Fallon cases referred to in the preceding footnotes, see the more recent decisions of *Crowell* vs. *Benson*, 285 U. S. 22 (1932), and *West* vs. *Chesapeake and Potomac Tel. Co.*, 295 U. S. 662 (1935).

this is a matter of prime significance. If concentration continues, regulation will doubtless be extended; moreover, when regulation is not possible or successful, there is usually a demand for outright public ownership. The all-important question becomes, therefore, "How much freedom do legislatures have in declaring additional businesses to be 'affected with a public interest' and in making them subject to governmental regulation?" A definite answer cannot be given. Due process of law determines whether the attempted regulation is legal or unconstitutional. Since the case of *Munn* vs. *Illinois*,[1] a "business affected with public interest" has been subject to public regulation of its rates, service, and profits. During the last fifty years, the number of regulated undertakings has been added to rather considerably. When an enterprise is associated with transportation, when it has monopoly characteristics, when its indispensability to the business community or the general public is great, then public control is likely to be upheld by the courts.[2] It is not sufficient that a majority in the legislature should decide that regulation would be in the public interest. American law-making bodies, unlike those in other countries, cannot extend public control when and as they think best. The judiciary must be satisfied that regulation is really necessary. Otherwise, courts will hold the statute invalid as depriving the business of its property and private character without due process of law.

THE PUBLIC-UTILITY CATEGORY

The number of regulatory laws thrown out as invalid is not large, but their potential significance is very great. The legislature never knows when new extensions of public control will be ruled unconstitutional. Ice might be thought to constitute a public necessity, but a majority of the Supreme Court, against a vigorous dissent, held that it was essentially and unalterably private.[3] New York's millions became very much dissatisfied with the brokerage charges they had to pay to agents for theater tickets. The best seats can be purchased only from brokers, who are few in number.

[1] 94 U. S. 113 (1876).
[2] Cf. Walton Hamilton, "Affectation with Public Interest," *Yale Law Journal*, XXXIX (June, 1930), 1089, and B. P. McAllister, "Lord Hale and Business Affected with a Public Interest," *Harvard Law Review*, XLIII (March, 1930), 759.
[3] *New State Ice Co.* vs. *Liebmann*, 285 U. S. 262 (1932).

However, the country's highest court, again against a strong minority disagreement, held that theaters are inherently private.[1] They are luxuries rather than necessities. New Jersey attempted to regulate employment offices, on the theory that people out of work were in no position to protect themselves from exorbitant fees that might be asked. The Supreme Court ruled that the employment business is a private one and cannot be regulated.[2] Since that time, the employment business has become more and more a public responsibility, with a national network extending from local centers to the U. S. Employment Service.

There is a curious anomaly about the American constitutional system. In some cases regulation is not permitted because it is held to be an invasion of private ownership; on the other hand, the courts have established no limitations upon the state's power to buy and operate any business it chooses. Governments have more freedom to own than to regulate. What significance may this fact have for the future of American life? North Dakota went into the manufacturing, grain-elevator, insurance, and banking businesses, and its power to do so was upheld by the Supreme Court.[3] Recently, we as have seen, the federal government's entry into the generation, transmission, and sale of power was sustained by the highest court. However, there is this important difference between the T. V. A. and the North Dakota cases: the federal government may go into business only when the enterprise can be related to some express power or powers; the states and their subsidiaries, on the other hand, are free to undertake any enterprise authorized by legislation and not prohibited by constitution or charter.

ENTRY INTO BUSINESS

In his dissenting opinion in the Tyson case, Mr. Justice Holmes said:

> The proper course is to recognize that a state legislature can do whatever it sees fit to do unless it is restrained by some express prohibition in the Constitution of the United States or of the state. . . . Courts should be careful not to extend such prohibitions beyond their obvious meaning by reading into them conceptions of public policy that the particular court may happen to entertain. . . .

[1] *Tyson* vs. *Banton*, 273 U. S. 418 (1927).
[2] *Ribnik* vs. *McBride*, 277 U. S. 350 (1928). [3] *Green* vs. *Frazier*, 253 U. S. 233 (1920).

The New York milk case,[1] decided since that time, seems to accept substantially the Holmes position. In this decision, the state's right to control milk prices and virtually regiment the business, was upheld. These extensive powers were permitted without actually declaring dairying a public utility. The court said that a "state is free to adopt whatever economic policy may reasonably be deemed to promote the public welfare." Does this mean that hereafter the courts will take an "economic" rather than a purely legal view of "business affected with a public interest"?

Both the commerce clause and the anti-trust laws have an important bearing upon the interests of organized labor. In the famous Debs case,[2] for example, obstruction of interstate commerce and of carrying the mail were grounds given by the court for issuing an injunction against the union in the serious Pullman strike of 1894. After the passage of the Sherman Act, a boycott by the Danbury Hatters' Union was held to be a violation of the Anti-Trust Act and triple damages were assessed.[3] Prior to that time, labor did not suspect that the law preventing combinations was applicable to their activities. One reason for the enactment of the Clayton Act was that organized labor wanted it made clear that its activities were exempt from the application of the monopoly laws. Their efforts were of no avail. Labor won the legislative fight but lost the court test. The Duplex Printing Company[4] decision held that a secondary boycott was not permitted by the Clayton Act.

THE INTERESTS OF ORGANIZED LABOR

The injunction has been the bane of labor's existence. The usual ground for granting it is that someone's property is being threatened with "irreparable damage." Contrary to the practice in the cases involving corporate combinations, the threat may be potential as well as actual.[5] Since the passage of the Norris Anti-Injunction Act a few years ago, however, the use of this weapon

[1] *Nebbia* vs. *New York*, 291 U. S. 502 (1934).
[2] *In re Debs*, 158 U. S. 564 (1895).
[3] *Lawlor* vs. *Loewe*, 235 U. S. 522 (1915); cf. Edward Berman, *Labor and the Sherman Act* (New York and London, 1930); and Alpheus Mason, *Organized Labor and the Law* (Durham, N. C., 1925).
[4] *Duplex Printing Co.* vs. *Deering*, 254 U. S. 443 (1920).
[5] This whole question is dealt with by Felix Frankfurter and James M. Landis in *The Labor Injunction* (New York, 1930).

against organized labor has been greatly restricted; moreover, the employer's right to prosecute unions for torts, even though the union is unincorporated,¹ has been offset by the incorporated union's right to request and be granted an injunction against the employer.²

Due process has been of greatest importance in cases involving legislation restricting the hours of work or giving special consideration to women workers. The judiciary has exercised broad discretion and has checked the legislatures when it has thought they had gone too far. A Utah law limiting the hours of labor for men engaged in mining was upheld.³ Although the owners contended that an eight-hour maximum day violated their property rights and freedom of contract, the Supreme Court ruled that mining was a dangerous employment and, hence, could be regulated under the police power. Seven years later, however, the same court declared unconstitutional a New York statute limiting bakers to a ten-hour day. In the famous Lochner case,⁴ the state argued that baking is a dangerous employment, for men tending ovens are subject to respiratory troubles and their vitality is lowered; moreover, it was contended that their health is extremely important, because they handle a food product in universal use. The majority of the Supreme Court thought otherwise. Baking, they said, is no more hazardous than many other occupations and, hence, does not need the protection of the police power. Is this adjudication, policy making, or fact finding?

HOUR RESTRICTION AND WOMEN WORKERS

The most famous case concerning women in industry resulted from the District of Columbia minimum wage.⁵ The legislation provided that a board should fix minimum wages for all women gainfully employed. The Supreme Court case involved a woman employed as an elevator operator. It was particularly interesting because the government submitted a long brief dealing with the

[1] *United Mine Workers* vs. *Coronado Coal Co.*, 259 U. S. 344 (1922).
[2] *Texas & N. O. Ry. Co.* vs. *Railway Clerks*, 281 U. S. 548 (1930); see Alpheus Mason, "Organized Labor as a Party Plaintiff in Injunction Cases," *Columbia Law Review*, XXX (April, 1930), 466.
[3] *Holden* vs. *Hardy*, 169 U. S. 366 (1898).
[4] *Lochner* vs. *New York*, 198 U. S. 45 (1905).
[5] *Adkins* vs. *Children's Hospital*, 261 U. S. 525 (1923).

sociological aspects of woman labor. Their contention was that the future of the race and feminine independence and morality depend upon woman's being given a living wage and hours that are not injurious. The majority of the Supreme Court, however, found that the law was too comprehensive, that elevator operators do not require protective legislation, that the relation between a living wage and morals is a doubtful argument, and, hence, invalidated the entire law. The sociologists were wrong! The police power bowed to due process![1]

The taxing power is an important means of regulation and social amelioration. At first this seems surprising. Is not the purpose of taxation that of securing revenues to run the government?

TAXATION AS A SOCIAL INSTRUMENT

True, but taxation may be used to level down differences in economic status and to drive out articles of trade which are injurious to the community. The federal government, moreover, has extended the power as far as permitted, because through it Congress hoped to attack problems which could be dealt with in no other way. When problems are numerous and powers are few, lawmakers must needs be ingenious about making the best use of express provisions! Some of these legislative efforts have succeeded and others have failed.

The first income-tax law was upheld by a majority of the Supreme Court.[2] The legislation was bitterly fought, because the income tax is one of the best instruments for levelling vast financial aggregations and for taxing according to ability to pay. Fourteen years later, Congress enacted another income-tax law. This one was declared unconstitutional by a divided court.[3] The income tax, held the majority, is in reality a tax upon the property itself and not merely upon the use of the property; hence, it is a direct tax. The Constitution provides that direct taxes must be apportioned according to population. As this was not, it was invalid.

---

[1] Citing this case as the precedent, a majority of the Court recently held that the New York minimum-wage law was likewise unconstitutional. In view of this decision, the constitutional validity of all minimum-wage legislation is doubtful, at least while the personnel of the Court remains unchanged. *Morehead* vs. *Tipaldo*, 56 Supreme Court 918 (1936).
[2] *Springer* vs. *U. S.*, 102 U. S. 586 (1880).
[3] *Pollock* vs. *Farmer's Loan and Trust Co.*, 158 U. S. 601 (1895).

It was necessary to pass the Sixteenth Amendment, declaring that income taxes need not be apportioned, in order to overcome the objections of the Supreme Court. The two income-tax decisions and the Legal Tender Cases represent the clearest instances in all constitutional history of the Supreme Court's reversing itself.[1] During the time between the two decisions, changes in court membership had occurred, which seems to have some presumptive importance.

The federal taxing power has made possible the expansion of federal authority. In John Marshall's famous opinion in the case of *McCulloch* vs. *Maryland*,[2] the right of Congress to charter a national bank was upheld as a power properly implied, and the rule was laid down that states may not tax any federal instrumentality. Conversely, the federal government does not tax state property. "The power to tax is the power to destroy." The case of *Veazie Bank* vs. *Fenno*,[3] decided soon after the close of the Civil War, involved the power of Congress to place a heavy tax upon state banknotes. It was argued that the tax would have the effect of driving them out of existence. As a matter of fact, this was the intention. The Supreme Court ruled that the federal government would clearly derive revenue from the Act and that it saw no reason to go into any other motive that Congress might have had. Federal control over banking has expanded ever since this decision.

"THE POWER TO DESTROY"

The oleomargarine case is of similar import. Congress laid a heavy tax on oleomargarine colored to look like butter, clearly intending to destroy the business. Whether Congress viewed the tax as a health measure or whether it was dictated by dairying interests is difficult to say. At any rate, the Supreme Court upheld the tax,[4] again ruling that intention was immaterial. Similarly, the control of narcotics by taxation was considered a proper measure.[5] The second child labor law met a different fate. Having failed in its effort to tie its earlier measure to the commerce clause, Congress imposed a tax on the net profits of estab-

[1] Cf. Charles G. Haines, *A Government of Laws or a Government of Men* (Los Angeles, 1929), pp. 16–18.
[2] 4 Wheaton 316 (1819).     [3] 8 Wallace 533 (1869).
[4] *McCray* vs. *U. S.*, 195 U. S. 27 (1904).     [5] *U. S.* vs. *Doremus*, 249 U. S. 86 (1919).

lishments operating in interstate commerce which employed children. The Supreme Court found the same fatal objections to the second effort as it did in the earlier case. It held that whether a commodity has been produced by children or by adults can be ascertained only by observing the manufacturing process, that Congress has no control over production, and that therefore the tax is an infringement upon state authority over commerce within its borders.[1] In this case, Congress's intention was the deciding factor. Can the holding be reconciled with the oleomargarine, narcotics, and banknotes cases? One thing seems clear: there was greater presumption for upholding child-labor legislation under the taxing power than under the commerce clause.

Taxation is used to fight large business combinations, particularly chain stores. For example, progressive taxes have been imposed upon chain grocery combines, the amount of the levy increasing in relation to the number of stores within the state. Such measures have generally been sustained when their validity has been judicially tested.[2] Apparently, the ulterior motive is not always subject to judicial cognizance.

The principal limitation upon the taxing power is that it must be for "a public purpose." This rule of due process also allows much leeway for judicial discretion. When the city of Topeka, Kansas, attempted to raise taxes for the purpose of giving financial assistance to a new manufacturing concern, on the ground that the new business increased local prosperity and the tax base, the Supreme Court ruled that the purpose was improper. When the federal government imposed a tax on the processing of farm products and impounded the receipts to be turned back pro rata to the farmers, the highest court held that the law was not a bona fide tax measure and declared the entire Agricultural Adjustment Administration Act unconstitutional.[3]

LIMITATIONS ON THE TAXING POWER

Courts are usually liberal about laws involving financial matters. Since taxes are the life blood of government, and public

[1] *Bailey* vs. *Drexel Furniture Co.*, 259 U. S. 20 (1922).
[2] *State Board of Tax Commissioners* vs. *Jackson*, 283 U. S. 527 (1931); cf. *Louis K. Liggett* vs. *Lee*, 288 U. S. 517 (1932).
[3] 297 U. S. 1 (1936).

authority cannot continue without money, courts are hesitant about upsetting the financial apple cart. This may be seen in the already famous "gold-clause" case.[1] Early in the Roosevelt administration, the dollar was devalued in terms of gold content. Holders of securities issued prior to devaluation brought suit to recover the shrinkage attributable to the country's having "gone off gold." The stakes involved were of staggering proportions. Repayment of a hundred billion dollars worth of obligations in terms of gold at the old content of the dollar would have added about 70 per cent to the debtor's burden, wrecked federal finance, and destroyed most of the benefits derived from the recovery measures. The plaintiffs relied upon the "contract clause" of the federal Constitution, which guarantees the inviolability of all contracts. A promise to pay an obligation in gold, they argued, cannot be changed by legislative fiat.

THE "GOLD-CLAUSE" CASE

The Supreme Court, in a five-to-four decision, ruled that no recourse lay to the Court of Claims for holders of private securities. The gold contract did not hold. Irrespective of how the Court might have decided if the Constitution and the precedents had been strictly followed, the decision was clearly a "practical" one. Payment in gold was impossible, because it had ceased to be currency; however, the court apparently left open the door to holders of government bonds in case it could be shown that their losses were other than "nominal."

Professor Elliott has described amusingly but pointedly the situation which existed prior to the Court's "gold-clause" decision:

> Most foreigners and many Americans were astonished to learn, at the dawn of 1935, that an economic issue affecting values of astronomical proportions was presently to be decided by a majority of nine elderly lawyers in Washington. To foreigners the thing seemed monstrous. "Yet you call yourselves a democratic country!" they said. "How can you keep up the pretence when you entrust to a court such a decision—one that may add sixty-nine billions of dollars or more to the debts of the American people? Are not these judges appointed for life and practically irremovable? Do they understand the vast and complicated

[1] *Norman* vs. *Baltimore & Ohio Ry.*, 294 U. S. 240 (1935).

problems of monetary policy in our present world? Are they really responsible to anyone but their own consciences? A 'democracy'—fantastic!"[1]

Yet this is the situation which obtains every time the highest courts of the land pass upon social legislation of far-reaching import to the well-being and future of American citizens.

The commerce, taxing, and police powers are the principal ones through which social reforms may be accomplished. The federal government's authority over interstate commerce and its taxing powers have been used in such a way that they amount to a national police power. In recent decisions of the Supreme Court, however, it seems apparent that the judges are unwilling to assume responsibility for further expansions of federal power by means of judicial construction. They have made it plain that if the people want Washington to have more authority, the voters should amend or reform the Constitution.

IS REFORM NECESSARY?

Said Chief Justice Hughes in the N.R.A. case:

If the commerce clause were construed to reach all enterprises and transactions which could be said to have an indirect effect upon interstate commerce, the federal authority would embrace practically all the activities of the people, and the authority of the State over its domestic concerns would exist only by sufferance of the federal government. ... It is not the province of the Court to consider the economic advantages or disadvantages of such a centralized system. It is sufficient to say that our Federal Constitution does not provide for it.[2]

There is much to be said in favor of restricting the judiciary to a strictly legal role. Apparently this is the attitude and determination of the highest court of the land. If it continues the people are faced with the alternatives of amendment or reform in the event that they want twentieth-century government for twentieth-century problems. One possibility is the reform of the Court's powers or other parts of its structure. The other alternative is to change the total distribution of powers between state and nation. Either one would require a constitutional convention or the use of the amending process.

[1] W. Y. Elliott, *The Need for Constitutional Reform* (McGraw-Hill, New York, 1935), p.151.
[2] The Schechter case, 295 U. S. 546 and 549 (1935).

The amending of the federal Constitution was clearly intended to be a difficult procedure. The British and French constitutions can be amended by a majority vote in the two houses of their national legislatures. In the United States, however, adoption of an amendment by both houses of Congress, followed by ratification by three-fourths of the states represents a conservative limitation upon majority rule. On the other hand, it has been demonstrated that when there is a strong demand for a constitutional amendment, the actual time necessary for adoption need not be very long. This is illustrated in the cases of the Eleventh and Twenty-first amendments. On the other hand, the Eighteenth and Nineteenth amendments required the strenuous efforts of their proponents for over a generation before success was achieved. But it is not the ease or difficulty with which individual proposals can be added to the basic law that constitutes the acid test of institutional fitness. The real question is whether the constitutional adjustments necessitated by changed social conditions are made effective without undue delay. It is to be expected that there will be a certain amount of social lag. The difficulty of amendment makes the lag period longer than would otherwise be the case.

THE AMENDING PROCESS

In 150 years, eleven amendments have been added to the federal Constitution. The Bill of Rights is really a part of the original document because Jefferson secured agreement to its provisions before the Constitution was finally ratified, and the adoption of the first ten amendments was taken care of by the First Congress. Between 1789 and the Civil War, there were only two additions; from 1860 to 1900, three amendments were adopted; and six have been ratified since the turn of the century. Of these six, four have been added in the last twenty years. The average rate of constitutional amendment has been one in fifteen years; in the last generation, it has been one in five years. This may suggest that the need for constitutional change has become increasingly apparent.

The eleven amendments which have been adopted since the Bill of Rights may be conveniently classified under four headings: machinery, powers, rights and privileges of citizenship, and governmental immunities. There is only one amendment which falls into the last-mentioned category: the Eleventh provided that no state shall be sued without its consent. This amendment was adopted a short time after the case of *Chisholm* vs. *Georgia*,[1] which excited fear in the several states that the federal courts might be used by citizens to invade sovereign immunities. The Twelfth Amendment changed the procedure in electing the President and, hence, represented an alteration in machinery. The Thirteenth, Fourteenth, and Fifteenth amendments added to the rights and privileges of citizens. The Sixteenth dealt with the income tax and was an addition to federal power. The Seventeenth provided for the direct election of Senators, a change in governmental machinery. The Eighteenth Amendment, establishing national prohibition, constituted an accretion of power. The Nineteenth gave the franchise to women, extending to a large bloc of the population the privileges of citizenship. The Twentieth did away with the "lame-duck" session of Congress—a mechanical alteration. The Twenty-first nullified the prohibition amendment, and, hence, was a change in governmental powers.

ANALYSIS OF AMENDMENTS

Three amendments, the Twelfth, Seventeenth, and Twentieth, have dealt with governmental machinery. A like number, the Sixteenth, Eighteenth, and Twenty-first, have been concerned with powers. Four amendments, the Thirteenth, Fourteenth, Fifteenth, and Nineteenth, have added to the rights and privileges of citizenship. One, the Eleventh, has created a governmental immunity. Since the Eighteenth and Twenty-first amendments canceled each other, there have been only nine amendments added to the permanent constitutional edifice in 150 years of American history.

A sound rule of constitutional government is that the basic charter should contain only matters of prime importance, namely, principles of government and protections to citizen rights. The federal Constitution comes close to satisfying this standard. A perfect record is spoiled by the Eighteenth and Twenty-first amendments, which represent restrictive legislation. They are concerned

[1] 2 Dallas 419 (1790).

with people's personal habits and, therefore, fall into the same category as do laws affecting eating and recreation. Compared to most state constitutions, however, the federal charter is superior indeed. State constitutions are almost invariably too long, too detailed, and contain much that belongs in the statute books rather than in the basic law.

No one of the federal amendments is a fundamental principle of constitutional government. This is not to belittle their importance. The amendments which have been added to protect human liberties are the most important ones. The others are chiefly concerned with mechanical changes which have little, if any, bearing upon governmental principle. Basic matters are exemplified by the separation of powers, federalism, cabinet responsibility, and judicial review of legislation. No amendment of this type has yet been adopted.

One possible way of adding to federal authority would be to adopt an amendment to Congress's enumerated powers giving the national authority jurisdiction of a broad character. Such an amendment has already been discussed and written about.[1] It would not be necessary to alter by specific reference the division of authority between the states and the national government; for example, Congress might have power "to pass all laws necessary for the social security of the individual and the economic stability of the country." A clause as sweeping as this would make the federal government virtually unlimited; however, it is an example of how fundamental change might be brought about with a minimum of textual addition or modification. Similarly, a clause might be drafted which would secure the essentials of responsible party government. However, this would be more difficult to do without modifying existing provisions.

EXPANSION OF FEDERAL POWER

A more far-reaching and continuous method of constitutional reform would be to adopt an amendment stipulating that a con-

[1] Lloyd Garrison, of the University of Wisconsin Law School, has suggested the following amendment: "Congress shall have power to promote the economic welfare of the United States by such laws as in its judgment are appropriate, and to delegate such power in whole or in part to the states. Existing state powers are not affected by this Article, except as Congress may occupy a particular field."

stitutional convention should be called at stated intervals, say every twenty years. Such a procedure would be particularly beneficial to state governments. The calling of the convention should be made mandatory. The delegates might adjourn after having concluded that minor, if any, changes were required. Even so, this would be a good investment of public money. Proposed reforms should be submitted in advance of the convention, giving the people a chance to think about the issues and providing the delegates with an opportunity to sound out public sentiment. Naturally, all delegates should be elected by popular vote. There should be a requirement that any changes proposed by the constitutional convention would require approval of the people at the polls. Legislatures should not be permitted to exercise this power, because some proposed changes might deal with the organization and relationships of the popular assembly. Such a system would encourage the careful and periodic consideration of basic governmental questions, would be an educational force of considerable importance, would do away with the complaints of those who say that constitutions are rigid and belong to the "horse-and-buggy" age, and yet would be surrounded with sufficient checks to give reasonable assurance that ill-considered or precipitate alterations would not be rushed through.

[sidenote: PERIODIC CONSTITUTIONAL CONVENTIONS]

At various times since Theodore Roosevelt's presidency, there have been proposals to limit the powers of the Supreme Court. For that matter, dissatisfaction with the judiciary's influence goes back to the early years of the nineteenth century. The number of justices on the Supreme Court bench has been added to in an effort to produce a majority favorable to the administration's program. This is theoretically possible at any time, and is a powerful reserved weapon; moreover, the President has the power of filling vacancies, an important means of controlling the judiciary. Executives see to it that judges are elevated who share their economic and social views. In more than one way, Mr. Dooley was right when he observed, "The Supreme Court follows the election returns."

[sidenote: PROPOSALS TO LIMIT THE SUPREME COURT]

There is no question that the Supreme Court is responsive to strong popular approval or disapproval; moreover, the tribunal is influenced considerably by current thinking and trends in the social, economic, and political fields. Most of the justices are assiduous readers. The influence of the average age of Supreme Court members is usually made too much of; Hughes, Brandeis, Cardozo, and Stone, for example, are certainly young in their outlooks and mental vitality.

What is to be done if the judiciary refuses to assume further responsibility for expanding the Constitution to meet new conditions? How can five-to-four decisions be justified? Will a democratic people long permit so few men to pass finally on the most vital social questions affecting the future of the country?

The objection to decisions by a bare majority might be met by requiring at least two-thirds agreement among the membership of the court. If there were nine members, as at present, this provision would mean that six justices must be in agreement before an act could be declared unconstitutional. Certainly, most people readily agree that five-to-four decisions are unsatisfactory; moreover, a number of the most important cases have been decided on this slender margin.[1] When one of these cases goes against the general public's interests, there cannot help but be disappointment and resentment openly expressed. A change to the two-thirds rule would assure a judicial veto when there was no question about unconstitutionality, and yet prevent some reversals which merely reflect the majority's doubt and differences due to their views on economics and government. It would take away much of the policy power from the courts and restore it to the legislature and the voters.

Another possible limitation would be to authorize Congress to re-enact any law declared unconstitutional whenever a two-thirds vote could be secured in both houses of Congress. So large a majority would be reasonably sure proof that the measure was really needed and demanded. "Whose government is it," people ask, "the people's or

LEGISLATIVE POWER OF RE-ENACTMENT

[1] Cf. "Judgments of the Supreme Court Rendered by a Majority of One," *Georgetown Law Journal*, XXIV (May, 1936), 984; Robert E. Cushman, "Constitutional Decisions by a Bare Majority of the Court," *Michigan Law Review*, XIX (June, 1921), 771; Felix Frankfurter, "The United States Supreme Court Moulding the Constitution," *Current History*, XXXII (May, 1930), 235.

the courts'?" Chief Justice Hughes, as Governor of New York, once said, "We are under a Constitution, but the Constitution is what the judges say it is." Repassage of a law by a two-thirds vote would restore the government to today's electorate. The Supreme Court would still have a great deal of preventive power. This proposal, however, is objectionable on the ground that laws repassed after a judicial decision could not help but hurt the prestige of the judiciary. It is of the nature of courts to be final. If either the legislative or executive branch were able to change its decisions, courts would lose one of their essential characteristics. Any reform dealing with judicial review should aim to increase the objectivity and prestige of the judiciary, not expose it to possible disparagement.

Several foreign jurists have expressed the wish that judicial review might be limited to procedural matters and to the protection of individual liberties, and still not be concerned with social legislation involving highly controversial matters.[1] Is a limitation of cases which courts will review a possible method of constitutional reform? The compromise is an attractive one, if it could only be made to work; but due process of law is the stumbling block. Even though Congress and the state legislatures were to amend the judicial statutes in such a way as greatly to restrict the review powers of the highest courts, the tribunals could still bring up cases and examine into their conformity with the due-process clauses. That is, of course, unless these provisions were to be removed by constitutional amendment. Still another possibility is that judges might limit their own review powers, but this seems quite improbable.

The most drastic reform would be to amend the Constitution in such a way that all power of judicial review over congressional legislation would be prohibited. This suggestion sounds radical to us Americans; but, after all, it is nothing more nor less than the rule which exists in most countries outside the United States. It would mean the acceptance of the principle of legislative supremacy. The people's elected representatives would be able to shape social destinies by expanding or altering the Constitution as the

[1] Cf. Charles G. Haines, *The American Doctrine of Judicial Supremacy*, pp. 505–31.

necessity and desire therefor arose. We would then be much nearer to popular self-government and democratic control than we are now. Do the people want it? Are we capable of it?

Irrespective of whether the judicial power is curbed or which of several alternatives is adopted, it is important that the improvement of public confidence in the objectivity of judges be made a prominent consideration. A distinguished French professor, Edouard Lambert, has pointed out that judicial review of legislation results in the Supreme Court's being drawn into the center of the political arena, where passions run high and powerful groups are resentful, no matter which way the decision goes.[1] This is inevitable, he says, so long as courts are called upon to be social umpires and expanders of the fundamental law. Judges can be objective only when they are relieved of the responsibility of shaping social and economic policy. If they permit themselves to make policy, they cannot expect the respect and deference due to men who hold the scales of justice.

An ideal constitutional system is one in which there is a full and immediate response to the people's will, yet one in which government operates through established legal principles. Can this compromise be effected more satisfactorily than it is at present?

SELECTED READINGS

Beard, Charles A.: "Social Change v. the Constitution," *Current History*, XLIV, No. 4 (July, 1935), 345–52.
Brown, R. A.: "Due Process of Law, Police Power, and the Supreme Court," 40 *Harvard Law Review* 943 (May, 1929).
———, and Hall, H. L.: "The Police Power and Economic Reconstruction," 1 *Chicago Law Review* 224 (November, 1933).
Cohen, Morris R.: *Law and the Social Order* (New York, 1933); a collection of essays included here because it embodies a stimulating philosophy of the nature and function of legal institutions.
Corwin, Edward S.: *The Commerce Power versus State Rights* (Princeton, 1936); argues the thesis that as a result of Supreme Court interpretation, the Constitution not only does not mean what it did originally, but is inadequate to meet the demands of the modern day.

[1] Edouard Lambert, *Le Gouvernement des Juges et la Lutte Contre la Legislation Social aux États-Unis* (Paris, 1921), pp. 234–36.

Corwin, Edward S.: "Social Planning Under the Constitution—A Study in Perspectives," *American Political Science Review*, XXVI, No. 1 (February, 1932), 1–27.

———: *The Twilight of the Supreme Court* (New Haven, 1934); a history of American constitutional theory, with particular emphasis upon the potentialities of the federal spending power.

Cushman, Robert E.: "Constitutional Decisions by a Bare Majority of the Court," 19 *Michigan Law Review* 771 (June, 1921).

Dickinson, John: "The Constitution and Progress," *Annals*, CLXXXI (September, 1935), 11–18.

Frankfurter, Felix: "Social Issues Before the Supreme Court," *Yale Review*, XXII, No. 3 (Spring, 1933), 476–95.

———: "United States Supreme Court Moulding the Constitution," *Current History*, XXXII, No. 2 (May, 1930), 235–40.

Garrison, Lloyd K.: "The Constitution and Social Progress," 8 *American Law School Review*, 486 (May, 1936).

Goodnow, Frank J.: *Social Reform and the Constitution* (New York, 1911), chaps. I, V, VI, VII, and VIII; though written many years ago, is none the less valuable; chapters cited are concerned with the constitutional aspects of government ownership, regulation, taxation, and the exercise of the spending power for social purposes.

Holmes, Oliver Wendell: *The Dissenting Opinions of Mr. Justice Holmes* (New York, 1929), especially chaps. I and IV; opinions here mentioned cover questions of social experimentation and the usurpation of power.

———: *Representative Opinions of Mr. Justice Holmes* (New York, 1931); chaps. I, III, and VIII include opinions on such issues as legislative freedom, trade combinations, and state taxation.

Lerner, Max: "The Supreme Court and American Capitalism," 42 *Yale Law Journal* 668 (March, 1933).

McAllister, B. P.: "Public Purpose in Taxation," 18 *California Law Review* 136 ff., 241 ff. (January, March, 1930).

Pound, Roscoe: "The Constitution in the Light of To-day," 68 *U. S. Law Review* 304 (June, 1934).

Powell, T. R.: "Constitutional Reform," 8 *American Law School Review* 472 (May, 1936).

———: "The Constitution and Social Security," *Annals*, CLXXXI (September, 1935), 147–58.

———: "The Scope of the Commerce Power," in *Essays on the Law and Practice of Governmental Administration*, Charles G. Haines and Marshall E. Dimock, eds. (Baltimore, 1935).

Reed, Thomas H.: ed., "The Constitution in the 20th Century," *Annals*, CLXXXV (May, 1936), *passim*.

Rohlfing, Charles C., and others: *Business and Government* (Chicago,

1934), chaps. I, II, XIII–XV, XVII–XXIV, XXVI, and XXVII; written from the point of view of the economist, these sections deal with constitutional protection of business, taxation, and labor problems.

Sayre, F. B.: "Labor and the Courts," 39 *Yale Law Journal* 682 (March, 1930).

Twentieth Century Fund: *Labor and the Government* (New York, 1935), chaps. VI–X and XII–XIV; these sections are concerned with the problems of industrial disputes, including past and present intervention by the government.

Witte, E. E.: "The Federal Anti-Injunction Act," 16 *Minnesota Law Review* 638 (May, 1932).

CHAPTER VIII

☆ ☆ ☆

## THE ENDS OF THE STATE

*"The ultimate problem of political theory is one of ends and not of means."*
—G. D. H. COLE

IN THE COURSE of this functional treatment of modern politics, several points have been raised which need to be brought together before continuing into the treatment of administration in this age of complexity. We have pointed out that the *raison d'être* of government is rule and service, with the latter playing an increasingly important part, and that the great problem is one of preserving individual freedom while state activity is increasing. Discussing a number of alternatives, we have emphasized the American social-democratic view of the function of government as the guaranty of equality of opportunity, a view in which the desires of the people and the ability of government to fulfill them are the only proper limits on the "proper" activities of the state. The intervening chapters have dealt with the difficulties of carrying on these functions in a democracy of which industrialism and urbanism are the dominant features, and they have discussed the adequacy of our constitutional representative system, as used at present, for fulfilling the needs of the people. Implicit in all these issues is a question touched on intermittently during the discussion: what is the objective of state action, to what purpose these services which have received so much of our attention? We cannot leave our treatment of modern politics without dealing with this problem.

Government, the instrumentality of the state, is neither good nor bad. It is both admired and hated. At its worst, it is tyranny; but at its best, it is social co-operation and makes possible the good life. It may be used for selfish purposes and to oppress the populace, or it may be the means of securing liberty and equality. The massed power and passion of a people sometimes take the form of destructive

THE NATURE OF GOVERNMENT

warfare; but, on the other hand, public authority preserves peace and order. The abuse of power may lead to injustice, but more frequently the public umpire helps to secure fair settlements. Government, like individuals, is a combination of opposites and of in-betweens.

When oppression has existed for a long time or it seems impossible that justice can ever prevail, people become cynical about the role of government. They begin to think that it has an inherent nature, is the instrument of the oppressor, and they regard government as brute force; to them it is asocial and amoral. "Since government cannot become anything else," they argue, "it had better be destroyed."[1] The community life would then revolve around social groupings nearer to the people and be nonpolitical in character.

Government has no fixed, unalterable nature, nor are the ends which it serves inherent or predestined. It is no more inevitable that political power should be used for oppression than that it should be the servant of justice. There is no miraculous life energy which irresistibly carries government toward the goal of community. What government does and becomes depends upon many factors, such as racial homogeneity, freedom from foreign oppression, the social characteristics of the folkways, the type of religion, the distribution of wealth, the nature of the leadership, and the dominant political myths and traditions.

It is likewise a mistake to think that government is merely "social action," and it is erroneous to consider it an end product, a dynamic control which has no roots or permanence. The institution of government is not superficial and transitory. The relation between government and society is better thought of as one of interaction, rather than as a superstructure on top of a bedrock foundation. Government appears in the roles of both controller and controlled. What it does and does not do leaves a deep mark on the ideology, attitudes, traditions, and economic well-being of the people. All the basic social factors are molded by government

[1] The ideas of the anarchists and syndicalists are explained by Francis W. Coker in *Recent Political Thought* (New York, 1934), chaps. vii and viii; for a more extensive treatment of political philosophies, see William A. Dunning, *A History of Political Theories*, 3 vols. (New York, 1902–20).

while they in turn furnish the motive power and problems which cause the political mechanism to run.

The state is the total political community, of which the government is but the instrument. The ends of the state consist of the persistent desires and aspirations of the people. How do we know that they exist? Their reality can be seen in the literature, song, religion, and political behavior of any nation. The ends of the state may be studied in the history of ideas. They are a composite of tradition, attitude, emotion, myth, and rational desire. The ends of the state are like a people's ideology; they commonly crystallize by a gradual process, though at times they rapidly take form. The French Revolution and the American Declaration of Independence are examples in point. In periods of great emotional excitement and spiritual exaltation, men's political ideals become fixed and lead them on through life. Their sons become inheritors of these visions and aspirations. During the new generation's lifetime, the national ideology may be changed somewhat, as new needs or great emotional crises arise; but the main body of crystallized sentiment moves on.

The larger the government the more influential these myths of the people become. One would hardly use the expression, "the ends of the municipality." The local government is too near at hand, too observable, too practical. True, people sometimes idealize it, but they are more likely to do so with something far away. The state is remote, all-inclusive, easily turned into a myth. It is associated with the patriotic fervor which nations cultivate from the earliest days of its citizens' childhood.

In a way, it is unfortunate that so much of our thought and attention are lavished on the national entity. No doubt we emphasize the state partly because it is far away, symbolic, and, hence, readily idealized. Political scientists are swept away by these same influences. The consequence is that we are inclined to overemphasize some aspects of government and not give sufficient attention to others. National governments involve the struggle of classes, the competitions of élites, war and peace, diplomacy—all very colorful and exciting. Local governments are more prosaic; they are concerned with street paving, water supply, garbage collection, educational facilities, and health services. They are practical, mundane. Service is their theme. National governments, on the other hand, are dramatic, powerful, highly prized. People become idealistic and sentimental about the national symbols.

The ends of the state are the common objects sought through all governments, whether local or central. Most social objectives, whether they be health, safety, equality, recreation, or liberty, can be achieved only through the co-operation of several governments.

Although the desires and objectives of people are felt as well as thought, it is desirable that so far as possible they take on a rational content. Should the state be a servant? Then, first of all, we must determine what to expect of it. Efforts and services are likely to be confused and ineffectual until goals have been defined. Which should be placed first in our scheme of values, maximum individual liberty or a higher cultural standard for all achieved through social co-operation? If we are to live successfully in a civilization which is built upon science and the corporation—both of which are high forms of co-operation—and if we are to solve the problems of industry and urbanization which almost overwhelm us, we must think deeply and concretely concerning the point toward which we wish to move and the steps needed in reaching that position. Policy is the derivative of objective. Once a community knows what it seeks, the choice of the requisite laws and means is greatly simplified.

<small>THE IMPORTANCE OF CHOOSING OBJECTIVES</small>

Ends usually signify complete certainty and a definite stopping place. We do not mean to suggest either of these implications. Ends of government are, like their functions, subject to human wishes and desires which change as time goes by. They are man-made and man-achieved. They are the result of our thinking, feelings, and actions. The more we think about them, the more steadily are we likely to progress.

Do individuals have inalienable rights? Is public authority to respect and safeguard certain fundamental interests, such as liberty, freedom of conscience, the enjoyment of health, the opportunity for free public education, and the right to work? If these rights are inalienable, why do people keep trying to add to the number of public obligations?

<small>ARE ENDS REAL?</small> If the individual has the right to be guaranteed a livelihood, for example, by what method is this hypothetical duty to be enforced? This is the crux of the whole matter. Ethical arguments as to whether or not the state is bound by an inescapable duty do not seem to get us very far. Those who adopt the affirmative side of the issue sometimes argue that the individual is sovereign, and that the government is merely the agent, and that any means necessary to enforce an inalienable right is morally justified. This was the view of John Locke and the American revolutionists. The negative side replies that ethical and moral rights are a mirage, that they never have existed, never will exist, and the only real right the individual possesses is the one he has the power to enforce.

Social rights which the state must guarantee to the individual actually exist so long as a sufficient number of people in the body politic believe that they exist and possess the means to make their effectuation possible. We may go further than this. If the community believes that individuals have certain inalienable rights, they may be said to exist, although their effectuation may be fraught with difficulties. The ends and objectives of the state are real insofar as people believe them to exist and strive for their accomplishment.

There are some objects of government which are traditional, well-nigh universally accepted. Public authority shall maintain order, resolve conflicting interests, administer justice. In addition, government is expected to provide for the <small>TRADITIONAL OBJECTIVES</small> indispensable needs of the community. This is the motif of local government, which political scientists are likely to underemphasize. "To promote the general welfare," said the city manager of Cincinnati in his 1935 annual report, "is the final function of government in the United States, according to our Constitution. The government of our city will be good, mediocre, or poor in proportion as it can affect favorably the safety, health, welfare, security and happiness of our people."

"The mold in which the modern state was cast is broken or is breaking." To appreciate this, one needs but to analyze outstanding functions of government and study their underlying purposes.

**THE CONTEMPORARY OBJECTIVES**  The largest group of public servants in the country are educators, numbering a million. The object of free public education is to produce useful, happy citizens. The postal service accounts for the next largest number, and public works also is very important. Their objects are to serve community needs and produce social assets. Health services prevent contagion and improve the nation's physical vitality. Recreation adds to enjoyment, moral tone, and aesthetic appreciation. We might go through the whole list of governmental services in this fashion. This is one method of determining what the ends of the state are in our generation.

The ultimate end of the state should be to foster the "good life" for the individual. The good life may be defined as the maximum enrichment of the individual personality. This certainly does not **THE ULTIMATE END** mean that there is one type of personality and one pattern of experiences and ideas which are best for all individuals. Enriched human personalities cannot be produced on a social assembly line. Enrichment comes from wide opportunities, varied experiences, freedom to think and choose, and release from fear.

The enrichment of the individual personality is not a neglected emphasis in political science. Locke, although primarily concerned with protecting personal liberty from an arbitrary ruler, and Rousseau, despite his romantic exaltation of life in the state of nature, were philosophical forbears of the ideals of community and equality which we think of in terms of the improvement of the individual through society. Unlike Hobbes, they did not assume that man is essentially "brutish" and at conflict with his kind— and, hence, despair of his prospects.[1]

In the political theory of the last hundred years, emphasis upon the good life, as the ultimate end of the state, has not been very conspicuous. One school of thought has emphasized the legal and

---

[1] An excellent brief account of their ideas will be found in Geza Engelmann, *Political Philosophy from Plato to Jeremy Bentham*, trans. by Karl F. Geiser (New York, 1927).

institutional nature of government. The individual was almost completely left out of the picture. Men exist for institutions, it would appear. "Our intelligentsia," said a recent critic of the social sciences, "are preoccupied with the externals of social control and thus have an unrealistic view of human experience." There is a great deal of truth in this indictment, for the juristic-institutional approach is not concerned with values. This is likewise true of the other principal emphasis in political theory of recent years, namely, that government is a struggle for power and position. The central truth of political science according to this view is that human beings are self-seekers, using government merely for their own ends. The psychological approach also divorces itself from ethics, and expresses a good deal of scepticism about the prospects of human nature. "If our practical object is social control, it is not so important to know what men wish to enjoy as to understand what they can do," according to a proponent of the human-nature approach. "The wishes and purposes of men are legion; what they can do is alone limited and, hence, capable of study."

Political theory divorced from ethics is bound to be incomplete, if not misleading.[1] Is it "unscientific" to say that the state should have as its primary purpose the cultivation of the good life for the individual? Policy needs an ultimate norm by which it can be tested. This one seems simple and reasonable. Conservatives, liberals, and radicals should have no difficulty agreeing that the most important object of the political state is to enrich human personality.

It may appear that this is a return to the individualism of Herbert Spencer. It is not. There is no real theoretical difficulty in reconciling the relative claims of society and the individual. The good life for the individual is the ultimate goal. Since the individual we are talking about is every individual, this end can be secured only by making society as a whole more just, contented, and cultivated. To the extent that general well-being depends upon social emphasis, to

SOCIETY VERSUS INDIVIDUAL

---

[1] Ethical philosophies are reviewed by W. W. Willoughby in *The Ethical Basis of Political Authority* (New York, 1930).

that extent society's claims should be recognized. As in most cases, it is not a choice of alternatives, it is a matter of interaction. Society produces the individual; personality would not exist if there were not other personalities and factors in the social environment. A person's basic opportunities are created by society. The better social conditions become and the more opportunities there are for general cultural improvement, the more outstanding personalities there are likely to be. On the other hand, society cannot advance without great leaders, men who stand out in their day. This is a universal need of every form of government, whether it be monarchy, fascism, communism, or democracy.

The practical difficulties of deciding, in countless cases, between the rival claims of society and the individual should not be minimized. The inherent difficulty of the adjustment must be the explanation of its having been the most perplexing problem of political theory through the ages. But it should be noted that the choice between society's claims and those of the individual is made easier when the ultimate objective is clearly recognized and widely accepted. Society's demands often become merely of an institutional, routine, or legalistic character. For example, the stringent limitations upon individual liberty caused by the passage of the Defense of the Realm Act in Great Britain continued long after the emergency had passed. Society should constantly be asking, "What is best for the individual?" This seems like a very simple and indecisive question, but if, without forgetting what is included in the "good life," it were kept constantly to the forefront of policy determinations and individual reckonings, men's social relations would be much more satisfactory. Society needs to guard against institutionalism, the individual against selfishness.

This compromise is furthered as the state takes on dominant service characteristics and minimizes its police aspects. Institutions are influenced by the type of work they do. The man who swings a night stick is not likely to be sensitive to individual feelings. As a rule, the person who sells transportation must please the customer, or else be unsuccessful. The city nurse who ministers to family welfare would not stay in her arduous task long unless moved by real sympathy. Institutions are made up of persons who become what they are largely because of what they are expected to do.

A functional analysis thus reveals that the objectives of the modern state are numerous. Prominent among them are protection of life and property, dispensation of justice, provision for equality of opportunity and intellectual enlightenment, improvement of health and physical well-being, supply of necessary economic services, and attention to matters aesthetic and cultural. How large a part has conscious design played in the establishment of social objectives?

A reinterpretation of man's significance in the scheme of things is one of the needs in political theory. The matter has been well expressed by a former sociologist:

THE SIGNIFICANCE OF MAN
We have lost faith in ourselves. When Copernicus persuaded men that they were not at the central point in the universe; when Newton convinced men that the reign of law was the same for other planets as for our own; when the industrial revolution subordinated man to the machine, and culture to commerce, then the human race suffered a serious deflation of its self-esteem. The climax came when, in the wake of Darwin who had found man a place among the animals, the new psychology made thought an instrument of the organic drives. Not only, then, have we lost faith in the accepted ends of life, but we have lost faith even in our ability clearly to formulate the ends of action for ourselves.[1]

Professor Aubrey is quite prepared to accept these scientific and intellectual discoveries. He points to the necessity of a new orientation, the formulation of a set of values which will satisfy man's intellect and also improve his status in the total environment. This need is very great in political science.

The problems of most social institutions are basically the same. We must "attempt to control those social processes which determine the well-being of the individual." The identical questions can be put to the state, economic order, education, church, and home. "Do your processes produce the good life for the individual?"

[1] Cf. Edwin E. Aubrey, *Present Theological Tendencies* (Harpers, New York, 1936). This book deals with some recent political theories.

Some of the elements in a reconstructed ideology may be suggested. The first one is the supreme worth of human personality. This is the absolute value. Then, individual well-being is a social product. All institutions are merely instruments, not ends in themselves, and governmental policies are to be tested by their ability to enrich the total experience of the individual.

<small>ELEMENTS OF A RECONSTRUCTED IDEOLOGY</small>

The danger of overemphasizing institutional processes and customary responses is a very great one. The divorcement of ethics from political science tends to have this result. So much attention is given to processes that, before one knows it, they are assumed to be inherent, unalterable. They become ends in themselves. The position we are suggesting keeps constantly asking, "What is the effect of this process upon personality and individual well-being?"

One further assumption may be mentioned. In man's effort to bring about a reinterpretation of his own place in the world, it is important that renewed emphasis be placed upon individual responsibility. Some psychological theories would seem to take adults back to the childhood stage so familiar to all parents. "I couldn't help it," is the familiar refrain of the adolescent. Irresponsibility and defeatism will kill democracy. The most important thing about any people is its temper. If the general run of people are like whipped dogs or sly foxes, nothing but exploitation may be expected. If they are self-confident, optimistic, and outspoken, democracy will have a long life. Fortunately, this is the temper of American pioneers.

### SELECTED READINGS

Coker, Francis W.: *Recent Political Thought* (New York, 1934); chap. xx, entitled "Empirical Collectivism," considers the ideas which have motivated or accompanied the increased amount of social legislation in the Western world.

Hobhouse, Leonard T.: *The Elements of Social Justice* (London, 1922): outlines the faith of a liberal philosopher and sociologist regarding the functions of the government.

———: *The Metaphysical Theory of the State* (New York, 1918); a declaration of faith in the democratic ideal.

Ickes, Harold L.: *The New Democracy* (New York, 1934); a progressive's ideas on the relation between the individual and society.
Laski, Harold J.: *Liberty in the Modern State* (New York, 1930); a statement of the pluralist position.
Lippmann, Walter: "The Government of Posterity," *Atlantic Monthly*, CLVIII, No. 5 (November, 1936), 543–54.
———: "The Providential State," *Atlantic Monthly*, CLVIII, No. 4 (October, 1936), 403–12.
Lorwin, Lewis L.: "The Plan State and the Democratic Ideal," *Annals*, CLXXX (July, 1935), 114–18.
Merriam, Charles E.: *The Role of Politics in Social Change* (New York, 1936); discusses the implications of the lack of a "working relationship between politics and economics and the larger social whole."
Perry, Ralph B.: "The Alleged Failure of Democracy," *Yale Review*, XXIV, No. 1 (Autumn, 1934), 37–51.
Robinson, Daniel S.: *Political Ethics* (New York, 1935); a semipragmatic approach to the problem of state activity.
Roosevelt, Franklin D.: *Looking Forward* (New York, 1933); a collection of addresses which embody a liberal conception of the ends of the state in America.
Thomas, Norman: *America's Way Out* (New York, 1931); a picture of democratic socialism for America.
Wallace, Henry A.: *New Frontiers* (New York, 1934); a progressive discusses the place of government in the modern society.
Willoughby, W. W.: *The Ethical Basis of Political Authority* (New York, 1930), chaps. I–XVII; develops a theory of the proper basis and scope of political coercion.
Wilson, Woodrow: *The New Freedom* (London, 1916), especially chaps. I–XII; an eloquent appeal for the restoration of American politics to their original strength and vigor.

# PART II ☆ ADMINISTRATION

CHAPTER IX

☆ ☆ ☆

## THE EXECUTION OF POLICY

*"The fight of public administrators for high standards is a fight waged on behalf of every citizen in a society that is over one-half urbanized."*
—JOHN M. GAUS

THE CONTROLLING INFLUENCE OF ADMINISTRATION

IN THE LONG RUN, men's thinking determines governmental action. It is all too easy to overemphasize the nonrational character of political behavior. "Soon or late," concludes John Maynard Keynes, "it is ideas, not vested interests, which are dangerous for good or evil." But when ideas have crystallized into policies, and policies have turned into laws, it is by no means certain that the attempted execution of the program will succeed. Some laws break down completely, while others are only partial successes. No doubt many policies should never have been written into the statute-books at all. The American people have a "passion for lawmaking." We naïvely believe that all we have to do is to enact a law and the reform is as good as accomplished. We blindly worship law, despite many bitter lessons in its ineffectualness.

Making the policy official is frequently the least difficult part of the task of satisfying a social need. This is especially true in our loosely-knit legislative system, where there is no real party responsibility and interests can lobby through their programs by trading votes and applying pressure. Moreover, responsible governments naturally make genuine efforts to execute government-sponsored acts. There is not always this presumption in the American system. A law may be passed merely to pacify a militant minority, but the lobby demanding the bill finds it more difficult to control the administrative agency than the legislative body. Furthermore, the legislative and executive departments may fail to co-operate, and the courts may invalidate the act—many are the hazards and uncertainties in carrying through a program.

What the people can accomplish through the governmental mechanism is limited by administrative effectiveness. The popular proverb, "It is not what you say but the way you say it that matters," might be paraphrased, "It is not what government does but the way it does it that counts." Both of these aphorisms, of course, are exaggerated, for the substance and objectives of policies matter mightily; however, the saying properly draws attention to the importance of the means. It points to the fact that one must consider the listener or the citizen, as the case may be, and take sufficient account of the effect of the statement or action on his interests and attitudes.

Administration is government's contact point. It is the focus at which effect is given to legally approved policies. Hence, the whole problem of whether or not compliance can be secured arises to encourage or defeat the measures of the administration. The execution of the law must not be thought of as a dry-as-dust procedure, as mere routine. It is not dull or stereotyped by any means. On the contrary, it is thoroughly human. If a law, for example, is popular and generally favored, the persons who compose the administrative service will try harder to secure its successful execution. Citizens will go out of their way to co-operate, virtually assuring the success of the program. The most important question in the enforceability of a new program is whether it makes the administrators enthusiastic and the people grateful recipients. Surely these are thoroughly human considerations.

*FACTORS CONDITIONING SUCCESS*

The public is very impressionable. Do not people go to the stores where they get the best service and attention? If they can possibly afford to do so, they will pay a few cents more for the same article just to enjoy the satisfactions which come from pleasant human association. The same factors apply in governmental administration. If an organization has likable people in it, and if they are devoted to their work, then the enterprise will have spirit and atmosphere; people will enjoy dealing with it; and it will succeed. This statement, however, needs one qualification. In the long run, the success of the enterprise will depend upon the value of what the organization has to sell; but this has already been implied by saying that governmental programs succeed when they are popular. Unless those who administer them also are popular, capable, and considerate of human feelings, however, a popular measure may lose its appeal. On the other hand, when the personnel and the methods are just right, a policy lacking in popularity may be put over with success and general approval. Public administration should attempt to be flexible internally and responsive to externals. The people who execute a program should have personality and "customer sensitivity." Governmental services would then produce "atmosphere." The human elements should constantly be pushed to the forefront, the mechanical ones kept out of sight. There is no reason why such an ideal should be too high for any organization of a public character. Other large organizations succeed in these respects. People can be made to respond with equal success to government's efforts if they are approached the right way. Perhaps the principal fault with governmental administration is the attitude of resigned pessimism which Americans are taught to take toward it.

Administration is a way of viewing government. It is a concept as well as a process.[1] The problem of America in the twentieth century, with a large population working in industries and living in congested cities, is automatically one of organization. We must organize and learn to co-operate in order to succeed. How can government organize best to fill the wants which complexity casts into its hopper? But organization is not confined to the mere structure of government. How are government and business to fit together, to supplement each other? How are planning and policy to be transmitted through the entire circuit without losing too much force? How can people be assured of good service and still keep power in their own hands?

ADMINISTRA-
TION AS A
CONCEPT

Administration is essentially an engineering concept. Imagine a river that causes flood damage, damage corresponding to the maladjustments that give rise to society's problems. "Can we put a dam across it? What will be the pressure of the impounded

[1] The conceptual view of public administration was early emphasized by Woodrow Wilson. Read his brilliant essay, "The Study of Administration," *Political Science Quarterly*, II, No. 2 (June, 1887), 197–222.

water?" questions the hydraulic engineer. The social engineer asks, similarly, "What are the social tensions, the force of public opinion, the basic design and tensile strength of the materials of control?" How are we going to organize to build the dam? Experience and accumulated knowledge are of great assistance. Who are the workmen to be? Instead of asking what is to be done with the by-products of the dam, hydroelectric power, for instance, we ask in administrative terms, what will be the effect upon business or some other organized interest?

The administrative concept is the over-all view. It looks to problem, cause, design, building material, method, result. All of them are fitted together, like pieces in a pattern. The job, however, is more difficult than the construction engineer's, because the principal factors in the political scientist's problem are human beings.

The advantage of looking at administration conceptually is that it reveals interrelations, the continuous process from raging river to stalwart dam. This does not mean that administration includes all of government, as the desirability of specialization in itself forbids that; but the over-all view does make it clear that certain processes, materials, and forces are found everywhere in government. Policy is engineering design; law is cement; people are workers and users. Leadership assures results; money provides the machinery, pays the workers, limits the size of the dam; but, most important of all, one must not lose sight of the fact that law and policy run throughout. Suppose that the dam is finished and the powerhouse is installed, but there is no ready market for the power. Or, to draw another illustration: labor threatens to quit work unless union wages are paid, but the engineer finds that his budget will not permit higher wages. Here is a difficult decision in the middle of a job! In many cases, the administrator cannot go back to the policy agency for advice but must make the decision himself.

Government as administration is a concept which has been caught by Gardiner C. Means, a social scientist trained as a professional economist. "The realm of political science is, or lies within, the realm of social associations or administrative organizations,"[1] he says. Traditional economics, on the other hand, "is essentially a science of economic organization through the market place and abstracts from all problems of administrative organization." Dr. Means points out that the classical economist has simply disregarded such co-ordination of economic activity as is brought about by administration—yet administratively controlled areas comprise 70 per cent to 80 per cent of all industrial wealth. "Gradually but steadily great segments of economic activity have been shifted from the market place to administration."[2] In the development of further administrative co-ordination in the economic order, concludes Dr. Means, economists "must come to political scientists for aid. We ask that you apply to the field of economic administration the technique of analysis and principles of organization which you have developed in the study of the state."[3] The researches of political scientists may prove helpful, because administration is generic. Whenever social organizations are formed, common problems of organization, leadership, control, personnel, finance, and public relations are bound to arise; moreover, the relationships of government and industry are so inextricable that the borderline becomes the most strategic salient.

The administrative stage theoretically begins after the legislative stage is completed. The executive does not set to work until the law is actually in his hands; however, we need to get a realistic idea of the continuity of governmental processes. There are ten steps which are usually involved in the development and fruition of a governmental policy. The first five are concerned with policy making and the last five with program execution:[4]

RELATION OF AD-
MINISTRATION
TO THE WHOLE
OF GOVERNMENT

*Germination and Fruition of Governmental Policy*

| | |
|---|---|
| Social need | Administrative stage |
| Philosophical stage | Executive stage |
| Conscious stage | Clerical stage |
| Political stage | Manual stage |
| Legislative stage | Social satisfaction |

[1]Gardiner C. Means, "The Distribution of Control and Responsibility in a Modern Economy," in a symposium edited by Benjamin E. Lippincott, *Government Control of the Economic Order* (Minneapolis, 1935), pp. 1–17.
[2]*Ibid*, p. 5. [3] *Ibid*, p. 8.
[4]This is the analysis of B. W. Walker Watson, "The Elements of Public Administration," *Public Administration*, X, No. 4 (Oct., 1932), 397–408.

This analysis will be readily understood by American readers, with one possible exception. The English construe the term "executive" more narrowly than the word "administrative." The executive stage is the dynamic one, where the work is actually being done.

This analysis gives us a good idea of precedence and continuity, but it is merely the skeleton. In order to understand how government actually operates, we need to examine carefully the middle area in which politics and administration are adjoined.

CONTRIBUTION TO LAW-MAKING

Administrators contribute to the lawmaking process, and policy makers share in the execution of programs. Government is a functional unit, even when its external appearance is institutionally compartmentalized. There are several reasons for this. In the first place, law flows throughout government. Areas of discretion are bound to exist in all stages, and since discretion involves policy determining, all three departments help to make law and construe policy. In the second place, most important laws are broad and general in their wording. "Skeleton legislation" is more the rule outside the United States than at home, but even in this country is it decidedly on the increase.

When the executive branch is called upon to fill in a broad outline with executive orders, administrators add to law and to policy. In the third place, the executive is elected as the official leader of the party and is expected to prepare policy measures for the legislature and try to get them enacted into law. This is true in the United States, and it is even more often true in countries which choose the executive from the legislature and then expect the cabinet to dominate the chamber. Finally, the policy-making branch reaches over into administration to secure advice and to observe and censure its operations. Both policy and law go through a series of interpretations and alterations from the time they are thought of until the courts decide cases involving them or the administration accomplishes all the objectives.

In drafting laws involving social control, public works, taxation, regulation, natural resources, public welfare, transportation, or the reallocation of duties, administrative officials are almost invariably consulted, or the bill may even be drawn in one of the executive offices. This is now the usual method of framing important legislation. So much reliance is placed upon administrators that some writers fear that legislatures have abdicated their most essential duty, that of deciding policy matters.[1] But when one looks at the matter practically, the reasons for drawing administrators into the legislative process become instantly apparent. Those who carry out laws learn from experience about enforceability and are able to recommend how a similar program might be better undertaken another time. Then, too, the work of government is technical, requiring the special knowledge of experts. Usually the combination of expertness and experience is found only in administrators. Legislators may have the theoretical knowledge, but they rarely have the practical understanding of administrative factors necessary for the effective instrumentation of policy.

A governor is elected on the promise that he will regulate public utilities more effectively. If he was sincere about his promises and concludes that his political survival depends upon his ability to carry out his campaign pledges, he will call together his closest advisers and draft a new public utility law. The chances are that the actual drawing of the bill will be done by someone other than a member of the legislature; however, the party floor leader or a committee chairman will be "in" on all of the proceedings. The executive and the legislature take the initiative and the responsibility; the law is actually drafted by an obscure administrator or consultant.

Let us take another example. The city council of a municipality with a half million population decides that a comprehensive park system is needed. All it decides in principle is that the need exists and that all parts of the city should be treated equally. The city manager then gets busy and talks with the head of the recreation department or the park commissioner. He passes on the assignment to the men in his office. The engineer

[1] Cf. James Beck, *Our Wonderland of Bureaucracy* (New York, 1932); Cecil T. Carr, *Delegated Legislation* (London, 1921); Lord Hewart, *The New Despotism* (London, 1929); Ramsay Muir, *How Britain Is Governed* (New York, 1930), pp. 37–80; and the *Report of the Committee on Ministers' Powers*, Cmd. 4060, 1932, a classic that deserves careful study.

in the planning commission, the landscape architect, the playground director, the forester, the draftsman all are consulted and all make a contribution. Then the city manager receives the plans. If he approves them, he passes them on to the council, the councilmen study the proposals, public hearings are held, and an election is called to vote bonds.

The chairman of the Senate committee on interstate commerce decides that the only salvation for the railways is public ownership. He wants to introduce a bill providing for a government-owned corporation to take over the railways. A good bill will require time, research, and knowledge of other efforts along the same line. The Senator clearly needs help and he calls upon the Interstate Commerce Commission which employs experts who are familiar with all the factors involved. The committee chairman goes to the head of the commission. There are conferences with some of the leading members of the staff. The administrators may not be at all sympathetic with the objects of the bill, but they are expected to contribute their knowledge as objectively as would a doctor or a lawyer. When the wording of the draft bill is complete, the Senator asks that changes be made, for otherwise, he says, it would not receive a sympathetic reception. The draft goes back for further work and is finally introduced into the Senate as "Senator Blank's Bill," and officially it is.

Close co-operation between the legislative and administrative departments is inevitable, irrespective of whether or not this fact be reflected in constitutional theory. And what possible harm is there in calling upon administrators to assist in the law-making process? Their function corresponds to that of a consultant; they are anonymous, serving not because they have authority but because they possess knowledge. The official responsibility is the legislator's, and the praise or blame goes to the party. So long as this is true it would seem that the more proficient policy formation becomes, the better for everyone concerned.

Now for the other side of the picture. Policy extends over into administration. Lawmakers contribute to the executive process. They pass skeleton laws which need administrative supplementation, but when new problems or important decisions arise, the legislature may again step in. This may take the form of supplementary legislation, a resolution, advice to the executive from prominent members of the assembly, or financial control. If the legislature is suspicious or citizens are dissatisfied, legislative committees may be appointed for the purpose of looking into the administration of the act and uncovering faults or violations. Legislatures are like fathers who give their sons allowances when they go to college. There are periodic opportunities for an accounting. Sometimes this means "laying down the law."

<small>ADMINIS-
TRATORS
AS POLICY
MAKERS</small>

Public administration involves policy formation and the formulation of supplementary orders and regulations having the force of law.[1] Consider, for example, problems growing out of the illustrations just used. Should bathers in public parks be permitted to wear abbreviated suits? Is $50,000 too high a salary for the general manager of the United States Railways? Will the new public utility commission be allowed to employ special experts on a *per diem* basis? The several acts do not say, and administrators must decide. Their decisions create rights and duties, regulate human conduct—which is essentially what law does.

Action possessing legislative and judicial characteristics is indispensable in modern administration, and in the future it may be expected to increase. Administrators enact sub-legislation.[2] They weigh the rights of individuals, hand down final awards, and perform functions which are almost identical to those of law courts.[3] Discretion is the very essence of some fields of administrative action.[4] When solutions depend upon technical knowledge, unforeseen contingencies, local differences, the necessity of speed, and flexibility of administration, the administrator must possess

---

[1] Cf. James Hart, *The Ordinance-Making Powers of the President* (Baltimore, 1925); and John P. Comer, *Legislative Powers of National Administrative Authorities* (New York and London, 1927).
[2] Frederick F. Blachly and Miriam E. Oatman, *Administrative Legislation and Adjudication* (Washington, 1935).
[3] John Dickinson, *Administrative Justice and the Supremacy of Law* (Cambridge, Mass., 1927).
[4] See my essay, entitled, "The Nature of Discretion in Modern Administration," in a symposium by John M. Gaus, Leonard D. White, and Marshall E. Dimock entitled, *The Frontiers of Public Administration* (Chicago, 1936).

discretionary and determinative powers; otherwise a program cannot succeed.

More and more, laws give administration permissory powers, authority which need not be used but which may be if found necessary. To the extent that government is given responsibility for the regulation of public businesses, social security, and economic stabilization, such powers are seemingly indispensable. The success of social legislation frequently depends upon the administration's having sufficient authority to make supplementary rules, regulations, and standards; to collect evidence, testimony, and facts; and to decide cases and controversies arising in the ordinary course of duty. The work of the Interstate Commerce Commission and that of the state industrial accident commissions afford good examples.

Lawyers have grown increasingly unhappy about the government's repeated reliance upon administrative adjudication. We find the special committee on administrative law of the American Bar Association stating in 1933, for example, that all power involving judicial procedures and characteristics should be the monopoly of the judicial department and that where administrative tribunals now exercise these powers, courts should be put in their place. There are various possible explanations of this attitude. One is that the legal profession seems to consider the separation-of-powers theory essential to our constitutional system and professes concern over its liberalization. Another possible explanation is the self-interest of the legal profession, which naturally looks upon the substitution of the administrative for the judicial process as a blow at its business and income. Administrative justice is cheaper and speedier. But there is still a third explanation, namely, lawyers may not realize that quasi-legislative and quasi-judicial characteristics are natural and necessary elements of public administration.

Administration is more than mere mechanics. It involves the recommendation of policies; the issuance of orders having the force of law; the choice between alternatives; the hearing of cases and controversies arising in the course of execution. These practices are all part and parcel of the administrative process.

One possible reason for attempting to strip administration of its legislative and judicial characteristics is to make the social control of business ineffective. Persons desiring only a half-hearted or ineffectual enforcement of laws regulating businesses affected with a public interest will prefer legislative or judicial action to administrative power. Governmental policies relative to the control of business have been experimental, and cut-and-dried formulas have not been considered as either possible or desirable; hence, there has devolved upon administration the task of establishing its own rules and standards, of recommending additional legislation to the lawmaking body, and of exercising discretion and quasi-judicial powers as unforeseen conditions and controversies arose. As Mr. Justice Cardozo of the United States Supreme Court said in an important decision, "In the complex life of today, the business of government could not go on without the delegation, in greater or less degree, of the power to adapt the rule to the swiftly moving facts."[1] Would that there were more judges who recognized that the requirements of administrative action bear a direct relationship to the social purposes which the community has expressed in the form of legislative enactments!

PROS AND CONS OF ADMINISTRATIVE JUSTICE

The base of common-law jurisdiction has grown progressively narrower as administrative justice has been substituted for court adjudication. This development needs to be accompanied by measures amply safeguarding the customary rights and immunities of the individual. In any administrative proceeding affecting a person's property or interests, there should be notice of the process, an opportunity to be heard, the right to confront witnesses, a public hearing, a decision by impartial persons, and appeal on bona fide questions of law. Fortunately, the administrative law of the United States provides for all of these requirements.[2] Even more important, however, is the recruitment of administrators who can be depended upon to act with objectivity and consideration.

[1] *Panama Refining Co.* vs. *Ryan*, 293 U. S. 441 (1935).
[2] Cf. Ernst Freund, *Administrative Powers over Persons and Property* (Chicago, 1928); also Frederick J. Port, *Administrative Law* (London and New York, 1929).

Discretion is freedom to choose between alternatives. It is the opposite of strict legal stipulation. The courts make a distinction between discretionary acts and ministerial acts of administrative officers. The latter are completely defined by the law, leaving no room for choice; hence, ministerial acts will be enforced by the writ of mandamus—a court order to an inferior court or officer commanding him to perform a certain act. On the other hand, when a realm of activity is discretionary, this mandatory writ will not be used. Instead, the courts will inspect the action by certiorari (bring up the record) and, if they find that the officer is acting within his jurisdiction, they will not interfere with his discretion.

<small>ADMINISTRATIVE DISCRETION</small>

Administrative discretion is particularly necessary in emergency situations, such as threatened epidemics or serious fires. It is indispensable also in public-utility regulation, certain fields of taxation, immigration cases, workmen's compensation, and generally where qualitative or technical factors are involved.

There are several important qualifications which administrative discretion must meet. First of all, if the officer does not have jurisdiction, he is acting *ultra vires* (beyond his power) and his actions are unlawful. Secondly, administrators must be able to show that they are following a "standard" which persons concerned can understand. For example, before an inspector can order a factory owner to install new safety equipment, the department clearly indicates what type of machinery constitutes a reasonable standard. The purpose of the "standard" rule is to assure equal treatment and avoidance of discrimination and arbitrary action. "Reasonableness" is a third general rule which courts apply to administrative discretion.

Several legal remedies are open to the individual who believes his rights are being violated by administrative officials. Habeas corpus is used to bring a case of detention before a court and to raise the question of jurisdiction. Certiorari is the means of bringing a case to a higher tribunal and reviewing the record. Mandamus forces action. Injunction prevents further proceedings. Quo warranto

<small>LEGAL REMEDIES</small>

inquires into title of office and authority to act. Prohibition prevents action. The last-mentioned two extraordinary remedies are now very rarely used.

The increasing extent to which discretion, standard making, sub-legislation, and administrative adjudication are found tends to bring about a fundamental change in the force and effectiveness of the separation-of-powers doctrine. The number and influence of administrative tribunals have been chiefly responsible for this development. The Interstate Commerce Commission, for example, makes its own rules of procedure, creates standards to fill in the interstices of Congressional legislation, develops policies which it either submits to Congress or puts into effect on its own authority, and yearly decides dozens of cases involving millions of dollars in railway properties and users' fares.[1] It combines legislative, administrative, and judicial powers. It is an *ad hoc* body, suspended amidst the three departments of government. The administrative tribunal is a "no man's land." There are scores of such tribunals in the United States, having degrees of authority varying from that of the Interstate Commerce Commission.

Another similarity between the legislative and administrative stage is that pressure groups make their impact upon both. Although their principal opportunity for effectiveness occurs during the lawmaking process, special interests also are active and vigilant so far as the work of departments and independent establishments is concerned. In the light of the analyses we have been making, the explanation should be obvious. Every bureau has its clientele, and since administrative officials have considerable influence in the lawmaking stage, it is, therefore, natural that the interest groups attempt to prevail upon the administrative establishments for support. Farm organizations approach the Department of Agriculture, business groups make use of the Department of Commerce, labor relies upon its own official mouthpiece;[2] more-

INTEREST GROUPS AND ADMINISTRATION

[1] Cf. I. L. Sharfman, *The Interstate Commerce Commission*, 4 vols. (New York, 1931), particularly II, 345-489.
[2] The best book on this subject is E. Pendleton Herring, *Public Administration and the Public Interest* (New York, 1936).

over, important interests are involved in the exercise of discretion, standard making, sub-legislation, and administrative adjudication. For example, the Secretary of the Interior consults the cattle interests before drawing up regulations concerning grazing rights on public lands.[1] Administration is not a thing apart. It works in close co-operation with the interest primarily served. Pressure groups try to "pull the teeth" of regulatory laws. Their impact is constantly felt by the Federal Trade Commission, Interstate Commerce Commission, state public-utility boards—in fact by all agencies engaged in social control of business.

So effective do interest-group pressures become that express provisions of law are sometimes never given effect. This was true, for example, of that important clause in the Federal Water Power Act of 1920 which stipulated that the commission should have permissory power to fix rates on power produced by licensees. Many times in public utility regulation it has appeared that the interests supposedly controlled were actually doing the controlling.[2] They try to dictate new appointments. They use their influence to keep the tribunal's budget low, thereby assuring the ineffectualness of its work. Laws which are against the interests of pressure groups can sometimes be "strafed" with less expense and more secretly by attacking their administration than by openly fighting them during the legislative stage.

It must now be sufficiently clear that there is much in common between politics and administration. Both processes involve procedures which have the characteristics of all three governmental departments. The development of law and policy is found throughout the entire governmental system.

An understanding of how politics and administration are connected is of the utmost importance. Only when the influence of administration on lawmaking and the importance of policy in administration are appreciated does one get a complete and realistic view of government in action. If this analysis has helped to reveal some of the elements which are found throughout gov-

[1] Cf. J. P. Comer, *Legislative Functions of National Administrative Authorities*, pp. 248–50.
[2] Evidence of this is to be found in a large number of studies. See, for example, W. E. Mosher (ed.), *Electrical Utilities* (New York and London, 1929); Keezer and May, *The Public Control of Business;* and Herring, *Public Administration and the Public Interest.*

ernment, the emphasis is well justified. Moreover, we have dealt with some of the components of administration: organization, discretion, sub-legislation, quasi-judicial determinations, group pressures, control by the judiciary. We now need to isolate the important elements of administration.

Government consists of politics and administration, policy formation and policy execution. The two processes are co-ordinate rather than exclusive. It is important, however, to recognize significant differences of function and of institution. Political offices are usually elective and temporary, while administrative positions are usually appointive and permanent. Politics draws up the laws and programs of government, while administration is concerned with all matters involving the successful accomplishment of these policies and programs.

PUBLIC ADMINISTRATION DEFINED

Public administration may be defined as that instrumentality or that body of knowledge which is concerned with the problems and powers, the organization, and the techniques of management involved in carrying out the laws and policies formulated by the policy-making agencies of government.[1]

A clearer idea of the meaning and content of public administration can be obtained by breaking down the definition into its principal component parts. A suggested enumeration of these is as follows: (1) the laws and policies which the administration is authorized to carry out, and the problems, legal, sociological, etc., arising thereunder; (2) the relation between areas or subdivisions of administration—such as federal, state, municipal relations—and contacts with nongovernmental agencies; (3) the problem of overhead and departmental organization, the focus of attention here being upon vertical relationships and integration; (4) the problem of finance, including revenues, appropriations, taxes, indebtedness, accounting, purchasing, and profits; (5) the personnel requirements of administration, including all matters designed to improve the service of government and the morale of employees; (6) the techniques of management, con-

[1] See my essay, entitled, "The Meaning and Scope of Public Administration," in the symposium, *The Frontiers of Public Administration*.

sisting of the art of executive leadership, "top" control, the use of machinery and labor-saving devices, and a knowledge of technical skills in the various "line" services of government; (7) the public-relations activities of administration represented by public reporting, the handling of complaints, press releases, etc.; (8) the control over administrative agencies and officials, including judicial, legislative, interest-group, and "inner" control. The last type of control is that exercised by higher administrative officials or by their professional standards.[1]

"Administration" and "management" are words which can be used more or less interchangeably. Writers on business organization consider the term "management" as the broader of the two. For example, Henri Fayol has said that there are six operations in management.[2] They are technical, commercial, financial, security, accounting, and "administrative." The administrative is at the apex of the hierarchy, planning and controlling all the other operations. In public administration, on the other hand, we use "administration" as the generic term, and refer to management as the special skills by which the actual accomplishment of co-ordination and objectives is made possible. Administration is comprehensive, management dynamic.

Despite differences in terminology, all fields of social co-operation experience much the same problems of administration. There are principles of large-scale organization which industry, church, army, school, voluntary associations, and government do well to follow.[3] Government can learn from other social groupings, and they, in turn, can profit from the attention given to administration in political science. For example, large business corporations have made use of the civil-service idea, particularly testing techniques, classification schemes, and retirement plans.

PRINCIPLES OF LARGE-SCALE ORGANIZATION

A principle of administration is a rule of procedural conduct whose validity has been widely tested and universally found to

[1] See my essay, entitled, "Forms of Control over Administrative Action," in *The Law and Practice of Governmental Administration*.
[2] Henri Fayol, *Industrial and General Administration* (London, 1930), pp. 8–10.
[3] Cf. James D. Mooney and Alan C. Reiley, *Onward Industry* (New York and London, 1931); also Mary P. Follett, *Creative Experience* (New York, 1924) and *The New State* (New York, 1918).

hold true.[1] Some of the more important lessons of large-scale organization may be mentioned. (1) *Problems and Powers:* The success of a program depends in large part upon how thoroughly the difficulties have been studied and the objectives defined. Planning is the first and most important step in administration. Men should be secured who are familiar with the kind of work to be done. (2) *Administrative Areas:* Field areas and the relation of their offices to headquarters should be clearly defined. Headquarters should confine its attention to planning, research, staff functions, co-ordination, and control. Field offices should be given as much operating independence and opportunity for initiative as possible. The number of regulations should be reduced to a minimum. The authority of any unit should be coextensive with the problem and responsibility.

Prediction is much more possible in some aspects of administration than in others; and, where such is the case, principles are more numerous and better substantiated. Organization stands out above all the others. (3) *Organization:* The work should be divided according to the predominant functions. There should be only one head of the organization and he should assume full responsibility. The number of department heads reporting directly to him should be kept as low as possible, consistent with functionalization. Lines of authority should be created but should not be rigid. Authority and responsibility should be equal. Line authority should not be divided.

In a very large organization, the intelligence with which the staff services are handled is more important than any other factor. When their duties and responsibilities require it, line executives should have staff assistance.[2] The principal staff services are planning, personnel, finance, law, and public relations. The function of the staff person is to be helpful. He does anything the line executive delegates to him. He is the eyes and ears of the responsible

ORGANIZATION PRINCIPLES

[1] Cf. Leonard D. White, "The Meaning of Principle in Public Administration," in the symposium, *The Frontiers of Public Administration*.
[2] A "line" official is one who is actually engaged in providing a direct service, as distinguished from a "staff" official, whose work is that of servicing those on the firing line. A policeman belongs to the line, while a personnel officer is an example of a staff person.

executive. His work is largely research, and under no circumstances does the staff official give orders down the line on his own responsibility. He is anonymous, the *alter ego* of his chief. When he begins treading on the toes of line executives, his influence and value will soon disappear.

The greater a person's responsibility, the more he needs to delegate tasks. This is one of the cardinal principles of organization and management. Most executives say they delegate, but few actually do to the extent that they should. The function of the executive is to be free to plan, to meet the public, to see the enterprise in all its ramifications, to keep in touch with what is taking place in all parts of the organization. Obviously, he cannot do any of these things successfully if he is buried under a mass of detail all day long and has no time to get outside his office.

It is sometimes stated as an inflexible rule that an organization should be built along functional lines, not along the line of individual capabilities. It is doubtful whether so sweeping a statement is supportable. The better rule seems to be that functionalization should be theoretically determined, but the actual division of responsibility should be adjusted to the particular aptitudes of the higher officials. When an organization is so fortunate as to get a man of outstanding capacity, it is wise to use that individual's talents to the fullest extent. Men make jobs, not jobs men. A final suggestion regarding organization is that the best use should be made of all its personnel. As obvious as this rule is, in practice it is frequently violated.

Nothing operates without funds. (4) *Finance:* Over-all planning and budgeting should be closely associated in the administrative organization. The finance officer is a staff official and, hence, should take care not to arrogate line authority. Accounting and auditing should be separate responsibilities. The chief finance officer should be concerned with efficiency as well as merely with honesty and legality. The financial department should not have unlimited authority over personnel and remuneration. Adequate budgeting and reporting procedures should be provided. The pay-as-you-go system should be used as widely as possible.

Human beings are the brains and energy of any organization.

## THE EXECUTION OF POLICY

(5) *Personnel:* Being a staff officer, the personnel director should confine his attention to efforts which will be helpful to the chief executive. The objective is to recruit the best men and to improve morale. When personnel work takes on line responsibilities, it gets outside its proper province. It should not attempt to be a control agency. Thinking, planning, and advice are the principal services to be rendered. Too much standardization is to be avoided. Individual initiative should be encouraged and special reward for special effort and ability should be the rule.

The actual execution of the program is obviously the crucible in which all other elements are tested. (6) *Management:* The spirit and tempo of the organization are set by the chief executive. His principal responsibilities are to choose likely men for important positions, keep close track of public attitudes and complaints, plan strategy of execution, and co-ordinate all parts of the enterprise. The lines of control should be definite, the purpose being to provide as much autonomy as is consistent with conformity to general objectives, but there should be adequate provision for free and direct communication across these lines. The executive should lead by personal example. The development of institutional morale, pride, and spirit should be encouraged. Organization should remain flexible to changed conditions and consumer demands. Everything possible should be done to secure the whole-hearted interest and co-operation of the rank and file of employees. Technical efficiency should be subordinated to customer satisfaction. The organization should define its objectives, develop a philosophy in conformity therewith, and then take a long view of what is to its advantage.

RULES FOR MANAGEMENT

The purpose is to serve; "the customer is always right." (7) *Public Relations:* The enterprise must find out what the public wants and try to give it to them. Complaints and dissatisfactions should be brought to light and remedies applied to their basic causes. The public should be made familiar with the objectives of the enterprise and with its institutional philosophy. Users should understand what they are getting for their money. The best advertisement is a sincerely enthusiastic employee—

personality is the symbol which has the greatest universal appeal. Advertising and propaganda, if overdone, will act like a boomerang on the undertaking. It is worse to overdo public relations than to be incompletely appreciated. This is particularly true when government is concerned. People expect public procedures to be dignified.

Administrators are agents, servants. Their masters are the public. (8) *Popular Control:* The official should be kept close to the people; aloofness or a feeling of superiority are socially objectionable. Regular checks should be provided for the prevention or punishment of illegality, arbitrariness, discrimination, or discourtesy. The official should have no master save the public welfare. He should serve all, and none with special favor.

It is to be expected that there are matters of importance which we have not mentioned; moreover, all principles are subject to exception. When an organization has at its head a man of extraordinary energy and human appeal, it is not so necessary that principles of organization and management be followed. Exceptional leadership qualities are sometimes a substitute for tried-and-true management principles; however, when the two are combined—extraordinary leadership qualities plus sound administrative procedures—the results are bound to be superior. In order to produce the best service, the objectives, organization principles, and distinctive contributions of each unit should be understood by everyone in the enterprise.[1] In other words, principles of administration should be made known to the low as well as to the high in the organizational pyramid. It will be found that these principles are applicable to business corporations and other large-scale enterprises as well as to governmental administration. These hypotheses have been brought together in one place so that the author's assumptions would be expressed clearly in the beginning in order to make his basis of evaluation explicit.

Organization principles, broadly construed, include almost everything of importance in administrative lore. We have already suggested that organization is a social-science concept. When

[1] Cf. John M. Gaus, "The Principle of Organization in Public Administration," in the symposium, *The Frontiers of Public Administration*.

human life becomes complex, salutary organization techniques become an indispensable requirement. Organization is the connecting link between human desire and social satisfaction.

CENTRAL IMPORTANCE OF ORGANIZATION
Alexander Pope exaggerated when he said, "For forms of government let fools contest, whate'er is best administer'd is best." Basic design controls results. Unless organization is adapted to social purpose and is made to follow tested rules of administration, the best efforts of human beings will be handicapped. Inflexible organization sometimes defeats the most brilliant of men.

Four basic types of organization may be distinguished: the military, committee, functional, and integrated. Let us consider their fundamental premises and differences. (1) *Military Type:*

FOUR THEORIES OF ORGANIZATION
Social organization has probably been influenced more by military methods than by any others, because military organization is so old and has had so much opportunity to be tested. Its initial assumption is that all authority is vested in the commander. A second hypothesis is that orders travel down the hierarchical pyramid from one level to another. Thirdly, each man in the organization receives orders from only one person, the superior next above him. Lines of authority are simple and clear, a very important characteristic. Monarchies and dictatorships follow this pattern, as does the "close" corporation, that is, one in which the owner is the operator and has all the power and responsibility.

Authority may be concentrated or it may be widely diffused. (2) *Committee Type:* When several persons of equal authority run an organization, administer it, we call it the "committee type." As in the military form, the policy-forming agency and the executing unit are the same. All authority is rolled into one. The committee decides and it also executes; but unlike the military, no one person is at the top. Administrative duties must therefore be divided. The committee type is exemplified in the commission form of municipal government, in administrative tribunals, such as the Interstate Commerce Commission, and in municipal and state departments headed by boards. Committees, boards, and commissions are all based upon the same organizational ideas.

Authority may be compartmentalized. (3) *Functional Type:* When the intrinsic nature of the various processes in an enterprise is analyzed and some person is given responsibility for heading each one, we have the functional method of organization. In its extreme form, functionalization divides responsibility, tending to diffuse it as does the committee type. The executive is not as strong as he is in military organization. Several functional heads may deal with the same subordinate in the organization. The privates have several superiors issuing orders, instead of just the corporal. The weak-mayor form of municipal government, when built upon functionalized departments rather than upon boards, is an example of this type. The federal government resembles it, as do most state governments. In other words, the executive does not exert firm control over administrative matters, the heads of departments are left pretty much alone, staff services issue orders to line officials, and line responsibility is not clear-cut.

Modern organization method is a compromise. It attempts to combine what is best in earlier forms. (4) *Integrated Type:* For most cases, the ideal organization is one in which administrative authority is concentrated in the chief executive; lines of responsibility are hierarchical, staff officers clear through officials of the line, adequate attention is given to staff services, sufficient freedom is given to heads of operating units, and the entire organization is meshed at different levels and simply controlled at the top. This may be called the "integrated form." From the military, it takes the ideas of strong leadership, hierarchy, authority issuing from only one superior, and the necessity of putting responsibility upon the person who actually furnishes the end result. Emphasis upon staff services has been the product of the last fifty years, and has been contributed jointly by military organization and by some of the more progressive business corporations. Examples of modern organization theory are found in the better city-manager municipalities and in the objectives which the more successful state reorganizations have sought.[1]

MODERN THEORY

---

[1] Cf. John M. Pfiffner, *Public Administration* (New York, 1935); also A. E. Buck, *Administrative Consolidation in State Governments*, rev. ed. (New York, 1930).

The committee type should not be used for performing work functions. The board is designed for policy formation and judicial procedures. When work is to be directed, however, the single head is preferable to the multiple head. Unity is necessary for consistency, initiative, and real responsibility. Divided councils hurt employee morale. Citizen advice and participation, however, are very important, and provision should be made for their utilization in advisory and voluntary capacities.

Most governments could provide better services and save taxpayers' money if they were reorganized along modern lines. The difficulty is not in deciding what should be done but in creating sufficient interest and determination to effect the reforms. Reorganization movements coming up from the citizenry are all too frequently aimed merely at reducing the number of public services, rather than furnishing better organization for existing ones. Taxpayers' associations usually want less government, and not infrequently less interference with business; hence, reorganization turns into a fight over social control, instead of being a matter of good housekeeping.

Most citizens are aware of the need for governmental reorganizations, but those whose influence counts heaviest are usually opposed to some changes which the experts say are necessary.

ADMINISTRATIVE REORGANIZATION

This is because every bureau has its clientele. We are not likely to want interference with those agencies of government which are most useful to us. "Don't stir things up or we may lose out," is the shortsighted reasoning that stops most reorganization movements. Business corporations usually do not experience this difficulty. The board of directors says to the president, "You are the boss. Do what you think is necessary." Can we trust mayors, governors, and other chief executives to do the same thing? In some cases, we have given them limited powers of reorganization and on the whole the results have been encouraging.[1]

It is sometimes contended that, after all, reorganization is not very important. Get the right kind of employees, it is argued,

---

[1] For principles of reorganization, see Ministry of Reconstruction, Viscount Haldane, Chairman, *Report of the Machinery of Government Committee* (London, 1918).

and everything else will take care of itself. This may be true in small private enterprises, but it is not so in public ones. Authority must be secured to make basic organization changes. Unless they are made, the administration will be fundamentally defective. It is just like trying to build a good house on a weak foundation. There is a combination of elements in government which should constantly be sought: power corresponding to need, and responsibility corresponding to secure popular control. Both these depend upon strong executive leadership and organization lines which will assure unified control and responsibility.

Most people will agree upon the objectives of good administration. They want their needs met, desires fulfilled, laws faithfully executed. Citizens want to be treated politely and considerately. They want the most service for the least money.

OBJECTIVES People like to feel that they are being served, not ruled.

Administration needs to be flexible, responsive to attitudes and points of view. It must feel that it has something to sell and that its success depends upon popular satisfaction and appreciation. How can anything like these results and attitudes grow out of government red tape?

Red tape is delay, numerous regulations, inflexibility, unresponsiveness to customer desires. A certain amount of it is inherent and ineradicable in any large-scale enterprise, public or private. The reasons for government red tape are

CAUSES OF
RED TAPE definite and apparent. In the first place, it must act through law and adhere to statutory provision. Private businesses can usually make exceptions, but public employees must abide by the law or be punished. The second reason is that government is expected to treat all persons equally, none with special favor. Here, again, business enterprises are not so circumscribed in what they can do; but if government began playing favorites, there would be no end of it, and popular indignation would become greater than it does with the grossest cases of red tape.

Public employees often find that it is more important to be consistently correct than to be constantly trying to please the customer. It should be possible to do both, of course, but the customer-is-always-right attitude is sure to result in petty inconsistencies and breaches of regulations. Government could stand such exceptions more than it does. When the executive is progressive and fearless, customer responsiveness and consistency are combined. The nervous-old-woman type at the head of public departments is what hurts government's reputation.

In the third place, red tape is an inevitable by-product of faulty organization. Delay is usually caused by the employee's need to get authority or confirmation for a certain act. When authority is direct and immediate, government can be as prompt as any other organization of equal size. The object should be to simplify lines of responsibility, to delegate authority farther down the line. Difficulty arises when a staff service, such as finance, comes to have operating responsibilities. Then, instead of serving the responsible executive, it ties him up in Lilliputian threads.

Another case in which red tape is a reflection of bad organization is found when many duties or services are thrown into the same department, causing both the public and the officials to become confused. Contrast this with an organization which furnishes only one service, such as telephone communication. The objective is clear—the best telephone service at the cheapest price. Everything in the organization can be planned to that end, and all service is judged by that standard; but when the services are many, the adequacy with which any one is handled suffers correspondingly.

The police functions of government give it a reputation for red tape. Restriction is universally disliked. "Officiousness" is a symbol of governmental administration. As service functions increase, there is less of this. Salesmanship becomes the motif. Moreover, it is possible to train control officials in manners and more acceptable attitudes. The greatest change in police administration during the last generation is the training of patrolmen to consider what the public thinks and feels. The idea of policemen being given lessons in politeness may seem funny, but this is actually what happens in the larger departments.

The eradication of government red tape is not hopeless. In a government of laws, there is always bound to be some of it; but if administrative faults were corrected and if public employees were convinced of the desirability of a sales attitude, the amount of it would be no greater than in other organizations of like size. But is there an unbridgeable gap between what might be done and what will be accomplished?

SELECTED READINGS

Beard, Charles A.: *American Government and Politics* (5th ed., New York, 1928), chap. III; a discussion of the role of administration in American society.

Beck, James M.: *Our Wonderland of Bureaucracy* (New York, 1932); a scathing criticism of the growth and practices of the bureaucracy in the United States.

Blachly, Frederick F., and Oatman, Miriam E.: *Administrative Legislation and Adjudication* (Washington, 1935); from the analytical and public-law standpoints, a good introduction to the role of administrative agencies in the governmental process.

Comer, J. P.: *Legislative Functions of National Administrative Authorities* (New York, 1927); a historical and critical treatment of the tendency on the part of Congress to delegate legislative duties to the executive.

Dickinson, John: *Administrative Justice and the Supremacy of the Law* (Cambridge, Mass., 1927); an excellent study of the development of administrative adjudication and its contacts with the courts; especially is chap. I a clear and concise statement of the problem.

———: "The Perennial Cry of Bureaucracy," *Yale Review*, XXIV, No. 3 (March, 1935), 448–63.

Fayol, Henri: *Industrial and General Administration* (London, 1930), Part I; an excellent contribution to the study of administration dealing primarily with definitions.

Freund, Ernst: "The Substitution of Rule for Discretion in Public Law," *American Political Science Review*, IX, No. 4 (November, 1915), 666–76.

Gaus, J., White, L. D., Dimock, M. E.: *Frontiers of Public Administration* (Chicago, 1936); a series of essays in which some phases and concepts used in public administration are subjected to a critical examination.

Goodnow, Frank J.: *Comparative Administrative Law* (New York, 1893), I, Book I, chaps. I–V, inclusive; II, Book V, chaps. I–IV, inclusive; this pioneering research on American and comparative administrative law stresses the methods and forms of administrative action.

———: *Politics and Administration* (New York, 1900); the first treatise in this country to emphasize the importance of administration;

explores the relationships between the formulation of policy and the execution of policy.

Gulick, Luther: "Politics, Administration and the New Deal," *Annals*, CLXIX (September, 1933), 55–66.

Herring, E. Pendleton: *Public Administration and the Public Interest* (New York, 1936), chaps. I and XXIII; an excellent case study of administrative agencies of the federal government and of the influences exerted by organized interest groups. Chapters cited deal with the delegation of legislative powers and proposals for the improvement of administration in the public interest.

Hewart, Lord: *The New Despotism* (London, 1929); written in the spirit of advocacy; points to the dangers to self-government inherent in the encroachment of the executive upon the powers of the legislature and the judiciary.

Laski, Harold: "The Growth of Administrative Discretion," *Public Administration*, I (April, 1923), 92–100.

Mooney, James D., and Reiley, Alan C.: *Onward Industry* (New York, 1931), chaps. I–VII, and XIV; a very interesting study of the principles of organization in the various fields of associated activity—political, military, feudal, ecclesiastical, and industrial.

Pfiffner, John M.: *Public Administration* (New York, 1935), chaps. I–III, inclusive; a general textbook on public administration; gives a good survey of the subject matter and provides at the end of each chapter a useful bibliographical appendix.

Muir, Ramsay: *How Britain Is Governed* (New York, 1930), chaps. I and II; an analysis of the developments that have taken place in the British system of government in the last half century; these chapters treat the increase in the range and power of the bureaucracy.

Pound, Roscoe: "The Administrative Application of Legal Standards," *Reports of the American Bar Association*, XLIV (September, 1919), 445–65.

Report of the Committee on Ministers' Powers (His Majesty's Stationery Office, 1932), Cmd. 4060, *Parliamentary Reports*, XII, 1931–32; an evaluation of the criticisms levied at the delegation of legislative power to the executive.

Robson, William A.: "The Report of the Committee on Ministers' Powers," *Political Quarterly*, III, No. 3 (April-June, 1936), 346–64.

Walker, Harvey: "An American Conception of Public Administration," *Public Administration*, XI, No. 1 (January, 1933), 15–35.

Urwick, L.: *Organization as a Technical Problem* (Geneva, 1933).

———: "A Republic of Administration," *Public Administration*, XIII, No. 3 (July, 1935), 263–70.

White, Leonard D.: *Trends in Public Administration* (New York, 1933), chaps. I–XI, inclusive; a survey of the changes in the institutions of public administration in this country since the beginning of the twentieth century.

Willoughby, W. F.: *Principles of Public Administration* (Baltimore, 1927), chaps. I, II, and V; an examination of the constituent elements of public administration and an attempt to formulate principles covering the entire field.

Wilson, Woodrow: "The Study of Administration," *Political Science Quarterly*, II, No. 2 (June, 1887), 197–222.

CHAPTER X

☆ ☆ ☆

## THE STRATEGY OF MANAGEMENT

"*The danger for management is a lack, not of activity, but of a plan of action.*"
—OLIVER SHELDON

MODERN GOVERNMENT is a huge public-service undertaking, supplying citizens with the necessary requirements of every-day life. Most of its activities would continue to be performed irrespective of the particular élite—proletarian, middle-class, plutocratic, or other type—that happened to control. As its service functions increase, government becomes increasingly a matter of administration and less an object of political manipulation.

GROWING IMPORTANCE OF ADMINISTRATION

Judged by the percentage of total expenditures and the relative number of persons employed, roughly three-fourths of American government consists of administration. Less than one-fourth of the total expenditures of the average city goes to the legislative and judicial branches; the balance is represented by administrative salaries, public-works expenditures, debt service, and other departmental outlays. If the number of employees be taken as the criterion, it will be found that only about 15 or 20 per cent is accounted for by the legislative and judicial branches. Municipal government is the nearest approach to undiluted administration.

Substantially the same ratio exists in the states and in the national government. For example, fully two-thirds of those employed by the Government of the United States may be classed as administrative personnel. The civil service alone numbers seven hundred thousand out of a total federal pay roll of about a million. Government is the largest of all business enterprises.

Despite the importance of administration, citizens in a democratic country are likely to neglect it. They associate efficiency with loss of liberty—justifiably in some cases—and are inclined to be apprehensive when strong political leaders arise. The relative frequency with which leadership changes makes it difficult to establish smooth administrative processes and skilled direction at the top. In any institution, the best functioning is never secured until there has been time for the organization to "settle down." A new organization tends to rely upon written regulations. It is slow and self-conscious. It naturally has to think about itself, because it feels gangling and disjointed. Only when institutional procedures have had time to mellow are the best results forthcoming. People learn to co-operate, natural leaders crop out, men know their jobs, experience replaces regulations, institutional morale emerges, and the focus of attention is shifted to the users of the service.

Administrative factors are likely to be neglected because government is compromise and expediency. This is particularly true when executives are party leaders. If the political party is to win votes and stay in power, it must judge all its moves by their possible effect upon citizen support. Governments of the day frequently know the wisest policy to adopt from an administrative standpoint, but they deliberately choose a less workable one if doing so will get them votes. Sometimes, this means carrying water upon both shoulders. The party passes a bill to satisfy one interest and then makes its administration ineffectual because other interests or established attitudes make it advantageous to do so.

<small>REASONS FOR NEGLECT OF MANAGEMENT FACTORS</small>

These compromises on administrative principle are sometimes more costly in the end than a firm stand on a workable program would have been. When programs break down because of faulty organization, leadership, finance, or public relations, the sponsoring group is alienated from the political party and the interests who opposed the policy in the beginning are still hostile because the party decision went contrary to their wishes. Compromise with administrative workability is almost always a losing game.

The political leader is schooled in compromise; it becomes his inner nature, and, when he finds himself in an executive post, he continues to make decisions as a politician rather than as a trained administrator. This is one of the unsolved problems of representative government. Is there a cure for it or is it a necessary price of popular rule? Monarchies and dictatorships can get away from it; they feel sure of their power, and efficiency and workability may be fearlessly, ruthlessly sought. Minorities and popular prejudices are not effective deterrents. In order to approach a golden mean, our democratic leaders need to be schooled in administration. Fortunately, municipalities are freer from expediency and compromise than are the higher levels of government.

Let us take a concrete example of how basic questions of public administration arise, complicating policy determination and fraying the nerves of overworked executives. The federal government, we shall say, decides in principle upon a program of social insurance. The first step is to bring together experts on the formulation and execution of old-age and unemployment-insurance laws. It immediately appears that the basic question for decision is whether the system of collections and benefits shall be administered primarily by the federal government or by the several states. We shall assume that doubts about unconstitutionality under either system are approximately equal.

<small>COMPROMISE VERSUS PRINCIPLE</small>

The consultants strongly recommend a federally administered law. They point out that if the states were free to set up any arrangements they chose, the burdens and benefits probably would not be equal in all the states. States might not even set up a sufficient fund to meet actuarial requirements as they fell due, jeopardizing the entire plan, as there would be no way for the federal government to coerce the state into meeting its obligations. If the payments in one state were high and in another state low or nonexistent, the difference in the burden upon business competitors would be such that the firm in the high-tax state might not be able to survive; moreover, it is taken for granted that the federal government will act as reinsurance agent, meaning that, if a state finds itself unable to pay its obligations, the national government will do so. This might conceivably invite states to run through their funds or not to set up sufficient ones in the beginning.

A unified system administered by the federal government would make the burdens and benefits equal, assure the solvency of the fund, and simplify administrative organization and co-ordination. What are the arguments against a federal system? In the first place, business organizations favor state control, because in some states, as is well known, their political power is so great that they can dictate the kind of law that will be passed. Then, too, while such a program is being considered, several new agencies have been set up increasing the powers of the federal government. People are concerned about the shrinkage of states' rights. The dilemma is apparent. On one hand, the experts say that only a federal system is likely to prove workable. On the other, political forces demand a state plan. If you were the responsible political executive, what would your decision be?

American governments neglect administrative factors because of inadequate organization. Since the chief executive himself is usually a political leader rather than an administrator, it is necessary for someone close to him to furnish constant advice concerning management problems. In most other countries, this function is performed by the permanent civil service head of the department. In Great Britain the highest officers in the Treasury and the Cabinet secretariat advise the Government on administrative matters of general import. Canada has her Deputy Minister in every department, an experienced civil servant who stays on irrespective of changes in party leadership. Our arrangements, as we shall see, are not so adequate.

INADEQUATE ORGANIZATION ARRANGEMENTS

How do our political executives go about their managerial duties? They take an oath to "execute the laws faithfully." When used in this context, does "faith" mean skill or blindness? Our executives are usually not trained administrators. We cannot expect them to understand the strategy of management, the things that the successful administrator does in carrying through a program to successful completion. All too frequently, they do not even seem aware of the importance of administrative aspects; moreover, our governments are not organized to supply the deficiencies which untrained laymen are bound to have.

## THE STRATEGY OF MANAGEMENT

A man from Mars would suppose that we expect our executives to be supermen. They are party leader, sponsor of the legislative program, patronage dispenser, and ceremonial figurehead, as well as administrator in charge of all program execution. At least the President and the governors of the forty-eight states theoretically perform all of these roles. In actual practice, it has been the executive function, the directive and co-ordinative work, that has been most neglected. The governor of one of the smaller states, if capable, can perform all the duties expected of him. He can be even the general manager of the state departments and services. In the larger states, however, and in the federal government, it is impossible for any individual to carry all the other obligations of office and still be an efficient executive.

Government demands much more of its leaders than it used to. The state is now positive and directive. When government fails to carry through programs capably and aggressively, the people are likely to suffer. The work which public authority now does requires a full-time executive who can devote his efforts and ability to planning, leading, and co-ordinating the manifold programs of administration. It is no longer a part-time job, something that can be done after political conferences are over, speeches made, and monuments dedicated.

The city-manager form of government provides a model for state and federal administrations. They need the dual executive, the figurehead elective official and the efficient appointive manager, much more than does the municipality.

**THE DUAL EXECUTIVE** After all, what city-manager cities have done is what almost every country outside the United States has found necessary and desirable. The elective head is a symbol of popular rule, of national unity; he relieves the efficient executive of most of the ceremonial obligations attached to political life, while the executive really gets the work done. The two men need somewhat different qualifications. Political leadership and a capacity for management are special skills; the two are almost never found together.

It may appear that if a chief executive only appoints capable department heads everything else will take care of itself. Why should managerial responsibilities be expected of our political executives? Many times in American political history, elected officials must have asked themselves the same question. They soon discover the answer. From the ranks of party workers, it is impossible to choose department heads who, without exception, are good executives. There are never enough to go around. Plums are handed out on the basis of influence, not sheer administrative ability. The chief executive always has men who disappoint him. Then, too, the administrative agencies are so numerous, the services so complex, and the details so overwhelming that it becomes almost impossible to keep all of them in mind. The chief executive cannot know what is going on unless he spends the time and energy needed to find out.

When administrative complexity exists and provision for an efficient executive has not been made, duplications of service and inconsistent policies are inevitable. For example, millions of dollars are appropriated to preserve wild-fowl and bird life, while at the same time other agencies of the same government are spending millions to drain the marshy places upon which the survival of wild life depends. Only the full-time executive is likely to provide for the co-ordination of planning agencies. The duplication of services increases expense. Taxes go up when the top executive falls down. There can be no such thing as responsible finance and executive budgets worthy of the name unless the President or Governor really has time for his administrative responsibilites.

Every group activity has an inherent tendency to expand, and the institution of government is an outstanding example. A frequent objection to the establishment of a new governmental agency is this, "Give it life and in a short time it will have grown beyond all reasonable bounds." Men who have spent their lives in minor administrative posts often remark, "The King incessantly attempts to extend his domain." What they mean is obvious; it is human nature for a leader to want more authority, responsibility, and power. Such an aspiration is not a bad trait in itself, for sometimes it indicates that a man really has more potential ability than he

*CONSEQUENCES OF INADEQUATE ATTENTION TO MANAGEMENT*

has had an opportunity to put into practice, but government has to guard against allowing it to run riot. The chief executive is the only one who can be expected to "trim the sails" of department heads. No one else should attempt to do so. But what if he does not have the time or ability to make the effort?

The larger an organization, the greater the need for strong leadership. One corollary to this is that capability and authority should be equal. The bigger the job, the more capable the person needed. Then, too, institutions which are not led invariably settle down into ruts, or retrogress. This danger is particularly great in government, where the rank and file of administrators are guaranteed permanence of tenure. There is the ever-present danger that institutional lethargy, rather than the captivating quality of executive leadership, will dominate them. If bureaucrats begin to feel that they owe no obligation save to the statute creating the office and the law guaranteeing security of tenure, it is idle to hope for progressive and wide-awake administration. The only thing that will keep bureaucracy out of a rut is the leadership qualities of the executive personnel. No matter what walk of life they may be in, most men have a need to be led. The inspiration of personal example is as necessary in an individual's affairs as stimulating food is to his body.

The dual executive is usually found in the business corporation, a fact which should be of some persuasive importance. The chairman of the board is the nominal head, while the president or general manager is the efficient executive. An analogy between government and business is appropriate. The board of directors corresponds to the legislature and the general manager is the equivalent of the political executive. Sometimes, corporations roll the offices of chairman and president into one, but when both executives understand their distinctive contributions and do not attempt to invade each other's fields, the dual executive has more to recommend it than the single one.

It cannot be said that at any time within the near future there is a likelihood of our providing dual executives for the larger states and for the national government. Despite the examples set by business, city-manager municipalities, and foreign

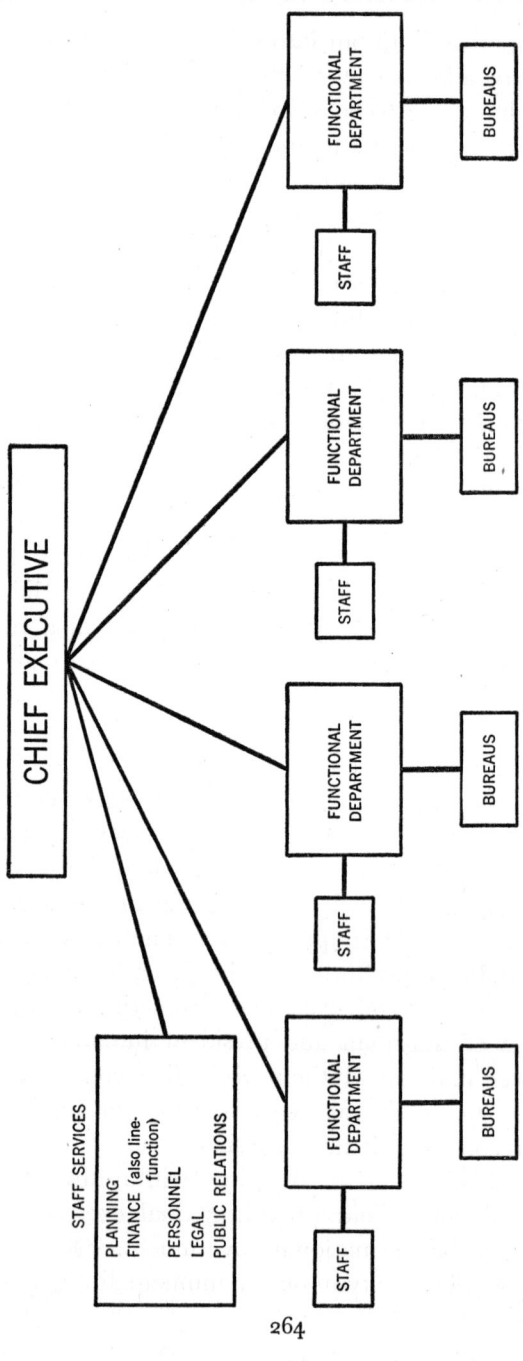

FIGURE 3.—ADMINISTRATIVE ORGANIZATION—ILLUSTRATING FUNDAMENTAL PRINCIPLES

governments, any such prediction would be unjustifiably sanguine; but there is a workable alternative.

Chief executives need staff assistance. (See Figure 3.) Just as the president of General Motors or of the American Telephone and Telegraph Company has close to him vice-presidents dealing with operations, finance, law, personnel, public relations, and all functional matters, so the nation's President requires administrative assistance which he can call his very own. The heads of the various departments do not fill this need. They have all they can do to learn about war, commerce, or whatever special field they work in during four years in office. True, they serve in the President's Cabinet, give their advice on questions of general importance, and help to introduce a measure of co-ordination into the work of the whole government. The National Emergency Council, President Roosevelt's "super-Cabinet," was intended to contribute to the same end, but no existing agency, either in Washington or in the several states, seems to supply what is clearly needed.

<small>STAFF ASSISTANCE A POSSIBLE SOLUTION</small>

Chief executives have their private secretaries, who serve a useful purpose, but not administration. Confidential secretaries answer correspondence, arrange calendars, meet visitors, mend political fences, and write speeches. They may learn a great deal about what is going on in the various departments and independent establishments, but rarely are they able to assist the executive in his role as managerial strategist.

Staff services should belong to the chief executive, not merely to the government as a whole. This is the original interpretation of the staff idea. The military commander had his advisers. Today's General Staff was yesterday's "General's Staff." Military and business management have not changed the original intention of the staff service; it still adheres to the top executive; but civil administration has not been so faithful to precedent. In state governments, treasurers are usually elected and operate independent departments. They do not feel that they are staff assistants of the governor. Civil-service commissions are described as "independent establishments." They are defenders of the merit system and, hence, frequently hostile or suspicious in their dealings with the chief executive. In some ways, this may be fortunate; but the larger point of administrative unity should not be overlooked.

Existing staff agencies have assumed "control" characteristics. They have ceased to be staff services in the truest and best sense of the term; moreover, the staff assistance available to chief executives is by no means adequate or integrated. These shortcomings are of even greater importance than the changed roles which finance and personnel have come to play.

The chief executive needs a staff unit corresponding to "operations" in a business corporation. The vice-president at the head of it reports to the president on all matters relating to the actual provision of service. In the A. T. & T., for example, the operations vice-president has charge of engineering, plant, traffic, and commercial activities. Most of the employees are in these four departments of the operating companies. They spend most of the money. They design, install, service, and charge for all telephone service. In other words, operations is responsible for all the service the user of a telephone gets. The other vice-presidents have small departments and their sole purpose is to contribute to better operations. True to theory, staff services are built around the line.

ANALOGY TO BUSINESS CORPORATIONS

In the federal government and in the larger states, the chief executive might be assisted by a staff official who would correspond to the vice-president in charge of operations. Mr. W. F. Willoughby has proposed a bureau of general administration for the federal government.[1] The head of it would correspond roughly to a city manager. His status, however, would be basically different because the President would continue to possess all responsibility and attempt to be the efficient executive. The bureau of general administration would merely act as the President's clearinghouse. Through it, the chief executive would be kept *au courant*, and down through it would go co-ordinating authority. It would inform, advise, help co-ordinate, and provide financial and personnel assistance.

PROPOSED DEPARTMENT OF GENERAL ADMINISTRATION

[1] W. F. Willoughby, *Principles of Public Administration* (Baltimore, 1927), pp. 52–80.

It is very doubtful whether a staff service should enjoy departmental status. True, the British Treasury is His Majesty's staff department for personnel, finance, and administrative consistency. The United States Treasury might be given similar authority; and, in fact, it has been relied upon to a considerable extent in recent years for advice of that sort; but if it were to become primarily a co-ordinating department, it would have to divest itself of many line duties which would otherwise prevent its fulfilling the intended function.

Co-ordination should take place above the departmental level. No department should be *primus inter pares*. Finance is only one aspect of management, and it can be overemphasized, just as any other factor can. A pinch-penny attitude, for example, can completely wreck the morale of everyone in the public service. This is short-sighted economy. To put it another way, finance should be first, but it should not dominate. The chief executive should control; therefore, he needs staff agencies in his own office, close by his side, and reporting to him alone. "No man can serve two masters."

There should be a co-ordinator, corresponding to the operations vice-president. Law is already taken care of in the office of the Attorney-General. Then, there should be staff officers responsible for finance and personnel. Planning as the primary staff service should be fittingly recognized. These five—planning, co-ordination, personnel, finance, and law—are probably the chief staff functions which should be ensconced near the chief executive. Public relations is important, too, but the social value of such an agency is probably not sufficiently well understood at the present time to make such a proposal acceptable.

<small>A SUGGESTED PLAN</small>

Planning and execution need to be co-ordinated; therefore, both should be under the general supervision of the President's administrative assistant. Two types of planning activity may be distinguished. The first is long-term, the execution of programs taking many years. City and natural-resource planning are of this kind. Then, there is applied planning for the execution of immediate programs. Every kind of organized effort must partake of this kind of forethought. This may be called "administrative planning," as contrasted with problem planning; it deals with organization, personnel, financial procedures, and the sequence in which various steps shall be taken in getting the work done. It is often difficult to draw a line between what we have called "long-term problem planning" and "applied administrative planning." In any case, the two should be placed under the same organizational roof, because they are complementary. It is particularly important, moreover, that administrative planning be closely integrated with the co-ordinator's responsibilities. This kind of planning comes up from the bottom and cannot be separated from day-to-day execution. If it were, administrative programs could not be expected to succeed.

The purpose of co-ordinated administrative planning is to secure consistency and co-operation and to prevent duplication. We do not visualize all planning rolled into one organization. Far from it. It is merely the integration of separate planning agencies that is needed. Long-time planners, such as those concerned with agricultural chemistry or reforestation, would continue to enjoy independent status. A liaison relationship would be established with the co-ordinator's office, which, of course, would involve some regroupings. If all the existing agencies of the federal government were represented by liaison officers, the assemblage would be another League of Nations. The work of the President's administrative assistant could succeed only if his staff were kept within workable limits. The representation of the most important departments and planning programs is the greatest consideration. In order to make this possible, consolidations and reallocation of functions are clearly necessary in some cases. Everything that has been said in this discussion applies as well to the problem of administrative management in the larger states.

Staff work is hard to explain. Large-scale organizations in which this function is well performed are much better managed than those in which it is poorly done or virtually nonexistent. It is the most important institutional factor in management. Only the capacity of individual leadership is of more consequence. The success of staff services depends upon securing the right type of persons and upon their understanding the nature of the work. Good staff men are rare. Men with large egos, which

QUALIFICA-
TIONS OF STAFF
OFFICIALS

have to be paraded daily, do not qualify as staff officials. At the same time, a staff person is no good if he is a "yes man." He needs the will-power and forcefulness to withstand the aggressiveness of the executive type. A hard combination to find, is it not? The ideal staff man knows more than his boss; has more tact and as much determination as his chief; and, yet, permitting others to get the credit for his contributions, derives sufficient personal satisfaction out of the organization's achievements. Self-abnegation and complete satisfaction in good workmanship are rather rare qualities in this modern world!

Most men who possess the needed knowledge and leadership qualities feel effective only when in a position of command. This is the fatal mistake which so many staff men make. They give way to the urge to run things. The staff official must get his ideas over to the line official and make the latter think them his own original ideas. The inexperienced staff man tries to take a short cut; he issues an order. Every time he does this, he steps on the toes of an executive of the line. Then, the staff man begins to wonder why he is not called upon for as much help as formerly. If he persists in "swinging the club," line officials will probably boycott him altogether. When enmity exists between the line and the staff, the enterprise is sure to suffer from weakness. All the life is sapped from it, *esprit de corps* is lacking, and, in consequence, the organization fails to concentrate upon the customer's wants and attitudes.

The staff function will be well performed if the chief executive knows his job and has the personal qualities to lead a large organization. Despite all the emphasis we are justified in placing upon the staff function, not for one moment should

"TOP CONTROL"  we lose sight of the fact that human factors have more to do with setting the bounds of institutional effectiveness than do organizational ones. After an enterprise has been organized and lines of responsibility drawn between the line and staff functions, the executive personnel give the signals, set the energy in motion, and direct the teamwork. The executive is like the ship's captain standing at the controls and signaling the engine room. There is plenty of power down below, but what is done with it depends upon the skill of the man on the bridge. In terms of management, what the captain does we call "control" or "top control."

The word "control" seems to suggest dictation or domination. We need to get a more liberal construction of the term. The domineering executive usually is not the successful one. Control does not mean "bossiness"; it can and should mean leadership. The real leader gets whole-hearted response from his followers because he impresses them by knowing his job and because his knowledge of human nature makes it possible to appeal to those interests and emotions in the individual which secure the utmost effort. A man who understands human nature and who has the energy and personality of the born leader can usually be relied upon to surround himself with others of like qualities. That a person usually chooses those who are like himself, is a truism of management. This is not necessarily a good thing, however, because sometimes a lop-sided man requires someone who is lop-sided in the opposite direction to complement his deficiency. But let us not stray from the point. The right kind of leadership is the basic matter in any kind of co-operative effort. Communism, fascism, and democracy all can agree upon this.

The problem of control is that of co-ordinating activities at the various levels of organization in such manner that the number of persons reporting to the top executive will be no larger than is necessary to secure the highest measure of over-all unity consonant with the greatest amount of operating autonomy. It is curious how often the best results are secured by blending seeming opposites! The consistency of the whole and the independence of the component parts: this is a basic theory of management.

UNITY OF MANAGEMENT

Unity of management is indispensable. Consistency, responsiveness, and dynamic leadership depend upon it. Unity of management has two corollaries: all persons follow a single leader;

all units in an organization are integrated into a system which leads up to the chief executive. Divided leadership produces quarrels, resulting in impaired morale. The chief executive cannot be expected to produce a complete service unless all units are under his direction.

Government probably violates the principle of unified management more than any other tenet in public administration. Staff services are set up to control line officials rather than to service them. We create so-called independent boards and commissions, making effective top control out of the question. We popularly elect administrative officers whose work is indispensable to the chief executive, but whose co-operation cannot be relied upon. Staff assistance is almost invariably inadequate. Organization is so complex that levels of authority are practically nonexistent. The number of persons reporting to the chief executive makes real direction and responsibility humanly impossible. These are not merely theoretical faults, and unless government does something about these flagrant violations of principle, it can never accomplish the things the modern community expects of it.

Sound principles of administration demand unity of management, but government usually exemplifies diffused or nonunified control. The management of the Detroit street-railway system quite typically illustrates this point. Here we have an important public-utility service run by the city. Like a business corporation, the enterprise has a board and a general manager; but there the resemblance ceases. If it were a private business, the chief executive would exercise complete control over finance and personnel. The Detroit street railway, however, is not permitted complete autonomy or unity of management. The city treasurer controls most of the financial procedures, including authority to borrow money and to keep it on deposit. All personnel requirements are filled by the city civil-service commission, which enforces permanent-tenure and limits freedom of discharge. In other words, the chief executive cannot control all parts of the business, not even all the most important ones. The same is true of highway superintendents, public-welfare administrators, and, in some measure, of mayors, governors, and the President himself.

Let us be sure that the issue is clearly defined. We are not objecting to departments' relying upon "pooled" services, such as personnel, for the consolidation of a general, city-wide function is usually desirable. The important point is that the pooled services should be merely staff agencies. When they are converted into control devices and interfere with unity of management, the line departments cannot hope to function with so much proficiency as could otherwise be expected.

It is the need to secure unity of management and the accompanying advantages of autonomous finance and personnel that has caused public authorities to make wide use of the corporate device. Finding it difficult or impossible to gain financial freedom and opportunity for initiative under traditional organization method, governments have made use of the corporation, the symbol of private business.[1] We shall have an opportunity in Chapter XII to see how it works and how it compares with diffused management.

Successful enterprises invariably require great leaders. Businesses and public departments which have been mediocre or weak have been converted into outstanding successes almost overnight when a man of imagination, statesmanship, physical vigor, and strong personality has taken over the reins of authority. Conversely, highly successful public and private undertakings have become mediocre or weak when uninspired and dull leaders have come to head the organization. When a public or private business has a great leader, the outsider almost instantly becomes aware of his influence, as reflected in the atmosphere and *esprit de corps* of the institution as a whole, as mirrored in the attitudes and dynamic spirit of the employees, and as manifested in concrete form by the quality of service rendered to its users.

QUALITIES OF EXECUTIVE LEADERSHIP

As organizations grow larger, the requirements of executive leadership increase. In the business world, the owner of a small undertaking has no difficulty securing unity of management. He

[1] For a theoretical introduction, see Marshall E. Dimock, "Principles Underlying Government-Owned Corporations," *Public Administration*, XIII, No. 1 (January, 1935), 51–66, and "Public Corporations and Business Enterprise," same journal, XIV, No. 4 (October, 1936), pp. 417–28.

is both owner and operator, personally supreme over a small force, and if he lacks capacity his business fails. The modern corporation complicates this simple arrangement. It is like government in that the trusteeship principle is established. The owners trust the board of directors and the management for results. A professional administrative corps with trained executives handling specific functions comes into being. The size of the organization seemingly produces bureaucracies in all large-scale enterprises, whether private or public. Thinking business men say, "Bureaucracy is inherent; the only question is whether its objectionable characteristics are ineradicable." This, in turn, depends upon the type of leadership that can be produced.

The demand for effective leadership in both business and government is far from being filled. Mere technicians will not suffice. A person may know finance "from A to Z" or public welfare administration forward and backward, but unless he can also plan, co-ordinate, and contribute qualities of personal leadership, he will not meet the requirements of a large organization. Narrow-gauge executives plunge themselves into a mass of detail—detail which should be delegated to subordinate officials. The consequences become almost immediately apparent. Unprogressiveness, false starts, conflicting objectives, loss of morale among employees, and colorless service, are the penalties paid by an enterprise which is so unfortunate as to have a chief executive who is not big enough for his job. Human beings the world over are sensitive to the presence or lack of leadership and respond accordingly.

Organizations today are typically found to be growing by division, like certain lower forms of biological life.[1] This is particularly the case in government. Large-scale administration assumes the effective participation of hundreds of individuals who are continually joining it with little prior knowledge of what the organization is striving to do. Without such an awareness, satisfactory organization and conditions of morale are almost impossible to maintain. Then, too, bureaucracies such as the

[1] See the fascinating book by Ordway Tead entitled, *The Art of Leadership* (New York, 1935), especially pp. 10–20.

national government tend toward a more complex functionalizing of individual duties and toward the building up of a wide geographic hierarchy of administration. Ordway Tead does not make an overstatement when he says, "Only competent leaders can correct the tendencies which functionalism and division of labor create. Only the leader can keep the group committed to that unity of aim which alone produces the best results." One of the most significant features of military administration, it has been truly remarked, is that "the top sergeant is trained to feel that he, as truly as the general, must be a leader." Leadership is the antidote to bureaucracy.

Ten steps are involved in effective executive work. These are typically: (1) planning and defining policies and procedures; (2) organizing the activities of others; (3) delegating authority and responsibility; (4) controlling these in terms of the results desired; (5) supervising the general progress of results; (6) giving general orders or instructions; (7) interpreting and transmitting policies; (8) training key subordinates to carry the executive load; (9) co-ordinating all the various efforts and elements; and, finally, (10) the important task of stimulating and vitalizing all the individuals who are contributing their effort.[1]

WHAT THE LEADER DOES

The leader-administrator must have breadth of knowledge, power of penetration, and constructive imagination. He needs to be resourceful, tactful, and philosophical. He must combine the ability to plan with the dynamics of efficient execution. As Tead has expressed the same idea, "The leader must be able to translate aspiration into acceptable methods." If a person is to see and control an enterprise in all its ramifications, he must maintain that perspective which comes only from delegating the actual work program to others. One of the principal reasons for Henry Ford's success is said to be that he spends a large part of each day visiting the various units of the organization and forming opinions regarding the satisfactoriness of the several departments and the steps which might be taken to improve individual processes or the smooth working of the enterprise as a whole.

[1] *Ibid*, pp. 14–15.

## THE STRATEGY OF MANAGEMENT 275

The ability to co-ordinate large enterprises is possessed by very few people. It requires knowledge of all aspects of the undertaking, ability to see things broadly and comprehensively, facility in altering work programs and organization when necessary better to achieve objectives, success in delegating duties, sensitivity to faulty organization or processes, courage to upset existing arrangements irrespective of whose toes are stepped on, and sustained vitality and freshness of outlook.

The socially minded administrative leader realizes that the success of the enterprise depends upon the response of all his employees. This reaction is conditioned by the example of the chief and the consideration he gives the rank and file. Ordway Tead points out that command is an exercise of power *over* people, while leadership is the use and creation of power *with* people. Command is occupied solely with the result; leadership is equally concerned with the process by which the result is attained. The distinction is a very important one. Outstandingly successful enterprises are usually those in which the employees have a feeling of genuine affection for the chief. The wise leader learns to know personally as many men as possible in his organization. The great executive has a big heart and a democratic spirit, as well as an alert mind.

<small>SPIRITED RESPONSE</small>

It is sometimes said that large-scale enterprises must break down of their own weight, because there are too many functions, departments, and details for any one man to co-ordinate successfully. Herbert Morrison, Britain's Labor Minister of Transport, has warned, "We must beware of overly large units of industrial management." But, as we have already said, there is considerable reason to doubt whether the growth of large enterprises can be stopped or will be checked. Let us note what is of more immediate importance. Past failures to achieve the best results of large-scale organizations have been attributable in large part to lack of knowledge of the essentials of administrative integration, inadequate use of staff services, failure to delegate sufficiently, or inadequate emphasis upon leadership and incentives.

Dynamic leaders will be required in public positions more frequently and persistently in the future than in the past, because the newer and more important of governmental activities are economic and social services. Consider, for example, the new administrative agencies which were created by the Roosevelt Administration during the first two years of the New Deal. Of the sixty or more instrumentalities which were either created or modified, by far the largest proportion were concerned with economic planning, assistance, or provision of services supplied directly to the public. Irrespective of what the character of government employment has been in the past (and it is not what most people have seemed to think), the future clearly indicates that "routinism" will never suffice if the state is to foster the nation's industry and attempt to guarantee economic security to the individual. A positive, want-supplying government must provide planning, leadership, and initiative. These can be assured only by competent individuals, given sufficient freedom to produce unity of management.

The chief finance officer is usually the right-hand man of the executive, either in government or in business. The planning of work involves the expenditure of funds. Thus, one of the automatic limits upon an enterprise is the amount of money there is to be spent. What the management feels it can do for employees depends upon the balance sheet. Purchasing and contracts, which constitute a large part of administration, are within the special competence of the finance officer. Besides, control over expenditures is a control of human beings and their efficiency. In short, when the feasibility of a program is involved, the planning of work considered, the legality of an expenditure questioned, a higher compensation for employees desired, contracts to be entered into, purchases to be made, or the efficiency of processes or employees to be gauged, the chief executive must rely upon his financial officer.

RELATION OF FINANCE TO TOP CONTROL

A common fault in management is that the finance officer is given too much power. The danger is greater in government than in business. The outstanding lesson of English constitutional history is that "he who controls the purse strings controls the government." There is a natural tendency for the same thing to be true in large public or corporate organizations. As we have already said, the responsibilities of the finance officer are practically as broad as those of the chief executive. He may know even more about the details of what the units of the enterprise are doing than the executive himself. This is not surprising, because all vouchers and contracts come to his office. Again, so much emphasis is placed upon economy and efficiency that the person controlling expenditures is inevitably treated with great deference.

A weak executive will transfer large blocks of responsibility to his chief finance officer. This happens over and over again. When the board of directors or the legislature, as the case may be, asks for an account of financial stewardship, the executive is likely to find that he cannot handle the details so well as the comptroller. One of two courses is open to him. Either he will prepare the report with the assistance of the finance man, and present it himself, or he will pass on the whole responsibility to his financial chief. The principal test of executive ability and independence, however, comes when disputes arise between department heads and the comptroller. These disagreements are frequent and inevitable in any enterprise. It may be a difference about budget provisions, the terms of a contract, the best purchase, or the distribution of a joint cost. If disagreements do not arise, the chief executive can be fairly sure that his assistants are asleep at the switch or that the comptroller has been "bulldozing."

The morale of an enterprise will be wrecked unless the top executive steps in and settles disagreements between department heads and the principal finance officer. It is his inescapable responsibility. One test of good management is whether a department head feels absolute freedom to go to his chief and lay before him a dispute with the comptroller. The executive should then bring the two officials together and effect an agreement. If he "passes the buck" and does not question the ruling of the comptroller, he will soon find that progressiveness is disappearing and that a sense of injustice rankles in the memories of his line officials.

<small>RESPONSIBILITY OF THE CHIEF EXECUTIVE</small>

The finance officer is a staff employee and, hence, should not be permitted to dominate. His main duty is to be helpful to the chief executive. He helps plan, "digs up" detailed information, and provides a powerful tool of administrative control for the co-ordinator. But if he makes the mistake of trying to run the organization himself, the entire enterprise will suffer, whether or not he personally does.

The relation between financial administration and top control is not very satisfactory in most governments, because the underlying theory is wrong. Chief finance officers are usually elected by the people or appointed by the legislature to be that body's watchdog. Finance is expressive of the checks-and-balances theory rather than of principled management. The underlying idea is to restrain the executive, rather than to assist him. Finance is not considered an integral part of management. It is primarily the legislature's responsibility, and this body attempts to control expenditures directly and in a detailed manner as well as to make the funds available. But modernized governments have seen the light. In city-manager and strong-mayor cities and in some of the reorganized states, finance is usually considered an executive responsibility. The executive prepares the budget and assumes real responsibility for executing it. The legislature confines its attention to examining and enacting the budget and raising the revenues. Under this system, treasurers or heads of finance departments are, or in all cases should be, appointed by the chief executive.

The right relation between financial control and executive leadership is of the utmost importance to good government. Sound principles are to be discovered by thinking in terms of functions rather than about departments or offices, as seems to have been the case too often in the past. There are two functions of finance: one is to serve as a tool of management and the other is to provide an audit on legality and honesty. A sharp line needs to be drawn between the two. The treasurer and the auditor perform entirely different functions. The latter represents the citizens and the legislature; he checks up on the management. The former is the staff assistant of the executive—planning, keeping the books, helping the management in all the ways suggested above.

TWO FUNCTIONS OF FINANCIAL MANAGEMENT

The distinction between the management aspect of finance and the fiduciary one is recognized and observed in business practice. From the earliest days of the corporation, the treasurer has been considered an administrative officer and the auditor an outsider, elected by the owners and reporting directly to them. Administrative reform in government depends upon the consistent application of this principle.

Under the Budget and Accounting Act of 1921, the Comptroller-General of the United States performs duties which properly belong to the Chief Executive and the administration. He makes a pre-audit as well as a post-audit. The Comptroller-General rules upon discretionary policy matters, not merely upon legality and honesty. His power is analogous to that exercised by the courts when they rule upon due process of law as applied to social legislation. Moreover, the Comptroller-General has no connection with the executive branch. He is Congress's watchdog, appointed for a fifteen-year term and removable only by a joint resolution. This system violates fundamental principles of management. It is desirable that provision be made for pre-audit in management, but it should be a departmental one and be undertaken by persons responsible to the Chief Executive. Here, again, we come back to the principle of unity of management.

Outside financial control of day-to-day management results in tying the hands of the administrator, dividing responsibility, slowing down the work of departments, and exasperating line officials because of their feeling of helplessness and frustration. Overcentralization of financial control can be one of the principal causes of red tape. This has been demonstrated in business as well as in government. Washington reeks with overcentralized financial control. The General Accounting Office cannot keep up with its work. Pre-audits may take as long as a month, or even more. Frequently, the administrative expense of making "exceptions" costs more than the amount involved. A sound rule to keep in mind is that finance exists for management, not management for finance. In Washington, departmental accounting and pre-audits are clearly desirable, but before such a reform can be accomplished the basic distinction between finance as a tool of management and as a check on past actions needs to be accepted by Congress.

The budget is one of the principal tools of management.[1] It is, like the work of the finance officer, almost as comprehensive as all of government. The budget gives a record of past programs and results; plans future activities; helps the executive organize men and materials; provides the legislature with the basis for appropriation and revenue measures; gives the administration a powerful weapon of control; constitutes the basis of audits; reports on expenditures and accomplishments; and educates the citizenry. There are three principal stages in budgetary procedure: formulation, enactment, and execution. The first and last properly fall to the lot of management, and the middle stage is the task of the legislature. There are, however, three principal types of budgetary formulation: by the lesiglature, by the executive, or by an agency representing both. The executive budget is most desirable from the standpoint of governmental theory.

THE BUDGETARY PROCESS

The executive budget is a recognition of the planning and initiating obligations which fall increasingly upon administration. It places the duty of drawing up a budget upon the Chief Executive, who, as party leader and as head of the administration, is best suited to the responsibility. The legislative and commission budgets, on the other hand, diffuse responsibility.[2] As the executive budget has been increasingly substituted for the legislative, unity of management, responsible finance, and a more sensible interpretation of the separation-of-powers doctrine all have been furthered. So long as the budget can be changed at will by the legislature, we are still a long way from responsible government of the cabinet type, but on the whole, executive budgets have considerably lessened the amount of change that occurs after the appropriation bill reaches the floor of the chamber.

[1] Cf. A. E. Buck, *Public Budgeting* (New York and London, 1929), and *The Budget in Governments of Today* (New York, 1934).
[2] Cf. W. F. Willoughby, *The Problem of a National Budget* (New York and London, 1918), for the system as it existed prior to 1921.

Separate financial agencies are needed to help the executive formulate spending policy and to audit expenditures after they have been made. It is sometimes contended that, in addition, a bureau of efficiency reporting directly to the Chief Executive is desirable. This is very doubtful. The budgetary agency should be concerned with organization and efficiency, just as is the Bureau of the Budget in Washington. The auditor should make efficiency investigations, as the Comptroller-General is authorized to do under the Act of 1921, although he has failed to discharge this duty.

EFFICIENCY TESTING

A well-administered auditing department will be concerned with efficiency, not merely legality and honesty. In business corporations, the auditor frequently conducts cost studies, in which efforts are made to figure how much each unit of activity costs. Unit-cost studies are much needed in government, because they would show the citizen what he gets for his tax dollar and where various portions of it go. Some progressive administrations, particularly in cities, have made advances along this line. It should be understood, however, that most governmental expenditures cannot be broken down reliably into unit-costs. This is particularly true where control functions are exercised. Measurement is much more feasible in some forms of assistance or in public-utility management. The per-unit cost of family welfare relief or of water supply are cases in point.

Efficiency, however, is not merely a financial measurement.[1] Cost and profit are only one approach to social satisfaction; other factors, such as customer satisfaction, treatment of employees, and the difference between what is possible and what has been accomplished, also are important. These over-all considerations can be judged only by the Chief Executive. The help of his financial aides is basic; but, after that, he must secure the evidence of department heads, employees' representatives, and those dealing with public relations.

Modern budgetary procedure also assists public reporting. The most important potential use of budgeting is its educational

---

[1] See my essay, entitled, "The Criteria and Objectives of Public Administration," in *The Frontiers of Public Administration*.

value. Citizens need to be shown what they are getting and to be given a basis for judging how much more, if any, they should expect. There are two principal types of reports: managerial, or departmental; and public, or general. An example of the first is the annual report of the water commissioner to the city-manager; while an example of the latter is the joint report of the manager and council to the citizens. The latter is compiled out of data which are secured from the departmental reports.[1] Both types of reporting, if based upon a satisfactory budget system, render managerial and public control more effective. They show exactly what was spent and what was secured in return.

PUBLIC REPORTING

A good public report is short, interestingly written, graphically illustrated, and free from long rows of figures and boresome details. It tells citizens what the park department did with the $75,000 it spent, in terms which can be readily understood and appreciated. It does not talk about lump sums; it discusses swimming pools, tennis courts, services which show citizens what was accomplished and what was spent. Public reporting is one of the fields in which government has shown the most improvement in recent years. The better reports rely principally upon photographs, and all the modern graphic techniques of presenting statistical and financial data.

Public reporting, if widespread and well handled, could be an important instrument of citizen education and popular control. The progress along this line is encouraging, but adequate reporting needs to be extended to wider fronts. Then, too, governments have not solved the problem of how to get even the best reports into the hands of the rank and file of the citizens. Usually, they are content to make free copies available upon request, which is hardly sufficient. Probably they should be sent out through the mail to everyone in the city directory, but here the element of expense enters. Legislative bodies, even in progressive jurisdictions, have not been thoroughly "sold" on the necessity of explaining what government does.

[1] Cf. The National Municipal League publication entitled, "Public Reporting" (New York, 1931); also Herman C. Beyle, *Governmental Reporting in Chicago* (Chicago, 1928).

Citizens are traditionally suspicious of any effort by a public body to advertise itself. They seem to have entirely different standards for business and government. It is not considered dignified for public authorities to attempt to influence what people think of the service they get. "Quality speaks for itself." Under the guise of "educating" the voters, officials might mislead the public and throw a smoke screen around their own questionable dealings. Many are the reasons for public hesitance and suspicion; however, these objections, usually nothing more than attitudes, have begun to disappear.

PUBLIC RELATIONS

"Putting the best face on things" may not be an effort to cover anything; it is more likely to be an effort to please the customers. A public-relations attitude is the secret of administrative success. This is what we mean in talking about "responsive" management. It concentrates upon the users, rather than upon the techniques. Methods of management are but means to consumer satisfaction. Unless government is given freedom to "make the best of itself," an effective public-relations attitude cannot be expected of its employees. Even the best of service is not sure to be appreciated, it has been discovered, unless steps are taken to make sure that users will appreciate the efforts that are being made to please.[1] This can be done in a dignified manner, and with educational, rather than propagandist, intent.

Public-relations efforts should aim to discover and then to remedy. First of all, the management needs to find out about public desires, criticisms, and attitudes. The last-mentioned are particularly important, because they may have no real relation to the quality of service given. They may merely be vestiges of the past or the results of hostile propaganda. At any rate, the atmosphere needs to be cleared before the right relations between management and consumers will exist. Public relations, broadly considered, is an effort to learn what people do not like and how they can be better

OBJECTIVES OF PUBLIC RELATIONS

[1] Cf. Harold Whitehead, "Salesmanship and the Public Services," *Public Administration*, XI, No. 3 (July, 1933), 267–76; also S. H. Wood, C. K. Wright, and A. P. Ryan, "Intelligence and Public Relations," *Public Administration*, XIV, No. 1 (January, 1936), 41–65.

pleased. Discovery leads to remedy. It may be necessary to combat an unfounded attitude by means of advertising designed to present facts. Sometimes nothing more is needed than the reiterated assurance that the public agency is anxious to serve and invites criticisms to that end. People feel that they own governmental services and, hence, that they are free to criticize them with more freedom than private businesses which they do not own and over which they can exercise no effective control. Therefore, public relations needs to open the channels to public criticisms which can be effectively registered and acted upon. The remedy may consist merely of effort to arouse interest in what is being done. Public relations is a two-way activity: it attempts to interest users and it hopes to stimulate the efforts of the employees.

Popular education and understanding depend largely upon the skill of the executive personnel in opening channels of public information. Representatives of the press are usually glad to have stories on day-to-day administration from the city hall if the mayor or manager treats reporters with sufficient deference. A busy executive, unless public-relations conscious, finds it hard to do this. Executives also must find time to talk with the various interests and explain the reasons for taking this action or that. The administrator-leader must expect to make many speeches and always be careful to say the right thing. A good administrator is also a good politician, if by politician is meant a "politic," tactful person.

THE PUBLIC AND THE EXECUTIVE

These methods of access to public opinion have always been open to administration. The use made of them depends primarily upon the personal qualities of the man at the helm. In addition to these outlets, however, public authorities may take positive steps of their own. In recent years federal officials and departments have made it a practice to employ press representatives, former newspaper men most of them, to advise on public relations and to prepare material for public circulation. The radio is used for educational broadcasts. Publicly owned stations have come into existence. Motion pictures are prepared by governments, showing citizens what is being done to meet pressing problems or to satisfy their needs. There seems to be a promising future for both educational films and broadcasts. In all probability, public-relations work will become a career in government, just as it has in private business. As more of government's work consists of sales and satisfactions, it is reasonable to expect that increasing attention will be given to citizen desires and attitudes.

Public relations is a responsibility which the Chief Executive cannot delegate very far. There are two aspects of management which he should keep closely tucked under his wing—public relations and personnel. Public attitudes depend upon the former, employee morale upon the latter. In one sense, public relations is the sum total of administration. The purpose of all administrative method is to provide a product more pleasing to the customer. If this rule is kept constantly in mind, every aspect of management will be tested by the public-relations yardstick.

SELECTED READINGS

Buck, A. E.: *The Budget in Governments of Today* (New York, 1934); a lucid and comprehensive study of the budget in leading foreign countries and the United States.

———: *Public Budgeting* (New York, 1929), chap. VI; a good discussion of the data and factors that enter into planning the budget.

Dent, A. G. H.: *Management Planning and Control* (London, 1935), chap. I; a study of budgetary control in industrial management, chapter cited dealing particularly with the planning factor in the preparation of the budget.

Dimock, Marshall E.: *Developing America's Waterways* (Chicago, 1935); an administrative survey of the Inland Waterways Corporation, dealing with the policies and the overhead management of the organization.

———: "Public Corporations and Business Enterprise," *Public Administration*, XIV, No. 4 (October, 1936), 417-28.

Fayol, Henri: *Industrial and General Administration* (London, 1930), Part II; a brilliant analysis of the principles and elements of administration.

Forbes, Russell: *Governmental Purchasing* (New York, 1929); presents a synthesis of the best existing practices in the purchasing systems of the federal, state, and local governments of the United States.

Haldane, Richard Burdon: *An Autobiography* (London, 1929); an inspiring record of a career in the public service, in which is found the distillation of Haldane's thought on the art of managing men.

Hart, James: "The President and Federal Administration," in *Essays on the Law and Practice of Governmental Administration*, Charles G. Haines and Marshall E. Dimock, eds. (Baltimore, 1935).

Mooney, James D., and Reiley, Alan C.: *Onward Industry* (New York, 1931), chaps. IV, VI, XXIII, and XXIV; an analysis of the process by which co-ordination is achieved, and a good discussion of the staff function in organization.

National Committee on Municipal Reporting: *Public Reporting* (Municipal Administration Service, New York, 1931); an illuminating study of public reporting in American municipalities.

Pfiffner, John M.: *Public Administration* (New York, 1935); chaps. VI, XIII, XIV, XV, XXII, and XXIII deal with methods of co-ordination, including budgeting and reporting.

Sheldon, Oliver: *The Philosophy of Management* (London, 1930); an excellent study of the principles of industrial management, industry being considered both as a productive unit and a social trust.

Taylor Society: *Scientific Management in American Industry*, H. S. Persons, ed. (New York, 1929), chaps. I–IV, XI, and XXVII; a treatise on the philosophy and technique of scientific management.

Tead, Ordway: *Human Nature and Management* (New York, 1929), chaps. I–XII; an exposition of the uses of psychology in determining managerial techniques.

———: *The Art of Leadership* (New York, 1935); written to assist those who direct others, this interesting book dwells upon the differences between the methods of command and the methods of leadership.

Urwick, L.: *Management of Tomorrow* (London, 1933), chaps. I–V; a stimulating discussion of the management aspects of business enterprises which examines the potentialities of a "scientific management."

White, Leonard D.: *Trends in Public Administration* (New York, 1933), chaps. XII–XVII; an examination of the role of American public executives and the agencies which have emerged to assist them in their administrative tasks.

Whitehead, Harold: "Salesmanship in the Public Service: Scope and Technique," *Public Administration*, XI, No. 3 (July, 1933), 267–76.

Willoughby, W. F.: *Principles of Public Administration* (Baltimore, 1927); chaps. III and IV deal with the chief executive as manager and a bureau of general administration as a tool of management.

CHAPTER XI

☆ ☆ ☆

MAN POWER

*"To operate the administrative machine alone will require the best brains of each generation."*
—LEONARD D. WHITE

THE SUSTAINED GREATNESS of a country depends upon the quality of the men and women who comprise the rank and file of its citizenship. The man who is supposed to have said, "let me pick your generals and I care not who your privates be," could not have observed the operations of large-scale enterprises very widely. Military strategists, even in these days of mass formations, say that an army composed of self-reliant, intelligent men is superior to one of resigned "sheep." So it is in the total culture. The spirit and independence of men and women are what make a people truly great. The advantages of position, wealth, or dominance early acquired, secure one's social status only so long, and then, unless ability and character survive, retrogression inevitably follows. The same thing is true of a nation's institutions and processes. Of themselves, they cannot sustain the vitality and advanced culture of a people. They help, but eventually an institution registers approximately the qualities of the people who operate it.

<small>HUMAN RESOURCES</small>

The man power of the nation is distributed among the various institutions and enterprises which provide for the wants and satisfactions of the whole people. We become so used to thinking of men existing for institutions, instead of the reverse, that it is desirable to orient ourselves with reference to the competition in the labor market. In the United States, there are forty or fifty million people gainfully employed out of a total population of one hundred twenty-five million. It need hardly be said that the percentage of those having jobs has fluctuated considerably in the last ten years. The greatest competition for brains and brawn is in industry and commerce; however, there is competition also between institutions, particularly between business and government. There are only so many men and women who can perform work requiring a certain level of training, proficiency, and experience. Increasingly it is a question of whether they will throw in their lot with business or with government. In all ranges of employment this is true, from unskilled workers, through clerical, professional, and scientific grades, to executives of co-ordinative ability. An understanding of the limited number of proficient people in various lines of work and of the competition for their services by business and government is basic to a study of public personnel management.

It is sometimes said that government is the largest employer. This is true if one considers the whole of government as a single unit, and if industry and commerce are not so considered. Approximately three and one-half million people are employed in the public service.[1] This is somewhere between a tenth and a fifteenth of the total working population. It is a safe generalization that about one-tenth of the population in the countries of western Europe is employed by the government. In these countries, all railway, telegraph, and telephone workers are usually state employees, which greatly swells the total. Even in the United States, however, the total number of public employees is greater than in any industry, such as transportation, communications, automobiles, or steel. With the exception of the U. S. S. R., the United States Government is the largest single employer in the world, employing about a million people.

GOVERNMENT AS EMPLOYER

Of the three and one-half million total, the largest single employment is in education. Approximately a third of all public employees are teachers or school officials. The Post Office Department, with roughly 300,000, constitutes the next largest vocational group. Police officials come third; then, there are thousands of public-welfare workers, engineers, medical officials, lawyers, scientists, and skilled workers. All clerical employees would make a very

VARIETIES OF WORK

[1] Estimates are presented in *Better Government Personnel* (New York, 1935), published by the Commission of Inquiry on Public Service Personnel; a good introductory book to read.

high total. Economists, statisticians, accountants, and researchers of many kinds are numbered in the thousands.[1]

There is a widespread misconception that most governmental work is clerical. To be sure, the management of any large enterprise involves much paper work, but insurance companies and mail-order houses have a far larger percentage of it than does government.

Somewhere in government, every kind of work, vocation, and employment is to be found. It has been truly said that modern governments assist at birth and provide funerals. In the Canal Zone, for example, public administration is "butcher, baker, and candlestick maker." It provides every service required by the population of that strategic strip across the isthmus.[2] But, in a way, this method of analyzing governmental work is misleading. Every kind of opportunity is presented, it is true, but there are enormous differences in the relative need for each kind of training and ability.

Some types of work are more or less inherent in government, just as railways find engineers indispensable, and telephone companies cannot get along without linemen. Analyze the positions in your local, state, or national government and you will find that teachers, policemen, public-works engineers, health officials, chemists, finance men, agricultural economists, lawyers, post-office workers, social-service employees, and stenographers are all indispensable. But it is impossible to make a final list, any more than the functions of government are determined once and for all. For example, in recent years, men trained in economics and administration have been very much in demand. The Tennessee Valley Authority alone, large public utility and planning agency that it is, employed more than 15,000 persons in about two years' time. A considerable portion of these were of necessity economists and administrators. Housing programs have been undertaken all over the country in recent years, and it was found that trained managers were not available. They have had to be trained—a

[1] Some estimates for the federal government are given in *University Training for the National Service* (Minneapolis, 1932).
[2] This interesting situation is described in my book, *Government-Operated Enterprises in the Panama Canal Zone* (Chicago, 1934).

new public profession has formed. The opportunities for planning and personnel officials have expanded in corresponding fashion. The wise man informs himself of the likely needs of a field before entering it and canvasses opportunities that are opening up which might appeal to his interest and ability.

The public service affords opportunity for a variety of careers. Sometimes it is said, "Government should be made a career." Judged by ordinary interpretations of the word "career," it is already one, for the term means opportunity for staying in a given skill group for most of one's active life. Tested by this definition, government stands high among the vocations and professions. Its turnover of personnel is far less than that of industry. In business, on the other hand, the proportion is sometimes staggeringly high. The turnover in government is lower than in some of the professions, law, for example. A very small percentage of those who begin to practice law continue to do so regularly. On the other hand, the scientific workers in the federal government are as secure in their careers as university faculties, if not more so. Statisticians who want to remain in the public service find an insatiable demand for their services. Public engineering, health, and social work have become lifetime professions, as has teaching. Even policemen and firemen usually remain in their chosen fields if they so desire.

ADMINISTRATIVE CAREERS

It is more accurate to say that if the highest administrative posts in government are to be made as attractive as the best opportunities in business and the professions, there are certain improvements that need to be made in the government-career service.[1] For the man or woman whose highest salary expectation is roughly $3,000 a year, public employment provides greater inducements than private business. A recent study revealed that in 1932 the average remuneration in the federal government was about $1,500 a year, while in the whole of industry it was about $1,200.[2] The industrial average does not, however, indicate the trend of wages as accurately as does that of government, because

[1] Cf. Leonard D. White, *Government Career Service* (Chicago, 1935).
[2] U. S. Bureau of Foreign and Domestic Commerce, *National Income, 1929–32* (U. S. Government Printing Office, Washington, 1934), p. 28.

the few very high salaries in industry unduly pull up the over-all average. A more significant comparison was made in another recent study in which it was found that for the same work in business and government, the average salary payment is higher in government until a salary range of $2,000–$3,000 is reached, when business remuneration progressively outstrips that of government.[1] In all of government, there is no salary of $200,000 a year or more, such as is sometimes paid to corporation executives. Construction engineers on public jobs have been paid as high as $75,000 a year. The highest-salaried city manager receives $25,000. In Washington, there are approximately one hundred administrators whose remuneration is $10,000 a year or more.

An increase of salary expectation for those who rise to the top of the administrative ladder would undoubtedly enhance career opportunities. Great Britain pays her civil-service heads of departments as much as most political ministers, what would correspond to $15,000 in the United States. We can afford to do no less. It would be money in the pockets of American citizens if we were to raise the prizes for those entering the administrative competition and thereby provide greater assurance of securing better executive ability.

IMPROVING CAREER OPPORTUNITIES

It is even more important to accord sufficient recognition of authority and distinction to top administrative posts than to boost the salaries which go with them. Far-sighted statesmen, such as Theodore Roosevelt, Woodrow Wilson, and Frank Lowden, have realized that American governments need to create the recognized and respected post of civil-service head for every department.[2] This office would correspond to that of permanent Under-Secretary of a British department or Deputy Minister in Canada. It would be the pinnacle of the administrative ladder, a position to be achieved by promotion from within. So attractive would it be,

[1] U. S. Personnel Classification Board, *Closing Report of Wage and Personnel Survey* (U. S. Government Printing Office, Washington, 1931), pp. 114–22.
[2] A plan has been proposed by ex-Governor Frank O. Lowden. See his article, "Permanent Officials in the National Administration of the United States," *American Political Science Review*, XXI (August, 1927), 529–36.

and so much esteemed in popular favor, that men would find it a very powerful incentive to put forth their superlative efforts.

In our municipal, state, and federal departments, we already have career men who roughly correspond to the permanent civil-service heads in other countries.[1] In many cases, they are guaranteed all the security that one could ask. Where our system does not quite measure up is in the title attached to the office, the deserved financial emoluments, and the complete authority over purely administrative matters. Since the transformation is not a difficult one to effect, it is surprising that progressive governments have not taken the necessary steps long ago. The top career man could be called "chief administrator," "co-ordinator" or be given some other expressive title. In the federal government, the salary of the administrative chief could be made to correspond to that of the politically appointed department head, $15,000.

The political appointee has superior authority in all dealings with the career official. The department head assumes responsibility for policies, appointments, expenditures, and every conceivable detail; but, in actual practice, he relies for almost everything upon the administrator's judgment, experience, and knowledge. Exactly what takes place between the expert and the layman is impossible for an outsider to know. The personal qualities of the two individuals concerned make a considerable difference. We can generalize, however, to the extent of saying that the civil servant runs the department as though it were his own, except when the political chief changes a policy or questions a move. The administrator soon learns what questions should go to the minister and what matters of internal administration are discretionary.

<small>RELATION OF POLITICAL AND ADMINISTRATIVE HEADS</small>

The right relation between the political executive and the civil-service administrator is largely a matter of experience and tradition. The greater the capacity and reliability of the top administrator, the more the political appointee is likely to depend upon him. Political leaders who have no special knowledge of the work of their own departments should be wise enough to

[1] Read Arthur Macmahon's studies entitled, "Bureau Chiefs in the United States Government," *American Political Science Review*, XX (August and November, 1926), 548–82 and 770–81; XXIII (May, 1929), 383–403.

realize how little they know and how much expert advice they need—at least until they "learn the ropes" thoroughly. In the United States, the deference paid to permanent administrators has tended to increase steadily in most jurisdictions. The political head relies upon them for facts, suggested remedies, speeches, drafts of letters, and usually takes their word about budgets and promotions. We are not far from a system in which the top administrator is given his due.

It may be valuable to characterize some of the skills. The manual, or "hand-minded," person usually excels in the "how" rather than in the "why." He is not interested in theory, and is more concerned with things than with people. This generalization usually holds true for clerical employees. Research workers are concerned with theoretical questions, ideas, abstractions, and, as a rule, their outstanding skill is not interpersonal relations. Professional people combine interest in subject-matter ideas and dealings with human beings; however, their primary skill is usually the manipulation of ideas and learned techniques. The staff assistant, like the researcher, is captivated by theory and ideas, but, like the professional person, also is able to deal with people. The executive type needs to combine characteristics of all these. He must know subject matter, the "how"; comprehend theory and create abstractions, the "why"; and, above all, he must know how to handle people.

<small>SKILLS DISTINGUISHED</small>

The "administrator" is no figment of the imagination. He possesses an unusual balance of characteristics and accomplishments which enable him to direct the work of others. He needs physique, nervous energy, special knowledge, imagination, theoretical ability, judgment, perspective, co-ordinating capacity, tact, strength to say "no," and ability to inspire others and to create confidence in employees and the public. This enumeration is by no means exhaustive. The important point is that ability to recognize executive traits makes it possible to pick out those who should be groomed for administrative responsibilities.

<small>AN ADMINISTRATIVE CORPS</small>

Whether or not those who reach the top of the administrative career are university trained makes no difference to the public welfare, so long as in the selection and promotion processes the man possessing the necessary co-ordinating abilities is given preference. If physical stamina, personality, understanding of human nature, likability, mentality, broad interests, and sociability were all qualities and accomplishments with which individuals were born, formal education would make no difference; but they are not. This is even more often true of the other characteristics mentioned than of physique and mentality, because the educational process can do more to produce them. Given two men of equal possibilities, one of whom provides himself with university training for administrative work and the other of whom decides he can dispense with it, and the percentages greatly favor the former.[1] Natural endowment is not everything, but neither is environment. Self-educated men are conspicuous because they are so rare. It is not to be doubted, however, that occasionally among their number one finds men who set levels of administrative capacity extremely difficult to equal.

Simply because good executives occasionally crop out among scientists and professional people, one should not assume that government and business might as well expect executive capacity in equal measure in all walks of life. The chemist of outstanding administrative capacity is the extraordinary person who might have succeeded either in the realm of ideas or in the world of management. His case does not make a new rule. It is fortunate that administrative ability develops in all skill groups, even though much more rarely in some than in others, for one would not want to head an organization of chemists with someone who knows nothing about the field.

Every line activity needs executive leadership and administrative co-ordination. The top executive should constantly be on the lookout for persons possessing co-ordinative and leadership qualities. So indispensable is good administration that persons who have these skills should be set apart as an "administrative corps." Government should recognize and encourage this top-

[1] Lewis Meriam takes issue with this viewpoint and with the emphasis upon university training. See his arguments in *Public Service and Special Training* (Chicago, 1936).

control classification in its personnel laws.[1] This does not mean that persons hoping to be administrators could expect to know only the theory of organization, personnel, and other aspects of public administration, and still be acceptable. Administrators must know also the subject matter of the field in which they hope to lead, be it public works, social service, public utilities, agriculture, police, or what not. The prospective administrator needs a double-barreled gun, so to speak.

The most important thing in public personnel administration is to keep objectives constantly in mind. Otherwise, means are likely to be mistaken for ends, which seems to have happened in the case of civil service. The choosing of the best man for the opening is a high standard which every good personnel system should try to reach. Business men usually have this objective in mind, even though they do not give competitive examinations and rate people mathematically. But selection on the basis of merit is only the first step in a complete personnel program. If civil service is not viewed as merely one part of personnel management, the reform for which it stands may be a positive disservice. Governments have been inclined to overlook the fact that what is done with people after they are in public service may be of more importance than the examinations given when candidates are admitted.

OBJECTIVES OF THE MERIT SYSTEM

The merit system stands for policies which appeal to every public-spirited citizen. The best man for the office; favoritism and partiality to none; no discrimination because of party affiliation or on any other ground—all these are sensible slogans and in line with American traditions of equality of opportunity. But it has been over fifty years since the federal Civil-Service Law of 1883 was passed, and still thirty-nine states and half of the country's municipalities are without civil-service laws; moreover, there are only 250 civil-service commissions in the country, and, of these, 175 were in existence before 1910. Until the League of Women Voters and other citizen organizations got busy a few years ago, people were wondering if the civil-service movement had not reached a stalemate.

[1] See the proposal of Leonard D. White, in *Government Career Service*, pp. 18–36.

Yet, the record is not so bad when one looks at it more broadly. More than two-thirds of all public employees may be said to work under a merit system of some kind.[1] Their qualifications are tested in some way, although not necessarily by a civil-service commission. The largest group, teachers, must present the necessary credentials. Who will say that universities and normal schools are not as good judges of teaching ability as civil-service examiners? This is not to say that teachers should not be examined by commissions, in addition to all the tests they take in getting their certificates. It merely points to the fact that there are other means of testing merit besides holding open competitive examinations. We have been inclined to confuse the three-headed commission and its examining techniques with the objective of securing the best qualified candidate, by whatever means.

The object of the merit system is not only to secure the best qualified candidates for the public service but also to prevent wholesale turnovers of administrative personnel when a change in party leadership occurs. The replacement of politically appointed department heads is to be expected, but the arguments are all the other way when it comes to the security of anonymous civil servants. The work of modern government is so complex and so indispensable that the community cannot afford the losses of experience, the interruptions in service, and the expense of breaking in new employees which result from the patronage system. An investor would feel very insecure if a business corporation changed its administrative force every two to four years, removing the most capable and experienced along with the general run. Imagine the effect upon a state income-tax division when 200 first-rate employees are forced out after several years of service and the victorious party puts in men with no special knowledge and experience, who have to learn the intricate work from the ground up. Yet this still happens in American states today!

In many states, of course, there is one-party government. Partisanship ceases to be an upsetting force in administrative departments. Virginia, for example, has a first-rate adminis-

[1] *Better Government Personnel*, p. 92.

trative personnel without the formality of a comprehensive civil-service law. Her merit system is based upon tradition. It is a reflection of the high regard Virginians have for government and for the national leaders the state has produced.

PARTIES AND PATRONAGE    When party strength is about equal and there are frequent changes from one to the other, partisanship and patronage present a much more serious obstacle to the success of the merit system. In recent years, parties have been more careful to select the best of their followers for patronage posts, partly because people demand better results and partly because the crusade for the merit system has made party headquarters feel the growing heat of public opinion. The application of the merit system, while confining appointments to the incumbent political party, cannot be regarded as a satisfactory permanent solution. Citizens know that when the opposition party comes in, there will be a turnover in personnel, and the whole process will be re-enacted.

Can the party system survive without patronage? Civil-service reform should not be considered merely a matter of efficiency and ethics; it also impinges upon the most important questions of representative government. Party victory requires the full-time efforts of hundreds or even thousands of organizers and canvassers. They expect appointment as their reward, and since the number of higher positions is very limited, most of the faithful must be placed in administrative posts. Party leaders sometimes succeed in accomplishing this purpose even when there is a civil-service law in existence. Merit legislation, like any other kind, is not inviolable. Moreover, when political henchmen with no qualifications for the job once become placed, permanent tenure under the civil-service law affords them protection.

Partisan influence has been virtually eliminated in the central British government,[1] but it has played a larger part in local administrations since the World War. Local authorities, significantly, are not under civil-service laws. France has a professionalized bureaucracy, but partisanship enters into appointments

[1] Leonard D. White, "The British Civil Service," in *Civil Service Abroad*, Commission of Inquiry on Public Service Personnel, Monograph II (New York, 1935), 1–54.

and turnovers occur.¹ Under the Weimar Constitution, Germany probably set a new all-time record for merit selections and administrative proficiency;² under the Hitler regime, however, party fealty is the acid test. Switzerland has a very fine public service which is primarily the product of citizen interest in government and a tradition of public efficiency.³

A rapid survey of foreign governments, as well as of our own, will show that the strict civil-service idea is still on trial. If people do not take citizenship seriously, a proficient administrative service is not likely to exist. Streams rise no higher than their source. Parties have not learned to get along without the power of patronage appointments; moreover, there is increasing skepticism as to whether nonpartisan appointments produce a bureaucracy which can be trusted when competitions between classes are probably at a higher pitch all over the world than at any previous time.

The merit system cannot succeed in the long run unless the absolute neutrality of the civil service can be relied upon. That such an ideal may not be too high for the human race is suggested THE NEUTRAL- by the loyalty of the British civil service during ITY OF PUBLIC the general strike of 1926. The strike weapon has SERVANTS never been used in the central governments of Great Britain nor in the United States, although it has been employed several times in France. But the strike is only one aspect. More important is the question of whether the civil service could be relied upon to put forth its best efforts if the policy to be executed were diametrically different from any that had been tried before.

Suppose, for example, that a British Labor government were to nationalize all banks, as they say they will do. This program could not be carried through without the unswerving support of the highest administrative officials. The "administrative class," about 1,100 strong, is recruited almost entirely from Oxford and Cambridge graduates, who come mostly from middle- or upper-

¹ Walter R. Sharp, "Public Personnel Management in France," *Ibid.*, pp. 83–157.
² Fritz Morstein Marx, "Civil Service in Germany," *Ibid.*, pp. 161–275.
³ Carl J. Friedrich and Taylor Cole, *Responsible Bureaucracy: A Study of the Swiss Civil Service* (Cambridge, Mass., 1932).

class conservative homes. The most important point is the following: The government of the day may be able to bank on administrative neutrality, but the accomplishment of some programs requires zeal.

Russia, Italy, and Germany are able to get "spirited" administration. A dictatorship does not produce anemic public servants; but vigor can be purchased at too high a price. What a democratic country wants is unswerving loyalty, combined with consistently energetic efforts. There is no question that this is expecting a great deal. It has been said, "No government demands as much from the citizen as democracy and none gives as much back."[1]

Despite the fact that a civil-service law cannot be expected to work miracles, all the larger governmental jurisdictions should be urged to adopt legislation establishing the merit system. The staunchest supporters of civil service sometimes seem to be carried away with religious fervor and to confuse means for ends, but this much may be said for the crusading approach: administrative services cannot be made efficient, *esprit de corps* produced, and a career service worthy of the name brought into being, until partisan removal of competent employees is effectively prohibited either by law or custom. Law gives custom a chance to grow. It does not transform human nature or produce good citizenship overnight, but it does give the merit system a chance to develop inwardly. When a fight against the patronage system is won, it is better to retain all employees, even some obvious party hangers-on, rather than perpetuate the system of removing those who do not see things your way. Reform from within and care in future recruitments can remake an administrative service in a remarkably short time.

TAKING STOCK OF CIVIL SERVICE

Before civil service will be accorded universal and whole-hearted support, its shortcomings need to be remedied. Many people who are in favor of the merit principle are opposed to a civil-service law because they are skeptical about the examination techniques and fearful of the deadening effects of permanent tenure. Among business men, particularly, one hears it said, "We try to land the

[1] James Bryce, *Modern Democracies*, II (New York, 1921), 608.

best men in the market, but we would not choose a man principally on the basis of a written examination; moreover, we would not tell a man he was to have permanent tenure when he might later prove disappointing. Naturally, we hold on to good men, because it is in the interest of the company to do so, but when weak men are fired, outstanding men try all the harder. Nothing hurts morale more than to have unequal men working side by side, both drawing the same pay." There is much truth in these analyses. True friends of civil service must assume the responsibility for correcting the weaknesses within the system or they cannot hope to sell their program.

The examining techniques, however, are now more reliable than most men in business are aware. Evidence of this is found in the fact that some large corporations have made studies of modern examining techniques and have introduced them into their personnel management. The essay-type of written examination has been largely superseded by short-answer and intelligence tests. A "completion" test, for example, not only reveals what a man knows, but indicates his ability to deal with abstractions of a simple sort. Then, too, the written part of the test is supplemented with an oral interview, which is what business men rely upon almost entirely. Finally, the candidate, even if successful in the competition, is only one of three on the selection list. The executive officer can choose any one of the three, thus allowing him some discretion regarding temperamental congeniality.

ADEQUACY OF EXAMINATIONS

Civil-service examinations are far more reliable for some types of work than for others. Testing techniques have been worked out successfully for skills which can be objectively tested, such as typewriting, manual dexterity, and for scientific knowledge. Other skills and personal traits are qualitative in character and are harder to define. The positions which call for the exercise of these traits are the "administrative" ones, involving the art of leadership, ability to co-ordinate, acumen in "sizing up" men and situations. Psychologists have expressed the opinion that executive ability is in the realm of "temperament." When asked whether objective, infallible tests can eventually be devised for determining existing or potential administrative ability, they usually say they believe so, but that it will take time to develop them.[1] The business executive remains skeptical. "Until you do work out reliable tests, why don't you confine your examining techniques to classifications for which they have been proved adequate?" The usual answer is that if some positions are treated as exceptions, the whole system will be endangered. On the other hand, we must remember that, if adequate leadership is not secured at the top, the services are bound to bog down.

The most vulnerable spot of civil service is its seeming inability to offset the objectionable results of permanent tenure. Civil service is sometimes characterized as "the perpetuation of mediocrity." Business men ask why public servants should be the only segment of society enjoying security of employment. The answer is, of course, that security for everyone is a desirable objective. But any system that cannot weed out the incompetent will suffer from lowered morale. Moreover, the efforts and abilities of workers should be proportionately rewarded. Men who have advanced part way up the ladder of success and who then stop giving their best after reaching a certain stage either should be demoted or others who are still trying should be permitted to pass them. A man who is producing better results than others on the same level should be rewarded by promotion or by increased compensation. These are requirements of any social system. Even Soviet Russia is now prepared to recognize their indispensability.

PERMANENT TENURE

The probationary period, usually of six months, is one check on errors of examination procedure which permit a misfit to get into the public service. Mistakes are bound to be made. If the probationary period were used effectively, however, incompetence and even mediocrity could be largely eliminated. In some cases, it has succeeded; but generally throughout the civil-service, removals or transfers during the trial period have suffered from inattention and spinelessness. It is not yet clear that there is cause for a

INADEQUATE USE OF PROBATIONARY PERIOD

[1] See, for example, the testimony of Prof. Louis L. Thurstone in *Minutes of Evidence* (New York, 1935), Hearings Before the Commission of Inquiry on Public Service Personnel, pp. 235–39.

feeling of despair, of complete hopelessness. It has been proved that probation can be made to work when the personnel officer is on the job. In other words, civil-service selection is only the first step in personnel management. When it is considered a complete system, probationary removals, among other necessary steps, are bound to be neglected.

In theory, it is possible to remove civil-service employees "for cause," just as private employers do. In practice, executives usually do not begin to exercise their authority to the extent that the good of the service seems to require. The most common causes of removal are for unlawful political activity or for moral dereliction. These are exceptional cases of gross misconduct. In addition to such disciplinary action, removals for incompetence, demotions for not trying, and replacements of mediocrity by outstanding ability need to be made effective rules of the public service. A large part of the blame for not securing these results falls upon executives who fail to exercise authority which is guaranteed to them.

<small>LIMITATIONS ON EXECUTIVE</small>

This is not the whole explanation; the system also is at fault. In many civil-service jurisdictions, any employee who has been removed or disciplined is entitled to an appeal to the civil-service commission. Incompetence, except of the grossest sort, is difficult to prove with evidence which a court would accept; yet the civil-service commission acts in the capacity of a court. Executives, therefore, hesitate a long time before dismissing persons who are not good but who are not thoroughly bad. Refusal of the commission to sustain the executive in a single case would jeopardize the deference of the organization to the chief. So what the executive usually does is to abolish the position or say that funds are not available with which to pay the undesirable individual. The necessity of resorting to such dodges is proof that something is vitally wrong with the system.

The master-servant relationship is as indispensable in government as in business or in any other field of co-operative effort. There is one leader and the rest are followers. The leader owes his superior status not to any deference due to him as an individual, but because he performs an indispensable function in large-scale organization. This relationship is analogous to the relation between citizens and governments. In democratic countries, we respect the state because it stands for co-operative aims which we hope to accomplish through it. In dictatorships, on the other hand, the citizen owes his respect to the person of the dictator. In popular governments, there is the need of respecting the office, the authority entrusted to the leader.

The master-servant relationship is not strong enough in most American governments. Executives are deterred from making necessary removals because of the inhibiting influence of employees' organizations. The organization secretary usually takes the position that any member who pays dues has a vested right to his job. The rank and file of employees seem to take the attitude that if removal for cause is countenanced, they may lose their positions. To a considerable extent, their attitude represents fear of partisanship, but this is not the only influence at work. An inherent characteristic of bureaucracy is to attempt to preserve itself, its privileges, and even the rate at which work is done. It is resistant to leadership from the top. Employees' organizations appeal to civil-service laws not only to prevent patronage but also to resist forceful executives. The wise executive knows that if he does not master the bureaucracy it will master him. It is no wonder, therefore, that executives frequently consider civil-service commissions their mortal enemies.

We must not be understood as condemning employees' organizations in a wholesale fashion. They may be a very useful aid to management. When the civil-service union has at its head a man INFLUENCE OF who understands that individual members will EMPLOYEES' prosper only if the efficiency of the entire organiza-ASSOCIATIONS tion is high, he will be willing to see removals and disciplinary action which raise the general level; but it is very difficult for union executives to take such a far-sighted policy.[1] Usually, they are driven by their members into a hostile, defensive attitude. The slogan seems to be, "Let no man lose his skin." Such a policy is fatal to progressive leadership and sound morale.

[1] Cf. Sterling D. Spero, "Employer and Employee in the Public Service," in *Problems of the American Public Service*, Commission of Inquiry on Public Service Personnel monograph (New York, 1935).

The solution in part, of course, is to secure secretaries of employees' unions who understand the principles of large-scale management and who, therefore, are prepared to pursue a far-sighted policy. Most executives are inclined to consider administration as a mysterious art which only they can fathom. If only they were astute enough to educate the rank and file in the essentials of co-operative enterprise, as the Whitley Councils tend to do,[1] they would secure much more reasonable responses from employees' organizations. Unions, like employers, may be either selfish or forward-looking.

Unions of public officials are usually found only in the larger governments—city, state, and national. The National Federation of Federal Employees, the largest in the country, has a membership of about 60,000. Several federal associations are affiliated with the American Federation of Labor. Their right to organize has been recognized since the Lloyd-La Follette Act of 1912. Since that time, they have become increasingly influential. The principal unions publish newssheets, carry on extensive social activities, provide insurance and benefit payments, support and oppose legislators, and lobby for higher wages and better working conditions before their employer, Congress.[2]

The employer-employee relationship in government raises some very puzzling ethical questions. Public servants enjoy a privileged relationship toward the center of governmental power; their position is almost tantamount to that of the armed forces. Particularly in countries where public authority operates all communication and transportation facilities, the strategic power of the bureaucracy is enormous. At the same time, the employees must see to it that they are treated fairly. A government intent upon economy is not likely to raise wages even when increased efficiency justifies it. Financial and other emoluments must be wrung out of the legislature. Under the cabinet form of government, it is possible to carry on what roughly amounts to collective bargaining; under congressional government, it is a matter of successful lobbying.

Of all forms of American government, the city-manager method

[1] See the conclusions of Leonard D. White, *Whitley Councils in the British Civil Service* (Chicago, 1933), chap. xviii.
[2] This is discussed in E. Pendleton Her  *Group Representation Before Congress*, chap. ix.

more nearly resembles that of the private corporation in its handling of personnel. The manager is assured of unified management. He can hire, fire, and discipline his employees. In most cases, the civil-service law, if any, is not permitted to interfere with his freedom of action on personnel questions. Employees deal with the manager when they think themselves entitled to salary increases or other benefits.

The improvement of public personnel programs requires comprehensive planning, in which all elements are dealt with and objectives and principles are determined. The first factor to keep in mind is that personnel work is staff work. It becomes apparent, therefore, that a quasi-judicial commission is hardly the proper agency to put at the center of the system. The chief executive needs an adviser on personnel matters, just as on law, finance, or planning. The apex of personnel management should be a personnel director. He should be responsible for administering the civil-service law, and the commission should either be abolished or retained in an ancillary relationship for disciplinary and removal cases. In addition to the personnel director, there should be assistants in all the principal departments. These departmental personnel men should be responsible to the executive heads of the respective departments and should be also the liaison between the latter and the personnel director.

NEED FOR A COMPLETE PROGRAM

Several American governments have already established unified personnel programs. In addition to city-manager administrations, St. Paul has a single-headed department, and it has produced one of the most progressive programs in the entire country. Two states, Maryland and Wisconsin, have directors of personnel, who have been outstandingly successful. Finally, several agencies in the federal government now boast of single-headed personnel divisions reporting directly to the chief executive. They are the Farm Credit Administration, Home Owners' Loan Corporation, Social Security Board, and the Tennessee Valley Authority. All these agencies have become pacemakers in modern personnel methods. The Department of Agriculture has had a personnel officer since 1923, and he has done outstanding work. The general rule in federal, state, and municipal departments, however, is that an assistant chief clerk or timekeeper is the only person with responsibility for personnel matters. These persons are merely clerks with no special knowledge of modern methods and no authority save over details.

The modern personnel director has an extremely important job, and the successful ones are necessarily men of outstanding ability. They must be good "pickers." They work out improved tests, conduct studies of compensation scales in comparable employments, devise collective bargaining plans, recreation programs, training opportunities, improved classification plans, and assist the line executives in deciding upon promotions. Personnel directors are constantly planning and contriving, the objective always being the same—to improve employee morale. Unless they serve the executive and the rank and file equally well, they cannot hope to succeed. The job of go-between is a difficult one.

Several years ago it seemed as though personnel management were afflicted with arteriosclerosis, but recently it has taken a new lease on life. The passing of a law is now realized to be only the beginning of a personnel program. Civil service is the first step. The real test of the personnel director is what he can do to improve morale after people are in the service. To accomplish this objective, the chief executive and his staff assistant must co-operate very closely. After C. A. Dykstra had been city manager of Cincinnati for six years, he was asked what his outstanding impression was after having turned from the teaching of public administration to the practice of it in America's best-governed city. His reply was that the reservoirs of human capability and responsiveness are much deeper than most people realize and, hence, that the success of management depends upon the right kind of appeal. The city-manager government of Cincinnati inherited machine-appointed employees, but when the charter group won, it did not replace the political appointees. Cincinnati became an entirely different city administration, because there was a totally different kind of appeal. The outstanding lesson of city-manager government in Cincinnati is that people are inclined to respond to what is expected of them.

Personnel administration has become red-blooded because some governmental agencies have been free and willing to experiment. The Tennessee Valley Authority has established a new standard for both business and government. Soon after the project was started, the directors secured one of the country's leading authorities on school administration as personnel director. They also gave him authority to recommend persons for the highest positions, a practice which is almost unknown in either business or the public service. Dr. Reeves then proceeded to scour the country for the best men in the various fields of employment needed by the enterprise; even from the higher brackets of large corporations, talent was sought.

<small>OUTSTANDING EXAMPLES</small>

The Tennessee Valley Authority, being corporate in its form and financial freedom, is able to offer salaries which are somewhat higher than those in the old-line government departments, but not so high as the salaries of public-utility executives. The personnel department had the courage to choose manual workers only after giving them intelligence tests. Private contractors laughed when they heard about it; after the plan had proved a success, some of the largest concerns came around and studied the plan thoroughly because they wanted to adopt it. Those who received high ratings in the intelligence examination and later showed leadership qualities were given training and promoted to supervisory positions.

A training school with a full-time faculty was established, and men in all kinds of employment were given an opportunity to improve themselves. Excellent cafeteria service, medical attention, and recreation opportunities were made available by the personnel division. Low-cost houses were constructed. The results of this can be seen from the fact that visitors from abroad observe the Tennessee Valley Authority and come away saying that the spirit with which all classes of employees go about their work is singular. Students of personnel management testify that the T. V. A. has brought together the finest group of public servants ever to be assembled. It is not under a civil-service law, but it represents the merit system at its best. The opportunities in personnel work are great for men of vision and resourcefulness.

In large-scale enterprises, it is necessary to work out a classification scheme, dividing all work into classes and grades, in order that there may be the same pay for the same work. If this were not done, persons in different departments doing identical work might be drawing different salaries. When such situations have been allowed to continue, employee dissatisfaction has become prevalent. Thus, one obligation of the personnel director is to work out a careful description of the tasks and responsibilities of every position within the service. These analyses are then used for making horizontal classifications of positions involving the same type of work and responsibility. General classes are established, and provision is then made for salary increments corresponding to the several grades within the class. The number of salary divisions within a class differs under various systems.

MERITS AND DEMERITS OF CLASSIFICATION

Classification schemes are of basic significance in the work of the personnel director. The necessity for them is undeniable. On the other hand, an oversimplified classification plan results in discouragement to individual ambition and hence a deadening mediocrity. Large organizations must constantly beware of "time servers." When a person knows that his salary increase or promotion depends upon the calendar or upon the rate of retirement of the men above him, there is not much incentive to keep above the recognized average. As we have said, special reward for outstanding accomplishment is a universal requirement of progressive management. There are two services that the personnel agency can perform: it can prevent the oversimplification of the gradations, allowing more frequent opportunities to consider the individual's claim for reward; and it can assist the line officials to discover persons of outstanding effort and initiative. Nothing in a large-scale organization is more tragic than the man of exceptional ability who gives the best he has and never receives any recognition for it.

The need for personnel assistance is in direct ratio to the size and complexity of the organization. The problems of morale are far greater than the line officials have time for. Consider the matter of promotions, for example. Those who receive regular promotions will eventually provide the leadership of the organization. If the rule of seniority were strictly followed, the chances are that some very good technicians would be elevated to posts which only co-ordinators can fill. On the other hand, if "B" men are consistently passed up, widespread discontent will exist near the top. The natural leader is almost as rare as the inspired inventor. The conscientious executive is given more sleepless nights over promotion choices than over any other question. He knows that the future of the enterprise depends upon those who will take over the reins when he steps out.

<small>THE PROBLEM OF PROMOTIONS</small>

Executives of long experience hesitate to suggest all the rules of promotion they have found advisable. Promotion from within the service is preferable, because it gives the prize to those who have given their lives to the enterprise; however, if the organization has grown stagnant or exhibits ingrowing symptoms, it may be wisest to infuse new blood from the outside. Men who evidence outstanding executive talent should be promoted rapidly, assuring a sufficient supply of ability at the top and safeguarding them against the dulling consequences of slow advancement. In the British civil service, cases have been known in which the eighty-fifth man on the seniority list was given the promotion. It takes courage to do this, but without it progressive management and responsive service have less chance of dominating an organization. On the other hand, if the next in line has the essential qualifications required for the job and no one near him has "the divine spark," the leadership should be accorded on the basis of seniority.

The executive should hesitate to rely solely upon his own judgment in deciding promotion questions. As we have remarked, one is likely to look for one's own qualities. Men with personality and not much else sometimes "take in" appointing officials. Promotion should be decided after balancing both objective record and personal traits. In making the decision, the personnel director, a promotion committee, and the judgment of the man's peers all should be weighed. Mistakes in promotion matters are one of the chief weaknesses of large organizations. In a small enterprise, the appointing officer knows his juniors intimately; in a bureaucracy, his opportunity is limited. Thus, the tendency is to rely upon promotion according to strict seniority. Illiberal classification schemes and promotion by rote can bind a bureaucracy so rigidly with red tape that only by drastic action can the fetters be removed.

Another serious problem of public personnel administration is to decide upon a sound theory of compensation. Several possibilities present themselves. Public employees might be paid on the basis of the marginal value of their contribution; the supply and demand of the labor market; the same amount paid in private business for the same work; more than private business, following the model-employer theory; the number of dependents an employee has to support; any amount necessary to secure the best employees; a "living" wage; a comfort-and-culture wage; or a prorata division of the national income. We can dismiss most of these theories without discussion. The marginal-value theory is impracticable, largely because of the difficulty of measurement; the labor-market one also is unworkable and less applicable to the "closed" public service than to industry; France and some other countries have experimented with allowances for dependents, but the social justification for such a policy is of dubious validity; "living" and "comfort" wages can be defined in a variety of ways, but if agreed upon would be of some service, though such standards are more valuable in setting minima than in determining more or less complete wage scales; and a division of the national income by official action is possible only in a controlled economy, such as Russia's.

THEORIES OF REMUNERATION

The two outstanding rivals are the exact-coincidence-with-industry basis of compensation and the model-employer theory.[1] The former is the yardstick used in practice, although governments sometimes pay lip service to the model-employer theory. If the latter were followed, public salaries would be higher than those in business, because the public would attempt to induce industry to raise wages and would attempt also to assure itself of the ablest employees. As we have said, the average remuneration up to the $2,000–$3,000 level is higher in government than in busi-

[1] U. S. Personnel Classification Board, *Preliminary Report of Wage and Personnel Survey* (U. S. Government Printing Office, Washington, 1929), pp. 69–74.

ness. Within this range, therefore, it might be said that government is consistently the model employer. This, however, is not quite an accurate interpretation, because the wages paid by government approximately correspond to those in the better-paid business concerns.[1]

A man's total income may depend upon other factors besides the size of his pay check. Among such emoluments of employment may be mentioned old-age retirement provision, annual allowance for sick leave, vacation with pay, insurance protection, and freedom from speeding-up measures. In all of these respects, government is a model employer—it leads business.[2] Pension systems, for example, were general in government when only a few progressive business firms had provided them;[3] moreover, vacations with pay were continued by most governments all through the depression, while business enterprises usually discontinued them.

All factors considered—security, retirement, remuneration, and non-monetary emoluments—government is a model employer. It does not offer dazzling financial prizes at the top, as does business, and it offers no opportunity for profit making. As a British civil servant once said, "The public service will not make me rich. But if a man wants enough to provide for the cultural requirements of his family, enough leisure to do the things he likes, security throughout life, and the satisfaction of feeling that he is serving humanity, I know of no career comparable to the civil service."

The incentives of public employment are a powerful force for spirited administration.[4] Before they can be completely released, however, understanding leadership must be assured and the inherent evils of bureaucracy need to be guarded against. Loyalty to the public service and to the welfare of the people have a strong appeal, because they are connected with patriotism and altruism. Pride of craftsmanship and the stimulating effect of distinction for work well done are both productive of outstanding results. Government

INCENTIVES

[1] *Closing Report of Wage and Personnel Survey*, pp. 114–20; 243.
[2] Cf. *Ibid.*, pp. 123–28.
[3] Cf. Lewis Meriam, *Principles Governing the Retirement of Public Employees* (New York, 1918).
[4] See my article, "The Potential Incentives of Public Employment," *American Political Science Review*, XXVII, No. 4 (August, 1933), 628–36.

needs to give more attention to the proper recognition of administrative heroes. The lawyers and doctors fill their corridors with photographs and busts of their great men. Business executives who have arrived at the top crave distinction more than anything else; their desire for money has been satiated. Recognition of the administrative genius of outstanding public servants is a tribute which democracy would do well to pay in fuller measure.

A constructive personnel program is one which is based upon a psychological understanding of the mainsprings of human action. Modern psychology, says Tead, points unmistakably to the conclusion that the true means of permanently influencing others and of getting the best results from their efforts lies in the direction of fostering conditions in which employees, in and through their own desires, come to seek the results which the leader also comes to desire, resulting in a permanent underlying enthusiasm which does not have to be constantly fed with new excitements and inducements.[1]

The most neglected factor in present-day life is the human one—the influence of personality, the release of potential incentives, and the deliberate cultivation of effective co-operation among people. Great administrators are humanists; they like people and hence are sincerely interested in helping them.

The personnel director is a planner, strategist, and psychologist. He should have the leisure and freedom to study employees at their work. His principal obligation is to use his knowledge and his ingenuity in proposing methods of producing more spirit, drive, contentment, understanding, co-operation, and atmosphere among all persons employed in the concern. This view of the opportunities and obligations of the personnel director is now relatively rare, but where personnel officers are found who have this humanized, psychological approach, the results are far superior to those found under routine record-keeping and employment-office methods.

The growing responsibilities of government in the economic realm make the training of leaders for fields of both private and public management increasingly similar. "The adaptation of

[1] Ordway Tead, *Human Nature and Management* (New York, 1929), pp. 4–7.

American democracy to the requirements of the new age," says Professor Holcombe, "calls for the recognition of a new profession, that of the public business man, and for the establishment of his proper position in the organization of the state."[1]

SELECTED READINGS

Beyer, William C.: "Municipal Civil Service in the United States," in *Problems of the American Public Service* (New York, 1935); published under the auspices of the Commission of Inquiry on Public Service Personnel; a convenient summary of the personnel practice in American cities.

Commission of Inquiry on Public Service Personnel (Report of): *Better Government Personnel* (New York, 1935); this landmark in the literature on public personnel is a clear analysis of the need for a career-service system in government personnel.

Dimock, Marshall E.: "The Potential Incentives of Public Employment," *American Political Science Review*, XXVIII, No. 4 (August, 1933), 628–36.

Finer, Herman: *The Theory and Practice of Modern Government*, II (London, 1932), chaps. XXVII–XXXVII; a comparative study of civil service in England, France, Germany, and the United States.

Friedrich, Carl J.: "Responsible Government Service under the American Constitution," in *Problems of the American Public Service* (New York, 1935); a discussion of the fundamental problems involved in the theory of the American public service.

—— and Cole, Taylor: *Responsible Bureaucracy: A Study of the Swiss Civil Service* (Cambridge, Massachusetts, 1932); presents an interesting analysis of bureaucracy as a concept, in addition to giving an able survey of the functions, organization, and practices of the Swiss civil service.

Graham, George A.: "Personnel Practices in Business and Governmental Organizations," in *Problems of the American Public Service* (New York, 1935); monograph, published under auspices of the Commission of Inquiry on Public Service Personnel; makes an interesting comparison of private and public personnel practices.

Harding, T. Swann: "Our Federal Civil Service," *Harvard Business Review*, XIII (January, 1935), 157–66.

Macmahon, Arthur: "Bureau Chiefs in the United States Government," *American Political Science Review*, XX, Nos. 3 and 4 (August and November, 1926), 548–82 and 770–81; XXIII, No. 2 (May, 1929), 383–403.

[1] See his challenging little book, *Government in a Planned Democracy* (New York, 1935).

Marx, Fritz M.: "Civil Service in Germany," in *Civil Service Abroad* (New York, 1935), published under auspices of the Commission of Inquiry on Public Service Personnel; a historical treatment of the German civil service which presents the main characteristics and practices of the system.

Meriam, Lewis: *Public Service and Special Training* (Chicago, 1936); a provocative discussion of training for the public service, in which issue is taken with the academic point of view.

Mosher, William E., and Kingsley, J. Donald: *Public Personnel Administration* (New York, 1936); a critical examination of personnel methods used in the public service; major emphasis on the rehabilitation of bureaucracy through the development of a positive personnel program.

Pfiffner, John M.: *Public Administration* (New York, 1935), chaps. VIII–XII.

Reeves, Floyd W.: "Personnel Administration in the Tennessee Valley Authority," *Southern Economic Journal*, II, No. 4 (April 1936), 61–74.

Robson, William A.: "The Public Service," *The Political Quarterly*, VII, No. 2 (April-June, 1936), 179–93.

Sharp, Walter R.: *The French Civil Service: Bureaucracy in Transition* (New York, 1931); an excellent treatise on the French bureaucracy and the sociological and psychological setting in which it operates.

Spero, Sterling D.: "The Employer and Employee in the Public Service," in *Problems of the American Public Service* (New York, 1935); an enlightening discussion of the problem of the civil servant and his position in society and government.

Tead, Ordway, and Metcalf, Henry C.: *Personnel Administration* (3d rev. ed., New York, 1933); a study of human-relations problems in modern industry in which particular stress is placed on motivations and attitudes.

White, Leonard D.: "The British Civil Service," in *Civil Service Abroad* (New York, 1935); a general survey of the British civil service emphasizing the place of the administrative class in the service.

———: *Government Career Service* (Chicago, 1935); a constructive proposal for the building of a career service in the administrative group in our national government.

———: *Whitley Councils in the British Civil Service* (Chicago, 1933); an examination of Whitleyism in the British civil service and a portrayal of how staff unionism and Whitleyism interact.

CHAPTER XII

☆ ☆ ☆

## ADMINISTRATIVE REGULATION

*"The need for some degree of governmental supervision is conceded."*
—JOSEPH B. EASTMAN

GOVERNMENT execution involves knowledge from all fields of science, technology, business, the crafts, and the professions. The administrator must master the subject matter of his field before he can put his knowledge of management method into operation. There are as many line activities of administration as there are functions and programs of government. The multitudinous departments and agencies of government, however, can be classified generally under the fourfold division of functions, namely, protection, regulation, assistance, and service. This chapter will deal with the regulatory activities.

<small>ADMINISTRATION AND THE FUNCTIONS OF GOVERNMENT</small>

We shall not attempt to consider the distinctive administrative problems connected with all four of the major functions of government. In preceding discussions, we have already given considerable attention to the age-old responsibility of protecting individuals, and we have discussed also the importance of modern forms of assistance. In the present group of three chapters, we shall be particularly concerned with the functions of regulation and direct service, and the relationship of government and the economic order. In the present chapter, we shall explore the theory and results of administrative regulation; while, in the two succeeding ones, we shall be concerned with governmental proprietary services, the planning and directive responsibilities of public authority, and efforts to add to the economic security and well-being of the individual.

The outstanding social development of the last fifty years has been the increasing interdependence of business and government. Technology, urbanism, intensive industrialization, and the modern corporation make this articulation inevitable. The proper division of responsibility between business and government is the most portentous social question in the process of solution. The primary concern in both fields is the same: can management be made as efficient as complexity demands and still be kept responsive to the desires of the rank and file of the citizenry? The American people are still searching for the best methods of organization, control, and human relationships with which to meet the complex social conditions brought about by the rapid economic changes of the last half century.

Several possible methods have appeared which attempt to offset the centralization of business power and to reshape the economic pattern along more democratic lines. A large segment of the population still has a nostalgic desire for small business. Senator Borah and others have demanded that "teeth" be put into the anti-trust laws. Then there are large groups of people who demand that the category of "business affected with a public interest" be considerably added to, including such basic industries as steel and coal. Regulation first needs to be made more effective, they say. Those who espouse the "public-utility concept" of industrial organization believe we can solve most of our problems by extending limited monopolies and public regulation.

There seem to be considerable possibilities in the type of control exemplified in the Independent Grocers' Alliance (I. G. A.). Each unit continues to be owned and managed by the individual grocer, but purchasing and distribution are taken care of by the same large-scale methods employed in chain-store organization. An extension of the independent grocer method of business procedure would seem to hold promise of securing the benefits of both individual initiative and large-scale rationalization. Can democracy survive unless most people are owners rather than employees, economically independent rather than industrially dependent?

The consumers' co-operative movement is another important economic development which bids fair to provide an important element from which the new economic-political compound is to be fashioned. Consumers' co-operatives, which in turn own and control their own productive facilities, have become of central significance in most of the countries of the Western world. In some, the co-operative movement already dominates the economic life of the nation.[1] There are now seventy million members of consumers' co-operatives in almost fifty countries. Great Britain has some seven and one-half million members of consumers' co-operatives, a million of whom are in the London area. English co-operatives now do an annual business of over one billion dollars, which is 15 per cent of the total volume of trade. The co-operative movement has taken hold in the United States and is now growing rapidly, the business of consumers' co-operatives having now reached an annual figure of about four hundred million dollars. The Rochdale plan is essentially democratic, because each member has only one vote and store profits are distributable in direct proportion to the individual's share of the total purchases.

Centralizing tendencies in business and government are offset by regional developments, such as those sponsored by the federal government in recent years. A balanced economy of agriculture and industry is one which people are likely to seek in many parts of the country. Howard Odum's book, *Southern Regions*, and the National Resources Board's report, *Regional Factors in National Planning and Development*, tell about some projects which are already under way.

An extension of public ownership is still another method of limiting the concentration of economic power and of organizing the industrial life of the people. Movement in this direction has been pronounced in recent years. "Upwards of 70 per cent of all Europeans are now living in the shadow of state-controlled enterprise," Stuart Chase has pointed out. According to the Marxist analysis, business becomes larger and larger, the rich richer and the poor poorer, until the people inevitably take over and operate the country's basic industries. How much truth is there to the "inevitability" theory? Already, seven-hundredths of 1 per cent of the nonfinancial business corporations control half of American corporate wealth.

[1] See Marquis W. Child's arresting book, *Sweden: The Middle Way* (New Haven, 1936).

So much heat is engendered by the public ownership controversy that most people are led to think that regulation of private business and public operation of business are the two alternatives between which we must choose in future economic development. It is to correct this limited notion that we have referred to the importance of the I.G.A. form of organization, consumers' co-operatives, and a regionally balanced economy. It is not suggested, by any means, that these forces are the only ones worthy of note; nor would we minimize the importance of the struggle between regulation and public ownership for preferment by the public as the method for dealing with some of our major economic problems.

<small>REGULATION VERSUS PUBLIC OWNERSHIP</small>

If regulation is considered in its generic sense, namely, as control of, or interference with, the individual, nearly all of government would be included in the definition. We shall use the term in its generally accepted sense, as the creation of standards of law for, and the enforcement of determinations concerning, the actions of persons or corporations organized for commercial or other profit-making purposes. We shall not deal with regulations of safety, health, and morals, however, such as those exemplified in required safety equipment for factories, inspection of public eating places, and motion-picture censorship. Our attention in this chapter will be devoted to the public control of business, to the regulation of public utilities. Has it been a success, a failure, or a partial success? When government acts as regulator of powerful economic interests, what is the result likely to be? The inquiry is important for future guidance, as well as for taking stock of the present.

For the last seventy years, regulation has been the outstanding development in the American governmental system. Soon after the Civil War, railroad commissions were created, because the extension of transportation to the West coast led to complaints from farmers and merchants about the power and practices of the railways. So extensive has public control of business become since that time that regulation is now considered a natural and inherent function of government in the United States.

Regulation and liberalism have come to be considered synonymous. Regulation is the middle ground between purely private

business and state socialism. American governmental and business leaders have constantly reiterated from platforms and through the press that regulation is the distinctive contribution of the IMPLICATIONS  American people to the evolving relationship be-
OF REGULATION
FOR POLITICAL  tween business and government. Public control,
THEORY         as compared with direct ownership and operation, Herbert Hoover says, represents the typical American preference for moderation and a happy compromise.

Regulation represents a distinct theory of political economy. Government is the policeman, the referee; its responsibility is that of enforcing the law, maintaining liberty, and catching and punishing those who break the rules. In so doing, the government is but maintaining the economic balance which is supposedly the result of natural laws and automatic forces. Regulation is "interference"; for economic enterprises, irrespective of their nature or characteristics, are essentially private. These are accepted canons of the early economics and of right-wing liberals.[1]

Social action is controlled by social necessity, as well as by the competitive processes described in economic theory. Railroad building made a market for nation-wide concerns, which soon came to be called trusts and monopolies. As competition was reduced or eliminated, prices became increasingly inflexible. Discriminations helped certain interests and sections, and hurt others. When business threatened to control government itself—the last recourse which the small merchant and the consumer had to protect their interests—the public awakened to the fact that if combinations were not regulated by the government, the country as a whole would be at their mercy.

The public-utility category was established in American law with the decision of *Munn* vs. *Illinois*,[2] decided by a divided Supreme Court in 1877. In this outstanding case, the authority of the State of Illinois to regulate the rates charged by grain elevators was the matter under consideration. When the state legislature passed the law imposing restrictions upon the business, owners argued that theirs was a private business and, hence, that the law

[1] See, for example, *Britain's Industrial Future* (London, 1928), a formulation of policy for the Liberal party.
[2] 94 U. S. 1113 (1877).

was unconstitutional because it deprived them of their liberty and property. The Court held that the public interest was the dominant consideration. It pointed out that certain businesses connected with common carriers had been subject to public regulations and restrictions under the English common law. Grain elevators were held to be closely related to transportation and to commerce; they were said to be "bottlenecks" through which the crops of Middle Western farmers were forced to pass on their way to market. Hence, there arose the tendency toward control of monopoly and prices. In a word, the total situation was so different from that envisaged by Adam Smith and the classical economists that no other course of action could have saved the business men and farmers of the middle section of the United States from the capricious and virtually unlimited domination of the elevator interests. Thus began a rapid modification of the hundred-year-old theory that *laissez faire* is the natural and proper condition of economic enterprise.

<small>WHAT PUBLIC UTILITIES ARE</small>

Public-utility status is attached to a business by the legislature. Since the courts have the power to review the reasonableness of the designation, however, the public-utility concept is largely a legal or judicial one. When a business is related to the common carriers, when its indispensability to the business community and consumers is very great, and when valuable privileges have been granted to it by public authority, regulation is likely to be upheld. An electricity-supply company, for example, is usually granted a complete monopoly to serve its entire area; it is given rights of way and may exercise the power of eminent domain; its rates are fixed by governmental action instead of by competition; and if consumers do not pay their bills the service may be removed.

Not all indispensable businesses and not all those possessing monopoly characteristics are considered public utilities. In the excluded group may be classed milk supply, housing, steel, banking, and several others. If indispensability alone were the test, certainly the provision of food would be a "business affected with a public interest." In many cases, however, there are some minor forms of public control. The most important features of a utility are the granting of public

<small>AMBIT OF UTILITY CONTROL</small>

# ADMINISTRATIVE REGULATION

privileges, chief of which is freedom from competition, in return for which government fixes the rates it may charge.

Stuart Chase has compiled a list of thirty-two industries which have hitherto been subject to regulation by virtue of being "affected with a public interest":

| | |
|---|---|
| Steam railroads | Ice companies |
| Trolley lines | Telephone and telegraph companies |
| Carriers by water | |
| Wharf and dock companies | Radio broadcasting |
| Terminal companies | Messenger service |
| Express companies | Market ticker service |
| Bus and taxicab companies | Produce exchanges |
| Toll bridges | Stockyards |
| Ferries | Gristmills |
| Canals | Grain elevators |
| Booming and rafting companies | Creameries |
| Gas companies | Commission merchants |
| Power companies | Hotels |
| Heating companies (in large cities) | Insurance companies |
| | Cotton gins |
| Water companies | Laundries |
| Sewage companies | Irrigation companies |

"Why," he inquires, "these particular industries? Granted that nearly all furnish an important commodity or service to the public, why are ferries included, and filling stations neglected; why is a cotton gin more affected with a public interest than a shoe factory; or a laundry more than a bakery? True, some listed industries are natural monopolies, like the water supply, but hotels and taxis are notoriously competitive. The only pattern discernible is the general inclusion of transportation, communication, and municipal utilities. The rest seem to have wandered out of private enterprise haphazard. Anthracite coal is a monopoly, but it is not included; neither is Mr. Mellon's airtight aluminum combine. . . . There is obviously no consistent body of theory here at all."[1]

[1] Stuart Chase, *Government in Business* (New York, 1935), pp. 122-23. Used by permission of The Macmillan Company, publishers.

During the '70's, legislatures soon discovered that they would have to entrust regulatory power to administrative agencies if public control was to be made continuous and effective. Hence, there has developed what is usually referred to as "administrative regulation." The process of regulating service, rates, and extensions is far too complex for a legislative body itself to handle. In theory, therefore, the regulatory body becomes the agent of the legislature, administering in its name and advising the assembly on matters of public policy.

So numerous and varied are administrative tribunals that our political system may almost be called "government by commissions." There are scores of regulatory bodies in the United States, most of which have been created in the last fifty years. In the federal government, we find the Interstate Commerce Commission, Federal Communications Commission, Federal Power Commission, Securities and Exchange Commission, Federal Trade Commission, Federal Reserve Board, Petroleum Administrative Board, not to mention others which have been absorbed or have disappeared. Public-utility commissions, under differing names, are found in forty-seven out of the forty-eight states. Their principal authority is over electricity, water, and gas companies, telephone and telegraph systems, busses and trucks, waterway users, urban and interurban railways, airplane companies, pipe lines, stockyards, warehouses, docks and terminals. In addition, there are regulatory tribunals dealing with workmen's compensation, banking and insurance, admission to the professions, and various athletic enterprises. Public-utility commissions dealing with local questions, such as franchises and service, are found even in some of our municipal governments. Commissions constitute a large part of the American bureaucracy.

EXTENSION OF ADMINISTRATIVE REGULATION

After seventy years of public-utility regulation, this form of public control is still on trial. During the last ten years, there have been more official investigations and more public dissatisfaction than in any preceding period. The Federal Trade Commission's investigation of electrical utilities, begun in 1928, has produced shocking disclosures of holding-company practices and propaganda activities.[1] New York, Pennsylvania, California, and several other states have carried on similar sweeping inquiries. The Insull crash, nation-wide in its injurious consequences, will long be remembered. Even more significant in its long-run consequences is the increasing number of experts and friends of utility regulation who have become discouraged about making it succeed. Some who have worked longest and hardest in the cause of effective control have had to conclude, "public-utility regulation is a failure."

A BALANCE SHEET

Sweeping generalizations about the success or failure of administrative regulation are difficult to justify. The criteria of success have not been clearly enough defined. There are so many kinds of public-service enterprises—more than thirty—that generalization is hazardous. Then, too, within the same industry, there are extremes of good and bad, from the standpoint of honesty and attachment to the public interest.

When people generalize about public utilities, they usually have in mind either railways or electricity-supply undertakings. Both are essential, because business prosperity follows improved and cheap transportation, while cheap power gives a nation an advantage in world-wide competition and enables business to produce more goods for home consumption. In addition, the regulation of these two industries is typical of that exercised by the federal and state governments over other public utilities. Suppose, then, that we confine our analysis largely to the administrative regulation of the railway and electrical utilities.

Technological improvements have been reflected in the service rendered by public utilities. American railways, for example, have been introducing new types of equipment, following a long period in which there were virtually no improvements. Streamlining and increased speed are largely explainable by the competition which highway users have given the railroads. Utility management, however, has been generally efficient and progressive. The electrical industry, particularly, has been characterized by the aggressiveness of private enterprise. There has been the desire to please the customer and to get as much business from him as

[1] For books in which the findings are summarized, see footnote on p. 82, *supra*.

possible, which is very important during the developmental stages of a new industry. Finally, public-utility management has contributed a great deal to the industrial supremacy of the United States.

There are some respects in which we fall below other countries. Perhaps the principal one is in the confinement of utility services to those areas in which profitability is greatest. In other countries governments have made service more universal, more democratic. This is generally true of telephone, telegraph, electricity, and even railway services. For example, in the United States rural electrification has been extended to only about one-tenth of our farms. In western Europe and the Scandinavian countries, rural electrification is usually between 30 and 90 per cent.[1] American utilities figure that they are justified in confining their expansion to those areas where lucrative returns are assured. In many cases, it appears that they would rather do less business at a higher price than more business at a greater net profit. This has meant that the small towns and the countryside have not had an even break with the cities. Our public utilities have more vestiges of purely private business than those in most other countries, because the profit-making aspect of the various utility services is emphasized to such a great extent.

ECONOMIC RESULTS

It is not our intention to deal primarily with the economic and financial aspects of utility development. Our proper concern is with the legal and administrative aspects, with the rules of the game which obtain, with the sufficiency of the regulatory process. Here we find some serious shortcomings, sources of discouragement to those who favor regulation instead of government ownership.

In reaching a conclusion regarding the merits of public-utility regulation, we need to consider the following factors: (1) the effectiveness of the administrative tribunal as a control device;

[1] The extent of rural electrification in some representative countries is as follows: Germany, 90 per cent; Scandinavia, 50 per cent; New Zealand, 66 per cent; Ontario (Canada), 15 per cent; Holland, practically 100 per cent; The United States, 11 per cent. See the testimony of Morris L. Cooke before the House Committee on Interstate and Foreign Commerce, hearings on *Rural Electrification* (Washington, 1936), pp. 8 ff.

(2) the relation between the commissions and the courts; and (3) the underlying assumptions of American regulation.

Our method of public-utility regulation is singular; it is based on the theory that the legislature creates an independent commission of experts with powers and procedures very much like those of courts. In other countries, regulation is entrusted to one of the regular departments of government, which would correspond to the Department of the Interior in the United States.

Among the principal foreign countries, there is only one that has dealt with the regulatory problem in a manner similar to that of the United States. In Great Britain, regulatory tribunals are found dealing with railways, road transport, and electricity; and from one of these tribunals, namely, the Railway and Canal Commission, the United States derived its precedent for public-utility regulation. The public-utility commission, however, is not the principal method of public control in Great Britain; the Ministry of Transport has the greatest responsibility. Moreover, in recent years, a great deal of dissatisfaction has arisen with the tribunals which have been mentioned, and the public-utility trust is now preferred to regulation.[1] In other leading Western countries, the administrative tribunal is unknown, so that the distinctive character of the American regulatory commissions, or perhaps we should say the striking emphasis in the United States upon regulatory commissions, is readily apparent.

THE REGULATORY TRIBUNAL

In most of the countries of the world, administrative regulation of economic enterprises is a relatively unimportant matter. The reason for the difference is found primarily in the widespread extent of government ownership and operation. According to the constitutional law of almost every country in Europe, communication facilities are a state monopoly and, hence, the telephone, telegraph, and radio service are publicly operated. In Great Britain, moreover, two-thirds of the electricity supply is owned by public bodies; whereas in Germany the proportion is three-fourths. With the substitution of management for regulation, the problem of control virtually

PUBLIC CONTROL ABROAD

[1] See my study entitled *British Public Utilities and National Development* (London, 1933).

disappears. Monopolies are treated as though they were thoroughly public rather than basically private.

The ministers responsible for internal affairs handle matters pertaining to the regulation of public services. This method of public control, it will be observed, is the natural outgrowth of a system of responsible government wherein the minister is responsible to the cabinet and Parliament. Under responsible government, there is no proper place for a so-called independent establishment to which important powers relative to public policy are delegated. In discharging his regulatory duties, the responsible minister is usually assisted by a consultative board for the particular public service concerned. In France, for example, there is an advisory board on electricity development composed primarily of representatives of the operators, whose purpose it is to advise the minister with reference to proposed policies and to give him the advantage of suggestions relating to improvement of established policies. Through this device, the regulatory process is made representative and the parties principally affected are consulted, while at the same time policy and practice are kept unified and responsible.

The practice of establishing independent regulatory tribunals in the United States has had the effect of making American government even more irresponsible than it is basically because of the separation-of-powers theory. There is serious question as to whether the commission is a sound administrative device. It becomes a "no man's land" between the legislative and executive branches. It is like all committees—every person can point his finger at someone else and no one is finally responsible. Calling it "independent" does not take it out of politics. Its members are appointed, and, hence, the opportunity for partisan influence is as great as if a head of a department were being appointed. It does not get away from political influence and it diffuses responsibility. Is it any wonder, then, that one of the commonest complaints against public-utility commissions is that they become "controlled" by the very interests they are supposed to control?

Our regulatory commissions are frequently referred to as "expert tribunals." Their members are supposed to have special competence, and, hence, the legislature delegates responsibility to them and the courts are not supposed to interfere with the tribunal's findings of facts. But as a matter of fact, their members are not very expert; the average member can be described as a layman of somewhat more than average intelligence. A survey of the backgrounds of public-utility commissioners in the several states, made in 1929, revealed that there were 79 lawyers, 13 engineers, 5 journalists, 29 business men and bankers, 17 farmers, 12 industrial workmen, and 9 government employees.[1] Of the federal tribunals, E. Pendleton Herring has said, "The members of our federal regulatory boards are widely recruited. But this process is almost casual in its lack of system. Little consideration is given to increasing the internal strength of the commissions. Great emphasis has been placed upon pleasing groups or sections that are politically powerful. Moreover, our chief executives have habitually appointed men whose views harmonized with their own."[2]

HOW EXPERT ARE COMMISSIONS?

Only five American states have incorporated into their public-utility statutes requirements concerning training and experience. There are very few commissioners who are trained in public-utility economics, engineering, and finance, and, hence, who deserve to be called "expert." If more men of ability and independent judgment could be placed upon regulatory bodies, there would be far more chance of producing results which are satisfactory to the public.

Commissions range in size from one to eleven members—the latter being the present membership of the Interstate Commerce Commission. The average salary of public-utility commissioners is only $5,000, while the maximum is $15,000. In many cases, "good men" have left their posts to accept employment as public-utility executives at salaries of $25,000 to $75,000 a year.

Is it too much to expect commissioners to be expert, if there is sufficient skill and training among the members of the technical staff? Should not the expert be "on tap, not on top?" The obvious

[1] Francis X. Welch, "The Trend from Lawyers to Laymen as Commissioners," *Public Utilities Fortnightly*, IV (Dec. 26, 1929), 801.
[2] E. Pendleton Herring, *Federal Commissioners: A Study of Their Careers and Qualifications* (Cambridge, Mass., 1936), p. 96.

answer is that, so long as the members of our regulatory bodies are supposed to act as judges, we must expect them to be trained and competent. After all, public utilities probably constitute about one-fifth of the business capital of the United States. Thus, not only does sheer size present major problems, but questions of valuation, depreciation, and finance are very technical. Professor Herring found that the two major faults in our present system of regulation are: (1) the average brevity of service and (2) the lack of intimate knowledge of administrative duties on the part of most appointees.[1] "The ideal interstate commerce commissioner," said an incumbent of outstanding ability, "should be caught when young and trained a lifetime."

Our commissions cannot be adequately expert or effective because they are understaffed and underfinanced. The struggle between the tribunals and the utility managements is an unequal one. The financial resources of the public-service industry are virtually unlimited; they can add the cost of court battles to rates which the consumers pay. Their attorneys are the best available; but because their salaries are so low, those representing the public are frequently young and inexperienced. The annual expenditure on public-utility regulation in the several states is approximately five million dollars. In one case, the New York telephone controversy, a single utility company spent more than this amount in its court battle. This case dragged on for ten years, and others have been prolonged for similar periods.

FINANCIAL LIMITATIONS

One of the principal criticisms of regulation is that commissions are not self-starters—they do not investigate on their own initiative and aggressively safeguard the helpless consumers. Regulatory tribunals become so much like courts that they expect problems to be brought to them, instead of going out and discovering what is wrong. To a considerable extent, commission lethargy is due to the fact that the objectives of regulation are not clearly defined. Should the tribunal be the policeman and prosecutor as well as the judge? Is it the guardian of the public interest or merely the trial court? In most cases these questions remain unanswered. In

[1] *Ibid.*, p. 98.

addition, investigations cost money, and the regulatory agencies do not have it. Court fights usually take such a large percentage of the commission budget that there is not enough left for thorough investigations. The public interest is likely to go by default, because eternal vigilance is the price of effective regulation.

Two types of complaints, informal and formal, can usually be lodged before the public-service commission by consumers. If a passenger on a train cannot find a seat or is treated discourteously, he may merely write a letter to the railroad commission. The chances are that the tribunal will not do anything unless several such complaints are received. When the matter is of a more serious nature, such as alleged exorbitant rates, the commission may institute an inquiry, and the case is classified as a formal complaint. Hearings are held, evidence is introduced, witnesses are heard, a ruling is made. The formal proceeding is not unlike that of a court.

Many regulatory bodies have not been given jurisdiction over some of the most important utilities and matters related thereto. Sixteen commissions have no power over the issuance of securities by utility companies.[1] This is surprising when one considers that financial manipulation of one kind or another has been such a common complaint. It would seem that all commissions should be given effective powers with reference to such matters as overcapitalization and "stock watering." "This power has been granted to the commissions in only twenty-five of the states," William E. Mosher has pointed out in his survey entitled *Electrical Utilities*, "and there only over the issues of operating companies. The fifteen states in which the commissions have control over electrical companies without control over financial manipulations are deprived of one of the most effective functions of regulation; but even in the case of the twenty-five equipped with the authority, there is no guarantee that it will be exercised effectively." In one-third of the states, public regulation of the electricity industry is "either totally lacking or limited in some degree," again quoting Professor Mosher.

LIMITED JURISDICTION

[1] William E. Mosher and Finla G. Crawford, *Public Utility Regulation* (New York, 1933), pp. 118 ff.

Only four state commissions have been given jurisdiction over holding companies, while interstate electrical holding companies were not brought under even limited federal control until 1935. This survey is by no means exhaustive, but it gives a sufficiently clear idea of the glaring gaps in public-utility control.

In the informality of their procedure, the liberality of their rules of evidence and their greater dispatch and freedom from unnecessary expense, the most successful public-utility commissions afford an example for ordinary courts. The Interstate Commerce Commission, and the public-service commissions of Wisconsin, Massachusetts, New York, and California, may justly be called outstanding. From the standpoint of effective judicial procedure, some of the best tribunals deserve commendation. The fundamental question for the public, however, is the effectiveness of the instrument as a means of protecting the public interest.

Public-utility regulation has many administrative shortcomings and deficiencies. The objectives of regulation are not sufficiently well defined, the commissioners are not expert, the tribunal is irresponsible, jurisdiction is far from complete, tribunals are underfinanced and inadequately staffed, and few commissions show sufficient initiative.

SUMMARY OF ADMINISTRATIVE DEFICIENCIES

From the standpoint of governmental administration, there is still a further basic weakness in the American system of regulation by independent commissions. Reorganizations of state governments which have taken place in recent years have attempted to secure a reduction in the number of independent boards and commissions. Greater responsibility and economy are secured thereby. These beneficial results have been largely offset by the continual increase in the number of regulatory tribunals in most states. These *ad hoc* bodies must be related to the departmental structure or superseded by another method before integration and simplification can be achieved.

So numerous and detached are the administrative tribunals that they are lost from public view in the maze of independent establishments. They become a prize for political appointments and lead to irresponsible administration, a multiplicity of agencies, and inconsistency in social policies.

The work of regulatory bodies is crippled by the frequent court interference with powers which have been granted by the legislature. Felix Frankfurter calls excessive appeals, "the heart of the difficulty." "The present enfeeblement of utility administration by the states," he says, "is in no small measure due to interference in administration by the lower federal courts."[1] The tribunal's judgment with regard to facts is supposed to be final and not subject to judicial nullification. Despite the fact that such stipulations are put into public-utility statutes, the courts find reasons to try cases *de novo*. In the field of public-utility regulation, administrative finality seems to be on the retreat.

The law of the land is still undefined. Not all the responsibility for constant judicial interference with the regulatory process is attributable to the courts themselves. One of the basic difficulties is that legislatures have not defined fundamental policies to be followed with reference to valuation and rates. The so-called "law of the land," as set forth in the *obiter dicta* of *Smyth* vs. *Ames*[2] provides no definite rule whatever. It merely enumerates all the factors entering into valuation, leaving it to future decisions to emphasize any ones considered important by the court.[3] Hence, the commissions and the courts have seesawed back and forth between the extremes of the original-cost and the reproduction-cost theories. The result has been a high degree of uncertainty, amounting almost to regulatory chaos, with estimated differences in rate bases, depending upon the theory of valuation to be followed, as great as 50 per cent.

THE COMMISSIONS AND THE COURTS

A utility is entitled to "a fair return on a fair value." Before rates can be fixed or returns computed, a valuation must be established upon the utility property. The Interstate Commerce Commission worked on railway valuation from 1913 until 1930 only to have its methods and results disapproved by the Supreme Court

[1] Felix Frankfurter, *The Public and Its Government* (New Haven, 1930), p. 121.
[2] 169 U. S. 466 (1898).
[3] Mr. Justice Brandeis has said, "The so-called rule of *Smyth* vs. *Ames* is . . . legally unsound. . . . The experience of the twenty-five years since that case was decided has demonstrated that the rule there enunciated was delusive. In the attempt to apply it, insuperable obstacles have been encountered. It has failed to afford adequate protection either to capital or to the public. It leaves the door open to grave injustice." Quoted from the case of *Los Angeles Gas* vs. *R. R. Com. of Cal.*, 289 U. S. 287, 290 (1933).

in the O'Fallon case. Valuation is the present basis of public-utility regulation, but it is not satisfactory, and we have not yet discovered a workable substitute.

The Indianapolis Water Company case is one of the most famous in American constitutional law involving administrative finality. It dealt with the question of valuation, and produced disagreement between the commission and the judiciary as to the proper rate base. The facts decided by the regulatory tribunal were reviewed by the Supreme Court and the commission was overruled.[1] The consequences are instructive. Investors thereafter received a return of 38 per cent upon the book value of the common-stock investment in the holding company.[2] This case was one of a series of decisions which have cut the ground from under the commissions. In recent years there have been several such reversals.[3] Instead of merely "trying the trial" and trusting the expert competence of the tribunal, the judges substitute their own judgment on the facts for those of the commissioners.

Even after a valuation has been fixed, the courts may disagree with the regulatory body concerning a "fair return." Any rate of return below the one considered "fair" is held to be "confiscatory." In the Baltimore Street Railway case,[4] for example, the Maryland commission found that a return of 6.26 per cent on a street-car line was sufficient. The Supreme Court, however, ruled that the return should be 7.44 per cent. What is a fair return upon a gilt-edged security? The public utility has a monopoly; competition is prohibited by law; income estimates can be figured closely. Public utilities usually do not suffer from flexibility of demand. If honestly administered, a public utility should be the safest kind of investment. With the investment market being what it has been, it would seem that 3 or 4 per cent might be a reasonable rate of return; but, of course, this depends upon the economic ideas of a majority of the judges!

Appeals to the courts are so frequent that commissions are

[1] *McCardle* vs. *Indianapolis Water Co.*, 272 U. S. 400 (1926).
[2] Dexter M. Keezer and Stacy May, *The Public Control of Business* (New York, 1930), p. 170.
[3] See especially *Crowell* vs. *Benson*, 285 U. S. 22 (1932); *Chesapeake & Potomac Tel. Co.* vs. *West*, 296 U. S. 661 (1936).
[4] *United Railways and Electric Co. of Baltimore* vs. *West*, 280 U. S. 234 (1929).

usually content with a compromise between what the utility contends for and what the tribunal's engineers think the real valuation is. A public-service commission's boasts that it has "saved" consumers so many thousands of dollars may mean nothing more than that, by a process of compromise, rates have been reduced below what they were formerly. It does not necessarily mean that the rate base which has been allowed and the rates which have been imposed represent a fair return upon capital actually invested.

One of the principal barriers to effective public-utility control has been the extension of the holding company device. According to the Federal Trade Commission, "no substantial progress is being made, or can be made, by the states generally, toward effective regulation of holding companies."[1] The same report continues, "The holding company in the utility field has been the chief device by which the control and ownership of operating companies has been rapidly concentrated into fewer and fewer hands with every prospect that the process will continue on to a nation-wide monopoly unless there be government regulation." Bonbright and Means, writing in 1932, said, "today ten great groups of systems . . . do approximately three-quarters of the electric light and power business of the entire nation. A somewhat similar but less extreme centralization prevails for the gas business, where sixteen holding company systems, most of which also do an electric business, control 45 per cent of the gas output of the country."[2]

HOLDING COMPANIES

By means of the holding company, public-utility operators have been able to draw many of the teeth from the laws subjecting utility properties to control by public-service commissions. It is the form of corporate organization that, under present law,[3] is least subject to public control. Yet practically all the electric energy transmitted across state lines, amounting to about one-sixth of the total consumed, is controlled by holding companies and, thus, is in two ways beyond control by the states. Through the

[1] Federal Trade Commission, *Utility Corporations*, No. 73-A (U. S. Government Printing Office, Washington, D. C., 1935), p. 63.
[2] James C. Bonbright and Gardiner C. Means, *The Holding Company* (McGraw-Hill, New York, 1932), p. 91.
[3] *Ibid.*, pp. 337 ff.; see also the case of *Smith* vs. *Illinois Bell Tel. Co.*, 282 U. S. 133 (1930).

holding-company device, a few individuals may gain a degree of control and reap corresponding profits, greatly disproportionate to their actual investment. By "pyramiding" holding companies, for example, the Insull interests controlled operating companies with as little as two-hundredths of 1 per cent of the securities of the bottom company.[1] Transactions between different companies within the same holding company structure also serve as a convenient medium through which write-ups of capital assets may be effected. Moreover, capital inflation is far from uncommon. The Federal Trade Commission found an average write-up of 22 per cent on the capital assets of operating companies in the electrical field.[2] The abuses of the holding company fall chiefly into two classes: (1) Unsound and needless financial structures and practices which are a detriment, and frequently a menace, to the investor or the consumer, or both; and (2) the milking of operating companies through the device of numerous forms of contracts and arrangements. The Federal Trade Commission's investigation disclosed that the profits thus exacted have in some instances ranged from 50 per cent to 300 per cent of the cost of such services.[3]

Cryptically the commission concludes, "the detriment of utility-holding companies to the public has exceeded, thus far, their value to the public." Continuing, it points out, "It is not easy to choose words which will adequately characterize various ethical aspects of the situation without an appearance of undue severity. Nevertheless the use of words such as fraud, deceit, misrepresentation, dishonesty, breach of trust, and oppression are the only suitable terms to apply if one seeks to form an ethical judgment on many practices which have taken sums beyond calculation from the rate-paying and investing public."[4]

Can the regulation of public-utility holding companies be made successful? "The holding company," say Bonbright and Means, "has now become such an essential part of the structure of large-scale business that its abolition would be serious, if not fatal, to the effectiveness of American industry."[5] One effective contribution

[1] Federal Trade Commission, *Utility Corporations*, No. 72-A (1935), p. 160.
[2] *Ibid.*, p. 299.   [3] *Op. cit.*, No. 73-A, p. 64.   [4] *Ibid.*, pp. 63-4.
[5] Bonbright and Means, *op. cit.*, p. 338.

it makes is to facilitate the decentralization of authority and responsibility, hence improving operating efficiency.

We can expect no substantial improvement in the public-utility situation until there is a recognition on the part of the managements, as well as on the part of the public, that monopolies which secure invaluable services from government are public businesses. The "cock-fight" theory of public-utility regulation is wrong. The touchstone of all policy is the cheapest and best possible service to the customers, not the highest possible profits for the owners. A public utility is a trusteeship, a fiduciary relationship to the government and to the users of the service; in the fiduciary relationship, the incentives of exploitation and profit making have no proper place. A low rate of interest on capital is all that can possibly be justified.

THE RULES OF THE GAME

The rules of the game need to be changed. The present rules encourage evasion, subterfuge, and sharp dealing. Public-utility regulation, at present, appeals to the "cops-and-robbers" instinct in men. From beginning to end, the regulatory process is one in which the public officials act as policemen and the utility operators try to see how much they can "get away with." This is likely to remain the atmosphere so long as public utilities are considered essentially private; the directors and stockholders keep prodding the management to earn higher rates of return; administrative regulation is regarded as "intervention," a necessary evil which should be circumvented as far as possible.

A phalanx of animosity develops. Each addition to the ranks of "business affected with a public interest" tends to add to the number of interests resistant to public authority. "Every increase in the area of regulated enterprise increases the difficulty of control by strengthening the opponents of the State and weakening its advocates. Thus, an industrial system completely regulated on behalf of consumers is almost inconceivable. As soon as the body of the regulated enterprises becomes large enough, the whole regulatory system must be vitiated of power."[1]

Public-utility regulation is defective from the standpoint of social theory; it creates the wrong atmosphere, promulgates incon-

[1] W. E. Atkins and others, *Economic Behavior* (Houghton-Mifflin, New York, 1928), p. 366.

sistent rules of the game, and fosters a power pyramid which is interested only in earnings. This is only one objectionable aspect of the situation; another has to do with the administrative deficiencies which result from the regulatory process.

One of the first conditions for the success of any economic enterprise is that it should have a unified management. Regulation violates this rule by tending to divide responsibility between the regulators and the operators. In the public mind, the effectiveness of public control is measured by the number of interferences placed upon the enterprise. The regulatory tribunal may come even to share the responsibility for management. This situation has been reached in the case of the Interstate Commerce Commission, which, since the passage of the Transportation Act of 1920, has had power, among other things, to formulate and enforce a required system of keeping books, to bring about an interchange of freight cars between all parts of the country, to fix maximum and minimum rates, and to control extensions and discontinuances.

Men of executive capacity chafe under constant interference from an outside authority. Among an increasing number of administrators who have had experience with regulated undertakings, there is a conviction that "a regulated business is worse than no business at all." A prominent member of one of the federal regulatory tribunals once told the writer that public control over that particular utility had suffered primarily because the managers had a feeling of contempt for, and a lack of confidence in, the members of the regulatory body. The commissioners are considered "academic" and not capable of appreciating the practical managerial problems which arise. He then admitted that there was a great deal of truth in this assertion, "because," he said, "the commissioners are rather mediocre and untrained and they can never be expected to know as much about running the business as the best of the public-utility executives."

Rigidity of rules and absence of flexibility are likely to result from regulation. Rules laid down by the legislature or the commission usually outlive their usefulness long before they are changed. Regulations tend to become static; inertia saps the life of the regulated undertaking, injuring both it and the public.

Efficiency is the modern substitute for administrative regulation. By efficiency, we mean the most effective management possible within a system of public control which provides adequate safeguards for the fundamental public interest, but which guarantees the unity of management and independence of action required in progressive administration. This combination can be achieved.

DESIDERATA OF PUBLIC-SERVICE MANAGEMENT

Inner control, or limitation through the powers and duties provided for in the incorporation, should replace constant interference from the regulatory tribunal. Concretely, this means that the basic forms of protection to the public interest need to be safeguarded in the charter which is granted when the utility is created. Federal incorporation is to be desired, if for no other reason, to escape from "liberal" state charters which are the cause of so many abuses. The basic considerations are the establishment of a "prudent" investment, the prevention of "watering," the substitution of a fixed interest rate on invested capital in place of speculative profits, the flexibility of rates depending upon basic price levels, the guarantee of reduced rates when costs are lowered, and the substitution of the "public trustee" for the director whose chief concern is profit making. Statutory or inner control is already found in the public-utility trust and the newer corporate developments.

Once the fundamental powers and limitations have been fixed by the legislative body, the management is as free from outside interference as is the ordinary private business. This is the goal which should be sought. Profit making is the principal stumbling block. Can the rules of the game be changed and public control be made a success? If so, public utility officials will need to be more far-sighted than in the past.

Recent economic analysis points to fundamental weaknesses in the theory of regulation. According to Professor Henry Simons:

Public regulation of private monopoly would seem to be, at best, an anomalous arrangement, tolerable only as a temporary expedient. Half-hearted, sporadic, principle-less regulation is a misfortune for all concerned; and systematic regulation, on the basis of any definite and adequate principle, would leave private ownership almost without a significant function or responsibility to discharge. Analysis of the problem, and examination

FUTURE OF REGULATION

of the experience to date, would seem to indicate the wisdom of abandoning the existing scheme of things with respect to the railroads and utilities, rather than of extending the system to include other industries as well.[1]

In this economist's opinion, "the state should face the necessity of actually taking over, owning, and managing directly, both the railroads and utilities, and all other industries in which it is impossible to maintain effectively competitive conditions. For industries other than the utilities, there still remains a real alternative to socialization, namely, the establishment and preservation of competition as the regulative agency."

Even though Simons's analysis should prove correct, there will still be the necessity of public regulation in many directions. Health and morals are two fields that have been mentioned. Then, too, regulation may be found efficacious in some public-utility industries and not in others. Leonard White was probably correct in prophesying that "The enlarging positive program of the state does not imply by any means a corresponding diminution of its repressive and regulative activities." In liberal-democratic countries, there should be room for many kinds of experimentation. Only a doctrinaire person thinks that all problems should be treated with the same formula. Unregulated private business, regulated utilities, co-operatives, and government proprietary services may well exist side by side. A doctor tries to discriminate between the needs of his patients; a biologist distinguishes between lower and higher forms of life. Adaptation is the secret of survival.

SELECTED READINGS

Bauer, John, and Gold, Nathaniel: *Public Utility Valuation for Rate Control* (New York, 1934); an excellent treatment of public-utility valuation from the standpoints of law, economics, administration, and public policy.

Bonbright, James C., and Means, Gardiner C.: *The Holding Company* (New York, 1932); a scholarly treatment of the social implications of the holding company.

Clark, John M.: *Social Control of Business* (New York, 1926); chaps. i–v are especially good as a critical interpretation of the philosophic considerations underlying control over business.

[1] Henry Simons, "A Positive Program for Laissez Faire," Public Policy Pamphlet No. 15 (University of Chicago Press, 1934), p. 11.

Commager, H. S.: "Farewell to Laissez Faire," *Current History*, XXVIII (August, 1933), 513–20.
Dickinson, John: *Administrative Justice and the Supremacy of Law* (Cambridge, Mass., 1927); chaps. VI–VIII deal with court review of administrative determinations in connection with the regulation of public utilities and unfair trade practices.
Dimock, Marshall E.: "British and American Utilities: a Comparison," *Chicago Law Review*, I, No. 2 (November, 1933), 265–82.
Dykstra, C. A., and others: "Public Utilities and Their Control: Symposium," *National Municipal Review*, XXIII, No. 11 (November, 1934), 567–70.
Frankfurter, Felix: *The Public and Its Government* (New Haven, 1930); chap. III focuses attention upon important problems in public-utility regulation.
Gaskill, Nelson B.: *The Regulation of Competition* (New York, 1936); an evaluation of the effects of court decisions in four leading cases upon the effectiveness of the Federal Trade Commission as a regulatory device. The author is a former chairman of the Commission.
Glaeser, Martin P.: *Outlines of Public Utility Economics* (New York, 1927), chaps. I–XIII; a treatment of the problems of public utilities from the economico-legal point of view.
Gray, John H., and Levin, Jack: *The Valuation and Regulation of Public Utilities* (New York, 1933); traces the history of public-utility regulation with emphasis on the principles and mechanics of valuation.
Herring, E. Pendleton: *Public Administration and the Public Interest* (New York, 1936); chaps. VII–XIV examine the effectiveness of *ad hoc* commissions as a means for securing regulation in the public interest.
———: *Federal Commissioners: a Study of Their Careers and Qualifications* (Cambridge, Mass., 1936); an interesting study of the qualifications of the personnel of the regulatory commissions.
Hormell, Orren C.: *Control of Public Utilities Abroad* (School of Citizenship and Public Affairs, Syracuse University, Syracuse, New York, 1930); a brief discussion of the essentials of public-utility regulation in Great Britain, France, Germany, Sweden, Norway, and Switzerland.
Keezer, Dexter M., and May, Stacy: *The Public Control of Business* (New York, 1930); a concise and stimulating treatment of the problem of government control and of the confusion that exists in the law of government control.
Lilienthal, D. E.: "The Cost of Regulation," *Public Utilities Fortnightly*, X, No. 12 (December 22, 1932), 723–32.
McFarland, Carl: *Judicial Control of the Federal Trade Commission and the Interstate Commerce Commission 1920–1930* (Cambridge, Mass., 1933); a study of the relations of the federal courts to administrative tribunals.

McNinch, F. R.: "The Evolution of Federal Control of Electric Power," *Journal of Land and Public Utility Economics*, XII, No. 2 (May, 1936), 111–19.

Mosher, William E., and Crawford, Finla G.: *Public Utility Regulation* (New York, 1933); a general treatise on the scope and effectiveness of present methods of regulating public utilities.

Mosher, William E., and others: *Electrical Utilities: the Crisis in Public Control* (New York, 1929), chaps. I–VI.

Olds, Leland: "The Public Utility Issue," *Yale Review*, XXIV, No. 4 (June, 1935), 704–23.

Patterson, Ernest M., ed.: "Power and the Public," *Annals*, CLIX (January, 1932).

Prendergast, William A.: *Public Utilities and the People* (New York, 1933); deals with controversial questions in the field of public-utility regulation, emphasizing the shortcomings of governmental regulation.

Rohlfing, C. C., Carter, E. W., West, B. W., and Hervey, J. G.: *Business and Government* (Chicago, 1934), chaps. IV–XII; an exposition of the important economic relations and adjustments inherent in the changing relationship between government and business.

Rooks, Irvin, and Booth, Harry R.: "Current Problems of Public Utility Rate Regulation," *Oregon Law Review*, XIII, No. 2 (February, 1934), pp. 122–33.

Sharfman, I. L.: *The Interstate Commerce Commission*, 4 vols. (New York, 1931–36); an exhaustive study and appraisal of the Interstate Commerce Commission as a governmental agency.

CHAPTER XIII

☆ ☆ ☆

## THE PROVISION OF ECONOMIC SERVICES

*"No door to service is closed so
tight that it cannot be reopened."*
—WILLIAM ANDERSON

GOVERNMENT is a trader, selling economic commodities and services. The citizens are both owners and consumers. Government as enterpriser is by no means a new role for public agencies, but only in the last fifty years have the number and variety of economic services become so extensive that people talk about "government in business."

GOVERNMENT AS ENTERPRISER

It is frequently difficult to draw a line between the so-called business and the traditional services of government. The process of transition from private to public enterprise has taken place gradually. Not so long ago, public roads, education, and water supply were considered part of the profit-making structure of private business. Now, in most countries, citizens are satisfied that these are essentially public. We no longer pay tolls for using roads or fees for sending our children to school. Instead, these charges appear on our tax bills, after the total expenditures on these services have been divided among all the rate payers. Of the three services, water supply is now the only one that people still pay for over the counter, in the manner of private business.

We pay for all the activities of government, whether they be protection, assistance, regulation, or direct services. A person has two pockets; in one of them he keeps the money with which he purchases groceries, gasoline, and shelter from private business concerns; in the other he keeps the funds with which he buys police protection, schooling, and good roads from public agencies. The only difference is that the costs of most of his purchases from government are lumped together in the form of a tax bill.

The trading activities of public authorities are most clearly distinguished when consumers pay cash for them, settle accounts at the end of the month, or buy metered or measured services. In most cases, municipal transportation, water, and electric services are paid for in this manner. When we pay over the counter, there is very little difference between going to the office of a private utility and the collection office of a municipal utility; moreover, the methods of operation and management are essentially the same.

Business is not only a method of supplying and collecting payment for services, but, in popular thinking, it has come to be identified with skill and efficiency in getting things done. People talk about "businesslike" management, the adjective being used to convey the idea of accuracy, punctuality, efficiency, and the desire to please the customer in order that one may sell something. We are justified, therefore, in speaking about the "business management" of government services. The concept is even broader. We customarily refer to a businesslike housewife, or club, or Russian oil trust, or co-operative association. Business is not only a particular type of enterprise or a system of profit making; it is a method and spirit of serving consumers. It has been discovered that to the extent to which public bodies achieve the highest standards of private enterprise, the public is prepared to entrust additional services to government if occasion arises.

Reasons for the extension of public commercial activities have been numerous, and rarely in any two cases do we find the same combination of explanations. Dissatisfaction with the profits and charges of privately operated services is probably the most common cause. This is particularly likely to be true if the business is monopolistic in its character. Both roads and water supply became so essential that people tired of contributing profits to private companies. There is now general satisfaction with the manner in which highways are improved, a supply of water is made available, and schools are run. These services have passed over into the sphere of completely accepted and legitimate public activities.

<small>CAUSES OF THE CHANGE TO PUBLIC OPERATION</small>

People get the idea in some cases that a service is public by its very nature. This is one of the most important explanations of why, in about a century's time, water supply has been transferred

## THE PROVISION OF ECONOMIC SERVICES 343

from private hands to public operation. In 1800 there was one municipally owned waterworks in the United States; in 1900 there were almost 2,000; at present there are only two important plants, Hackensack and Indianapolis, under private operation. Water supply is more than 95 per cent public. Warren M. Persons, who has written a book attacking government enterprise, says, "Other undertakings, such as the post office, sell services to the public, but . . . for special reasons connected with the nature of the business, their conduct by the government is not questioned."[1] Wells Fargo did not take this complacent view of the matter!

A conversion from private to public operation sometimes takes place when citizens become dissatisfied with the existing service. This is likely to be the case when the private management is highhanded or neglectful. Here, again, this situation rarely arises except in monopoly or semi-monopoly services. Slothfulness is an inherent danger of large enterprises. They feel sure of their position; competition does not keep them on their toes. One common complaint has been that private operators are not interested in extending the market. They would rather take their money with less work than extend the service and run the risk of not netting more profit. Public ownership of electrical utilities, particularly in Great Britain, is largely explained, on the one hand, by the unwillingness of private owners to expand and, on the other, by the tradition of democratic service in government-operated enterprises.

Public utilities have become government-operated when the people were satisfied with the efficiency of their governments and, hence, had confidence that an additional service would be well managed. The widespread municipal ownership in Great Britain and Germany, for example, is largely explained by the excellence of local government. Hardheaded conservatives, such as Joseph Chamberlain, have been and still are, proponents of municipal ownership. In the final analysis, it is the over-all efficiency of private versus public operation that determines where the dividing line shall be drawn.

[1] Reprinted by permission from *Government Experimentation in Business*, by Warren M. Persons. Published by John Wiley and Sons. (New York, 1934), p. 3.

Party policies and programs also have caused an extension of government trading. The Socialists, for example, deny the necessity of the profit incentive and contend that certain types of industry are especially "ripe" for public ownership. They have confidence—sometimes naïve and unsupported—that economic enterprises can be managed as successfully by public managers as by private ones. The long-time consequences of the Socialist analysis are clearly very important. In studying the causes of public ownership, however, one is bound to be misled unless the numerous factors we have been mentioning are taken into consideration.

Even conservative economic analyses make allowance for public enterprise. Said Adam Smith himself: "The third and last duty of the sovereign or commonwealth is that of erecting and maintaining those public institutions and those public works, which, though they may be in the highest degree advantageous to a great society, are, however, of such a nature that the profit could never repay the expense of any individual or small number of individuals." To this point, his utterance is thoroughly orthodox. The father of modern economics added, "The performance of this duty requires, too, very different degrees of expense in the different periods of society."[1] Would Henry Simons's analysis, above, be considered orthodox theory by Adam Smith if he were alive today?

Government has frequently been saddled with enterprises which private owners were anxious to dispose of, usually because profitability had disappeared. In the early stages of government enterprise, this explanation was the commonest one.

GOVERNMENT HOLDS THE BAG When the turnpike ruined the canals, and, later, when the railways destroyed the business of the toll-road owners, those who suffered in each case were glad to sell out to the government. Now we find an important block of railway investors in the United States favoring government ownership of carriers because they hope to get a treasury guarantee of dividends which have not been forthcoming for some time. One of the principal trusts of public officials is to keep owners from unloading worthless properties upon the public. When one looks at this angle of the matter, one is not likely to be so much impressed

[1] *The Wealth of Nations*, Book V, Part III, chap. I.

by the contention that public enterprise is solely a deep-laid conspiracy on the part of those who would destroy private enterprise. In a book written for the Edison Electric Institute, Warren Persons has traced the history of profligate grants of public funds to railways, canals, and many other forms of private venture, in which taxpayers were frequently left to "hold the bag."[1] Public ownership has been, to a considerable extent, a catchall for bones which private enterprise has thrown to it.

Government as enterpriser has also pioneered. It has been the risk taker. Mr. Persons's book is full of such examples, and countless other illustrations can be supplied from the history of every country. The Australian Government has developed an export market for agricultural products, providing the necessary machinery and capital. The British Post Office, with its ample resources, is rapidly putting television within reach. After the World War, Germany passed a law making superpower available all over the country, laying the foundation for industrial recovery and for recapturing world markets. The Government of the United States made the building of Western railways possible, has financed the growth of the merchant marine, and owns and operates the barge lines on our inland waterways, a responsibility it undertook when private enterprisers were unwilling to risk a battle with the railways. Yes, government pioneers. When it succeeds, public enterprise rarely gets its share of the credit; when it pays the losses, people are not permitted to forget about it.

PIONEERING AND RISK BEARING

Even the severest critics of public enterprise admit the satisfactoriness of governmental responsibility for older services, such as highways, the post office, and education. These functions are now taken as a matter of course, and the public is led to expect satisfactory and efficient service. Ventures such as these do not encroach upon private interests; the profit-making and speculative factors have almost completely disappeared. The situation is completely altered, however, when state enterprise impinges upon private interests. The intensity and magnification of the attack upon public enterprise is in direct ratio to the private interests

[1] Warren M. Persons, *op. cit.*

affected and the profitability of the business. This is why we hear so much about electricity but relatively little about railroads.

Publicly operated economic services now constitute so large a part of the total want-supplying mechanism and are such a large proportion of administrative services that political scientists need <small>TASK OF THE POLITICAL SCIENTIST</small> to give more attention than they have in the past to the theoretical and practical problems arising therefrom. Can government serve the economic wants of the community satisfactorily, or are there insuperable handicaps which limit the effectiveness of the service? To what extent can business management be introduced into public enterprises? These problems and their solutions are primarily administrative. The questions of organization, finance, personnel, and control, however, go to the very roots of constitutional and representative government.

It is estimated that state-controlled enterprises now affect the lives of nearly 70 per cent of all Europeans. A staggering figure, this! At first, it seems as though there must be a mistake, but the facts and figures support this estimate.[1] <small>STATE ENTERPRISE ABROAD</small> It is no surprise to be told that in Russia 80 to 90 per cent of industry and agriculture is operated by government; but it may cause surprise to learn that Sweden, for example, is "now 50 per cent collectivized—including the co-operatives as public business." We can grasp the extent of public enterprise more clearly, perhaps, if we deal with basic industries and utilities. Telegraphs and telephones are owned and operated by public authorities in all countries save Spain, Brazil, and the United States—"an incongruous trinity." There are about fifty state-owned and operated railway systems; the United States and Great Britain are the only countries of any size in which they are not public in whole or in part. Municipal ownership of water, gas, light, and power utilities is well-nigh universal. In Great Britain, for example, two-thirds, and in Germany three-fourths, of the electricity supply is publicly owned and operated. Local transportation comes close to falling into the same category. National or local governments in almost a dozen

[1] See Stuart Chase, *op. cit.*, pp. 3, 70 ff.

countries now operate banks. Several countries, including some of our American states, operate insurance systems. As early as 1914, the government of New Zealand did one-half as much insurance business as all private companies combined.

What Sidney Webb said in 1914 is even more clearly true today. Governments are found "manufacturing in one place or another every conceivable commodity for the use of the consumer." It would become tedious if we were to attempt a complete list of government economic enterprises. Public authorities, national or local, operate quarries, brick works, iron and steel mills, lumber industries, tin and copper smelters, flour mills, bakeries, shoe factories, slaughter houses, distilleries, breweries, clothing factories, furniture mills, rubber plantations, restaurants—why prolong the list?[1]

Where does the United States stand? There are approximately three and one-half million public employees in the United States, and of this number 3 per cent work for municipal utilities.[2] There are now in the neighborhood of 2,400 municipal electric-light plants. Water supply, as we have said, is now almost wholly governmental. Several American cities, including San Francisco, Detroit, and Seattle, own and operate their own systems of local transportation. In 1935 the annual report of the Treasurer of the United States showed that federal proprietary corporations, such as the Inland Waterways Corporation, represented investments of over four billion dollars and had assets of eleven and one-half billions. The Reconstruction Finance Corporation, alone, listed assets of over five billions.

GOVERNMENT PARTICIPATION IN THE UNITED STATES

The city of Milwaukee, although it has had a Socialist mayor for a generation, does not operate more municipal enterprises than several other American cities. Consider some of the public services it makes available! Milwaukee operates a stone quarry, printing press, bindery, and an asphalt plant. It manufactures traffic

---

[1] Cf. Harry W. Laidler, *Public Ownership Here and Abroad* (New York, 1924); Carl D. Thompson, *Public Ownership* (New York, 1925); A. Emil Davies, *The Collectivist State in the Making* (London, 1914); and Stuart Chase, *op. cit.*
[2] Katherine A. Frederic, "Trained Personnel for Public Service," National League of Women Voters' pamphlet (Washington, D. C., 1935), p. 8.

signals, alarm boxes, fire engines and equipment, radios, blueprints, and fertilizer. The city runs a 160-acre nursery. It does all its own mechanical and repair work. The local government administers the port facilities, which at present handle commerce totaling about seven million tons. Milwaukee runs hospitals, twenty centers for second-run motion pictures, open-air dance halls, baseball diamonds, golf courses, outdoor operas and festivals, housing projects, a real-estate department, and a coal yard which supplies indigents.[1] This reads almost like a chamber of commerce advertisement! Milwaukee is not in a class by itself, however, for in conservative Colorado Springs, where this chapter was written, the city operates the electric-light-and-power utility and a municipal golf course. Local residents are convinced that they are the best managed of any in the country.

Between the middle of the nineteenth century and the outbreak of the World War, there was a steady expansion of municipal trading functions in many countries, including the United States. The municipality is a corporation, a business enterprise. Even its traditional services, such as public works, have been primarily economic or businesslike in their nature. Running a city government does not involve deeply disputed political issues; local government is a matter of good housekeeping; moreover, people are likely to act more rationally on questions that are near to them. Under these circumstances, it has been easy and natural for municipalities to assume the responsibility for water supply, gas and electricity, street railways, and even services less customarily supplied by the municipality.

SIZE AND ADMINISTRATIVE DIFFICULTIES

In recent years, there has been also a rapid extension of the field of economic activity on the part of national governments. Most of the countries of Europe, including Great Britain, Germany, France, and Italy, now have nation-wide interconnected systems of electricity transmission under government ownership or sponsorship. Radio broadcasting has been added to the national government's jurisdiction over communication facilities. Central

[1] See James L. McCamy, "Economic Enterprises in Milwaukee," *Public Management*, XVIII (March, 1936), 76–81.

governments have extended their sway in transportation, while mining, banking, and insurance have received widespread attention. In the United States, the outstanding development has been increased federal participation in the realms of banking and electricity. Nation-wide problems require national solutions.

As might be expected, the creation of nation-wide and regional trading enterprises has raised new and difficult problems of public management. Sometimes it seems that the difficulties of administration are in direct proportion to size. Large-scale enterprise, either private or public, produces problems which either have not existed or are found only at low intensity where business is small-scale. They may all be resolved into the caption "the inherent dangers of bureaucracy." Large public enterprises find it difficult to secure unity of management, flexibility of prices and administration, corporate morale, adequate executive leadership, freedom from excessive regulations and red tape, sufficient financial autonomy, integration in the superstructure of government, and consistency with general policies. Because of their bigness, the British Broadcasting Company, the Tennessee Valley Authority, and the German national electrification system are confronted by these administrative problems. How can they furnish the flexible, responsive service associated with good private management and still comply with general governmental policies and administrative controls? Municipal services, in greater or less degree, have long had to face and solve these same basic problems. Generally speaking, they have succeeded very well. Large enterprises have inherent administrative handicaps, but experience shows that they can be overcome if sufficient invention and principle are applied to their procedures.

"The state by its constitution and character, being subject to democratic control, is fundamentally unfitted to act as trader in the ordinary meaning of that word."[1] Not content with this generalization, Archibald Hurd continues, "The essential objection to nationalized trading is that the state is not organized and cannot be organized for successful trading." Variations of this theme are found in the

TRADITIONAL SHORTCOMINGS

[1] Archibald Hurd, *State Socialism in Practice* (London, 1925), p. 152.

writings of most of those who have attempted to analyze the prospects of governmental economic enterprise.

The traditional method of operating a public commercial activity is through the ordinary department of government. The Post Office and municipal waterworks, for example, are departments within the national and the local governments, respectively. Until recent years, governments have not given special consideration or distinctive administrative treatment to trading services. Their internal organization and relation to the general government have been precisely the same as that of the so-called political departments. The newer corporate developments which we shall analyze had not taken place at the time Hurd wrote.

In recent years, there have been criticisms of the administrative relationships and methods of both the British and the American post office systems. It has been proposed in Congress that our Post Office be given corporate form. In 1932 a Royal Commission reported on post-office management in Great Britain. The main question considered was whether there should be a change from departmentalism to corporate organization.[1] The issue was brought to a head by the writings and public utterances of Lord Wolmer, then Assistant Postmaster General. In his book, *Post Office Reform*, Lord Wolmer made an analysis of the administrative and financial handicaps from which, in his opinion, the British Post Office suffered. "... Parliamentary control must be held to be the root of all inefficiency in the Post Office. It involves the changing Postmaster General, Treasury Control, overcentralisation, civil-service conditions, and the conversion of a communications service into a tax-collecting machine."[2] The Royal Commission concluded that financial autonomy could be secured by permitting the Post Office to retain its net profit (amounting to between fifty and seventy-five million dollars) for betterments and extensions; that administration should be decentralized by creating a functional board at headquarters and by giving regional officials greater independence; and that parliamentary responsibility is

[1] Royal (Bridgeman) Commission on the Post Office, 1932, Cmd. 4149 (H. M. Stationery Office, London); for a summary and interpretation, see Marshall E. Dimock, *British Public Utilities*, chaps. IV–V.
[2] Viscount Wolmer, *Post Office Reform* (London, 1932), p. 300.

worth preserving. The Post Office was commended for its efficiency and urged to give more attention to public relations. All these reforms have now been put into effect.

The operation of economic services through the agency of an ordinary department of government has been frequently criticized on the grounds of an excess of democratic control, the unsuitability of civil-service methods, and the hurtful rigidity of financial control. The assumption underlying the first of these criticisms is that successful businesses cannot be run under a democratic system. A change in party control may mean a turnover of department heads, and this instability makes difficult the use of successful business methods. The practice of changing department heads has been particularly common in the Post Office, whereas longer terms are characteristic of municipal enterprises, such as water, gas, and electricity. The frequent change of Postmasters General, however, is not quite so upsetting as it might appear, because, except in the United States, there is a permanent administrative head who manages the enterprise irrespective of political fortunes. There is no doubt that instability of executive leadership is contrary to the best interests of the enterprise. It interrupts constructive programs and means that new occupants of the office must acquire their knowledge afresh. Insofar as frequent turnovers occur, traditional governmental methods deserve criticism.

DEMOCRATIC CONTROL

Management by the government department entails criticism and questioning by members of the legislature. Because we do not have responsible government, there is not nearly so much of this in the United States. In Great Britain, the Postmaster General is interrogated by members of Parliament during the regular "question" time. Matters of policy and administration, which sometimes seem to have little, if any, general importance, have to be explained and justified on the floor of the national legislature. "Imagine trying to run a business under those conditions," says the business man. There is, however, something to be said for it. Legislative questioning keeps the organization "on its toes," provides a useful channel for sensing consumer attitudes and desires, and furnishes one of several means by which mistakes can be rectified and oversights corrected. On the other hand, it should be clearly recognized that democratic control can be carried too far, and that constant interference would demoralize the undertaking and impede seriously the carrying on of the enterprise.

Some business men say that civil servants are not qualified to run a successful business. The civil servant has been trained in general administration, so it is said, rather than in the art of making money. He does not have the mysterious qualification, "financial acumen"; moreover, permanent tenure is likely to make the public servant neglectful of salesmanship. In the absence of the freedom which private enterprises have in hiring, firing, and disciplining without restriction, it becomes extremely difficult for the executive head of the state service to secure the co-operation, unquestioning response, and effective leadership which are found in private business.

<small>CIVIL-SERVICE CONDITIONS</small>

The very rigidity of civil-service regulations militates, it is alleged, against the development of outstanding capacity for executive leadership. Men of great energy and force are said to be the product of rough-and-tumble commercial competition, a condition which cannot exist in the public service. The department of government, says Hurd, "is staffed by civil servants without knowledge of, or aptitude for, commerce, habituated to routine methods which, if they be a necessary evil in the War Office and the Admiralty, would be absolutely destructive to a trading department, especially if the latter were in competition with private enterprise."

There is much truth in these statements. What is referred to as "the civil-service type" is clearly not the one that is successful in business. On the other hand, it has been proved over and over again that the type is not fixed, that public servants can be made energetic public businessmen. When there is inspiring leadership at the top, autonomy in management and finance, a complete personnel program stressing morale and customer satisfaction, and an enlightened public-relations policy, the civil servant loses his stodginess and becomes responsive. The British Post Office has learned this lesson, as did municipal trading departments, long

THE PROVISION OF ECONOMIC SERVICES 353

ago. Whether the enterprise be public or private, service depends upon management methods and effective incentives.

The third outstanding defect of governmental departmentalism is rigidity of financial operations. The ordinary department is subject to the control of treasury and accounting officials and is governed by all the regulations relative to the expenditure of public funds. Business enterprise, on the other hand, requires free and unified finance. "Every enterprise," according to Hurd, "and every business needs what may seem unnecessary and profitless expenditure. . . . On the other hand, every state department has necessarily to justify every penny of its expenditure to the Treasury, from whom it must draw all its funds and surrender any profits it may make, and it must eventually satisfy the Accountant-General as well as Parliament. . . . Estimates of expenditure for one financial year are submitted to Parliament, and consequently there is no means of providing the capital essential to any trading concern. . . ."

AN EXCESS OF FINANCIAL CONTROL

Still a further defect of financial practice and procedure is that all capital and operating costs which should be considered are not always included in the balance sheet; moreover, in case the enterprise fails to produce a satisfactory showing, the government "can recoup any loss by the simple process of appropriating public money which has been derived from the taxpayer." This is what the United States Post Office does. Although the extent of the financial shortcomings referred to is usually greatly exaggerated, it will be recognized by anyone who has made a study of governmental practices that there is considerable validity in the general criticism. In large numbers of cases, however, it has been proved that sufficient capital, adequate accounting, and businesslike freedom can be secured in the trading departments of government.

Public commercial administration is said to be "political" management. Probably no attack upon the state's conduct of economic activities is launched more frequently than this one. "Public management," says Warren M. Persons, "is apt to be political management. Elected officers are not apt to delegate full responsibility for the conduct of a government undertaking to the appointed officials in

"POLITICAL" INFLUENCES

actual charge of the work." That partisan influences, the spoils system, rotation in office, and the influence of pressure groups are injurious to the successful operation of government-owned utilities admits of no doubt. Judging from the length of tenure of representative trading departments which have been studied, however, it seems likely that the turnover is much higher in comparable private utilities. It seems contradictory to criticize the civil service for too great security and then to turn around and contend that partisan removals are characteristic.[1]

Granting the partial validity of all the criticisms which have been considered, it is nevertheless true that the general results of departmental trading are better than most people (in the United States, at least) seem to realize. This is particularly true of municipal services.

RESULTS OF MUNICIPAL TRADING

Municipal electricity undertakings, although most of them are still operated as ordinary departments of government, have been generally successful from all points of view. Some of them have been conspicuously so. In Great Britain, for example, no privately operated electricity companies can be mentioned which, from every standpoint of business management, equal the standard set by the municipal plants of Birmingham, Manchester, and Leeds. In Germany, dozens of municipal electricity enterprises have established standards of efficiency, good service, and attention to consumer desires which would be difficult to surpass. Experience in the United States is similarly reassuring. Studies which have been made of the Los Angeles Department of Water and Power, the largest municipally owned utility of its kind in the world, point to its efficient management and record of continuous enterprise.[2]

At the present time, the more than two thousand municipal

[1] "Germany from the days of Bismarck has never known 'politics' in the management of federal and municipal enterprises. 'Reasonably high salaries, permanent tenure of office and professional reputation have, it is agreed, placed public operation on a plane as high as that of private enterprise at its best.' There is no campaign by private utility interests in Germany or England or Sweden against government ownership as *inefficient*. It would be laughed out of court as preposterous nonsense." Stuart Chase, *op. cit.*, p. 247. Used by permission of The Macmillan Company, publishers.
[2] See Martin G. Glaeser, "The Los Angeles Bureau of Power and Light: Development of Market Area," *Journal of Land and Public Utility Economics*, VII (August, 1931), 249–54.

electric plants in the United States serve a population of more than ten million persons. Although relatively few intensive studies of these enterprises have been made, analyses which are available point to the conclusion that public plants more than hold their own so far as rates, service, and general efficiency are concerned.[1]

The old-fashioned Post Office Department sets a creditable standard of efficiency. The Post Office, let it be remembered, is one of the largest business concerns in any country. Even in the United States, where it has been customary to reward the party chieftain and patronage dispenser by making him Postmaster General, the satisfactory character of the service is a matter of no little surprise even to businessmen. The American postal service is regular, speedy, well co-ordinated, and, particularly in recent years, progressive and aggressive. Evidence of the last-mentioned characteristic is found in the active advertising and business-getting campaign which has resulted in no little objection from transportation and communication agencies. For examples of the efficiency which is possible, however, one needs to turn to outstanding post-office services, such as those of Great Britain and Germany.

In the last half-dozen years, the British Post Office has rectified its greatest weakness, namely, failure to emphasize advertising, sales promotion, and public-relations techniques. This has been done by engaging the services of one of the most successful firms of public-relations consultants—an indication of how other public enterprises can master a deficiency which was once thought inherent.[2] The reason the Post Office did not emphasize public relations prior to 1930 is because it was not permitted to do so. This illustrates an important point: the management of public services is likely to be no better than those in control of the general government desire.

[1] Federal Power Commission, *Comparative Rates of Publicly and Privately Owned Electric Utilities*, Rate Series No. 5 (U. S. Government Printing Office, Washington, D. C., 1936); also: Frederick L. Bird, *The Management of Small Municipal Lighting Plants* (New York, 1932); Donald M. Whitesell, *Municipal Electric Utilities in Michigan* (Ann Arbor, 1934); and Howard Chandler, "Municipal Electric Utilities in Illinois," unpublished MS, University of Chicago Library, 1936.
[2] See the excellent article by Harold Whitehead entitled, "Salesmanship in the Public Service: Scope and Technique," *Public Administration*, XI (July, 1933), 267–76; see also Marshall E. Dimock, "Selling Public Enterprise to the Public," *National Municipal Review*, XXIII (December, 1934), 660–66.

What is there about the management of private business that public services would do well to copy? They should seek unity and flexibility. We have said that the ultimate objective of good administration is to respond to the customers' desires and produce a pleasing service. Another, of course, is the making of a satisfactory financial showing. Our immediate concern, however, is with the methods of procedure by which these end products are secured. The answer, as suggested, is that business has greater freedom to unify all parts of the enterprise and to adjust it quickly to changed conditions.

<small>OBJECTIVES OF BUSINESSLIKE MANAGEMENT</small>

A businesslike enterprise should rally around a single leader. There should be no outside controls which divide the authority of the management. Autonomy and independence are the conditions under which successful administration is produced. Only when management is unified is it likely to be spirited and progressive. The leader can make the most of his talents; unity creates corporate spirit and undivided loyalty; the channels of control and inspiration are simple, direct, effective.

Ordinary government departments violate the unity principle. The civil-service agency usually becomes a "control" agency. Autonomy of finance and purchasing are prevented by placing the trading department under the control of the central finance officers. The head of the government may even withhold important management responsibilities from the executive head of the government utility. Now, to be sure, when there are central staff agencies, such as personnel and finance, it may be cheaper and more efficient to use them. This is particularly true in small municipalities and trading enterprises; however, this needs to be done while still preserving the autonomy and unity of the economic enterprise. A separate budget, bank account, capitalization, and set of books, plus greater freedom of personnel management and purchasing than is usually granted to ordinary departments, will give the government utility the freedom and unity needed.

A well-run business is flexible. Its organization, finance, and procedures are responsive to changes in technology, the market, and consumer desires. Business, particularly when competition exists, is a matter of survival. When new scientific discoveries are made, better goods are produced, and consumer demands fluctuate, the management must adjust itself quickly or run the chance of losses and even financial failure. A business succeeds in proportion as it accurately judges these changes, desires, and attitudes and responds quickly to them. Flexibility is the unwritten law of business success, and unity of management is a condition precedent to it. A successful enterprise is always changing and improving its organization and methods. When the gradual process of change stops, then the business is almost sure to go into a decline.

Experience shows that trading departments can secure considerably more unity and flexibility within the framework of the general government than most of them have achieved heretofore. Central controls are desirable, but they need to be made less rigid for economic activities. The general government should oversee, not share, in the management. The head of the government, the legislature, and the personnel and finance agencies should exercise general surveillance, but should interfere only when affairs are not going well. If the indispensability of unity and flexibility are understood, and if the desire exists to make the commercial activity succeed, the necessary adjustments and relaxations can be effected.

The organization and procedure of state enterprises are more changeable and varied than was once thought. Government is now making extensive use of the business corporation, the device which secures unity and flexibility. In recent extensions of state trading, the government-owned corporation, the public-utility trust, and the mixed undertaking have been preferred to the old-line department. It has been demonstrated that new economic services need not be added to the central organization of government, but that they may be undertaken through the instrumentality of a corporation owned in whole or in part by the government.

THE PUBLIC CORPORATION

The chart on the following page shows graphically how the public corporation fits into the economic organization of society and the gradations from the simon-pure private business to old-style socialism.

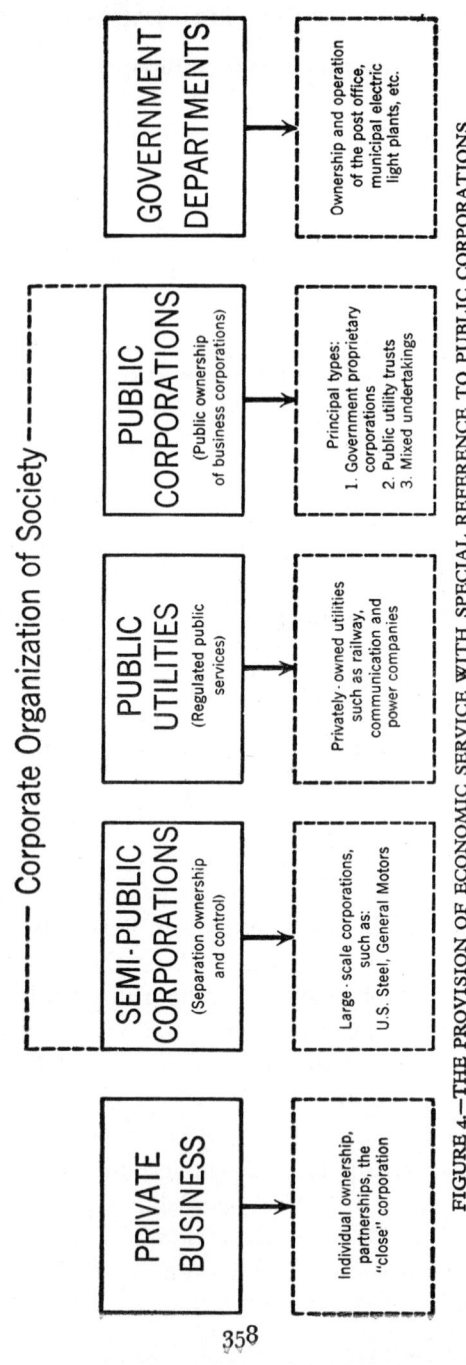

FIGURE 4.—THE PROVISION OF ECONOMIC SERVICE WITH SPECIAL REFERENCE TO PUBLIC CORPORATIONS

The public corporation differs considerably from the regular department acting as a trading organization. The newer forms of public-service enterprise are not subject to those offshoots of democratic control which result in the impermanence of the chief executive, extensive and direct questioning by the legislature, treasury control, strict civil-service procedures, and inability to retain the net profit of the year's enterprise. The newer public commercial undertakings are modeled after the private business corporation and differ from it only with respect to restrictions upon earnings and other limitations of finance and control which have been imposed for the purpose of safeguarding the public interest. In their internal management and ability to respond to consumer requirements, they are free.[1]

The government-owned corporation is a public proprietary service which is chartered and operated along the same lines as an ordinary private corporation. The chief factor which distinguishes it from other corporations is that all the stock is owned by the government, and sometimes a portion of its net profit is turned over to the general treasury. The development of the government proprietary corporation has advanced furthest in the United States. The extent to which the federal government has utilized this device is indicated below:

GOVERNMENT CORPORATIONS OWNED BY
THE UNITED STATES

Panama Railroad Company
Inland Waterways Corporation
Farm Credit Administration (Production Credit Corporations, Banks for Co-operatives, Federal Farm Mortgage Corporation, and others)
Reconstruction Finance Corporation
R.F.C. Mortgage Corporation
Federal Deposit Insurance Corporation
Federal Savings and Loan Insurance Corporation

Home Owners' Loan Corporation
Tennessee Valley Authority
T. V. Associated Co-operatives
Federal Surplus Relief Corporation
Emergency Housing Corporation
Federal Subsistence Homesteads Corporation
Commodity Credit Corporation
Export-Import Bank of Washington
Rural Rehabilitation Corporations
Federal Prison Industries, Inc.

[1] See my article, "Public Corporations and Business Enterprise," *Public Administration*, XIV (October, 1936), pp. 417-28.

In addition, there are some instances in which corporate entities have been created by states, groups of municipalities, and individual cities.

In 1935 the assets of federal proprietary corporations constituted approximately 15 per cent of the total corporate wealth of the country. The significance of this is better understood when it is realized that, with the exception of the Panama Railroad Company and the Inland Waterways Corporation, all the public corporations listed above have been created within the last ten years. The oldest existing one is the Panama Railroad Company, chartered in the State of New York by private enterprisers in 1849 and purchased by the United States Government in 1904. It has made a remarkable financial and administrative record.[1] Since being taken over by the government, the corporation has continued to enjoy the freedom and autonomy it had under private ownership. It operates a railway, steamship line, department stores, telephone and telegraph system, hotels, fueling stations, manufacturing enterprises, in fact, all services needed by the isthmian population and by world shipping passing through that strategic strip. This model has undoubtedly done a great deal to encourage the wider use of government-owned corporations and to demonstrate how they should be run.

The public-utility trust is corporate in form and management, but with important differences in ownership and control. It has no voting stockholders, although its securities are privately subscribed. The directors or trustees are appointed by the government and are expected to represent consumers, workers, and the government as well as the investors. The earnings of the public-utility trust are circumscribed—a fixed interest rate, usually from 3 to 5 per cent is established. A share of stock becomes in effect a bond, for the rate of return is guaranteed and is nonelastic. This form of public enterprise is found primarily in Great Britain. The outstanding examples of it are the Central Electricity Board, British Broadcasting Corporation, London Passenger Transport Board, and

PUBLIC-UTILITY
TRUST

[1] See my study, *Government Operated Enterprises in the Panama Canal Zone* (Chicago, 1934).

Port of London Authority.[1] Like the government proprietary corporation in the United States, the British public-utility trust is primarily a development of the last decade.

The principal difference between the government-owned corporation and the public-utility trust is that the securities of the latter are owned by the investing public. So far as the constitution and powers of the board are concerned, there is no appreciable difference; both are run by directors who are government appointed. The government proprietary corporation, however, is tied into the government by a cabinet member's sitting on the board and voting the stock, whereas the public-utility trust is not connected with the government. A designated Minister merely exercises surveillance and possesses reserved powers to investigate.

The mixed enterprise is created as a corporation and enjoys the freedom of business management. Its ownership, profits, and management are divided between the public and private investment, in relation to the amount which each contributes. In France, the government participation is fixed by law at less than 50 per cent; while in Germany it is usually more than half. Mixed enterprises are found in a dozen countries of Europe, including Great Britain. They have been the outstanding public-utility development of recent years. The leading example of the mixed undertaking in Great Britain is the Manchester Ship Canal, jointly owned and operated by the city of Manchester and a private company. Although the term is not yet commonly employed in the United States, examples analogous to the mixed enterprise are found in the early United States banks and the present Federal Land Banks.

MIXED UNDERTAKINGS

A mixed undertaking is one in which public and private resources and management are joined in order to form a public-utility enterprise. There appears to be no limit to the kinds of business which can be owned and operated by this type of joint control. Among those which are common in Europe are housing, railway, gas, water, electricity, street-railway, aviation, and even garage businesses. The percentage of ownership determines the proportion of the total number of directors which the government

[1] Cf. *British Public Utilities and National Development*, chaps. I, VII, VIII.

and the private investors shall select, and controls the division of earnings. If the government's investment were 60 per cent, for example, it would receive $60,000 if the total profit were $100,000, and it would appoint six directors if there were ten on the board. In France, it is customary for the president of the board to be chosen by the private investors and for the vice-president to be selected by the government; in Germany, the opposite situation obtains. In case of disagreement between the representatives of the government and the investors, there is an appeal to the cabinet official who is concerned with the public-utility enterprise. His decision, unless it involves a question over which the courts have jurisdiction, is final. The protection of the public interest is uppermost, irrespective of whether or not the government controls the major part of the investment.

The mixed enterprise possesses certain distinct advantages. The government is permitted to come to the aid of privately owned utility companies when the essential public services are jeopardized. This has been the principal reason for the growth of mixed undertakings. It is also a means whereby the public may invest in a public-service undertaking without assuming the indebtedness involved in owning the entire enterprise. Outright public ownership in Europe has been retarded since the World War because of the financial limitations of governments, particularly municipalities.

<small>RELATIVE ADVANTAGES OF THE THREE TYPES</small>

From the standpoint of administration, one advantage of the mixed enterprise is that it permits the financial and organizing initiative of individuals to come into play. This is supposedly one of the chief advantages of private management and there is an alleged deficiency in this respect in outright public ownership. Finally, the mixed undertaking is an effective means of public control. Government representatives are inside the organization rather than outside; they are familiar with the details of the business; the government has no trouble regulating capitalization accounts, earnings, or service, because it is able to exercise day-by-day control over the business. On the other hand, because of the representation of private investors, there is a check on the actions of the public representatives.

Over against these advantages there are certain shortcomings of the mixed undertaking which are not found in either the government-owned corporation or the public-utility trust. Because some directors are appointed to represent the investors and some the government, and because there is the same differentiation as regards the management, there is likely to be a clash of interest between the two groups, in which unity of management is destroyed. This theoretical difficulty has proved true in practice. In recent years, mixed undertakings have grown increasingly unpopular, primarily for this very reason. Still another complaint is that the consumer is not adequately protected when the government is a partner in a business from which it can secure a handsome profit. Governments have been so hard pressed for funds that there is a constant temptation to substitute utility profits for taxes. This criticism, however, can be made also of outright government ownership and operation.

The public-utility trust has more freedom than either the government proprietary corporation or the mixed undertaking. It is not tied to the government. The line of public control is very faint. Once profit making has been eliminated, the public-utility trust is set free to manage itself as independently and efficiently as possible.[1] It has as much unity, freedom, and flexibility as a "semi-public corporation," such as U. S. Steel, General Motors, or A. T. & T. Everything depends upon the government's choosing capable trustees. This Great Britain has been able to do. Political parties have even appointed majorities from parties other than their own, in order to obtain capable management which would hold the public interest uppermost and would not feel political obligations to particular parties. The qualifications of directors, as stated in the charters, are business ability, success in one's own business, and proved attachment to the public welfare. Trustees, to date, have been outstanding public figures in whom the people have confidence. This type of person has naturally selected a first-rate management and has then turned it loose to get results.

There are two distinct advantages which the government-owned corporation has, as compared with the public-utility trust. In the

[1] Cf. Herbert Morrison, *Socialization and Transport* (London, 1933), chap. IV.

first place, the inclusion on the board of directors of the cabinet officer whose department is most closely associated with the work of the corporation provides a necessary connecting link for governmental integration and public control. Except in the matter of voting the stock for the government, the cabinet officer has no more power or authority as a member of the board than any other. The other directors are businessmen and laymen, appointed by the President on the recommendation of the cabinet officer. Selections have compared favorably with those in Great Britain.

The advantage of having a department head on the board is that through him it is possible to keep the President, the Cabinet, and Congress informed regarding the corporation. This integrating factor is an indispensable one, and failure to provide for it will probably prove to be the greatest defect of the British public-utility trusts. Moreover, when the number of corporate undertakings becomes large, the problem of bringing about consistency with reference to social and economic policies becomes almost insuperable unless such a connecting link is provided. Public control may be said to be more adequately safeguarded when an official representative of the government is a member of the board of directors of a public corporation. Responsible government and the requirements of trusteeship would seem to demand such a provision.

A second advantage of the government-owned corporation is that it is not exposed to the constant pressures and temptations from interest groups nearly to the extent that the public-utility trust is. In the case of the Central Electricity Board, for example, it has been discovered that the pressure of the British electrical manufacturing interests is constant and effective. In their advertising and promotional campaigns, there has been a close working relationship between the board and the manufacturing interests. Needless to say, there are very great dangers in too intimate a relationship of this kind. The government-owned corporation which is under the eagle eye of a cabinet member, who in turn represents the administration and the legislature, is the safeguard against the undue influence of private interests in the awarding of contracts and the management of the business. There is a higher standard of ethics in government, relative to such matters, than has yet been developed in private business.

The use of the corporate device will not necessarily make the conduct of state enterprises eminently successful. All that can be said is that in the corporate organization, as compared with departmentalism, there are certain inherent advantages, the principal ones being less likelihood of political interference, greater financial freedom, and more liberty to experiment and improve in the field of management. On the other hand, unless the government-owned corporation follows principles of organization which have been found necessary in private corporations and in other public corporations, it cannot expect to make the best of its opportunities. The Inland Waterways Corporation, for example, does not have a full-fledged board of directors, and this is the principal obstacle that has kept the undertaking from being an unqualified administrative success.[1] The Tennessee Valley Authority has not drawn a dividing line between policy formation and its execution. Its directors have divided administrative responsibilities among themselves.[2] This violation of management principle, unless rectified, is likely to be injurious to the enterprise.

GENERAL CONSIDERATIONS

The chief advantage of a public corporation over an ordinary department is greater financial autonomy. The ability to raise capital funds, the right to expand the business, the necessity of earning money before it can be spent, the assurance that income depends upon economic factors rather than upon the benevolence of the legislature, the right to borrow money on the corporation's credit, the freedom to build up reserves for the replacement of plant and the expansion of the business, the knowledge that accounts can be kept on a business basis and audited in conformity with commercial practice, and the desire to run the business as efficiently as possible because the enterprise will be judged on its own financial showing—these are some of the respects in which

[1] See my monograph, *Developing America's Waterways: Administration of the Inland Waterways Corporation* (Chicago, 1935).
[2] Cf. *Regional Factors in National Planning and Development*, chap. IX, on the organization and management of the T. V. A.

the public corporation excels on the financial side. The Comptroller-General of the United States, however, has manifested a determination to treat government-owned corporations with the same rigor with which other federal agencies are controlled. If public corporations are to succeed, Congress must keep them financially unencumbered.

The traditional shortcomings of state enterprise are understood. They can be largely corrected within the regular framework of government and by continued use of the departmental type of organization. The principles of businesslike administration likewise are understood. Unity of management, autonomy of finance, flexibility of organization and procedure, and adequate attention to public relations are the most important factors to be kept in mind. Government has been characteristically efficient as enterpriser, but it has not devoted enough attention to public desires, attitudes, and relations. Usually it was not free to do so.

DECISIVE FACTORS

"If the Government had the brains, or could draw in the brains, and could organize the brains," a regular contributor to *Nation's Business* has said, "then government operation of all the multitudinous lines of business endeavor might be satisfactory."[1] Certainly the importance of brains and ability cannot be denied. There is a basic factor, however, which underlies securing administrative ability and sound management method. It all goes back to effective public opinion. When a community or a nation wishes a public commercial undertaking to succeed, it almost invariably does. If those in control of the government are thoroughly "sold" on an enterprise, it can be made as efficient as any private venture.

SELECTED READINGS

Bird, Frederick L.: *The Management of Small Municipal Lighting Plants* (New York, 1932); a reliable source of information on a subject seldom treated objectively.

Chase, Stuart: *Government in Business* (New York, 1935); traces the expansion of government ownership and control in Europe and the United States from the latter part of the 19th century to the present.

[1] W. M. Kiplinger, "What's Ahead in Washington?" in *Nation's Business*, XXI (December, 1933), p. 14.

Dalton, Hugh: *Practical Socialism for Britain* (London, 1935), especially chaps. III and V; the author, member of the National Executive of the Labour party, discusses that party's policies; sections cited treat socialization, the public corporation, and planning.

Davies, Albert E.: *The State in Business or The Collectivist State in the Making* (London, 1920); sets out the particulars of the successful operation of state and municipal undertakings up until the outbreak of the World War.

Dimock, Marshall E.: *British Public Utilities and National Development* (London, 1933); a study of British public-service undertakings in relation to national development, involving a consideration of the policy, organization, management, and control of the enterprises.

———: *Government-Operated Enterprises in the Panama Canal Zone* (Chicago, 1934); a study of the state as entrepreneur in the Panama Canal Zone with special consideration of the corporate device in managing a government-owned business.

Hart, Sir William: "Mixed Undertakings," *Public Administration*, X, No. 2 (April, 1932), 138–56.

Hurd, Archibald: *State Socialism in Practice* (London, 1925); a criticism of attempts at socialization.

Laidler, Harry: *Socializing Our Democracy* (New York, 1935); this book develops the thesis that a socialistic order can be constructed on the present capitalistic structure without resort to revolution.

Lilienthal, David E.: "Business and Government in the Tennessee Valley," *Annals*, CLXXII (March, 1934), 45–9.

Morrison, Herbert: *Socialization and Transport* (London, 1933); a realistic consideration of the concrete problems relating to the administration of socialized industries with particular reference to the London Passenger Transport.

Persons, Warren E.: *Government Experimentation in Business* (New York, 1934); a survey and evaluation of the accomplishments of the United States Government in business, tending to show that state and federal commercial undertakings seldom pay for themselves.

Pick, Frank: "Some Reflections on the Administration of a Public Utility Undertaking," *Public Administration*, XIII, No. 2 (April, 1935), 135–45.

Royal (Bridgeman) Committee of Enquiry on the Post Office: *Report*, Cmd. 4149 (H. M. Stationery Office, London, 1932).

Shannon, Joseph B.: *Government Competition with Private Enterprise*, House Report No. 1985, 72d Congress, 2d session (1933); an enumeration and discussion of the numerous fields in which the government competes with private business.

Thomas, Norman: *America's Way Out: a Program for Democracy* (New York, 1931), chaps. IX–XII; a discussion of the socialization of industry by America's outstanding Socialist leader.   Few practical problems are considered.

Van Dorn, Harold A.: *Government Owned Corporations* (New York, 1926); traces the growth and analyzes the possibilities of government-owned corporations, particularly those established during the World War period.

Wilcox, Delos F.: *The Administration of Municipally Owned Utilities* (Municipal Administration Service, New York, 1931); chiefly concerned with the principles underlying the successful operation of municipal utilities.

*Encyclopaedia of the Social Sciences* (New York, 1930–35). See articles entitled, "Government Owned Corporations" and "Government Ownership."

CHAPTER XIV

☆ ☆ ☆

GOVERNMENT CONTROL OF THE ECONOMIC SYSTEM

> "*There must be at the very center of the system a mechanism for maintaining a changing master plan.*"
> —LUTHER GULICK

"STATECRAFT," says one of the world's leading economists, "is concerned with the economic system as a whole and with securing the optimum employment of the system's entire resources. . . ."[1] A few years ago, such a statement would have fallen on incredulous ears; now, other economists are coming around to the same position. Gardiner Means believes that the most important decisions as to price and output must be made by government, but that this does not necessarily mean ownership. His reasoning is of the utmost importance to the political scientist. "Actually, the choice does not lie between private ownership and Government ownership," he says, "because the problem is primarily the distribution of controls, not the locus of ownership."[2] "The distribution of controls": how familiar this sounds to the student of government! The economist prescribes, and the political scientist then attempts to instrument.

RECENT ECONOMIC THEORY

In the past, government control of the economic order has been primarily concerned with rectifying the mistakes or shortcomings of the free market system. Now that business concentration and inflexibility of prices obtain, economists tell us that government may be expected to assume more positive, directive responsibilities. "The increased rigidity of prices, a rigidity that seems inevitably tied up with the administrative organization of economic activities, reduces the flexibility of the market place and destroys its efficacy

[1] John Maynard Keynes, *The General Theory of Employment, Interest, and Money* (Harcourt, Brace & Co., London and New York, 1936), p. 340. (All references are to the American edition.)
[2] Gardiner C. Means, *Industrial Prices and Their Relative Inflexibility*, Senate Document No. 13, 74th Congress, 1st session (U. S. Government Printing Office: Washington, 1935), p. 13.

as an over-all co-ordinator."¹ Means emphasizes prices; Keynes stresses investments. Says the English economist: "I expect to see the State, which is in a position to calculate the marginal efficiency of capital-goods on long views and on the basis of the general social advantage, taking an ever greater responsibility for directly organizing investment. . . ."² Once more the state is directed to assume responsibility for the nation's economic well-being!

John Maynard Keynes won his reputation as a leading modern exponent of classical economics. In this latest book of his, Keynes recants. ". . . The characteristics of the special case assumed by the classical theory happen not to be those of the economic society in which we actually live," he finds, "with the result that its teaching is misleading and disastrous if we attempt to apply it to the facts of experience."³ Keynes is temperamentally mild-mannered and conservative. In his new book, however, he is forced to conclude: "It is certain that the world will not much longer tolerate the unemployment which, apart from brief periods of excitement, is associated—and, in my opinion, inevitably associated—with present-day capitalistic individualism."⁴ But it may be possible by a proper analysis of the problem, he says, "to cure the disease whilst preserving efficiency and freedom."

SHORTCOMINGS OF *LAISSEZ FAIRE*

Efficiency! Most countries say they want it, but what is it? Stuart Chase states an interesting idea when, after suggesting that few public businesses are as efficient as the best-managed private industries, he says, "This is, however, only a minor part of the efficiency of a national economy. The major aspect is found in operating the whole plant at capacity without duplication; in building no more woolen mills than can supply the demand for wool; in constructing no parallel lines of competing railroad track and terminals; in drilling no more wells into a pool of oil than the best geological practice permits."⁵ Do we want this kind of effi-

[1] Means, "The Distribution of Control and Responsibility in a Modern Economy," in Lippincott, *op. cit.*, pp. 6-7.
[2] Keynes, *op. cit.*, p. 164.
[3] *Ibid.*, p. 3. In his Preface: "For if orthodox economics is at fault, the error is to be found not in the superstructure, which has been erected with great care for logical consistency, but in a lack of clearness and of generality in the premises."
[4] *Ibid.*, p. 381.
[5] Stuart Chase, *Government in Business*, p. 76, used by permission of the Macmillan Co.

# GOVERNMENT CONTROL OF THE ECONOMIC SYSTEM 371

ciency? Even if we do, we are warned that, "What may ruin the community . . . is the selection of unworkable models for public business and the setting of insuperable administrative tasks."

What do people want from the economic system? Have we defined the ends and objectives? In 1934 the president of the American City Planning Institute said, "124,900,000 of America's 125,000,000 people have discovered that the highest good in our bewildering social structure would be to secure a minimum livelihood, economic security, no fear of want; to know that every person is absolutely assured of food, clothing, and shelter, and these on a decent standard and with self-respect. . . . Conversely, only a very small minority crave to own a production plant except where that seems to be the means for security, as it has seemed to be with the farmer. The central objective of contemporary national planning, then, becomes: for everyone economic security, along with increase of opportunity to acquire and use good and better places to live, more and better personal property, and more of the cultural enrichments, from food and wine to music and travel. In shaping a national program these years, we are bound to hew to this line, letting the chips fall where they may." Are these reasonable expectations, or is this a description of Utopia?

"The outstanding faults of the economic society in which we live," says Keynes, "are its failure to provide for full employment and its arbitrary and inequitable distribution of wealth and incomes."[1] On the basis of his analysis, he reaches the following conclusions:

KEYNES' ANALYSIS

The extent of effective saving is necessarily determined by the scale of investment and the scale of investment is promoted by a *low* rate of interest, provided that we do not attempt to stimulate it in this way beyond the point which corresponds to full employment. . . .

Interest today rewards no genuine sacrifice, any more than does the rent of land. . . . I see, therefore, the rentier aspect of capitalism as a transitional phase which will disappear when it has done its work. . . .

. . . A somewhat comprehensive socialization of investment will prove the only means of securing an approximation of full employment. . . . But beyond this no obvious case is made out for a system of State Socialism which would embrace most of the economic life of the community.

[1] Keynes, *The General Theory of Employment, Interest, and Money*, p. 372, Harcourt, Brace & Co.

It is not the ownership of the instruments of production which is important for the State to assume. . . .

It is in determining the volume, not the direction, of actual employment that the existing system has broken down. . . . The central controls necessary to ensure full employment will, of course, involve a large extension of the traditional functions of government. . . .

Whilst, therefore, the enlargement of the functions of government, involved in the task of adjusting to one another the propensity to consume and the inducement to invest, would seem to a nineteenth-century publicist or to a contemporary American financier to be a terrific encroachment on individualism, I defend it, on the contrary, both as the only practicable means of avoiding the destruction of existing economic forms in their entirety and as the condition of the successful functioning of individual initiative. . . .

There are valuable human activities which require the motive of money-making and the environment of private wealth-ownership for their full fruition. . . .[1]

Can government secure the brains and the organizing ability to control investments, fix an "agenda," and determine production quantities and priorities? Equally important, can initiative and freedom be adequately safeguarded within an administered system?

The same thought and foresight which are devoted to successful individual establishments need to be applied to the larger field of economic enterprise. Business planning can secure effective co-ordination of effort only within the limits of each independent business enterprise. At present, there are control and integration only over those units of organization which are subject to a single financial control. As between the various units, however, there is no effective co-ordination, because no provision has been made therefor. Wesley C. Mitchell has analyzed the extent to which intelligence has been applied to our business system and the shortcomings which result from failure to make corresponding provision for the over-all plan:

Co-ordination within an enterprise is the result of careful planning by experts; co-ordination among independent enterprises cannot be said to be planned at all; rather is it the unplanned result of natural selection in a struggle for business survival. Co-ordination within an enterprise has a definite aim—the making of profits; co-ordination

[1] *Ibid.*, pp. 374-80.

## GOVERNMENT CONTROL OF THE ECONOMIC SYSTEM 373

among independent enterprises is limited by the conflicting aims of the several units. Co-ordination within an enterprise is maintained by a single authority possessed of power to carry its plans into effect; co-ordination among independent enterprises depends on many different authorities which have no power to enforce a common program, except so far as one can persuade or coerce others. As a result of these conditions, co-ordination within an enterprise is characterized by economy of effort, co-ordination among independent enterprises by waste.[1]

The thinking of Alfred Marshall, the English economist, proceeds along the same line. He has pointed out that one of the chief elements of success in private business is the faculty of weighing the advantages and disadvantages of any proposed course, and of assigning them to their relative importance.

PLANNING
IN BUSINESS

"He who by practice and genius has acquired the power of attributing to each factor its right quantity, is already well on the way to fortune; and the increase in the efficiency of our productive forces is in a great measure due to the large number of able minds who are devoting themselves ceaselessly to acquiring these business instincts." Perhaps from this source, government can secure the necessary brains and ability! In the present unco-ordinated system, Professor Marshall goes on to say, "the advantages thus weighed against one another are nearly all regarded from one point of view, that of the producer; and there are not many who concern themselves to weigh against one another the relative quantities of the interests which the consumers and the producers have in different courses of actions."[2] The ability may be there, but it is not marshaled!

Let us turn our attention to an analysis of the National Resources Board, the principal planning agency of the United States Government. "The frequent recurrence of economic crises and depressions is acknowledged evidence that the automatic functioning of our business system is defective. In view of recent events, no one longer holds that the business cycle is being ironed out. Instead, it appears that the difficulty of maintaining the necessary equilibrium among different factors in the enormously

[1] Wesley C. Mitchell, *Business Cycles: The Problem and Its Setting* (National Bureau of Economic Research, New York, 1927), p. 172.
[2] Alfred Marshall, *Principles of Economics*, 8th ed. (Macmillan, London, 1920), p. 491,

complicated mechanism is becoming greater rather than less." Among the factors tending to aggravate the situation, importance is attached to the following: the widening of markets, the growth of combinations, the trend of population from farms, the diminishing dependence of farm families upon what they can make for their own consumption, the resulting fact that general economic maladies afflict more people more seriously than they did in past generations, and the fact that an increasing part of the annual national production consists of semidurable goods which people can stop buying for a time if conditions are bad. "Business planning has found no effective means of preventing the growth of these factors that tend to make the business-cycle hazard more serious. *Rather the hazard grows graver in large part because of business planning.*"[1]

The initial and final stages of the industrial process are the only ones which are not carefully planned. Obviously, they are the most important. The initial problem is to determine, for

GAPS IN PLANNING

whole industries and for the country's entire economy, what the relation should be between possible production and possible consumption, between wages and profits, agriculture and manufacturing, and international trade and domestic business. The ultimate question, inextricably related to the first, is: for what purpose or for whose benefit is the economic system to be operated? If the highest good of production is consumption, then surpluses will not rot while people are in need, and money will not lie idle in banks while the capital-goods industries stagnate. If, however, the ultimate test of economic transactions is profitability, then production and credit both may be brought to the verge of collapse whenever profits cannot be made from producing goods or loaning money.

Some economists say that government must be expected to socialize investments and plan production, in order that unemployment may be abolished. This necessitates control, but control in turn means planning. You cannot control intelligently unless

[1] [Italics ours.] National Resources Board, *A Report on National Planning and Public Works in Relation to Natural Resources* (U. S. Government Printing Office, Washington, D. C., 1934), p. 82.

the objectives, the instruments, and the methods are carefully worked out in advance. Luther Gulick has compared the national government to a holding company.[1] Its function is not so much to execute as to plan and to service other operating agencies. "There must be at the very center of the system a mechanism for maintaining a changing master plan." The modern holding company plans the major strategy and provides advice on engineering, operating, financial, and personnel matters. The holding company is an assemblage of experts and consultants whose business it is to do research, to think, and to plan, in order that individual units of the whole enterprise may be more efficient. The analogy between the holding company and government control of the economic system is an appropriate one.

What is planning? The term has a variety of connotations and implications. It may mean merely arranging a row of figures or it may involve the ordering of a country's entire economic life.

WHAT IS INVOLVED IN PLANNING? According to the dictionary definition, the verb "to plan" means "to devise, project, arrange beforehand"; and the word "planning" is defined as "a formulated or organized method according to which something should be done." Planning, according to the National Resources Board, consists in the systematic, continuous, forward-looking application of the best intelligence available to programs of common affairs in the public field, as it does to private affairs in the domain of individual activity. This seems to suggest that planning is merely a matter of the right administrative arrangements.

The most important element of a plan is the decision upon the all-embracing purpose or objects of planning. A purpose involves agreement by those affected on what it is they want. Until this is done, legislative and administrative programs are likely to be merely a matter of shooting in the air. As Earle S. Draper, the land planner, has pointed out, planning is a means to an end; the means are elastic, but the ends are steadfast; planning is visualizing or foreseeing; and the thing planned is movement. Planning

[1] Luther Gulick, "Politics, Administration, and the 'New Deal'," *Annals*, 169 (September, 1933), 55–66.

is dynamic and not static. All these theorems of planning, **Draper** has counseled, are combined in the all-embracing purpose of laying the physical basis for optimum human living through extending the range of choice.

Planning may be defined as the application of intelligence to social and economic change on a large enough scale to be effective. This conception is certainly not doctrinaire or cut-and-dried. It suggests that the amount of planning necessary depends upon the extent to which complexity and planlessness exist. "Planning does not involve setting up a fixed and unchangeable system, but, on the contrary, contemplates readjustment and revision, as new situations and problems emerge." The principal argument in favor of planning is that it brings about a fresh release of opportunities, rather than narrowing the choice or freezing the existing mold. "Large-scale planning," it has been truly said, "should extend the range of choice and increase the freedom and opportunities of the citizenry."

"Planning is a distinctly American idea. The Constitutional Convention gave us our national plan of Government. Hamilton's 'Plan of Manufactures,' Jefferson's and Gallatin's 'Internal Improvements,' Clay's 'American System,' the American Homestead Policy, the Conservation Movement, and the 'economic mobilization' of the World War are all examples of national planning. Business planning is similarly a distinctively American idea in the form of 'scientific management' and 'management engineering.'"[1] "The War made it clear that business is business without a great deal of difference who owns it or administers it, provided those in control are interested in delivering specified goods to specified places at specified times."

**ADVANTAGES WHICH AMERICA POSSESSES**

We may look to the scientific management movement for assistance in stabilizing our economic life. Engineering has contributed two important tools, namely, mechanical technology and the techniques of scientific management.[2] With the first of these methods we have been able to discover ways by which a surplus can be

[1] National Resources Board, *A Report on National Planning and Public Works*, p. 80.
[2] Harlow S. Persons, "The Approach of Scientific Management to the Problems of National Planning," *Taylor Society Bulletin*, No. 17 (December, 1932), pp. 204–28.

produced and with the latter the total production has been swelled; but the surplus is so unevenly divided, Mr. Persons says, that industry itself is threatened.

In all our history and in almost all our institutions from the church to formal economics, the assumption has been that there would always be a scarcity of things. It is now apparent that the real problem is the intelligent distribution and use of the surplus which technology has made possible. The principles of scientific management need to be applied to the economy as a whole: first, the economy of surplus production must be maintained; second, the same techniques which produced the surplus economy will be able to solve the distribution of the surplus; and, finally, these same techniques or processes must forthwith be directed to the problem. Scientific management has successfully extended its scope from shop to industrial corporations. Can it help solve the larger problem of planning the political economy?

Over-all planning would not be as difficult as we are first inclined to think. "Never were there such mountains of data to assist in plotting relationships. Never was there so great a margin of safety between population and food supply." The importance of statistics as a planning tool became apparent during the World War, and there have been many opportunities to put it to the test since. Its twin is accounting, which tells us how much a service costs, what the profit is, and how much value capital and labor add to raw materials.

Once a business becomes too big for one brain to handle personally, accounting takes over the job. The principles of cost accounting are uninfluenced by political or moral passions. There they are—for Mr. Sloan's use, or Mr. Stalin's use, or the use of the Danish co-operative societies. All large corporate organizations are now run by remote accounting control. On the records as they come hourly, daily, weekly, monthly, to the central office, the front line administrators stand or fall. Question: What difference does it make to a front line administrator—say the manager of the A and P store in any town—whether the stock in the vast impersonal corporation for which he works is owned by Tom, Dick, Harry, or the State? Answer: The only difference to him is which corporate control gives him the better break.[1]

[1] Stuart Chase, *Government in Business*, p. 237; used by permission of The Macmillan Co.

During the World War, the War Industries Board divided all basic industries into seventeen groups and set quotas for each. The amount each was to produce depended upon the demands of all the other groups, and the total output was adjusted to the total need. We as a people were surprised to learn how much we could produce and consume, and how efficiently processes could be co-ordinated.[1] Something similar to this could be done in peace time.[2]

FASHIONING THE INSTRUMENTS

Granting the necessity of forethought, co-ordination, and ability to provide the planners and the skilled processes, the most difficult question is that of control. Can over-all planning be effected without compulsion and without fundamental changes in ownership? Those whose ideas we have been examining take it for granted that increasing government control will be brought about without seriously disturbing the private ownership of industry. This method has been called "control without ownership." In spite of certain dangers which inhere in it, says Stuart Chase, "control-without-ownership seems to have wide application for public business in the power age. If it were inaugurated wherever possible, it would save the State the burden of administrative detail, and so apply the principle of least work."[3] John Maynard Keynes believes that, ". . . if our central controls succeed in establishing an aggregate volume of output corresponding to full employment as nearly as practicable, the classical theory comes into its own again from this point onwards . . . . It is not the ownership of the instruments of production which it is important for the State to assume."[4] Gardiner C. Means, as we have noted, agrees that "the problem is primarily the distribution of controls, not the locus of ownership."

CONTROL WITHOUT OWNERSHIP

According to the Marxian analysis, control without ownership is a costly delusion. Planning involves coercion; the few must conform in order that the many may prosper. So long as basic

---

[1] Cf. Bernard M. Baruch, *American Industry in the War* (Washington, 1921).
[2] Stuart Chase has proposed an "Agenda," *op. cit.*, pp. 118 ff; see also Harold Loeb and associates, *The Chart of Plenty* (New York, 1935); and Brooks Emeny, *The Strategy of Raw Materials* (New York, 1935).
[3] Stuart Chase, *op. cit.*, p. 232.        [4] Keynes, *op. cit.*, p. 378.

industries and finance are privately owned, individuals will withdraw from co-operative programs whenever in their opinion it is advantageous to do so. An analogy may be drawn between a confederacy, in which the right of secession is recognized, and a union, in which all parties must "stay on the ship." Has it not been found that there is a point beyond which the rentier class will not permit leveling taxes to rise? How much less likely would they be to permit "regimentation," if it were not invariably to their financial advantage. The economic radical has a low estimate of the co-operative characteristics of human nature in a capitalist society.

The liberal is the one who has faith in men's willingness to put the common good above immediate personal advantage. He believes that private owners can be convinced of the wisdom of taking the long view, instead of the short-range one. The liberal believes that people will give up minor immediate advantages in order to share the greater benefits which foresight and co-ordination promise. Which analysis is correct? What will human nature do in the United States? The most important question of the future is, what shall be the relationship between business and government and to what extent will the techniques and ideology of each infiltrate the other?

Insofar as organized business has expressed itself on planning, it is to favor the "self-government of industry." The Swope plan and the official recommendations of the Committee on Continuity of Business and Employment of the United States Chamber of Commerce best exemplify the present thinking of big business on this subject. They believe that the stabilization of profits and employment should be undertaken primarily by trade associations and chambers of commerce. A national economic council would be created, which would be built upon the foundation of trade associations and chambers of commerce. Three cardinal principles would underlie the establishment of the council. It would be appointed by business and supported by it, although it would work in close co-operation with the government and have as ex officio members the Secretary of Commerce, Secretary of Agriculture, and

THE SELF-
GOVERNMENT
OF INDUSTRY

Attorney General. It would, however, be independent of Congress and the Executive. In the second place, the national economic council would have only advisory powers. Finally, the members of the council would be appointed by groups selected by the United States Chamber of Commerce, but they would not in any sense be responsible to the appointing groups; moreover, the council would not be broadly representative even of the various branches of industry, because the pressure of special interests would cause the body to lose its ability to take a broad view.[1]

Very few business men have given much thought to stabilization and planning. This was apparent at the hearings before the La Follette committee, at which time the above ideas came out. Most of America's prominent industrial and financial leaders admitted they had not, and simply could not, give any thought to such complex questions. The pressure of their own jobs made it impossible. How many of them, we wonder, knew that, following the World War, national economic councils with powers far greater than the one suggested were created in most of the principal countries and that very little has ever been heard from them?

What do the owners of small business enterprises think? How representative is the following view? "What is the matter with business?" asked the president of the Truscon Steel Company a year before the great depression. "From time to time the business cycle is rolled out and we are told that depressions must always follow periods of prosperity. Is it necessary that there be depression at all?" This businessman stoutly maintains that it is not. "Our unrest comes principally from the want of proper guidance," and since the government is the "trustee of our welfare," the "only body that can guide us all, . . . every solution to the problems of bad business must emanate from a guiding central authority—namely, our government."[2] "This is a highly individual point of

GOVERNMENT RESPONSIBILITY

[1] Cf. *Establishment of National Economic Council*, Hearings Before a Subcommittee of the Committee on Manufactures, Robert M. La Follette, Jr., Chairman (U. S. Government Printing Office, Washington, D. C., 1931); see also Gerard Swope, *The Swope Plan* (New York, 1931).
[2] Julius Kahn, "A Plea for More Government Regulation," *Nation's Business*, 16, No. 2 (February, 1928), 20–22.

view," said the editor, "an interesting point of view, but not the point of view of *Nation's Business*." This is one of the few times that the editor has been willing to admit that his journal does have a point of view!

Secretary Ickes has expressed in terse language his ideas on the ultimate objective of public control of the economic system:

> Government planning must be for all the people, that is for the greatest good of the greatest number. To put it into economic language, planning should be for the consumer. The major part of the activity of all of us is that of consuming. It is as consumers that we all have a common interest, regardless of what productive work we may be engaged in. In the pioneer stages of our development it was only natural that the emphasis should have been upon our productive activity rather than upon our interests as consumers. In those times we produced what we could and consumed what we had. But in a day when there is plenty, when production in some directions is being curtailed rather than expanded, we are in a position to live lives of greater comfort and leisure.[1]

Is our thinking still tied to a "scarcity economy"?

A form of control should be chosen which gives the greatest assurance of fostering all interests, the well-being of the community as a whole. The answer which the United States Chamber of Commerce gives is that, "What's Good for Business is Good for the Country." From this slogan it is deduced that when the owners of industry are enriched, the community as a whole stands to benefit automatically and proportionately. Anyone who has given serious thought to this contention or who has observed the results produced by it, knows that there is no such automatic process. Andrew Mellon's sieve gets stopped up.

The most powerful interests within the respective trade associations and chambers of commerce eventually dominate, determine policy and action. This admission was implicit in the proposal for a national economic council. The trade association, moreover, can have at best only a partial view of the total economic situation. Its objective is to further the interests of the particular industry or craft. The trade association is not designed by its constituency or

DRAWBACKS OF ECONOMIC GROUPS AS GOVERNORS

[1] Harold L. Ickes, *The New Democracy* (Norton, New York, 1934), p. 142.

tradition to consider large questions of economic policy and industrial control. Trade associations and chambers of commerce, like labor unions and professional groups, are important factors in representation, but no one of them is capable of doing government's work for it. The liberal is right when he contends that control should be vested in that agency which has the community, or over-all, view.

Planning needs to be made the most important staff agency in our larger governing units.[1] What is primarily needed is co-ordination. The planning of natural resources, of social controls, and of administrative methods already takes place at many points in the federal government. Individual units usually do their work well. In the Central Statistical Board and the statistical division of the Department of Agriculture, we have planning agencies which would be difficult to surpass for their comprehensiveness and excellence. Clearly what is needed is a small planning group close to the President, thinking out and co-ordinating the control of the industrial order and the operation of government. This strategy board would be assisted by the existing, decentralized planning units in the departments and independent establishments.

ORGANIZING FOR PLANNING

There are two principal kinds of planning, basic and dynamic. Most of the existing planning work is basic; it is pure research. This is not to suggest that it lacks practical importance or that it fails to meet many present needs. Dynamic planning is the co-ordination of basic data, plus the perfection of administrative methods, in order to attack and control some immediate problem. The planning of the national economy requires both kinds of activity. The fundamental analyses should continue to be made by the Bureau of Chemistry and Soils, Geological Survey, Forest Service, Bureau of Agricultural Economics, Corps of Engineers, Bureau of Standards, and Bureau of Foreign and Domestic Commerce. Over-all agencies, such as the National Resources Committee, the Central Statistical Board, and the Census Bureau, are the nucleus around which planning at the top should form.

[1] For a discussion of staff agencies, see pp. 265–69, *supra*.

Planning is a two-way process; it proceeds from the bottom up and from the top down. Traffic both ways is indispensable. The bureau chiefs and department heads decide what they would like to do in the next year or five-year period; consultation occurs with the finance and budgetary officers, who draw up estimates and financial programs; staff officers responsible for planning and co-ordination check the work programs which come up to them; the chief executive and the legislature review the proposals put before them and decide what shall be done. Most planning, at least at present, is of this upward-heading sort. On the other hand, the legislature and chief executive come into office with certain broad programs which they hope to carry out. They then ask administrative agencies to work out details of execution. This is planning from the top down. The most successful planning is likely to be that in which there is a heavy two-way traffic.

The importance of imagination, vision, and co-ordinating ability at the top can hardly be overemphasized. Top planners will fail if they content themselves with being gristmills. They need to take the initiative. Where is such ability to be secured? Both from business and from government. This is an inescapable procedure in control without ownership. The available talent is probably more adequate than we suspect. The United States excels in the fields of statistics, cost accounting, business planning, and executive management. What is needed are men who can be relied upon to take the broad, social view. As Arthur Holcombe says, we must set about training "public businessmen."[1] On this point, Secretary Ickes' thinking is interesting and challenging:

PROVIDING THE BRAINS

> In order that the Government may adequately plan and efficiently administer a program that will be devoted to the common good, it will be necessary for it to employ the very best brains available. Our colleges and technical schools will be taxed as they have never been before to produce able men who can think into the future and who are endowed with a social conscience that will make them eager workers for the better development of our great country. . . . After all, I suspect that what those who decry the use of brains in government fear is not brains as such, but brains that are used for the benefit of the masses

[1] See his book, *Government in a Planned Democracy* (New York, 1935).

of our people instead of the privileged few. They want brains without heart, brains without soul, brains without conscience, brains without social responsibility. They want brains that, if they cannot be bought or bullied, are content to lead a quiet existence remote from the practical affairs of life.[1]

Sounds like Teddy Roosevelt, does it not?

The state's ability to carry out a program of national planning revolves largely around the question of administrative capacity. "If government could secure the right men with the right kind of brains and ability," said a business leader recently, "no task would be too great." This is probably true, assuming that the co-operation of those who control economic power can be relied upon. Government, however, has no magic, even when its programs are supported. Government is no better than its administration. If the machinery and personnel of government are adequate, the task will be done satisfactorily; otherwise it will not. The administrative organization and practices of government in the United States need to be greatly improved before economic stabilization can be achieved. Among the reforms which seem to be needed, in addition to the recruitment of an improved caliber of planning and executive capacity, are better co-ordination of administrative areas, reorganization of the federal government, and the establishment of over-all planning and control agencies.

ADMINISTRATIVE REFORMS

The whole is no stronger than its component parts. Sound conditions in individual countries are the condition necessary for revived world trade. In the past, says Keynes, international trade has been a "desperate expedient to maintain employment at home by forcing sales on foreign markets and restricting purchases, which, if successful, will merely shift the problem of unemployment to the neighbor which is worsted in the struggle. . . ."[2] There is all too much truth in this characterization. Theoretically and desirably, of course, each nation should specialize in those commodities and services in which it has a relative advantage. This

NATIONAL PLANNING AND INTERNATIONAL TRADE

[1] Ickes, *op. cit.*, pp. 145, 148.
[2] Keynes, *The General Theory of Employment, Interest, and Money*, p. 382, Harcourt, Brace & Co.

is the eventual goal. It is now apparent, however, that the principal nations must put their own systems in order before an effective world demand will be assured. "If nations can learn to provide themselves with full employment by their domestic policy . . . ," Keynes concludes, "there need be no important economic forces calculated to set the interest of one country against that of its neighbors." Because of its plenitude of resources and its geographical extent, the United States is in a better position to develop a balanced economy than any other great nation.

Our hope of general prosperity is in rediscovering and giving concrete form to the concept of political economy. Well-being is an economic condition produced by the foresight and wisdom of the state. We need ". . . a national investment program directed to an optimum level of domestic employment which is twice blessed in the sense that it helps ourselves and our neighbors at the same time. And it is the simultaneous pursuit of these policies by all the countries together which is capable of restoring economic health and strength internationally, whether we measure it by the level of domestic employment or by the volume of international trade."[1]

*Laissez faire* and economic individualism constitute a relatively short chapter in the long history of state responsibility for economic progress. Until the time of Adam Smith, "it seemed the right and proper policy for the state, through parliaments or kings and their servants, widely to regulate human activities." We need to make use of the best aspects of mercantilism and yet avoid its shortcomings. "The invisible hand of Adam Smith has failed us. Communities must now control their economic life according to some deliberate plan, or sink into decay." On the other hand, mercantilism was short-sighted in that it aimed at national advantage and relative strength. Heckscher, the greatest authority on mercantilism, says that, "*Within* the state, mercantilism pursued thoroughgoing dynamic ends." Production and prosperity were increased. "But the important thing is that this was bound up with a static conception of the total economic resources

THE REVIVAL OF POLITICAL ECONOMY

[1] *Ibid.*, p. 349.

of the world; for this it was that created that fundamental disharmony which sustained the endless commercial wars. . . . This was the tragedy of mercantilism."[1] We know better now. Self-sufficiency is not a desirable goal. Everyone loses when the principle of relative advantage is flaunted. On the other hand, nations cannot do a thriving business with one another when, for want of good housekeeping, the internal economy is faulty.

Let no one minimize the degree of statesmanship required if national planning and international trade are to be given their proper emphases. If economic complexity is neglected, suffering and even revolution are invited; if national planning turns into exclusiveness, war is the likely result. To pursue a middle course between the two horns of the dilemma is a difficult maneuver. It seems, however, the only way open, if economic progress is to take place.

The problems which the political economist is expected to help solve are staggering in their difficulty and importance. The alliance between economics and government obviously needs to be more firmly cemented. Speaking for the vanguard of economists, Gardiner Means, as we have noted before, has said, "It is in the development of further administrative co-ordination that we must come to political scientists for aid. We ask that you apply to the field of economic administration the technique of analysis and principles of organization which you have developed in the study of the state." From a political scientist comes the following analysis:

"All the problems of control may be reduced to three fundamental ones; the problem of liberty, which is both moral and psychological; the problem of administration, which in its most basic expression is moral and psychological (incentives); and the problem of economic progress, which is at bottom psychological (incentives) where it bears upon the desire to invent and to save, and which is administrative and economic where it involves synchronizing invention and the new methods of organization for the purpose of material economic advance."[2]

[1] Eli Filip Heckscher, *Mercantilism*, II (London, 1935), 25.
[2] Benjamin E. Lippincott, *Government Control of the Economic Order* (Minneapolis, 1935), p. 118. There are other ways of classifying controls, but this one has a great deal of suggestiveness.

GOVERNMENT CONTROL OF THE ECONOMIC SYSTEM 387

In the two remaining chapters, we shall be concerned with the attempted reconciliation of these interests and controls.

SELECTED READINGS

Brady, Robert A.: *The Rationalization Movement in German Industry* (Berkeley, 1933), Parts I and III; a general discussion of the rationalization movement in Germany, showing the cultural and political implications of the movement.

Clark, John M.: *Economics of Planning Public Works* (U. S. Government Printing Office, Washington, 1935); a consideration of public expenditures with special reference to programs of public works and their probable economic effects.

Cole, G. D. H.: *Economic Planning* (New York, 1935); an account of the principles and desirability of a planned economy, with a consideration of the prospects of planning in the United States.

Corwin, Edward S.: "Social Planning Under the Constitution," *American Political Science Review*, XXVI, No. 1 (February, 1932), 1–27.

Douglas, Paul H.: *Controlling Depressions* (New York, 1935); an analysis of the causes of depression together with suggestions as to how it may be eliminated or reduced in the future.

Holcombe, A. N.: *Government in a Planned Democracy* (New York, 1935); examines the premises from which planning proceeds in a democratic society and suggests the recognition of a new profession, that of "public businessman."

Joint Planning Conference, Proceedings of: *Planning for City, State, Region, and Nation* (American Society of Planning Officials, Chicago, 1936); refer especially to the sections dealing with regional and national planning.

Keynes, John Maynard: *The General Theory of Employment, Interest, and Money* (New York, 1936); a well-considered attack on some of the underlying assumptions of classical economics.

Lippincott, Benjamin E., ed.: *Government Control of the Economic Order: a Symposium* (Minneapolis, 1935); an analysis of the economic ventures of government in Great Britain, Germany, Russia, Sweden, and America.

Lorwin, Lewis L.: "Social Aspects of the Planning State," *American Political Science Review*, XXVIII, No. 1 (February, 1934), 16–22.

Merriam, Charles E.: "Planning Agencies in America," *American Political Science Review*, XXIX, No. 2 (April, 1935), pp. 199–211.

Mitrany, D.: "Political Consequences of Economic Planning," *Yale Review*, XXIII, No. 4 (June, 1934), pp. 685–705.

National Resources Board: *A Report on National Planning and Public*

*Works in Relation to Natural Resources* (U. S. Government Printing Office, Washington, D. C., 1934).

National Resources Committee: *Regional Factors in National Planning and Development* (U. S. Government Printing Office, Washington, D. C., 1935).

Patterson, Ernest M., ed.: "National and World Planning," *Annals*, CLXII (July, 1932), entire number.

Salter, Sir Arthur: *The Framework of an Ordered Society* (New York, 1933); in this stimulating little book, the ground plans for an ordered society are sketched.

———: *Recovery* (New York, 1932), Part I, chaps. II and III; Part II, chaps. IV-VI; and Part IV; an eminent economist discusses for the layman his views on reform of the economic system, these sections dealing with planning without sacrifice of initiative and provision of economic services through the mixed enterprise.

Soule, George: *A Planned Society* (New York, 1932); an excellent little treatise on the philosophy and technique of planning.

Tugwell, Rexford G.: *The Industrial Discipline and the Governmental Arts* (New York, 1933); develops the argument for a co-operative individualism under an industrial democracy.

Wallace, Henry: *America Must Choose* (New York, 1934); presents the choice between the advantages and disadvantages of nationalism, world trade, and a planned middle course.

———: *New Frontiers* (New York, 1934); an exposition of the New Deal, stressing the need for experimentation and defending the idea of national planning.

Woll, Matthew, and Walling, William E.: *Our Next Step—A National Economic Policy* (New York, 1934); an attempt to formulate the national economic policy of American labor.

Wooton, Barbara: *Plan or No Plan* (London, 1935); one of the early efforts to analyze the necessity of planning.

CHAPTER XV

☆ ☆ ☆

## THE EXPERT AND THE LAYMAN

*"Always and inevitably in a democracy, the people must seek the balance between expert service and popular control."*
—LEWIS MERIAM

Democracies are proverbially inefficient. They take roundabout methods of reaching goals which monarchies and dictatorships grasp by direct means. Popular government is built upon compromise, debate, trial and error. Authoritarian governments, on the other hand, are usually characterized by orthodoxy, force, and dispatch. The administrative methods of democratic systems are, as a rule, less efficient. They reflect compromise and conflicting counsel. Their personnel is drawn from the rank and file, rather than from those who can contribute most to the power and efficiency of the ruling élite.

<small>RECONCILIATION OF EFFICIENCY AND POPULAR CONTROL</small>

We are prone to exaggerate the relative inefficiency of popular government. Progress which grows up from the bottom is more permanent than precipitate action dictated from above. That the governmental methods of democracies can be made efficient is demonstrated by an imposing array of evidence. Public administration in Great Britain, the Scandinavian countries, Switzerland, Germany under the Weimar Constitution, or in our own best-governed units of government sets a high standard of human accomplishment. Democracies are inclined to be modest and self-effacing; dictatorships, proud and arrogant.

The goals which democracy seeks are more difficult to achieve than those which satisfy an authoritarian government. The latter pursues efficiency and compliance; the only limit on its own designs is the fear of revolution. In a democracy, on the other hand, the broadening of the base of those who are politically active and the effective carrying out of the objects of government are equally indispensable. The compromise between popular control and efficiency is a difficult one to make. It is something of a dilemma.

"All democracies want a plenitude of service from Government, but at the same time they fear Government, and desire that the electorate have unlimited freedom of interference with the planned activities of Government. Having willed an end they prefer not to will the means. . . . Democracies demand both an efficient Government and immediate popular control of that Government; their efforts to achieve the latter constantly stand in the way of achieving the former. Hence we have in democratic governments a constant combination of amateurs and experts, of engineers and politicians, of scientists and partisan administrators, and of untrained officials interfering with problems that demand the skill of experts."[1]

The more complex society becomes and the more difficult governmental problems are, the greater is the need for trained officials. Sometimes it seems that our common problems are so stupendous and the rate at which they are solved so slow that it would be better if we were to hand over the government to those experts who seem to know what is needed and how to go about getting it. On sober second thought, however, we are reminded of Sir William Harcourt's amusing but sound advice, "The country would be extremely well governed by the permanent officials for twelve or eighteen months and then the public would hang all the heads of the Civil Service to the nearest lamp-posts. The value of the political heads of departments (laymen) is to tell the permanent officials what the public will not stand."[2]

Democratic peoples are usually too tolerant of inefficiency. They are inclined to say, "We would rather be free than efficient." And if it were absolutely necessary to choose between one or the other, experience teaches us that freedom would be the better choice. It is not so simple as that, however, for if government becomes too inefficient, we may expect democracy to be replaced by some other form of government. Unless popular government is made effective, the ends of the state cannot be achieved. Anomalously, perhaps, the continuance of freedom is dependent upon the effectiveness of democratic programs.

[1] T. Swann Harding, *T.N.T., These National Taxeaters* (New York, 1934), p. 73.
[2] A. G. Gardiner, *The Life of Sir William Harcourt*, II (New York, 1923), 587.

Now that government's functions are increasingly positive and directive, the need of competence is correspondingly greater. Complexity creates specialization and the necessity of expertness. This is as true of government as of business or the professions. "Every man to his own last." We would not think of letting a rodman design a bridge or permit a veterinarian to diagnose baffling human ailments. How much more reckless it would be to employ plumbers as public-health officers or grocery clerks as planning officials! How foolish it is to elect as lawmakers men who know little about government, economics, or sociology. Our legislators and administrators can do infinitely more harm than quack doctors, because their actions affect many more people. A noted surgeon once said to the author, "Personally, I should be glad to pay government experts more than the highest-paid physician. We cure individuals, but they are expected to save all of us."

THE INDISPENSABILITY OF COMPETENCE

Expertness in government is the result of training and experience. Men will not make the sacrifice to train themselves unless they can look forward to permanence and promotion; they will choose another career. Likewise, they expect to be treated as experts; a highly trained man asks that his advice be respected and that he be given authority and responsibility. Following the training and internship period, professional competence is acquired by experience—by facing problems and solving them. The better the expert's background, the greater his experience, and the more difficult the problems he can solve, the greater the reliance that can be safely imposed upon him.

Expertness, professionalization, specialization, teamwork, hierarchical authority—these are the earmarks of bureaucracy. In any large government, business, or social institution, bureaucracy is indispensable, for bureaucracy is an essential concomitant of expertness. The fundamental question we are considering can be stated in slightly different terms: how are democratic control and bureaucratic efficiency to be reconciled in the best interests of society? It is frequently said that bureaucrats destroy the people's liberties. Is this true? Professionalization causes a gulf to rise between the body of public officials and the citizens. Is this inevitable? Specialization and permanence produce officiousness and nondemocratic attitudes. Need this be? When the people turn over the administration to experts, they leave no jobs for themselves and, hence, their participation and interest disappear. Serious, if true!

Efficiency and expertness are needed in democracies because the alternatives are frustration or dictatorship. This is the case, at any rate, in a democracy which has positive and difficult obligations. Failure of the governmental processes invites either disorder or a proscription of liberty. Whether it be too little effectiveness or too rigid control, the people as a whole stand to lose. These alternatives, of course, are usually a long time in appearing. If citizens looked far enough ahead, they would see that only an efficient democracy can prevent confusion and eventual dictatorship. Democracy is so soothing to the senses, so reassuring; it tends to make us so complacent. We appreciate it more after it is gone.

<small>ALTERNATIVES TO EFFECTIVE POPULAR RULE</small>

The alternative to efficient minority rule is a neutral, self-disciplined bureaucracy. A democracy needs to fill its higher administrative posts with men who look upon their positions with the same objectivity and professionalism that we expect from a good lawyer or doctor. They should be the masters of their respective skills; give their advice only when it is asked for; carry out the laws with consistent loyalty and effort, irrespective of their private opinions; and have no master save the public welfare. Although this may be asking a great deal of mere men, nothing else seems sufficient to vouchsafe both democratic control and effectiveness. That such a goal is a reasonable one is proved by the present approximation to such a standard by thousands of municipal and several national governments.

If people realized that the choice is between a democratically controlled body of experts and class rule, there is not much question what their choice would be. All too few are aware of the administrative implications of a democracy which has heavy burdens. They corrupt and revile the terms "politics" and "bureaucracy." They do not seem to realize that wise policies and neutral administration are all that stand between them and chaotic social conditions, on one side, and the slave trail of dictatorship, on the other.

In this day and age, proficiency is bound to come to government, either through democratic channels or from a willful minority. The task of democratic statesmanship the world over is to effect a happy admixture of democratic control and efficiency, in order that proficiency may not be bought at too high a price. What are the factors which need to be taken into account?

The ultimate objective is to maintain effective popular control. True liberals will agree that, in case of a choice between democracy and efficiency, the decision should be in favor of popular control. Assuming that both can be realized under the same governmental system, the problem is then one of making proper provision for both factors. It is extremely important that society should prevent a gulf from forming between the public administrators and the rank and file of the citizenry. Ways and means should be devised to prevent officiousness and other characteristics which sometimes attach themselves to large organizations.

PROBLEMS TO BE SOLVED

There are three principal aspects to the problem of balancing administrative effectiveness and citizen control: first, the machinery of popular control needs to be constructed in such a way that both objectives can be achieved; second, the public servants must be educated concerning their obligations; third, education for citizenship should inform men and women what is expected of them if the golden mean is to be made a reality.

Some writers, such as Lord Hewart and James M. Beck,[1] charge that legislatures have "abdicated." By this they mean that administrators have been given increasing influence in the drafting of laws, in the promulgation of rules having the force of law, and in freedom to exercise discretionary power without strict control by the lawmaking body. In a preceding chapter, we explained why it is that these shifts in the balance of power have taken place.[2] If we are to follow the common-sense rule of utilizing the knowledge

THE MACHINERY OF POPULAR CONTROL

[1] Lord Hewart, *The New Despotism* (London, 1929); and James M. Beck, *Our Wonderland of Bureaucracy* (New York, 1932).
[2] *Supra*, pp. 232–35.

and experience of those who are best prepared to solve complex problems, the influence of administrators over the policy-making process may be expected to increase still further. The real task is to use the best brains, in whatever department they happen to be, and still preserve intact the power of decision and review which the legislature holds in trust from the voters.

The effectiveness of democratic control is not measured by the amount of detailed work which the legislature does for itself. Rather, too great attention to picayune matters may lead to inadequate consideration of basic issues and failure to observe closely the use made of power given to executive agencies. Legislatures should become more closely analogous to boards of directors of private corporations. That is, they should rely upon the advice of the management in drafting programs, and perform their most useful function in criticizing, modifying, approving, and controlling the measures advanced by the administration. Legislatures are representative of many points of view, constituted largely from inexperienced laymen, and famed for reflecting democratic attitudes rather than for their knowledge of social engineering and statecraft. This is no reflection on representative bodies. Their function is indispensable, because legislators bring to public administration the common sense, simple wisdom, and sense of humor which experts too frequently lack. The legislature is the most important institution of government; it decides; it assumes responsibility; it keeps the administration on the straight and narrow path. Is this not a desirable division of work?

The existing shortcomings of representative government are due not so much to the arrogation of power by administrators as to inadequate organization for legislative decision, responsibility, and control. "Bureaucracy triumphant" is the figurative man of dark complexion in the woodpile, conjured up to divert attention from the failure of most legislatures to modernize their organization and practice.

SHORTCOMINGS OF LEGISLATIVE PROCEDURE

Bureaucracy becomes a threat to liberty when it is left irresponsible. If the number of administrative agencies is so great that people become confused in attempting to untangle the web, then the threat to democratic control is doubly great. Departments headed by responsible ministers stand in the limelight of legislative and public attention. Independent establishments, *ad hoc* boards and commissions—all these detached agencies of which there are so many in the United States—constitute the irresponsible, confusing bureaucracy. Democratic control could be increased if the short ballot, administrative simplification, and the abolition or consolidation of detached commissions were put into effect more widely throughout the country.

The greatest assurance of popular control is in vigorous and responsible party leadership. It would be a tragic loss for democracy if efficiency were carried so far that party leadership shriveled and died. Sometimes, when public administrators discuss city government, they talk as if politics and parties should be completely eliminated. When this impression is conveyed, the result is to be regretted. Too much emphasis upon national parties hurts good local government; but, on the other hand, sound municipal government cannot be expected to continue long unless an effective citizen organization is running affairs. This group may not bear a traditional party label. It may be called "Fusion Group," "Charterites," or "Nonpartisan League," but unless it fulfills the functions of the regular party organization, the control of the city hall is sure to change hands. Even if the group contents itself with emphasis upon "businesslike management," its existence and activity are indispensable if the administration is to have a working mandate, loyal support, and the backing of public opinion.

PARTY RESPONSIBILITY AND POPULAR CONTROL

Professional administrators, like other professional people, are estopped by etiquette and self-interest from defending their every action whenever criticisms are made. Civil servants are cloaked in anonymity, and unless the expert administrator has behind him someone who assumes the responsibility and who is willing to take up the cudgels of public defense, his is a sorry lot indeed. This the party does for him. The assumption of responsibility by the politically appointed department head is absolutely necessary if a proper balancing of democratic control and expertness is to take place. The administrator who is forced into the political arena usually loses his job as a result.

Legislative control can be increased by requiring periodic confirmations of discretionary administrative acts and by providing for more frequent progress reports. John Stuart Mill was strongly of the opinion that a legislative body's most important function is that of criticizing and controlling administrative actions. The legislature itself should not attempt to administer; but it can help the executive; increase its lawmaking competence; and protect the citizen interests by exercising a careful surveillance and check. In this process, legislative committees are found very useful. Members of a committee take a special interest in that particular field of activity, and the more able members try to master the subject matter. Whether it be a large corporation or a government, the control activity of committees is very important to the success of the whole. Cabinet governments, in which there is no proper place for legislative committees as initiating agencies, stand in need of committees for review, criticism, and control purposes.[1]

<small>LEGISLATIVE CRITICISM, REVIEW, AND CONFIRMATION</small>

Review of administrative action by legislative committees is a function of popular control which is relatively well performed in American governments. This procedure takes several forms. There may be periodic progress reports, accompanied by hearings before the committee. Another method is to force the spending agency to return to the appropriation committee and give a report on its stewardship before additional sums will be forthcoming. Finally, hearings are frequently held at which the use made of broad powers or realms of discretion are explained and defended by executive officers. We lack, however, the British system of "Provisional Orders," according to which Parliament periodically confirms the licensing and ordinance acts of department heads. Something similar to this method—only more effective— could be adopted with benefit by our larger legislative bodies in the United States.

The publication of executive orders and regulations, growing

---

[1] Cf. Ramsay Muir, *How Britain is Governed* (New York, 1930), pp. 229 ff.

out of "delegated legislation," is a popular safeguard. Administration issues more ordinances having the force of law than the legislature does session laws. Ramsay Muir, for example, has pointed out that in 1927 Parliament enacted only 43 public acts, whereas administrative orders and regulations numbered 1,349.[1] Because of our vast bureaucracy of commissions and independent establishments, the amount of "administrative legislation" is very great in the United States.[2] It is fortunate, therefore, that recently the federal government established *The Federal Register*, in which all such orders creating legal rights and obligations are reported. Other American governments would add to democratic control and official responsibility by doing likewise.

There is very little that the courts can do toward democratizing expert administration. Rather, the judiciary's contribution is in enforcing the terms of the law, preventing excesses of power, and giving redress to any citizen whose rights have been invaded. These forms of protection and control are exceedingly important, but are designed to prevent abuse rather than to improve the method and spirit of administration.[3] In a democratic country, government acts through law and holds its officials subject to court prosecution. These are indispensable safeguards to democracy, even though they add little to the reconciliation of expertness and popular control.

JUDICIAL CONTROL

The democratization of administration is assisted by the use of citizen advisory committees. This is a device which is being used very extensively, both here and abroad. Almost everyone is familiar with the famous slogan, "The expert should be kept on tap, not on top." There is a great deal of experience and sound advice in this play on words; however, it really needs to be accompanied with the reminder that if laymen interfere too much with the technical

CITIZEN ADVISORY COMMITTEES

---

[1] *Ibid*, p. 61.
[2] See Frederick F. Blachly and Miriam E. Oatman, *Administrative Legislation and Adjudication* (Washington, 1934); and James Hart, *The Ordinance-Making Powers of the President* (Baltimore, 1925).
[3] This subject is broadly treated in "Forms of Control Over Administrative Action" in Haines and Dimock, *The Law and Practice of Governmental Administration* (Baltimore, 1935).

competence and discretion of the expert, it will be found difficult to find experts who will consent to stay on tap. Democracy and good administration are largely the result of learning what the expert should do and what the layman should control, and how each can supplement the other to the best advantage. The advisory committee has the virtue that it brings to the permanent administrator the fresh, broad outlook, and still leaves him free to act as his best judgment dictates. The function of the advisory committee is consultative, not directive.

Directive boards also are a connecting link between the citizenry and the officials. At one time, almost all state and municipal departments were headed by citizen boards. They are still numerous, and are found particularly in the fields of education, parks, police, libraries, and public welfare. Efforts are usually made to place on them citizens who have some knowledge of, or special interest in, the governmental function. The board has administrative power, actual authority to plan and direct the work program. The administrative head of the department is subject to the board's orders and pleasure.

DIRECTIVE BOARDS

There is a great deal of disagreement as to whether directive boards are a sound governmental device. Persons concerned with school, library, and public-welfare administration frequently express sympathy for the board system. The board of laymen automatically creates a devoted clientele of influential citizens who will defend and work for the particular service. Every public service needs its stalwarts, men and women who will rise to its defense irrespective of the intrinsic merits of the controversy. Besides helping to assure such a clientele, the directive board brings to the professional administrator the attitudes and desires of the general public, along with criticisms and suggestions which even an advisory board might not provide.

Over against these advantages, there are certain proved drawbacks to board administration. The multiple-headed department divides responsibility, whereas the single-headed commissioner cannot avoid it. The decision of a single individual is likely to be arrived at more speedily than that of a board, and there is more flexibility with which to meet emergencies and unforeseen contingencies. Most important of all, a board of inexperienced laymen is all too likely to invade the proper province of the paid official and to attempt to decide routine or technical matters for which it has insufficient competence. When the expert is overruled too frequently, he is likely to fight the interference or else give up in despair. Two heads are not invariably better than one—it depends upon the heads.

This important issue brings to focus the entire question of the proper admixture of professionalization and citizen participation. A wise decision will take adequate account of long-time results. An intelligent resident of one of England's best-governed cities recently said, "Our local government has become efficient and undemocratic—citizens are taking less interest and exercising less influence each passing year. In America, on the other hand, you have less efficiency, on the whole, but a larger number of control functions which citizens are still expected to perform." What will be the result over a long period of time? One possible answer is, "If service is as good as anyone could expect, why worry if experts do the job and laymen are eliminated?" On the other hand, "When citizen participation and interest are lost, the foundations of popular government have disappeared." Sheer efficiency, unless consistent with larger social interests, may result in loss. An excess of amateurism also may cost the people money and deprive them of a better life. Again we are brought face to face with the necessity of securing a proper blending of the two ingredients. May it not be wise to continue citizen boards, in some fields, even though they lessen the net efficiency of performance?

*NECESSITY FOR LONG VIEW*

Bureaucracy at its worst is officious and overbearing, careless and indifferent, detached and aloof. It loses touch with the average man and feels superior to the rank and file. Snobbery is the term which is sometimes applied to this sort of behavior; however, a feeling of superiority is only one possible explanation. Large organizations, public and private, are inclined to exalt rules above service and regulations above customer satisfaction. Since it is so large, the

*INHERENT DANGERS OF BUREAUCRACY*

organization's internal relationships and its contacts with customers tend to become routine and impersonal. Experts, moreover, are usually very poor salesmen; they are interested in knowledge, rather than in people; their objectivity makes them seem aloof. It is difficult to be the proverbial "man in the street" and a skilled technician, too. This combination of expertness and democratic attitude, however, is the one which should constantly be sought.

Concentration upon a special field of scientific or professional endeavor naturally tends to narrow a man's interests and outlook. When such persons are put in charge of a service which has continuous and numerous contacts with the public, it is not surprising if public relations and employee attitudes are neglected. The successful administrator has broad interests, enjoys meeting all kinds of people, and has a spontaneous interest in human nature. The coldly objective, preoccupied expert hardly fits this description. The blind spots of the highly specialized administrator have been described as follows by a British official: "It is not by any means a rule, but the more highly gifted the scientific head is, scientifically, the more he requires guidance and help in the plain matter-of-fact matters of administration and the less he is disposed to recognize that he requires it! Was it not Newton who made a large hole in the barn door for the cat and a small hole for the kitten?"

Specialized technicians need the help of general administrators, and the latter are incomplete without the back-to-earth influence of citizen advisers and critics. Almost all work is narrowing; concentration is the inexorable law of modern life. There is all the more necessity, then, for the market-place attitudes and non-deferential criticisms which the layman brings to the administration of a public service. The average person, particularly in the United States, fortunately has no feeling of awe or reverence in the presence of a so-called expert. The outspoken, matter-of-fact man of broad sympathies and general interests must supplement the professional administrator if serious mistakes are not to be made and departments are not to drift away from popular sympathy and understanding.

A large part of public administration is clerical, research, and staff work, which rarely brings officials and employees in touch with the general public. Many public servants, therefore, become "cloistered," in the manner of the proverbial university professor. This is an important contributing factor to the gulf which tends to widen between the public and the official. In a large number of services, it has more to do with aloofness than scientific temperament, rigid regulations, or impersonal attitudes. This gulf is the greatest threat to popular support and democratic control; officials need to be constantly devising means of filling it in. For this reason, public relations, broadly construed, is more indispensable to government services than to any other field of human relationships.

Much of the time, public officials cannot be blamed for losing their patience and for becoming cold and sarcastic. The public has a different attitude toward enterprises which it owns than toward those which are private. John Citizen seems to say, "This is mine, and concerning it I can do as I please and act as I please." In a way, this attitude is to be applauded. One result of it, however, is that citizens usually show less consideration for public employees than for those in a private establishment. In part, this attitude is explained by the fact that they have been led to expect indifferent treatment in return. The public's feeling of power and proprietorship, however, is undoubtedly an important explanation of the frequency of bullying treatment. Public officials should expect such behavior and make up their minds that tempers will not be lost, that clerks will not be "snippy," and that the customer will be considered right no matter how wrong he is. Not without reason are public officials called "servants."

Cloistered persons are likely to be unusually sensitive to criticism. The man in the rough-and-tumble of the market place must "learn to take it" as a condition of success and survival. Civil servants, however, are particularly vulnerable to criticism, as they are not hardened to it and, being unable to defend themselves publicly, have a feeling of injustice because of their helplessness. For these reasons, it is all the more important for political officers to be responsible and to be prepared to defend the actions of permanent officials. Nothing hurts morale more than a rankling feeling of injustice.

The right relations between the public and the service depend most upon the efforts made by the bureaucracy itself. If it disciplines itself, the problem of democratic attitudes and control can be solved largely without assistance from other quarters. The professional standards, ethics, philosophy, attitudes, and ideology of the public service are the surest means of securing a satisfying rapport. Group consciousness and responsibility, although they may lead to exclusiveness, are, paradoxically enough, the very forces which can correct the inherent defects of bureaucracy.

RESPONSIBILITY OF THE ADMINISTRATIVE CORPS

The philosophy of a bureaucracy either keeps it democratic or makes it arrogant. Professional standards and ethics provide "rules of the game" which do more to control action and attitudes than any amount of outside compulsion. The inherent tendency toward officiousness is offset by a philosophy of public service.

Public servants are what H. G. Wells calls the "priestly or educated persons." "Liberalism," he says, "is too apt to denounce 'priestcraft' as altogether evil. Yet the progressive and revolutionary initiatives of the past have been almost entirely of priestly origin." By the priest type, Wells is concerned not only with ministers of religion, but with "a vast world of quasi-disinterested effort, with teachers of every class, with the writers and creative artists, with scribes and journalists, with doctors, surgeons, and the associated professions, with judges and lawyers generally, with *administrators, and particularly that excellent type, the permanent official*, with technical experts, and finally, most hopeful, various and interesting of all, with the modern scientific worker."[1] The most distinctive element in the priestly, or educated, class of persons is the conception of self-abnegation, or devotion.

The individual is not supposed to work directly either for his own enrichment or for his own honour and glory. He belongs, he has made himself over, to an order consecrated to ends transcending any such personal considerations.

[1] [Italics ours.] H. G. Wells, *The Work, Wealth, and Happiness of Mankind*, I (Doubleday-Doran, New York, 1931), 344.

That is the essence of priesthood, of professionalism, and of all artistic and literary pretensions. . . . The element of devotion . . . is absolutely essential to the processes of civilization. . . . This . . . class of persona is moulded and its qualities are evoked out of germs of purpose which remain latent in all the less educated elements of the social mélange. That is the key-fact to the study of social psychology. . . . It is in *the ineradicable idea of disinterested integrity* which this priestly-learned class alone has fostered that the future of humanity resides.[1]

This statement expresses with deep insight and great clarity the heart of the public-service philosophy of the permanent administrative corps.

The cornerstones of this philosophy are corporate self-discipline, the creation of positive standards of ethics and conduct, unswerving attachment to the public welfare—in short, professionalization of the public service. Although the public servant's primary attachment is to the public interest, the practical touchstone of his activity is loyalty to the service which he represents. This is the highest ethic wherever professional public service has developed. Every action of the administrator is judged by its effect upon the prestige of the service and upon the public satisfaction with that service. It is at this point that corporate feeling and professional pride blaze most brightly. That professional standards can be made as compelling in the public service as in any other profession has already been demonstrated in this country as well as abroad. Once standards of ethics and conduct are developed, they become the most potent influences in producing integrity and satisfactory service. So seriously do city managers take their international code of ethics that in 1932, for example, seven managers resigned because the council interfered with appointments and another voluntarily left office because he was made an issue in a council election. The good of the profession is above the interest of any member!

<small>DEMOCRACY AND A PUBLIC-SERVICE PHILOSOPHY</small>

Positive incentives are more efficacious than outside compulsion. Laws and courts can punish erring officials, legislatures can "sweep out dirty corners," but only professional self-discipline can be relied upon to produce democratic attitudes and efficiency.

[1] *Ibid.*, pp. 345-47.

The most reliable guarantee of honest, efficient, intelligent, public-spirited administration is a corps of professional administrators. No amount of outside pressure can make an incompetent, unprincipled employee fulfill standards of conduct.

Perhaps the most important element in the ideology of the public service is that the citizens are the masters and the officials are merely their agents. When this thought burns in the consciousness of employees, they are not so likely to become aloof, neglectful, and overbearing. No matter how able an expert may be, he does not threaten popular rule so long as he is characterized by humility and democratic understanding. This combination of technical ability and altruistic philosophy is the salvation of democracy, as Wells says it is of humanity. Self-seeking minorities, either from the left or the right, do not supply this indispensable factor of social solidarity and community progress.

In the last analysis, of course, citizens will be masters of their own governments only if they show enough interest and activity. Most administrators would welcome increased citizen co-operation, but it cannot always be obtained. The proper balancing of administrative competence and democratic control requires citizen education, as well as self-analysis and discipline on the part of the bureaucracy. There is a close correlation between interest and activity; they are interacting, because interest expresses itself in action, and activity creates interest. A fundamental truth of group activity is that people should be given something to do if they are to be kept permanently interested. This is why too much professionalization has an inherent danger: everything will be done for the citizens and, hence, there will be nothing worth their doing.

*POPULAR PARTICIPATION*

If democracy had to rely upon human selfishness, it would fail. Minorities would attempt to grasp power and take what they could for themselves. Permanent administrators would be interested only in salary and security; citizens would do nothing about improving government unless they saw something in it for themselves. The fact is that the same forces which produce the public-service

*"PUBLIC PERSONS"*

philosophy produce also good citizenship. The aim of democratic education should be to produce "public persons,"[1] that is, individuals who put the common good above their own immediate advantage. Only the paternal, altruistic, patriotic impulses in people make government efficient and democratic. Unless large numbers of people will of their own accord support good government, and actually get out and work for it, popular control is doomed. That is why the work of the National League of Women Voters is so encouraging. The league knows that women will work for the community because its interests and the family's interests are identical. Give men and women something worth doing and you will have their whole-hearted support. Literally, then, the problem of democratic statesmanship is that of providing jobs—not patronage jobs, but nonremunerated ones which will capture the interest of public-spirited citizens.

Democracy is a race between education and selfishness. Unless our public schools can succeed in producing "public persons," the devil will certainly take a good many more than the hindmost. Education for citizenship, as Professor Merriam and a committee of the American Historical Association have made clear, is the rock on which democracy will either build or founder.[2] In what has since been proved a mistaken realism, our schoolteachers have taught that government is a dirty game and incurably inefficient. By all means, they should present the bad with the good, but not with such emphasis that what is the exception is mistaken for the rule. Democracy is so worth while that teachers are justified in propagating among students a favorable attitude toward it. A certain amount of "indoctrination" is inevitable in any society. There are minimum tenets of faith, such as a belief in popular rule, majority decisions, institutional adjustment to change, the intrinsic value of personality, and the indispensability of co-operation, which democracy is justified in actively propagating. If tomorrow's citizens are to assume their responsibilities with the changed attitudes and predilections made neces-

---

[1] A term used by C. A. Dykstra.
[2] Cf. Charles E. Merriam, *The Making of Citizens* (Chicago, 1931) and *Civic Education in the United States* (New York, 1934).

sary by rapid social change, the public-school systems must expect to bear the brunt of the burden.

How are citizens to be given more opportunities for participation? There are possibilities in government itself and also in organizations which influence and control it. More citizen advisory boards, more voluntary co-operation in public welfare and other fields, the spread of reform parties in municipal governments—these are examples of fruitful avenues of citizen service. Large sums of money must be spent if citizens are to be adequately educated concerning intricate public questions. Public forums, sponsored by the Bureau of Education and other agencies, are making encouraging progress. A few years ago, it was thought that the educational power of the radio would have a revolutionary effect, but the prediction has proved extremely disappointing. Here is an opportunity that a democratic people cannot afford to neglect much longer. Business men's clubs—Rotary and all the other internationals—could do a great deal toward bringing live issues before the male population. In this respect, they are falling far behind our womenfolk. Who is to pay for citizen education—the schools, the clubs, the churches, the universities, the philanthropic foundations, municipal and other governments? It is to be hoped that all or most of these agencies will contribute toward the maintenance of enlightened citizenship and popular control.

<small>PROVIDING OPPORTUNITIES</small>

Experience shows that the best opportunities for tempering expert administration with democratic influence are in organizations which are outside the formal framework but which influence what it does. The Parent-Teachers Association is probably the best example that could be mentioned of effective citizen contribution. Some of the activities of the League of Women Voters are along the same line, and affect many departments. Women sit on the bench as observers in delinquency cases, investigate the reasons for dilatory garbage collection, pry into vote frauds, look into violations of civil-service laws, attend meetings of the council and legislature. These are merely examples; on this diet, the organized women have made themselves a powerful contender for the title of guardian of the public interest.

The success of citizen education depends upon the ideology and values which the community embraces. If the highest honor a person could be paid were that of being called "valuable citizen," participation in politics and administration would be more general. In many communities this situation already exists. A civilized people respect a man not for his wealth but for his benefactions to community living. Outstanding citizenship is one kind of aristocracy, prestige, or call it what you will, from which no possible harm could come. Primary attachment to pressure groups or other special-interest organizations is incompatible with the larger allegiance of citizenship. Not until we get our relative values straightened out can we be confident of preserving the democratic system.

PUBLIC VALUES

SELECTED READINGS

Christie, Charles: "Democracy and the Expert," *Public Administration*, XI, No. 4 (October, 1933), 351–68.
Dewey, John: *The Public and Its Problems* (New York, 1927), *passim;* presents a philosophic discussion of the expert in a democracy.
Dimock, Marshall E.: "Forms of Control over Administrative Action," in *Essays on the Law and Practice of Governmental Administration*, Charles G. Haines and Marshall E. Dimock, eds. (Baltimore, 1935).
Floud, Sir Francis L. C.: "Sphere of the Specialist in Public Administration," *Public Administration*, I (1923), 117–26.
Frankfurter, Felix: *The Public and Its Government* (New Haven, 1930) chap. IV; a discussion of expert administration and democracy.
Gaus, John M.: "American Society and Public Administration," in *Frontiers of Public Administration* (Chicago, 1936), by John Gaus, Leonard D. White, and Marshall E. Dimock; deals with the elements of a reconciliation between expertness and democracy.
Hall, Maurice C.: "The Expert in Government," *Annals*, CLXVIII (September, 1933), 91–100.
Herring, E. Pendleton: *Public Administration and the Public Interest* (New York, 1936), chaps. I–III, XXI, and XXII; analyzes the democratizing influences that are brought to bear upon bureaucracy.
Hopkins, Sir R. V. N.: "The Expert and the Layman," *Public Administration*, III (1925), 10–22.
Laski, Harold J.: "The Limitations of the Expert," *Harper's Magazine*, CLXII (December, 1930), 101–10.

Meriam, Lewis: *Public Service and Special Training* (Chicago, 1936); lecture 2 deals with the expert in public service.

Merriam, Charles E.: *Civic Education in the United States* (New York, 1934); a study of the needs and possibilities of civic education in the United States.

Muir, Ramsay: *How Britain is Governed* (New York, 1930); chap. II discusses the professional administrator and the growth of bureaucracy in Great Britain.

Roberts, J. R. Howard, and Macgregor, A. S. M.: "The Professional Expert and Administrative Control," *Public Administration*, VII, No. 3 (July, 1929), 247–59.

Schultz, E. B.: "An Unsolved Problem in City Government: Political Leadership and Expert Administration," *Southwestern Social Science Quarterly*, XIV, No. 2 (September, 1933), 120–32.

## CHAPTER XVI

☆ ☆ ☆

## THE NEW INDIVIDUALISM

*"We cannot have a great citizenry until all are so situated that the attention of each is pitched at a level above the struggle for mere subsistence and a satisfying of animal wants."*
—C. A. DYKSTRA

"Liberty and equality sound well together—but they have never liked each other." It must be granted that this is true, but does it necessarily mean that they are hopelessly irreconcilable? RECONCILIATION Both liberty and equality are component parts OF LIBERTY AND of the essential American tradition—as they are EQUALITY in every country which aspires to general well-being. It must be admitted, however, that increasingly they seem to conflict. The current issue is made to revolve around the "liberty" of certain business interests to be left alone by government. In contrast with the emphasis upon personal rights which is found in the long course of Anglo-American history, the crux of the present conflict is further public control of the economic order. Are the traditional connotations of these grand old words to be altered, or will it be found on closer examination that liberty and equality, properly construed, can be made friends?

Liberty connotes freedom from restraint. A standard dictionary suggests, among other less pertinent meanings, personal liberty, non-slavery, independence, liberty of action, and power of self-determination. In general, liberty conveys both negative and positive implications. At one extreme, it may be solitariness, license, or utter disregard of conventions; on the other hand, liberty may result from psychological satisfactions within a high degree of order. Liberty is both a state of being and a state of mind. Liberty has long been associated with economic *laissez faire*, but even in this realm it is increasingly recognized that positive measures are entailed.

"Who may define liberty?" asks Herbert Hoover. "It is far more than Independence of a nation. It is not a catalog of political 'rights.' Liberty is a thing of the spirit—to be free to worship, to think, to hold opinions, and to speak without fear—free to challenge wrongs and oppressions with surety of justice." These traditional rights of the individual, not the freedom of business units from public control, are the essence of liberty. Mr. Hoover has repudiated the doctrine of *laissez faire*, which "may thrive as an economic or social philosophy in some countries today, but has been dead in America for generations. . . . There may be some reactionary souls who still yearn for *laissez faire*," but in general it may be regarded as "a dishonest polemic, as a straw man set up to be knocked down."[1] Individualism, in contrast, brings about "the development of the special qualities of individuals, their personality and character." However much one may disagree about the meaning of *laissez faire*, it is refreshing to have our one-time President re-emphasize the personal and spiritual qualities of true liberty.

<small>LIBERTY DEFINED</small>

In our complex society, liberty can frequently be secured only by effective public controls. This truth has been convincingly stated by the British Liberal party,

> Liberalism stands for Liberty; but it is an error to think that a policy of liberty must always be negative, that the State can help liberty only by abstaining from action, that invariably men are freest when their Government does least. Withdraw the police from the streets of the towns, and you will, it is true, cease to interfere with the liberty of the criminal, but the law-abiding citizens will soon find that they are less free than before. Abolish compulsory education: the child and perhaps his parent, will no longer be forced to do what they may perhaps not wish to do; but the adults of the next generation will be denied the power to read, to think, to succeed, which is essential to a real freedom. Repeal, to take one more example, the Shops Act: short-sighted shopkeepers will be allowed to trade for longer hours, but other shopkeepers and the whole class of shop-assistants will be robbed of their proper share of the leisure without which life is a servitude. Often more law may mean more liberty.[2]

[1] Herbert Hoover, *The Challenge to Liberty* (Scribners, New York, 1934), p. 53; see also *American Individualism* (Scribners, New York, 1923).
[2] Liberal Party Inquiry, *Britain's Industrial Future* (London, 1928), p. xix.

## THE NEW INDIVIDUALISM

When "liberty" results in unfair privilege or social injury, it is no longer true liberty.

Equality, similarly, is subject to many degrees of interpretation. At one extreme, it connotes absolute sameness, complete uniformity, which obviously is a denial of individualism. On the other hand, equality suggests the idea of balance, the proper adjustment of interests and quantities.

EQUALITY DEFINED

It is as unthinkable that all men should have exactly the same heredity, ability, or income as that liberty should mean chaotic license. In American usage, "equality of opportunity" is the limiting interpretation which is customarily employed. Men should have the same benefits if they possess the same ability and work equally hard. The important factor is that they should have like opportunities in which to develop their talents. In order to guarantee an equal start and to prevent unfair advantage, the government must regulate, tax, and control in many other ways.

Equality of opportunity is the essence of American democracy. Unless unbalancing inequalities, undeserved privileges, and unfair practices are prevented, individuals will not be free to make the most of their abilities and efforts. Equality of opportunity constitutes the happy balance between unregulated liberty and leveling equality. Herbert Hoover, usually regarded as a conservative, concludes that any actions taken by government to preserve equality of opportunity are "proper ones." The extensiveness of our regulatory machinery, he says, is a monument to the American passion for equality of competitive conditions.

Government is the great balance-preserver. There should be correspondence between effective demand and production, earnings and compensation, effort and reward, justice and mercy, tolerance and belief, persuasion and compulsion, efficiency and democracy, liberty and equality. Public authority should attempt to reconcile the subjective and objective, the personal and the utilitarian. Let us not lose the thought here in a multitude of words. "Utilitarian" represents the economic wants and necessities of society—using the full productive capacity of the economic system. "Personal" or "subjective" stands for the individual tastes and psychological satisfactions of those who make the wheels of industry turn. The problem of social change is to satisfy the utilitarian wants of the people and still gratify, insofar as possible, the customary incentives of the owners and managers. This ancillary problem well illustrates the adjustment that needs to be effected between liberty and equality on the larger front.

Because they are so largely subjective or psychological, liberty and equality cannot be expected to mean the same thing to all people. Equality, like liberty, is a feeling as well as a social status. It is possible to feel socially equal even when there is a big difference in worldly goods. What seems a large grant of liberty to a given person or group would seem unsatisfyingly small to others. Within the same society, different persons and groups are guided and compensated by totally different incentives, myths, ideologies. John Maynard Keynes explicitly recognizes these differences when, referring to the future of the profit-making drive, he says, "dangerous human proclivities can be canalised into comparatively harmless channels by the existence of opportunities for money making and private wealth, which, if they cannot be satisfied in this way, may find their outlet in cruelty, the reckless pursuit of personal power and authority, and other forms of self-aggrandizement. It is better that a man should tyrannize over his bank balance than over his fellow-citizens; and whilst the former is sometimes denounced as being but a means to the latter, sometimes at least it is an alternative."[1] The existence of these psychological differences, however, is no reason for giving up the search for a workable compromise between liberty and equality.

Several factors need to be emphasized in attempting to combine liberty and equality in a dynamic society. Social utility and the personal satisfactions of leaders and creative workers must, as nearly as possible, be harmonized. Equality of opportunity is both an objective and a happy balance. Reforms which break too sharply with traditional methods and attitudes are almost sure to cause wide-

ELEMENTS TO
BE ADMIXED

[1] Keynes, *The General Theory of Employment, Interest, and Money*, p. 374, Harcourt, Brace & Co.

spread dissatisfaction and objection. On the other hand, the system of industry and the effective rules of the game produce incentives, characteristics of human nature, and attitudes toward liberty and equality. It is, therefore, apparent that statesmanship alone can effect a satisfactory reconciliation. Time, psychological attitudes, and the relative number of those who adhere to various viewpoints are among the variables to be considered. How can this adjustment be made once and for all, when balance is primarily the product of appropriate responses to social and economic changes?

The ultimate norm is the greatest amount of economic well-being compatible with political democracy and general psychological gratifications. It is unlikely that everyone can be satisfied. The next best policy, therefore, is to combine as nearly as possible economic utility and the psychological satisfactions which come from the democratic way of life. Liberty, to be worthy of the name, involves freedom of choice and power to change one system for another. Therefore, unless the productive mechanism allows choices between vocations and provides every opportunity for the full initiative and ability of outstanding leaders, it fails to qualify as free and democratic. Likewise, if economic well-being can be secured only at the sacrifice of political liberties and freedom of choice, it fails to effect the necessary reconciliation, and the adjustment is only postponed. It is better that citizens should indulge their personal tastes and tolerate inefficiencies than that they should sell their liberties for larger quantities of consumable goods. Man's elevation above the animals is measured by his dignity, character, and culture, not his production totals.

As soon as one thinks that some disturbing conflicts have been reconciled, others crop up to cause theoretical complications. Equality of opportunity and economic balance are obviously dependent upon a government which is powerful enough to control those interests which would take unfair advantage, grasp special privileges, or upset the balance between individual and general well-being. Stated baldly, public authority must be stronger than any group or combination of interests, its strength being measured by compliance and co-operation, not by dollars and bullets. This means, concretely, that government must be able to enforce regulatory and restrictive laws, break up combinations, and make necessary adjustments between demand and supply. This is the necessary practical implication from the principles of equality of opportunity and economic balance. At this point many—Herbert Hoover, for instance—refuse to follow through from the premises to the logical conclusion. Even if one is prepared to grant the necessity and desirability of effective control over individual economic groupings, however, there arises the problem of democratic control in a powerful bureaucracy. This question we have discussed in the preceding chapter and, hence, there will be no necessity to repeat here. In attempting a realistic reconciliation of liberty and equality, it must be recognized that effective political power is indispensable to equality of opportunity and economic balance.

"Regimentation" is the modern equivalent of effective governmental control. To a considerable extent, the term is an emotive, propagandist one. However, insofar as it conveys the thought of effecting control and introducing order into the REGIMENTATION economic structure, its common acceptance is to be desired. It conveys an idea which, perhaps, cannot be otherwise expressed with so great economy. Regimentation, so defined, is another practical implication of regulation, control, and planning. It is an offshoot of democracy attempting to enforce economic balance and equality of opportunity.

After a certain stage of business concentration and social complexity, regimentation is seemingly inevitable. Both industry and government are regimenters, but each, as might be expected, blames the other for ordering and controlling the indispensable processes. It is the old case of "the kettle calling the skillet black." As we have already said in the chapter on government control of the economic order, it is apparently inevitable that either government or organized business should assume the responsibility for economic stabilization and planning. The real questions, therefore, are: Which one regiments more? What are the differences, if any, between the kinds of regimentation each one produces?

Which is in the best interests of society? Having already considered the regulatory, planning, and economic-control functions of government, let us turn to some of the implications of business regimentation.

"Stripping off false banners then, two sorts of regimentation are proposed to us. One is the brand which, while seeking to mobilize the American masses into an army of easily disciplined, easily underpaid, and easily junked economic robots, has proved itself complacently callous to the needs of any form of individualism but that of the freebooter acquisitive spirit. The other is the kind of regimentation which would regulate the operations of acquisitive genius in order to provide an economic security under which, for the first time since the dawn of the machine age, the latent individuality of the many will have some chance to set itself free. To say this, of course, is not to make simple an urgent problem of grave difficulty. It is inevitable that economic collectivism will bring with it restraints. The task is to see to it that in that collectivism the greatest freedom for individuality may be maintained. Difficult, yes. Impossible, no."[1] This statement is probably unduly critical of the motives of business leaders, and in some places the language is too strong, but it does present some aspects of business standardization which very much need to be considered.

The concentration of industrial and financial power in the hands of a relatively few corporations produces regimentation. It is found in what we eat, wear, read, and enjoy—nothing is exempt, not even the home, education, the church, recreation. "Today the consumer has lost much of his old direct control in industry. . . . In purchasing any one article he has few sellers to choose from. He no longer has the same means of testing quality as the seller; and, finally, *he is bludgeoned by all the arts of advertising to conform to the pattern laid down by one or another of the great units of economic organization.*"[2]

In the '20's, heyday of "Our Business Civilization,"

---

[1] Duncan Aikman and Hawley Jones, "The Bogey of Regimentation," *Harper's*, 169 (Nov., 1934), 649–50.
[2] [Italics ours.] Gardiner C. Means, in *Government Control of the Economic Order*, p. 14.

... the "key men" of individualism's golden age were not interested in individualism at all in so far as it might have any connection with individuality, as it might have implied any development of the cultural and intellectual differences among different individuals. They were interested in creating, marshaling, disciplining, and ordering about a population of mental and emotional robots, who would conduct their lives on two premises:

(1) That the American business man was the salt of the economic earth and the rightly ordained dictator of the contemporary economic era;

(2) that his acquisitive instincts, which were the essence of the nation's genius and, for all practical purposes, the total sum of that genius, must be left free and unfettered to dominate the intellectual, the æsthetic, the political, and the recreational life of our times.[1]

The term individualism has become so corrupted that sometimes it seems best to change to the word "individuality." Individuality means the freedom of the individual to develop the best cultural and social characteristics which his heredity and man-made environment can produce. The cry of individualism has become a shield for special privileges and for nonsocial activities. What is needed in the United States, therefore, is a new individualism, or what might be called "cultural individuality." The good old word "individualism" needs to be saved, its former connotations restored.

WHAT IS INDIVIDUALISM?

Cultural individuality represents the reconciliation of liberty and equality. The individual assiduously serves the indispensable requirements of society and at the same time is an individualist in his private life. The country needs "public persons" who are also individualists. In our highly complex and interrelated society, individuality and economic security tend to become interdependent—the opportunity for personal development depends upon social conditions which make possible the flowering of personality and culture. "We cannot have a great citizenry until all are so situated that the attention of each is pitched at a level above the struggle for mere subsistence and a satisfying of animal wants." For the present-day city dweller who is dependent upon others for all his services, rugged individualism not only seems to

[1] "The Bogey of Regimentation," *loc. cit.*, p. 644.

result in standardization and regimentation, but, in too many cases, want, insecurity, and despair. Hence, the new individualism is to be achieved only after economic security has been provided for people generally.

Individuality means self-expression in vocational activity, in recreation, and in avocations. The new individualism should produce persons who know no fear. As long as economic insecurity is the principal characteristic of our civilization, this kind of individualism is not widely possible. Persons who are controlled by fear do not have a chance to develop their personalities and cultural enjoyments.[1] True individualists are not "different" simply to be "smart"; they respond to natural instincts which flow spontaneously from freedom and from the joy of living.

Although there is a necessary and proper place for personal struggle and competition in society, this part of the citizen's life should be secondary to and controlled by his primary attachment to social well-being. Within socially fixed rules of the game, the individual has more "freedom," in the form of independence, fearlessness, and cultural expression, than he has under a destructively competitive one. The so-called individualism of the past was largely confined to a few captains of industry, but even they were not free. Most of them sought wealth, power, and authority simply because it was considered the thing to do; it was in accordance with the accepted rules of the game. Having thrown all of their nervous energy and abilities into the struggle for dominance, the development of their cultural and human characteristics rarely became possible. Nervous intoxication results in enslavement even for those who are called masters.

The real individualism of America is found in natural enjoyment of the unspoiled out-of-doors and in the creative and cultural activities which under present conditions are reserved to artists, professional people, and some of the independently wealthy. Although America was originally revolutionary, nonconformist, and experimental, it has become, since the businessman's regimentation of the last half century, increasingly stand-

---

[1] Cf. **Harold D. Lasswell**, *World Politics and Personal Insecurity* (New York, 1935); and John Dewey, *Individualism, Old and New* (New York, 1930).

ardized and expressionless. If we are again to produce fearless individualists, natural recreation, and original cultural expression, the country as a whole must have sufficient economic security to make possible the disappearance of fear and rigid conformity.

Genuine freedom is found in a satisfying sense of purpose. Both nations and persons are not likely to develop very far culturally unless they know where they are going and are anxious to arrive there. The Tennessee Valley Authority is frequently referred to as an example of socialism and regimentation, but one needs but to live in Norris, or in any other of the T.V.A. towns, to discover that true individualism flourishes there. The fact that most impresses visitors is that everyone has a sense of social purpose. This results in enthusiastic work, co-operation, ingenuity, and *esprit de corps;* the net result is contentment and happiness. One feels that the actions of the employees are spontaneous and natural, rather than routine. Cultural development depends to a large extent upon whether or not a man is happy in his work.

In any extension of public control, the most important factor to keep in mind is that individual initiative must be preserved and stimulated at all costs. It is often asserted that, in a complex society, initiative and creativeness will die out. Persons who make this assertion sometimes fail to consider all the fundamental matters which are involved. They falsely assume that rigid uniformity, uncompromising legalism, and hide-bound administration are somehow inevitable. Whether initiative and creativeness are fostered and given an opportunity to develop depends upon the intelligence of those who are responsible for planning large-scale policies and administration. There are three important matters upon which the result is likely to turn: preserving freedom of choice, providing attractive incentives, and developing flexibility of management.

CULTIVATING INITIATIVE

The most desirable characteristics of individualism, namely initiative and creativeness, are the result of providing the proper conditions for the individual. It will be noted that we have said "providing" the right kind of conditions, and of course this immediately implies intelligent planning and the proper environment,

Initiative and creativeness flourish when they are encouraged and given a chance.

The cultivation of the new individualism may be compared to the process which has been carried on in recent years in progressive schools. The purpose of the process is the education of men and women who will abound in initiative and originality. An important point to notice in the training program is that children are encouraged to experiment and to assert their individualities, but the conditions under which they play and study and the methods which are employed are determined by those in charge of the program. The theories and the planning which go into the success of the progressive school curriculum are certainly as important as the play habits and individual responses of the students. So it is in the relation between government and the individual.

The state is often accused of being paternalistic, but this should not be considered in itself a valid criticism. Paternalism, comparable to the relation between the teacher and the student, is the natural and necessary responsibility of the community. If teachers and states did not plan programs, establish rules of the game, exercise discipline, and insist that individuals put the public welfare above their own, there would indeed be conflict and disorder in the classroom and in the commonwealth.

There is no innate or miraculous quality of government which causes it to be either lacking in initiative or full of originality and experimentation. As in other matters, the record depends upon the amount of intelligence which goes into the planning and execution of policies. Some departments are battened down by precedent, whereas in a growing number of public enterprises there is as much initiative, experimentation, leadership, and invention as in the best-managed private concerns. Instead of assuming that *laissez faire* produces initiative, whereas co-operation results in lack of initiative, we should recognize that irrespective of whether an enterprise is public or private the emergence of progressiveness and morale depends upon the quality of administration. Initiative is not something that some people have and others completely lack. Recognizing, of course, that there are differences in health and ability, any additional responses which are elicited above bare mediocrity, depend upon such administrative factors as leadership, delegation of authority, and the effective utilization of inspiring incentives.

It is fortunate for mankind that genius is not dependent upon competition and high financial prizes. In a technological civilization, social well-being is largely dependent upon the skills and incentives of two groups, inventors and administrators. Both are characterized by pride of craftsmanship, rather than by the profit impulse. Sir Arthur Salter is right:

> Nor should we hastily accept the libel on human nature that it is only under the perpetual stimulant of daily fluctuations of loss and profit that man will do his best work. . . . How few indeed of those who do the world's work do so under the conscious stimulus of constantly varying profit! Entrepreneurs have this stimulus, but the men they direct work for wages and salaries which are stable for long periods and only differ from those of the public service in a somewhat greater insecurity, which is destined to be reduced. And such leaders of industry do themselves an injustice when they consider that their own motive is only or mainly that of unlimited profit, as the best of them always show when they have the opportunity of creative work under different conditions.[1]

Administrators and inventors are Wells's priestly persona!

Invention, either in the physical world or the social realm, is an expression of the highest form of individuality. Real invention is a very rare occurrence. Inventors, moreover, are not found primarily in business and industry. Authorities on invention classify research agencies into four groups, namely, universities and colleges, privately endowed laboratories, government agencies, and industrial research departments. "The universities are placed first in the above classification because it has been from them that the other agencies have drawn for their very existence . . . Universities are well suited to the search for fundamental laws."[2] The privately endowed research laboratories and governmental agencies also

INVENTIVE
CAPACITY

[1] Sir Arthur Salter, *Recovery: The Second Effort* (D. Appleton-Century, New York, 1932), p. 215.
[2] Franklin S. Harris and Newbern I. Butt, *Scientific Research and Human Welfare* (Macmillan, New York, 1924), pp. 359–60.

have borne a heavy responsibility for research and discovery. The scientific services of the federal government alone are spread through forty bureaus, of which eighteen may be called *primarily* scientific. The Bureau of Standards employs about seven hundred scientists and technicians and has an annual budget of three million dollars. In contrast, the principal function of industrial agencies has been the adaptation of pure research to marketable commodities. Seeing merely the end products of the industrial laboratory, the general public has not been aware that the fundamental research and discovery was for the most part being done elsewhere.[1]

Scientific inventions have done much to produce America's greatness. Most of these creative workers have been outside the private profit-making system and were not spurred by the hope of financial reward. Instead of new scientific discoveries being the product of large business corporations, large incomes and fortunes are based upon long-time fundamental researches which are carried on by universities, governments, and endowed agencies. There is no necessary connection between competitive profit-making enterprise and the progress of research and discovery.

Initiative and creativeness flourish within the confines of a social program when they are encouraged and given a chance. One of the great difficulties of the past has been that dominant groups did not want government to be creative and ingenious. An illustration may be interesting and appropriate. Not long ago J. R. McCarl, then Comptroller General, criticized the Tennessee Valley Authority for several of its expenditures which he considered inappropriate to a government enterprise charged with the purposes for which the T. V. A. was created. One of the issues which he emphasized particularly was the expenditures of the Authority for registered cattle. The Comptroller General challenged the board's authority to buy dairy herds, stating that this activity

FREEDOM AND INVENTIVENESS

[1] Cf. Report, Science Advisory Board (U. S. Government Printing Office, Washington, 1934), on corporate research, "Du Pont: An Industrial Empire," *Fortune* (December, 1934); and T. Swann Harding, "There is Research—and Research," *Scientific American*, CL (January, 1934), pp. 14–16.

had not been specifically mentioned in the T. V. A. Act. The legal merits of the controversy need not detain us, except that it may be noted that the Authority has been given the very broad power of undertaking the "social and economic development" of the Tennessee Valley. It may reasonably be argued, as the T. V. A. did successfully, that the purchase of a dairy herd for demonstration purposes is a legitimate exercise of that power. The important point is that this governmental agency took the initiative in purchasing the dairy herd, as part of its planning activity. It has been recognized for years that the people of the Southern states need to introduce diversified agriculture if their economic well-being is to be improved. The natural fodder of the entire region and the abundant supply of water seem to make the hillsides ideal for the cattle industry. But changes occur slowly in the life of the South; hence, if dairying is to become an important agricultural activity, it will be necessary for the T. V. A., or some other agency which has the funds and influence, to demonstrate by actual experience the desirability of this form of diversification. This newly created public agency had the foresight and determination to lead the way.

An analogous case arose in the activities of the Panama Railroad Company, which, among its numerous enterprises, conducts the dairy business in the Canal Zone. This public agency, which started out as a private corporation and has never been stripped of its freedom and autonomy, purchased high-priced dairy cattle in the United States and introduced them into tropical pastures. They soon died of tick fever; but this public corporation was not "licked." If someone had raised a hue and cry about the money that had been wasted or spent improperly, the public corporation might not have been able to continue its experiment—an experiment upon which depended the availability of milk and meat in case the zone were isolated during war time. The officers of the company, however, persisted in their efforts. They bought more pure-bred cattle from the mainland of the United States and at the same time purchased smaller, but more hardy animals from Cuba. Eventually they were able to establish a new strain which has proved highly successful, having the high milk-pro-

The ultimate objective of government is "community." It is a rule which rests upon the solid foundations of well-being and coöperation. The touchstone of all policies is the provision of conditions which will make "the good life" possible for people generally. In achieving these goals, the most important factor is the civic attitude of the population. When the time comes that good citizenship is put first, divisive tensions will begin to disappear and individuality will have greater chance to flourish. Democracy is a way of life—it extends into all activities and attitudes. Only as individuals adjust themselves to the implications of complexity will the creative state make further advances toward national well-being.

### SELECTED READINGS

Bryce, James: *Modern Democracies* (New York, 1921), especially I, chaps. VI and VII; these sections deal with liberty and equality; acquaintance with this work and with the classic *American Commonwealth* is recommended to every student.

Burlingame, R.: "Freedom and the Lone Wolf," *Harper's*, CLXIX (June, 1934), 82–90.

Dewey, John: *Individualism Old and New* (New York, 1930); discusses the need for an individualism consistent with our machine, business civilization.

Frank, L. K.: "Social Planning and Individual Ideals," *International Journal of Ethics*, XLV, No. 1 (October, 1934), 81–9.

Hoover, Herbert: *American Individualism* (London, 1923); discusses the distinctive character of American individuality.

———: *The Challenge to Liberty* (New York, 1934); develops the same ideas somewhat less objectively than in his earlier essay.

Maritain, Jacques: *Freedom in the Modern World* (New York, 1936); discusses how various philosophies reach the personal-social equation.

Meiklejohn, Alexander: "Liberty—for What?" *Harper's*, CLXXI, (August, 1935), 364–72.

Merriam, Charles E.: *American Political Ideas, 1865–1917* (New York, 1923); chaps. XI and XII discuss the relation between government and liberty.

———: *The Making of Citizens* (Chicago, 1931); the last chapter indicates what the individual must do to maintain independence and responsibility.

Mill, John Stuart: *On Liberty* (1859); a defense of individualism as individuality, which need not have an antisocial interpretation.

ducing characteristics of the registered cattle and the ability, acquired from the Cuban stock, to withstand tropical conditions. If government is to be creative and constructive, the Constitution and machinery must be kept flexible.

Liberty and equality are merged in the concept of "community." Where wealth is fairly equally distributed and education and cultural attainments are fairly consistent, community spirit and voluntary effort are conspicuous, and restraint virtually disappears. Community spirit is likely to be found in its most advanced form in a suburban municipality where the residents are economically and culturally on approximately the same plane. Examples are found in the neighborhood of any large city, whether it be New York, Philadelphia, Chicago, Los Angeles, or a foreign municipality. Community pride becomes particularly strong when the population is relatively permanent rather than transient—where second, third, and fourth generations live in the same locality. In such suburban areas, community spirit frequently becomes so potent that some very curious and interesting things happen. Suburban developments are usually populated by fairly well-to-do persons who presumably have rather conservative political and economic views. Many of them are active members of the chamber of commerce, for example, and at business men's meetings will subscribe lustily to the view that government "should not compete with its citizens." It is significant to note, however, how many of those suburbs have established their own electric-light plants and utilities. In the Chicago region, conservative Winnetka and Hinsdale are two illustrations which immediately come to mind. Business leaders residing in these communities will tell you that they have the finest electric-light plants in the country, and that the entire citizenship responds with equal pride to the triumph of community spirit and honest government.

<small>THE GOAL OF COMMUNITY</small>

The goal of community is realizable in the national state. Denmark, with her economic equality and general well-being, her consumers' co-operatives, and her governmental successes, provides "the good life" for her citizens. So do Norway, Sweden, Switzerland, and Holland, though perhaps in lesser degree.

Nolte, J. M.: "The People versus Individualism," *North American Review*, CCXXXVII, No. 6 (June, 1934), 545–56.

Ritchie, David: *Natural Rights* (3d ed., London, 1916); a criticism of some traditional political and economic conceptions, developing the thesis that rights are socially created.

Russell, William F.: " 'So Conceived and So Dedicated'—Liberty Versus Equality," *Atlantic Monthly*, CLV, No. 11 (May, 1935), pp. 515–22.

Smith, Thomas V.: *The American Philosophy of Equality* (Chicago, 1927); an eloquent discussion of the *right* of equality as necessary to the realization of individuality through the social process and to the continued vitality of the "American ideal."

Tawney, Richard H.: *Equality* (New York, 1931); an English socialist diagnoses contemporary social psychology, concluding that economic equality is a necessary objective.

Wallas, Graham: *Our Social Heritage* (New Haven, 1921); a stimulating analysis of the place of co-operation and liberty in the complexity of modern society.

# INDEX

# INDEX

☆ ☆ ☆

Accounting, planning tool, 377
Adjudication, administrative: and American Bar Association, 238; pros and cons of, 239
*Adkins* vs. *Children's Hospital*, 200 (*note*)
Administration: compromise in, 259 f.; definition of, 231 ff., 243; dynamic, 30; influence of, 229 f., 257; and interest groups, 241 ff.; and judicial control, 240, 397; and legislatures, 234 ff., 393 ff.; neglect of, 258 ff.; objectives of, 252; and party responsibility, 395; and planning, 245, 384; and politics, 30, 292 f.; and popular control, 248, 393; powers of, 238; principles of, 343 ff.; public and private, 356 f.; and public relations, 402; reorganization of, 251 f., 266; and university training, 294
Administrative areas, principles of determining, 245
Administrative careers, 290 f.
Administrative class, in Great Britain, 298 f.
Administrative corps, 293 ff.
Administrative discretion, nature of, 240
Administrative law, in the U. S., 239
Administrative legislation, nature of, 234 ff.
Administrative regulation, growth of in United States, 322
Administrative skills (*see* Skills, administrative, types of)
Administrative tribunal (*see* Regulatory tribunals)
Administrator (*see also* executive): characteristics of, 293 f.
Agricultural Adjustment Act and the taxing power, 203
Agricultural society, 73 f.
Agriculture, Department of, personnel officer of, 305
Aikman, Duncan, 415 (*note*), 416 (*note*)
Allport, Floyd H., 14 (*note*)
American Bar Association, and administration adjudication, 238
American Federation of Labor, and government employees' associations, 304
American Telephone and Telegraph Co., organization of, 265 f.
Anderson, William, 62, 63, 65, 66 (*note*), 134 (*note*), 171 (*note*), 341
*Anderson* vs. *Dunn*, 142 (*note*)

Anti-Saloon League, pressure politics of, 152
Anti-trust legislation (*see* Sherman Act; Labor; Supreme Court)
Aristocracy (*see* Great Britain): theory of, 41
*Arizona* vs. *California*, 193 (*note*)
Arneson, Benjamin A., 192 (*note*)
Ascher, Charles, 64
Associated Press, 86
Atkins, W. E., 335 (*note*)
Aubrey, Edwin E., 223
Australia: compulsory voting in, 105; export market developed by, 345; federalism in, 176
Authoritarian state, theory of, 41 f.

Bagehot, Walter, 14
*Bailey* vs. *Drexel Furniture Co.*, 203 (*note*)
Baruch, Bernard M., 378 (*note*)
Bates, Frank G., 56
Beard, Charles A., 47, 73 (*note*), 131, 168 (*note*), 179 (*note*)
Beard, Mary, 73 (*note*)
Beck, James M., 235 (*note*), 393
Belgium, compulsory voting in, 105
Berle, Adolf A., 79
Berman, Edward, 199 (*note*)
*Better Government Personnel*, 134 (*note*)
Beyle, Herman C., 282 (*note*)
Bicameralism, arguments on, 139 f.
Bird, Frederick L., 355 (*note*)
Blachly, Frederick F., 176 (*note*), 237 (*note*), 397
Bonbright, James C., 333, 334 (*note*)
Bossism (*see* Machine politics)
Brandeis, Louis D., 210, 331
*Britain's Industrial Future*, 319
British Broadcasting Corporation: administrative problems of, 349; a public-utility trust, 360
British Liberal Party, on liberty, 410
British Post Office, administration of, 345, 350 ff.
Brownlow, Louis, 64
Bryce, James, 74, 159, 299 (*note*)
Buck, A. E., 250 (*note*)
Budget: tool of management, 173, 280 f.; in reporting, 282; agency, testing efficiency, 281
Budget and Accounting Act of 1921, 279
Bureaucracy: discussion of, 274, 391 f.; dangers of, 394 f., 399 ff.; and public relations, 402

429

Business (see also Industry): affected with a public interest, 58 f., 197 f., 320 f.; concentration in, 78 ff.; government in, 198 f.; and government, interdependence of, 62 f., 81 f., 88, 91 f., 315 f.; public control of, 83 f., 192, 195 ff.; regimentation by, 414 f.; self-government of, 379 f.; finance in, 279; dual executive in, 263
Businessmen: attitude toward government, 40 f., 81, 91 f.; group consciousness of, 51; and political parties, 81, 117; and public opinion, 80 ff., 86 f.
Butt, Newbern I., 420 (note)
Byrd, Harry, 170

Cabinet, United States, 265
Cabinet government, advantages of, 174 ff.
Canada: courts in, 181; federalism in, 176; management problems in, 260
Cardozo, Benjamin, 216, 239
Careers, administrative, 290 f.
Carpenter, William S., 168 (note)
Carr, Cecil T., 235 (note)
Catlin, G. E. G., 11, 12, 18 (note), 48 (note)
Central Electricity Board, a public-utility trust, 360, 364 f.
Central Statistical Board, a planning agency, 382
Chamber of Commerce, United States: on economic planning, 381; on industrial self-government, 379 f.; an interest group, 40 f., 153
Chandler, Howard, 355 (note)
Chesapeake and Potomac Tel. Co. vs. West, 332 (note)
Chase, Stuart, 179 (note), 317, 321, 346 (note), 347 (note), 354 (note), 370, 377 (note), 378 (note)
Chicago, machine politics in, 119
Child, Marquis W., 317 (note)
Child labor, and the commerce power, 191 f.
Childs, Harwood, L., 25 (note), 82 (note), 153 (note)
Cincinnati: area-wide representation in, 135; city-manager government in, 306; proportional representation in, 107
Citizen boards, arguments for and against, 397 ff.
Citizenship and pluralism, 25
City-county consolidation, 138
City-manager plan: description of, 170 f.; effect of smaller councils in, 147; finance in, 278; as a model administration, 261; personnel in, 305 f.; separation of powers in, 170 f.

City managers: philosophy of, 403; salaries of, 291
Civil-service examinations: 300 f.; in government enterprises, 352 f.; and merit system, 295 ff.; neutrality of, 298; and probationary periods, 301 f.; and tenure of office, 301 ff.
Civil-service commissions, as staff agencies, 265 f.
Civil-Service Law of 1883, 295
Civil-service laws, state, 295
Class (see Great Britain; middle class; Rentier class)
Classification of personnel, 308
Clay, Henry, 376
Clayton Act, 194
Cleveland, proportional representation in, 107
Clough, S. B., 177 (note)
Coker, Francis W., 25 (note), 216 (note)
Cole, G. D. H., 215
Cole, Taylor, 298
Colorado Springs, government enterprises in, 348
Comer, John P., 237 (note), 242 (note)
Command and leadership, 275
Commerce, interstate, definition of, 191 f.
Commerce power: child labor under, 191 f.; and organized labor, 199 ff.; uses of, 192 ff.
Commission of Inquiry on Public Service Personnel, 134 (note), 288 (note), 303 (note)
Commission, regulatory (see Regulatory tribunals)
Committee on Ministers' Powers, Report of, 235 (note)
Committees, legislative, 145 ff.
Common law and common carriers, 320
Community: definition of, 17; goal of, 423; and government, 424; and social legislation, 188 f.
Compensation, in the public service, 310 f.
Comptroller General and administration, 279 ff.
Constitution of the United States: amending process, 206 ff.; distribution of powers, 54; due process and, 181 ff.; general provisions of, 161; judicial review and, 166 ff.; and legislative supremacy, 132 f.; as a "living constitution," 162; proposed reforms of, 174 ff., 205 ff.; social reform and, 187 ff.
Constitutional law, United States, influence of natural law theory on, 164
Constitutions: as changing social instruments, 161 ff.; definition of, 159; types of, 159 f.
Consumers' co-operatives, control of monopoly, 316 f.

## INDEX

Control: administrative, executive budget and, 280; top, definition of, 270; public-utility (see Regulation); administrative, relation of finance to, 276 f.; financial, 278 f., 353; results of over centralization of, 279; government, without ownership, 378 f.; judicial and administrative, 397; legislative, nature of, 396
Conway, A. P., 177 (note)
Cooke, Morris L., 324 (note)
*Cooley* vs. *Port Wardens*, 191
Coolidge, Calvin, 39
Co-operative marketing, growth of in United States, 74
Co-ordinator, administrative need for in national government, 291 f.
Corporations (see also Public Corporations): characteristics of, 78 f.; government-owned, 359 f., 363 ff.; management of, 78, 272; public and private compared, 359 f.; business, "banker control" of, 83; semipublic, definition of, 78
Corwin, E. S., 173, 187
Council-Manager plan (see City-manager plan)
Courts (see also Supreme Court) and the regulatory tribunals, 331 f.
Crawford, Finla G., 329 (note)
Creative state, concept of, 7 f., 44 f., 64 ff., 421 ff.
*Crowell* vs. *Benson*, 196 (note), 332 (note)
Cushman, Robert E., 167 (note)

Daudet, Leon, 41
Davies, A. Emil, 347 (note)
Dawson, Robert M., 176 (note)
*Debs, in re*, 199 (note)
Democracy: advantages of, 70; in agricultural society, 73 f.; alternatives to, 392 f.; American tradition of, 44 f.; bicameralism and, 140; and compulsory voting, 105 f.; conditions necessary to, 70 f., 156 f., 403 ff., 424; and efficiency, 388 f.; failure of in Italy and Germany, 133 f.; and individuality, 70; in an industrialized country, 69 ff.; interpretations of, 71 ff.; legislative supremacy in, 131 ff.; middle class as index of, 89 f.; modern approach to, 73 ff.; and monopoly, 79, 96; and public values, 407; and representative government, 27; as a social attitude, 71 f.; social legislation as an index of, 187 ff.; urbanism and, 77 ff.
Democratic control, and legislatures, 393 f.; of public enterprises, 351, 359
Department head, relation of to executive and comptroller, 277

Departmentalism: in British Post Office, 350; and corporate form, 359
De Tocqueville, Alexis, 99 (note)
Detroit Street Ry., organization of, 271
Dewey, John, 417 (note)
Dickinson, John, 196 (note), 237 (note)
Dictatorship, theoretical advantage of, 69 ff.
Dimock, Marshall E., 82 (note), 141 (note), 142 (note), 237 (note), 243 (note), 244 (note), 272 (note), 281 (note), 311 (note), 325 (note), 350 (note), 355 (note), 359 (note), 360, 361 (note), 365 (note), 397
Draper, Earle S., 375, 376
*Dred Scott* vs. *Sanford*, 190
Due process of law: compared to equity, 183; and labor legislation, 200 f.; and the police power, 184; public control of business and, 195 ff.; significance of, 181 ff.
Dunn, Samuel O., 63, 91
Dunning, William A., 216 (note)
*Duplex Printing Co.* vs. *Deering*, 199 (note)
Du Pont, 83 (note)
Dykstra, C. A., 69, 306, 405 (note), 409

East India Company, 46
Eastman, Joseph B., 315
Economic services, provision of, 341 ff.
Economic theory, and government, 369 f.
Education, public: as a governmental function, 60, 345; in democracy, 405; number employed in, 288
Efficiency: alternatives to, 392 f.; budgetary agency and, 281; and popular control, 389 f.
Election laws and political parties, 117
Electorate: volatility of, 112; qualifications of, 101 ff.
Élites, theory of, 48 ff.
Elliott, W. Y., 25 (note), 174, 175, 176, 178, 180 (note), 192 (note), 204
Emeny, Brooks, 378 (note)
Emergency Housing Corporation, 61
Employees' Associations, 303 f.
Employment offices, regulations of, 198
Engelmann, Geza, 220 (note)
Equality: American tradition of, 93; and community, 423; and liberty, 409 ff., 412 ff.; nature of, 411
Europe, state enterprises in, 346 f.
Examinations, civil-service, 300 f.
Executive: and lawmaking, 170; and legislatures, 174; deficiencies of, 261; place of in public administration, 302 f.; power of removal, 302; and the public, 284; qualities of, 272 ff.
Executive, dual: in business, 263; need of in United States, 261 f.; staff assistance as alternative to, 263 f.

Expert: and the layman, 388 ff.; in government, 391

Fact finding, importance of in legislative process, 149
Fayol, Henri, 244
Federal-city relations, 95
Federal government: functions of, 55 ff.; growth of, 93 ff.; proposals to expand power of, 208; research in, 55
Federal Housing Administration, 61
Federal Land Banks, a mixed enterprise, 361
Federal Power Commission: 355 (note)
Federal Register, The, 397
Federal Trade Commission, 322; on holding companies, 333 ff.; investigations by, 82
Federal Trade Commission Act, 194
Federalism: and planning, 178; functional analysis of, 54; governmental levels in, 30; judicial supremacy and, 177; problems of, 176 ff.
Fesler, James W., 180
Field, Oliver P., 56
Finance: and administration, 246; irresponsible, 173 f.; responsible, and the budget, 280; relation of to top control, 276 f.; separate functions of, 278; staff agency, 207
Financial control and government as enterpriser, 353
*Fletcher* vs. *Peck*, 181 (note)
Follett, Mary P., 244 (note)
Ford, Henry, 274
*Fortune*, 83 (note)
France: cabinet government in, 175; control of pressure groups, 154 f.; regulation of electrical utilities, 326
Franchise: failure to exercise, 103 ff.; proposals to limit, 101 f.
Frankfurter, Felix, 99, 181 (note), 189 (note), 196 (note), 199 (note), 331
Frederic, Katherine A., 347 (note)
Freedom: and inventiveness, 421 f.; nature of, 418
Freud, Sigmund, 14
Freund, Ernst, 349 (note)
Friederich, Carl J., 298 (note)

Gallatin, Albert, 376
Gardiner, A. G., 390 (note)
Garrison, Lloyd, 208 (note)
Gaus, John M., 229, 237 (note), 248
Geiser, Karl F., 220 (note)
General Accounting office, overcentralization of control in, 279
General Motors Corporation, staff assistance in, 265
General will, concept of, 27 ff.

Germany: administration in, 299; electrification system in, 325, 349; failure of democracy in, 133 f.; merit system in, 298; middle class in, 90; political leaders of, 52; political system of, 42
*Gibbons* vs. *Ogden*, 191
Giddings, Franklin, 14
Glaeser, Martin G., 354 (note)
Gooch, Robert K., 177 (note)
Goodnow, Frank J., 20
Gosnell, Harold F., 102 (note), 103 (note), 119 (note)
Governance, art of, 87
Governing class, obligations of, 87 ff.
Government (*see also* Federal government; Representative government; State government; Local government; Minority government; Municipal government; Party government): balancer of liberty and equality, 411 f.; administration in, 230 f.; as assistance, 59 ff.; assistance to business, 62 f.; and business, 88, 91 f., 198 f., 315 f., 341 ff., 380; businessmen and, 81; cabinet system, 174 ff.; classification of functions, 53, 288 f.; classification of processes, 19 f.; by committees, 145 f.; concentration in business and, 79 ff.; "conspiracy" theory of, 50 ff.; as control and power, 38, 47 ff.; control of the economic system, 369 ff.; control without ownership, 378 f.; definition of, 8, 19, 20 f.; dynamic theory of, 47 f.; as employer, 288 f., 311 f.; finance and top control in, 278; forms of, 26 f.; functions of by appeal to history, 45 f.; functions, dynamic theory of, 47 f.; functions of, historical, 7 f.; functions of, interest groups and, 65; functions of, proper, 37 ff.; functions, public interest as test of, 39 f.; functions of, relief of social tensions, 53; growth of economic activities of, 342 f.; historical role of, 45 f.; as a holding company, 374 f.; industrialization and, 75 ff.; initiative in, 419; institutional and dynamic approaches to, 32 f.; of "laws," interpretations of, 164 f.; levels of, 30 f., 53 ff.; in liberal-capitalist state, 10; in a modern society, 3 ff.; nature of, 8 ff., 215 f.; one-party, and administration, 296 f.; and paternalism, 57; pioneering of, 64 ff., 345 f.; powers of in United States, 53 ff., 134.; presidential system, 175 f.; as protector, 57 f.; as public-service corporation, 47, 56; *raison d'être* of, 6 ff., 215; red tape in, 252 ff.; as regulator, 58 f.; reorganization of, 251 f.; separation of power and, 168 ff.; as response to social problems, 4 ff.; "social lag" and, 5 f.; study

of, 11 f.; theories of the state and the functions of, 38; as tool of pressure politics, 25; 20th-century functions of, 370; ultimate objective of, 424; "umpire" function of, 39; unitary, definition of, 177; units of in United States, 30; violation of unity of management by, 271
Government as enterpriser: 64 ff., 341 ff.; and civil service, 352 f.; conclusions, 366; and democratic control, 351; and financial control; 353; flexibility of, 357; in Europe, 346 ff.; in Milwaukee, 347 f.; political influence on, 353 f.; problems of political science, 346; traditional shortcomings of, 349 f.; in the United States, 347 f.
Government corporations (see Corporations; Public corporations)
Government employee associations, 303 f.
Government-owned corporation: 359 f.; advantages of, 363 ff.
Government service, salaries in, 290 f.
Great Britain: administrative class in, 298 f.; aristocracy in, 41; art of governance in, 87 ff.; bicameralism in, 140; cabinet government in, 175; civil service in, 298; Conservative party in, 113; consumers' co-operatives in, 317; control of pressure groups, 154 f.; electricity supply in, 325; governing class in, 87 ff.; management problems in, 260; Labor party in, 118; legislative supremacy in, 165; Liberal party in, 42 f.; local government in, 145; public-utility control in, 325 f.; Royal Commissions in, 150; Treasury as staff department in, 267; unwritten constitution of, 159 f.
Group behavior, theories of, 14 f.
Group representation: definition of, 122; differentiated from lobbying, 122
Gruening, Ernest, 82 (note)
Gulick, Luther, 369, 375

Haines, Charles G., 159, 164, 165 (note), 166 (note), 167 (note), 202 (note), 211, 397
Haldane, Viscount, 251 (note)
Hamilton, Alexander, 63, 376
Hamilton, Walton, 197 (note)
Hammer vs. Dagenhart, 191 (note)
Harcourt, William, 390
Harding, T. Swann, 390 (note), 421 (note)
Harris, Franklin S., 420 (note)
Hart, James, 237 (note), 397
Hasbrouck, Paul De Witt, 142 (note)
Haynes, Frederick E., 116 (note)
Health, public, and government, 60 f.
Hearst, newspaper chain, 85
Heckscher, Eli Philip, 385, 386 (note)

Herring, E. Pendleton, 25, 26 (note), 40 (note), 82 (note), 121, 122 (note), 125 (note), 153 (note), 241 (note), 242 (note), 304 (note), 327, 328
Hewart, Lord, 235 (note), 393
Highways, a governmental function, 345
Historical method, political science, 32
Hitler, Adolph, 52
Hitler regime and merit system, 298
Hoan, Daniel, 170
Hobbes, Thomas, 220
Holcombe, Arthur, 116, 313, 383
Holden vs. Hardy, 200 (note)
Holding companies: abuses of, 334; and anti-trust laws, 195; regulation of, 333 f., 83
Holmes, Oliver W., 198
Home rule: charters of, 164; municipal, arguments on, 137 f.
Hoover, Herbert C., 4, 319, 410; on equality, 411, 414
House of Representatives, proposed limitations on, 175
Housing, governmental, 61 f.
Houston, East and West Texas Ry. Co. vs. U. S., 181 (note)
Howe, Frederic L., 78
Hughes, Charles E., 205, 210, 211
Human resources, 287 f.
Hurd, Archibald, 349, 350, 352, 353

Ickes, Harold L., 381, 384 (note)
Illinois, regulation of grain elevators in, 319 f.
Independent Grocers' Alliance, and monopoly, 316
Individual, place of in institutional studies, 11 ff.
Individualism: American, 417 f.; characteristics of, 418 f.; cultivation of, 419; and individuality, 416; the new, 409 ff.
Individuality, cultural; as reconciliation of liberty and equality, 416 f.; and urbanism, 77; and democracy, 70; and individualism, 416; and invention, 420 f.; meaning of, 417; and society, 221 ff.
Industrial democracy, 73
Industrial society: class differentiations in, 89; and government, 75 ff.; and democracy, 86 f.
Industrialism and municipal home rule, 137
Industrialization, effect on levels of government, 93 ff.
Industry: decentralization of in United States, 76; technological bases of, 84 f.
Initiative and public control, 418
Injunction and organized labor, 199 f.
Inland Waterways Corporation, 347; defects in administration, 365

# 434 INDEX

Insull, Samuel, 199, 323, 334
Interest groups: and administration, 241 ff.; and government, 65, 153
Interest representation: official recognition of, 155; political parties, 122 ff.
International trade, and planning, 384 ff.
Interstate Commerce Commission: 241; and difficulties of valuation, 331 f.; efficiency of, 330; membership of, 327
Interstate Commerce Commission Act, 92, 191
Invention: in America, 421; and freedom, 421 f.; and individuality, 420 f.
Investigating committees: as fact-finding agencies, 149; inquiries into lobbies, 154
Irresponsibility, American governmental, and regulatory tribunals, 326
Isaak Walton Leagues, 188
Italy: administration in, 299; failure of democracy in, 133 f.; political system of, 42; representative government in, 26; voting in, 73

Jefferson, Thomas, 44, 63, 168, 189, 376
Joeckel, Carleton B., 19 (note)
Jones, Hawley, 415 (note), 416 (note)
Judicial control and administration, 397
Judicial legislation and the United States Constitution, 162 f.
Judicial review: due process and, 183; in the United States, 166 ff., 190; proposal to abolish, 211 f.; and administrative regulation, 195 ff.; and social legislation, 167
Judicial supremacy and federalism, 177
Judiciary: importance of in the United States, 162 ff., 180 f.; and social reform, 189 ff.

Kahn, Julius, 380 (note)
Kandel, I. L., 60
Keezer, Dexter, 242 (note), 332 (note)
Kennedy, W. P. M., 176 (note)
Kent, Frank R., 116 (note)
Keynes, John Maynard, 229, 369, 370, 371, 378, 384 (note), 385 (note), 412
Kiplinger, W. M., 366 (note)

Labor: and anti-trust legislation, 199 ff.; due process and legislative protection, 200 f.; and the injunction, 199 f.
Labor party in Great Britain, 118
La Follette, Philip, 170
La Follette, Robert M., Jr., 380 (note)
La Guardia, Fiorello, 170
Laidler, Harry W., 92, 347 (note)
*Laissez faire:* Herbert Hoover on, 410; shortcomings of, 370; and state responsibility, 385 f.; tenets of, 59
Lambert, Edouard, 212

Landis, James M., 181 (note), 189 (note), 199 (note)
Laski, Harold J., 18 (note), 24 (note), 41, 87, 118
Lasswell, Harold D., 48, 417 (note)
Law: administrative, in the United States, 239; classifications of, 22 f.; "fundamental" and "statutory" distinguished, 163; and government, 9; meanings of, 22 f.; natural, 164; and political science, 23; sociological view of, 22 f.; statutory enacting of, 144
*Lawlor* vs. *Loewe,* 199 (note)
Lawmaking: process, 131 ff.; and administrators, 234 ff.; and the executive, 170
Lawrence, David, 20 (note)
Leadership: in legislative bodies, 172; in large organizations, 263; requirements for, 272 ff.
League of Women Voters: 405, 406; and civil-service laws, 295
Le Bon, Gustave, 14
Lees-Smith, H. B., 140 (note)
Legislation: administrative, nature of, 234 ff.; anti-trust, and the commerce power, 193 ff.; and organized labor, 199 ff.
Legislative control, nature of, 396
Legislative process: and administration, 148 f.; and committees, 145 ff.; and fact-finding, 149 ff.; and interest groups, 153; popular participation in, 156 ff.; specialized nature of, 148 ff.
Legislative reference bureau, 149 f.
Legislators: ability of, 133, 142; and lobbies, 124 f.; popular attitude toward, 143
Legislatures: and administration, 236 f., 322, 393 f.; atmosphere of, 138; bicameralism in, 139 ff.; defects of, 133 ff., 374 f.; deliberation in, 143 f.; efficiency of, 151 ff.; and executives, 174; functions of, 142 ff.; number in the United States, 134; and political parties, 146 ff.; power of internal organization, 142; powers of, 142 f.; and pressure groups, 154 f.; and private bills, 150; and the public, 133; proposed reforms of, 147 ff.; responsible leadership in, 172; and the representative process, 131 ff.; supremacy of in a democracy, 131 ff.; state, equal representation in, 135
Lepawsky, Albert, 77 (note)
Levin, Jack, 82 (note)
Liberal, nature of, 379
Liberal party, in Great Britain, 42 f.
Liberal Party Inquiry, 410 (note)
Liberalism, tenets of, 42 f.

## INDEX

Liberty: and community, 423; and equality, 409 ff.; nature of, 409 f., 413; threatened by bureaucracy, 394 f.
Library of Congress, as fact-finding agency, 149 f.
Lincoln, Abraham, 72
*Lindheimer* vs. *Illinois Bell Tel. Co.*, 196 (*note*)
Line activities, needs of, 294 f.
Lippincott, Benjamin E., 370 (*note*), 386 (*note*)
Lippmann, Walter, 28
Lloyd-La Follette Act of 1912, 304
Lobbies (*see also* Pressure groups; Pressure politics): as aids to legislators, 124 f.; congressional investigations of, 154; and legislative independence, 151 f.; place in representative government, 25 f.; tactics of, 123, 151 ff.
Lobbying: definition of, 122; differentiated from group representation, 122; of government employees' associations, 304
Local government: English system of, 145; functions of, 56; health activities of, 60; trading functions of in the United States, 348
*Lochner* vs. *New York*, 200 (*note*)
Locke, John, 219, 220
Logan, Edward, 117 (*note*)
London, consumers' co-operatives in, 317
London Passenger Transport Board, a public-utility trust, 360
Los Angeles Department of Water and Power, 354
*Los Angeles Gas* vs. *R. R. Com. of Calif.*, 331 (*note*)
*Louis K. Liggett* vs. *Lee*, 203 (*note*)
Lowden, Frank O., 291
Lowell, A. Lawrence, 28 (*note*)
Luce, Robert, 142 (*note*)

Machiavelli, 89
Machine politics: bossism 109; conditions favoring, 78, 105; in Chicago 119; methods of, 119 ff.; Theodore Roosevelt on, 109
MacIver, R. M., 17 (*note*)
McLaughlin, Andrew C., 167 (*note*), 168 (*note*), 190 (*note*)
Macmahon, Arthur, 292 (*note*)
McNutt, Paul V., 170
Madison, James, 108
*McCray* vs. *U. S.*, 202 (*note*)
*McCulloch* vs. *Maryland*, 202
McAllister, B. P., 197 (*note*)
McBain, Howard Lee, 160 (*note*)
McCamy, James L., 348 (*note*)
*McCardle* vs. *Indianapolis Water Co.*, 332
McCarl, J. R., 421

Man Power, 287 ff.
Management: "banker control" of business corporations, 83; the budget and unity of, 280; control in business corporations, 78; consequences of inadequate attention to, 262 f.; importance of unity, 270 f.; operations in, 244; and public relations, 283; rules for, 247; reasons for neglect of, 258 ff.; scientific, application of to national economy, 376 f.; strategy of, 257 ff.
Manchester Ship Canal, a mixed enterprise, 361
*Marbury* vs. *Madison*, 166, 167, 183, 189
Marshall, Alfred, 373
Marshall, John, 166, 179 (*note*), 191, 202
Martin, Everett Dean, 14
Marx, Karl, 4, 48
Marxian analysis and control without ownership, 378 f.
Mason, Alpheus, 199 (*note*), 200 (*note*)
Maurras, Charles, 41
May, Stacy, 242 (*note*), 332 (*note*)
Means, Gardiner C., 79, 232, 233, 333, 334 (*note*), 369, 370, 378, 386 (*note*), 415 (*note*)
Mellon, Andrew, 41, 321
Meriam, Lewis, 294 (*note*), 311 (*note*), 388
Merit system: and civil service, 295 ff.; executives' power of removal under, 302; objectives of, 295 f.; political parties and, 296 ff.; public employees under, 296
Merriam, Charles E., 3, 4, 20 (*note*), 37, 48 (*note*), 77 (*note*), 102 (*note*), 119 (*note*), 160 (*note*), 405
Methodology: in study of political science, 32 f.; sociological approach to democracy, 73 ff.
Metropolitan areas: city-county consolidation in, 138; problems of governing, 76 ff.
Middle class: as a balance in political equation, 90; as index of democracy, 89 f.; in United States, 90 ff., 113 f.
Mill, John Stuart, 396
Milwaukee, government enterprises in, 347 f.
Minnesota Rate Cases, 191
Minority government, theoretical advantages of, 69 ff.
Minority parties, handicaps of, 115 ff.
Mitchell, Wesley C., 372, 373 (*note*)
Mixed enterprise: advantages of, 362; nature of, 361 ff.; shortcomings of, 362
Monopoly: effect on press, 85 f.; suggestions for controlling, 316 f.
Montesquieu, Baron, 19, 168
Mooney, James D., 244 (*note*)
Morale, employee, importance of, 275

Morehead vs. *Tipaldo*, 168 (*note*), 201 (*note*)
Morrison, Herbert, 275, 363 (*note*)
Mosher, William E., 82 (*note*), 242 (*note*), 329
Muir, Ramsay, 42 (*note*), 235 (*note*), 396 f.
Mumford, Lewis, 73 (*note*)
Municipal electric plants, 354 f.
Municipal government: bicameralism in, 139 f.; charters of, 163 f.; home rule in, 137 f.; proportional representation in, 107; small councils in, 147
Municipal trading: results of, 353 f.; in the United States, 348
*Munn* vs. *Illinois*, 197, 319
Munro, William Bennett, 20 (*note*), 81, 150 (*note*), 180
Mussolini, Benito, 52, 71
Myers, William Starr, 116 (*note*)
Myths, use by political parties, 112 f.

National Emergency Council, 265
National Federation of Federal Employees, 304
National Municipal League, 282 (*note*)
National Resources Board, 317, 365 (*note*); on economic planning, 373 f., 376 (*note*)
Navigable waters, federal control over, 193
*Nebbia* vs. *New York*, 199 (*note*)
Nebraska, unicameral legislature in, 139
New Deal, and the Supreme Court, 190
*New State Ice Company* vs. *Liebmann*, 197 (*note*)
New York City, bicameralism in, 139 f.; and equal representation, 136; regulation of ticket brokers, 197 f.
New York Telephone Case, 196 (*note*)
Newspapers, circulation statistics, 85 f.
Nolting, Orin F., 171 (*note*)
Non-voting: reasons for, 103 ff.; significance of in a democracy, 105 f.; United States and Europe compared for, 103
*Norman* vs. *Baltimore and Ohio Ry.*, 204 (*note*)
Norris Anti-Injunction Act, 199
Norris, Tennessee, individualism in, 418
North Dakota, public ownership in, 198

Oatman, Miriam E., 176 (*note*), 257 (*note*), 397
Odegard, Peter H., 13, 14, 72, 121 (*note*), 152, 155 (*note*)
Odum, Howard W., 179 (*note*), 317
Ogburn, William F., 4, 5
*Ohio Water Co.* vs. *Ben Avon Borough*, 196 (*note*)
Olson, Floyd, 170
Oppenheimer, Franz, 50

Organization: committee type, 249; delegation of tasks, 246; functional type of, 250; importance of, 248 ff.; inadequate in American governments, 260; integrated type, 250; military type, 249; principles of, 245 f.; and red tape, 253 f.; staff and line, 245 (*note*)

Panama Canal Zone, administration in 289
Panama Railroad Company, 360, 422
*Panama Refining Co.* vs. *Ryan*, 239
Parent-Teachers Association, 406
Parliament, British: legislative supremacy of, 165; method of handling private bills, 150
Parratt, Spencer D., 77 (*note*)
Parties (*see* Political parties)
Party government, constitutional limitations on in United States, 108
Party responsibility and popular control, 395
Party system and responsible government, 110 f.
Paternalism, need for in a community, 419
Patronage: effect of on governmental enterprises, 353 f.; and machine politics, 117 ff.; and merit systems, 296 ff.
Personnel, classification of, 308
Personnel director, duties of, 305 ff., 308
Personnel management (*see also* Merit system; Civil service): under city-manager government, 305 f.; in government and business, compared, 305; objectives of, 295 f.; prerequisites to a study of, 288; principles of, 247; problem of promotions, 308 ff.; in the Tennessee Valley Authority, 307; theories of remuneration, 310 f.
Personnel programs: in American cities, 305; requisites of, 305
Persons, Harlow S., 376 (*note*), 377
Persons, Warren M., 343, 345, 353
Pfiffner, John M., 250 (*note*)
Philadelphia, machine politics in, 119
Pinchot, Gifford, 170
Planning: administration of, 372 f., 382; and administrative reforms, 245, 384; the executive budget and, 280; and federalism, 178; national, and international trade, 384 ff.; nature of, 375 f., 382; need for co-ordination, 267 f.; abilities needed for, 383 f.; economic, defects in, 374; Marshall on, 372 f.; National Resources Board on, 373 f.; need for, 372 f.; regional, federal authority over navigable waters and, 193
Platt, Tom, 109

# INDEX

Pluralism: and pressure politics, 25; and sovereignty, 24 f.; theory of, 24 f.
Police, functions of United States, 57 f.
Police power, due process and the, 184
Political behavior (*see* Psychology)
Political democracy, sociological approach to, 73 ff.
Political economy; definition of, 10; problems of, 386; revival of, 385 f.
Political man, characteristics of, 11 ff.
Political parties: campaign funds, 81; composition of, 109; economic interests of, 113 ff.; effect of sectionalism on, 121; factors determining membership, 111 ff.; importance of finances, 117; increased control of legislatures, 146 f.; influence of election laws on, 117; and the merit system, 296 ff.; minor, handicaps of, 115 ff.; organization of, 117 ff.; and patronage, 297 f.; platforms of, 110; power elements of, 117 ff.; relation to interest representation, 122 ff.; role in the representative process, 107 ff.; and sectionalism, 121; third-party movements in United States, 114; two-party system, arguments for and against, 115 ff.
Political power: and interest representation, 156; and the wealthy, 80 ff.
Political science: and methodology, 32 f.; nature of, 8 ff.; and problems of government as enterpriser, 346; psychological basis of, 11 ff.
Political theory: American conception of equality, 93; aristocracy, 41; concept of general will, 27; concept of sovereignty, 23 ff.; conspiracy theory of the state, 50 ff.; élites, 48 ff.; ends of the state, 215 ff.; interpretations of democracy, 71 ff.; liberalism, 42 f.; natural law, 164; pluralism, 24 f.; plutocratic philosophy, 40 f.; reinterpretation of man's significance in, 223 f.; relation to ethics, 221; social-democratic philosophy, 44 f.; socialism, 43
Politics: and administration, 292 f.; connotations of term, 21 f.; interaction with administration, 30; money power in, 81; as a "science," 11 f.; socialists' attitude toward, 111
Policy: execution of, 229 ff.; stages in formulation of, 233 f.
Pollock, James K., 81 (*note*)
*Pollock* vs. *Farmers Loan and Trust Co.*, 201 f.
Pope, Alexander, 249
Popular control: over administrators, 248; aided by short ballot, 395; alternatives to, 392 f.; and efficiency, 389 f.; and party responsibility, 395; as an ultimate objective, 393

Popular participation: and administration, 404; ways of providing for, 406
Population, urban, growth of in United States, 76
Porritt, Edward, 176 (*note*)
Port, Frederick J., 239 (*note*)
Port of London Authority, 361
Post Office (*see also* United States Post Office) as a government function, 345
Powell, Thomas Reed, 192 (*note*)
Power, economic, concentration of in industry, 415 f.
Power politics, 45
Practical socialists, definition of, 91 f.
President: proposal to increase financial power of, 174; and the Senate, 141; staff assistance, 265
Presidential system, disadvantage of, 175 f.
Press: circulation statistics, 85 f.; effect of monopoly on, 85 f.
Pressure groups (*see also* Lobbies; Lobbying): defense of legislatures against, 154 f.; influence of, 82; and the representative process, 121 f.
Pressure politics: influence of, 25 f.; methods of Anti-Saloon League, 152; and pluralism, 25
Probationary period, use of, 301 f.
Professional workers, concerns of, 293
Professionalization of the public service, 403 f.
Profit motive and genius, 420
Promotions in the public service, 308 ff.
Propaganda and public opinion, 28
Proportional representation, advantages and disadvantages of, 106 f.
Provisional Orders, 396
Psychology: and government, 11 ff.; of political behavior, 11 ff.
Psychological method, contribution to political science, 32
Public administration (*see* Administration)
Public and the executive, 284
Public corporations (*see also* Corporations; Public-utility trust; Mixed undertaking): 357 ff.; advantages over government department, 365 f.; owned by the United States Government, 359.
Public interest: nature of, 127; tests of business affected with, 320 f.
Public management of governmental enterprises, 349 f.
Public opinion: control of by business interests, 86 f.; difficulties in determining, 29; instruments of, 86; nature of, 27 ff.; and the press, 29; and propaganda, 28; and technology, 85

Public ownership: in American cities, 423; as control of monopoly, 317 f.; freedom from legal obstacles in United States, 198 f.; versus regulation, 318; and Socialism, 344
Public relations: difficulties of, 283; importance of to British Post Office, 355; objectives and importance of, 283; principles of, 247 f.
Public servants and strikes, 298
Public service: democracy and a philosophy of, 403; incentives of, 311 f.; numbers employed in, 288
Public utilities: conditions necessary to improved regulation of, 335 ff.; control of, abroad, 325 f.; definition of, 319 ff.; economic results of management of in United States, 324; federal regulation of, 195 ff.; government operated, 343 f.; a legal concept, 320; valuation problems, 195 f.
Public-utility regulation, dissatisfaction with, 322 f.
Public-utility trust: advantages of, 363; compared with government-owned corporations, 361; nature of, 360 f.; weaknesses of, 364
Public welfare, as a governmental responsibility, 62

Radio and public opinion, 85
Railways and the United States Government, 345
Reapportionment: in metropolitan centers, 137; need for in States, 135 ff.
*Recent Social Trends*, 4, 100 (*note*)
Reconstruction Finance Corporation, 62, 347
Reeves, Floyd W., 307
Reeves, W. P., 177 (*note*)
Regimentation: by business, 414 f.; as governmental control, 414 f.
Regional commonwealth, proposal for in the Un ted States, 179 ff.
*Regional Factors in National Planning and Development*, 179
Regionalism: and centralization in business and government, 317; growing importance of in United States, 180 ff.
Regulation: administrative, 315 ff.; governmental function of, 58 f.; holding companies, 83; importance of in United States, 318 ff.; improvement of, 335 ff.; and the police power, 58; and political theory, 319; versus public ownership, 318; of public utilities, dissatisfaction with, 322 f.; of utilities, extent of in United States, 321; of utilities, federal government and, 195 ff.

Regulatory tribunals: and the courts, 195 ff., 331 f.; development of, 241; distinctive character of in United States, 325; fact-finding function of, 149; financial limitations of, 328 f.; lack of expertness in, 326 f.; powers of, 322, 329; procedure of, 329; summary of deficiencies, 330
Reiley, Alan C., 244 (*note*)
Remuneration, in the public service, 310 f.
*Rentier* class, cohesiveness of, 51
Reorganization movements, weaknesses of, 251
Reporting, public, types and importance of, 282
Representation (*see also* Proportional representation): methods of apportioning, 134 ff.; nature of, 100 f.; political parties and, 108 ff.
Representation by area: relation to pressure politics, 123; shortcomings of, 123
Representation, equal: objections to, 136; in State legislatures, 135
Representative government: and civil service, 297; deliberation in, 143 f.; differentiated from democracy, 27; nature of, 26 f.; and pressure groups, 25 f., 82, 126 f.; problems of, 99 ff.; processes of, 109 ff.; shortcomings of, 394 f.
Representative process: interest groups and, 124 f.; role of legislature, 131 ff.
Research agencies, classification of, 420 f.
Research in federal government, 55
Research workers, concerns of, 293
Responsible government and British government enterprises, 351 f.
*Ribnik* vs. *McBride*, 198 (*note*)
Ridley, Clarence E., 171 (*note*)
Rogers, Lindsay, 141 (*note*), 170 (*note*)
Roosevelt, Franklin D., 39, 44, 170, 173
Roosevelt, Theodore, 44, 109, 157, 209, 291
Rosen, S. McKee, 86, 121 (*note*), 154 (*note*)
Rousseau, Jean Jacques, 27, 28, 220
Royal (Bridgeman) Commission on the Post Office, 350 (*note*)
Royal Commissions (*see* Great Britain)
Rural electrification in United States and Europe, 324
Rural Resettlement Administration, 76
Russia (*see also* Soviet Russia), administration in, 299
Ryan, A. P., 283 (*note*)

*St. Louis and O'Fallon Ry. Co.* vs. *U. S.*, 196 (*note*)
Sait, Edward M., 177 (*note*)
Salter, Sir Arthur, 420
Salter, John G., 119 (*note*)

# INDEX 439

Schechter Poultry Corp. vs. U. S., 191 (note), 205
Schneider, H. W., 177 (note)
Schuman, Frederick L., 52 (note)
Science Advisory Board, 421 (note)
Scripps-Howard newspaper chain, 85
Sectionalism and political parties, 121
Self-government of industry, drawbacks to, 381 (note)
Senate, United States: appointive power of, 145; characteristics of, 141 ff.; committee rule in, 146; equal representation in, 136; and the President, 141; proposed limitations on, 175; and the Supreme Court, 141
"Service" state, definition of, 39
Separation of powers: and administrative discretion, 241; city-manager plan and, 170 f.; judicial review and, 168 f.; and responsible government, 168 ff.; in the United States, 168 ff.
Sharfman, I. L., 241 (note)
Sharp, Walter R., 298 (note)
Sheldon, Oliver, 257
Sherman Anti-Trust Law: 92; history of application, 193 f.
Short ballot: movement for, 106; and popular control, 395
Shreveport case, 191
Siegfried, André, 99 (note)
Simons, Henry, 337 f., 344
Skills, administrative, types of, 293
Smith, Adam, 320, 344, 385
Smith, Alfred, 170
Smith, Bruce, 57
Smith, J. Allen, 108
Smith vs. Illinois Bell Tel. Co., 333 (note)
Smyth vs. Ames, 195, 331
Social change: class consciousness and, 114; factors in, 100 f.
Social democracy, 73
Social environment, control of, 99 f.
Social lag: legislative shortcomings and, 133; theory of, 5 f.
Social legislation: and community, 188 f.; as a concession, 188; creative aspect of, 187 f.; as index of democratic vitality, 187 ff.; judicial review and, 167, 184
Social reform: the Constitution and, 187 ff.; judiciary as umpire of in United States, 189 ff.
Socialism: guild and state, 43; state: Keynes on, 371; in Soviet Russia, 4
Socialists: and public ownership, 344; and political parties, 111
Society (see also Agricultural society; Industrial society): concept of, 15 ff.; individual in, 221 ff.; institutional organization of, 16

Sociology and political science, 15 f.
Sovereignty: concept of, 23 ff.; pluralism and, 24 f.
Soviet Russia: political system of, 42; state socialism in, 4
Specialization and legislative process, 148 ff.
Spencer, Herbert, 221
Spero, Sterling D., 303 (note)
Spicer, George, 171 (note)
Spinoza, B., 37
Springer vs. U. S., 201 (note)
Staff, qualification of officials, 268 f., 293
Staff agencies: alternative to dual executive, 263 f.; a plan for, 267 f.; shortcomings of existing, 266
Standard Oil Company vs. U. S., 194 (note)
State (see also "Service" state): authoritarian, theory of, 41 f.; "conspiracy" theory of, 50 ff.; creative, 7 f., 44 f., 64 ff., 421 ff.; as domination and control, 45; ends of, 215 ff.; as enterpriser, 64 ff., 198 ff., 314 ff.; historical role of, 45 ff.; idealization of, 19, 217 f.; juristic theory of, 23 f.; liberal-democratic problems of, 10; nature of, 8 f., 17 ff.; plutocratic philosophy of, 40 f.; social-democratic view of, 44 f.; socialist conception of, 43; as sovereign, 23 ff.; syndicalist view of, 4; traditional objectives of, 219 f.; as "umpire," 39
State Board of Tax Commissioners vs. Jackson, 203 (note)
Statecraft: definition of, 69; nature of,369
State governments: United States, decline of importance of, 179; finance in, 278; health activities of, 60; powers and functions of, 56
Statistics: as planning tool, 377; and political science, 32
Stone, Harlan, 210
Studenski, Paul, 77 (note)
Strikes by public servants, 298
Suffrage, woman, effect on voting, 103 f.
Supreme Court, United States: as a constitutional court, 189; expansion of commerce power by, 193 ff.; "gold-clause" decision, 203 f.; and the income-tax cases, 201 f.; jurisdiction of, 189; and labor legislation, 200 f.; and the New Deal, 190; periods of judicial review, 190; proposals to limit power of, 209 ff.; and public ownership, 198 f.; and regulation, 319 f.; and the Sherman Act, 193 ff.; and the United States Senate, 14; umpire of social reform, 189 ff.; and utility valuation, 332
Switzerland, public service in, 298
Swope, Gerard, 380 (note)
Swope plan, 379

Symbols: and political parties, 112 f.; types of, 112
Syndicalists, conception of the state, 4

Tammany Wigwam, activities of, 119
Taney, Roger B., 190
Tarde, Gabriel, 14
Taxation, as a social instrument, 201 ff.
Taxing power: limitations on, 203 f.; use of in extending federal authority, 202 f.
Tead, Ordway, 273 (*note*), 274, 312
Technology, influence on government, 84 f.
Tennessee Valley Authority: 76, 418; administrative defects of, 365; administrative problems of, 349; and Comptroller General, 421; constitutionality of, 193; as employer, 289 f., 307
*Texas and N. O. Ry. Co.* vs. *Railway Clerks*, 200 (*note*)
Thomas, Norman, 73 (*note*)
Thompson, Carl D., 347 (*note*)
Thompson, William Hale, 119
Thurstone, Louis L., 301 (*note*)
Trade associations and anti-trust laws, 195
Trade unions and guild socialism, 43
Trading by government, 341 f.
Tribunals (*see* Regulatory tribunals)
Trotter, Wilfred, 14
Turner, Frederick Jackson, 180
*Tyson* vs. *Banton*, 198

"Umpire" state, theory of, 39
Unemployment and radicalism, 121
Unicameralism, 139 ff.
Unions of public servants, 303 f.
*United Mine Workers* vs. *Coronado Coal Co.*, 200 (*note*)
United Press, 86
*United Rys. and Electric Co. of Baltimore* vs. *West*, 184 (*note*), 332 (*note*)
United States Bureau of Foreign and Domestic Commerce, 290 (*note*)
United States Bureau of Standards, 421
United States Classification Board, 310
United States Employment service, 198
United States Government as employer, 288 ff.
United States Personnel Classification Board, 291 (*note*)
United States Post Office Department, administration of, 353 ff.; number employed by, 288
United States Public Health Service, 61
United States Senate (*see* Senate, U. S.)

*U. S.* vs. *Doremus*, 202 (*note*)
Universal suffrage, desirability of, 100 ff.
Upson, Lent D., 56
Urbanism: effects upon the individual, 77; in United States, 75 f.; democracy and, 77 ff.; and municipal home rule, 137

Valuation and regulation, 331 f.
Values, public, and democracy, 407
Vaughan, W. F., 14
*Veazie Bank* vs. *Fenno*, 202
Virginia, personnel system in, 296 f.
Voting: citizen education in, 104 f.; compulsory, 105 ff.; of economic interests, 51; in Fascist Italy, 73; increasing participation, 104 f.; qualifications for, 101 ff.; suggestions for improving, 103

Wall street, power of, 80
War Industries Board, 378
Warner, K. O., 177 (*note*)
Washington, George, 108
Waters, navigable (*see* Navigable waters)
Waterworks, municipally owned, in the United States, 342 f.
Watson, B. W. Walker, 233 (*note*)
Webb, Sidney, 347
Weimar Constitution: 52; merit system under, 298
Welch, Francis X., 327 (*note*)
Wells, H. G., 139 (*note*), 402, 403 (*note*), 420
Werner, M. R., 119 (*note*)
*West* vs. *Chesapeake and Potomac Tel. Co.*, 196 (*note*)
Westphalia, Treaty of, 3
White, Leonard D., 171 (*note*), 237 (*note*), 245 (*note*), 287, 290 (*note*), 297 (*note*), 304 (*note*), 338
Whitehead, Harold, 283 (*note*), 355 (*note*)
Whitesell, Donald M., 355 (*note*)
Whitley Councils, 304
Willoughby, W. F., 148 (*note*), 266, 280 (*note*)
Willoughby, W. W., 23, 163, 167 (*note*), 221 (*note*)
Wilson, Woodrow, 44, 145, 169, 170 (*note*), 172, 231 (*note*), 291
Winslow, C. E. A., 61 (*note*)
Wolmer, Lord, 350,
Woman suffrage (*see* Suffrage, woman)
Wood, S. H., 283 (*note*)
Wooddy, Carroll, 94 (*note*)
Wright, C. K., 283 (*note*)